Contextual Bach Studies

A series of monographs exploring the contexts
of Johann Sebastian Bach's life and music,
with a particular emphasis on theology and liturgy.
Series Editor: Robin A. Leaver

Music has its own distinctive characteristics—melody, harmony, rhythm, form, etc.—that have to be fully appreciated if it is to be effectively understood. But a detailed comprehension of all these musical elements cannot reveal the significance of all the compositional choices made by a composer. "What?" and "how?" questions need to be supplemented by appropriate "why?" and "when?" questions. Study of the original score and parts, as well as the different manifestations of a particular work, have to be undertaken. But if such study is regarded as an end rather than a beginning, then the music itself will not necessarily be fully understood. One must go further. There are various contexts that impinge upon a composer's choices. Music is conditioned by time, place, and culture and therefore is influenced by particular historical, geographical, and social contexts; music written in fulfillment of a contractual agreement has an economic context; and so forth.

The music of Johann Sebastian Bach has been the object of intensive study and analysis, but in the past many of these studies have been somewhat narrow in focus. For example, the received view of Bach's music was to some degree incomplete because it was largely discussed on its own terms without being fully set within the contextual perspective of the musician's predecessors, contemporaries, and successors. It is only in fairly recent times that the music of these other composers has become accessible, allowing us to appreciate the nature and stature of their accomplishments, and at the same time giving us new perspectives from which to view a more rounded picture of Bach's genius.

The monographs in this series explore such contextual areas. Since much of Bach's music was composed for Lutheran worship, a primary concern of these monographs is the liturgical and theological contexts of the music. But Bach's music was not exclusively confined to these specific religious concerns. German culture of the time had more general religious dimensions that permeated "secular" society. Therefore, in addition to specific studies of the liturgical and theological contexts of Bach's music, this series also includes explorations of social, political, and cultural religious contexts in which his music was composed and first heard.

1. Cameron, Jasmin Melissa. *The Crucifixion in Music: An Analytical Survey of Settings of the* Crucifixus *between 1680 and 1800*, 2006.

2. van Elferen, Isabella. *Mystical Love in the German Baroque: Theology, Poetry, Music*, 2009.

3. Leahy, Anne, edited by Robin A. Leaver. *J. S. Bach's "Leipzig" Chorale Preludes: Music, Text, Theology*, 2011.

J. S. Bach's "Leipzig" Chorale Preludes

Music, Text, Theology

Anne Leahy

Edited by Robin A. Leaver

Contextual Bach Studies, No. 3

THE SCARECROW PRESS, INC.
Lanham • Toronto • Plymouth, UK
2011

Published by Scarecrow Press, Inc.
A wholly owned subsidary of The Rowman & Littlefield Publishing Group, Inc.
4501 Forbes Boulevard, Suite 200, Lanham, Maryland 20706
http://www.scarecrowpress.com

Estover Road, Plymouth PL6 7PY, United Kingdom

British Library Cataloguing in Publication Information Available

Library of Congress Cataloging-in-Publication Data

Leahy, Anne.
  J. S. Bach's "Leipzig" chorale preludes : music, text, theology / Anne Leahy ; edited
by Robin A. Leaver.
        p. cm. — (Contextual Bach studies ; No. 3)
  Includes bibliographical references and index.
  ISBN 978-0-8108-8181-5 (cloth : alk. paper) — ISBN 978-0-8108-8182-2 (ebook)
  1. Bach, Johann Sebastian, 1685–1750. Choräle von verschiedener Art, BWV 651–668.
2. Chorale prelude. I. Leaver, Robin A. II. Title.
  ML410.B13L34 2011
  786.5'18992—dc22   2011012617

Printed in the United States of America

#708648757

Contents

Abbreviations

AM	*Acta Musicologia.*
BACH	*Bach.* The Journal of the Riemenschneider Bach Institute.
Bachtagung	*Bericht über die wissenschaftliche Bachtagung der Gesellschaft für Musikforschung, Leipzig 23.–26. Juli 1950,* ed. Walther Vetter, Ernst Hermann Meyer, and Hans Heinrich Eggebrecht. Leipzig: Peters, 1951.
BC	*Bach Compendium. Analytisch-bibliographisches Repertorium der Werke Johann Sebastian Bachs,* ed. Hans-Joachim Schulze and Christoph Wolff. Leipzig: Peters, 1985–.
BG	*Johann Sebastian Bachs Werke. Gesamtausgabe der Bachgesellschaft.* Leipzig: Bach-Gesellschaft, 1851–1899.
BJ	*Bach-Jahrbuch.*
BkC	*The Book of Concord: The Confessions of the Evangelical Lutheran Church,* ed. Robert Kolb and Timothy J. Wengert. Minneapolis: Fortress, 2000.
BSLK	*Die Bekenntnisschriften der evangelisch-lutherischen Kirche,* 11th ed. Göttingen: Vandenhoeck & Ruprecht, 1992.
BWV	*Bach-Werke-Verzeichnis. Thematisch-systematisches Verzeichnis der musikalischen Werke von Johann Sebastian Bach,* ed. Wolfgang Schmieder. 2nd expanded edition. Wiesbaden: Breitkopf & Härtel, 1990.
Church Postils	*The Sermons of Martin Luther: The Church Postils,* trans. and ed. John Nicholas Lenker. Minneapolis: Lutherans of All Lands & Luther Press, 1904–1909; reprint, Grand Rapids: Baker, 1983.
CoG	*Commentary on Galatians: Martin Luther.* Grand Rapids: Zondervan 1924, reprint, 1988.
Dok	*Bach-Dokumente,* Bach-Archiv Leipzig:

1: *Schriftstücke von der Hand Johann Sebastian Bachs*, ed. Werner Neumann and Hans-Joachim Schulze. Kassel: Bärenreiter, 1963.

2: *Fremdschriftliche und gedruckte Dokumente zur Lebensgeschichte Johann Sebastian Bachs, 1685–1750*, ed. Werner Neumann und Hans-Joachim Schulze. Kassel: Bärenreiter, 1969.

3: *Dokumente zum Nachwirken Johann Sebastian Bachs, 1750–1800*, ed. Hans-Joachim Schulze. Kassel: Bärenreiter, 1972.

EKG	*Evangelisches Kirchengesangbuch* (1950).
House Postils	*The Sermons of Martin Luther: The House Postils*, trans. and ed. Eugene F. A. Klug. Grand Rapids: Baker, 1996.
JbLH	*Jahrbuch für Liturgik und Hymnologie.*
KB	*Kritischer Bericht* [of *NBA*].
LW	*Luther's Works: American Edition*, 55 vols. St. Louis and Philadelphia: Concordia and Fortress, 1955–1986.
Mf	*Die Musikforschung.*
MuG	*Musik und Gottesdienst.*
MuK	*Musik und Kirche.*
NBA	*Neue Bach Ausgabe.*
NBR	*The New Bach Reader: A Life of Johann Sebastian Bach in Letters and Documents*, ed. Hans T. David and Arthur Mendel; rev. and enl. Christoph Wolff. New York: Norton, 1998.
P271	Berlin Staatsbibliothek. Mus. ms. Bach P 271.
SLG	*Schuldiges Lob Gottes / Oder: Geistreiches Gesang-Buch / Ausgebreitet / durch Hrn. D. M. Luthern / und andere vornehme Evangelischer Lehrer* . . . Weimar: Mumbach, 1713.
WA	*Luthers Werke: Kritische Gesamtausgabe.* [Weimarer Ausgabe]. Weimar: Böhlau, 1883–1993.
WA TR	*Luthers Tischreden.* [Weimarer Ausgabe].
Zahn	Johannes Zahn, ed. *Die Melodien der deutschen evangelischen Kirchenlieder.* 6 vols. Gütersloh: Bertelsman, 1889–1893; reprint, Hildesheim: Olms, 1963.

The following designation of pitches is employed:

C	bottom c
c^0	tenor c
c^1	middle c
c^2	c above middle c
c^3	c two octaves above middle c

Beats within a measure are indicated thus: m. 1.1 = measure 1, beat 1, etc.

Editor's Preface

Robin A. Leaver

In the author's acknowledgments that follow this preface, the author, Dr. Anne Leahy, registers her sadness and shock at the untimely death of Professor Kees Vellekoop, her primary doctoral adviser at Utrecht University. It is with the same kind of sadness and shock that I have to acknowledge the death of Anne Leahy herself, whose untimely passing occurred as she was beginning to revise the substance of this book. It therefore seems appropriate to include here the substance of the obituary that I wrote for the newsletter of the American Bach Society.[1]

★ ★ ★

Anne Leahy (1961–2007) was a whirlwind of energy, drive, intelligence, friendship, scholarship, loyalty, and musicianship that overpowered you not by force but by charm, wit, positive feistiness, and an irrepressible sense of fun that permeated all things professional and personal. Contrary to normal whirlwinds, this extraordinary whirlwind was always constructive, never destructive, and she leaves behind an impressive wake of achievements that she accomplished during her all-too-short forty-six years.

I first encountered this whirlwind as a gentle breeze. Actually it was a telephone call. It was the mid-1990s, and my colleague Joan Lippincott at Westminster Choir College, Princeton, had recently been in Dublin as recitalist and judge for the international organ competition, and Anne was then visiting her in New Jersey. She introduced herself as an organist who had spent some time studying in the Netherlands and was currently a doctoral student at Utrecht University. Since I had studied in the Netherlands and was involved in Bach studies, she wanted to meet me. So Sherry and I invited her to come over for dinner, and she ended up staying the night with us. Within a short time we learned much about her: that she had completed her undergraduate studies at University College, Dublin; that she had graduated with distinction in music and mathematics; that she had spent some time in The Hague studying with the leading Dutch organist Ben Van Oosten; that she was the organist of St. Michael's, Dun Laoghaire, with its fine Rieger organ, where she had run the prestigious summer organ recitals for quite a few years; that she was teaching at the National University of Ireland, Maynooth, and the Dublin Institute of Technology (DIT) Conservatory of Music and Drama; that she was intrigued by the ingenuities and complexities of the music of Bach, which nevertheless has such strong emotional power; and a hundred and one other things that poured out while we sipped single malt scotch. The breeze was strengthening.

She learned that, with my colleagues, conductor Andrew Megill and baroque violinist Nancy Wilson, I was preparing a summer Bach festival at Westminster Choir College in Princeton, focused on the St. John Passion. Anne was determined not only that she would come but that she should also bring with her a group of friends and colleagues from Dublin—which, of course, she did, and she came more than once to these festivals, which became an annual event. The breeze had now become a steady wind. After the festival, she decided that this was exactly what was needed at the DIT, so she went to work on her colleagues in Dublin and, by force of personality, created the opportunity for the three of us to do something like our Princeton Bach festival with the DIT students, culminating in a performance of cantatas in the chapel of Trinity College. Over the years, we did the same kind of thing in Dublin on a number of other occasions, sometimes with Fred Fehleisen substituting for Nancy Wilson. These were notable experiences—for us as well as the Irish students who had not encountered the music of Bach in quite this way. But it was the hard work and infectious enthusiasm of Anne Leahy that made it all happen.

By this time she was well advanced on her dissertation, and she had become a member of the American Bach Society. The whirlwind was coming into her own, and the numbers on the Beaufort scale were steadily increasing. She completed her dissertation in 2002: "Text-Music Relationships in the 'Leipzig' Chorales of Johann Sebastian Bach"—her defense was a notable occasion, both for her feisty responses and for the social interaction between her family and friends with representatives of Bach scholarship. The following year she was awarded a Fulbright fellowship and became the first Gerhard Herz Visiting Professor in Bach Studies at the University of Louisville in the fall of 2003. During these years she attended many national and international conferences—at which she usually gave a paper—such as those arranged by the American Bach Society, the Internationale Arbeitsgemeinschaft für theologische Bachforshung, the Bach Network UK, the Biennial Conference on Baroque Music, the Society for Musicology in Ireland, and the Royal Musical Association, in such places as Eisenach (1996), Belfast (1996), Chicago (1997), Limerick (1997), Yale (1998), Belfast (1998), Exeter (1998), Waterford (1999), Løgumkloster (1999), Washington (2000), Utrecht (2000), Logroño (2002), Eisenach (2002), Maynooth (2003), Belfast (2004), New Brunswick (2004), Manchester (2004),Warsaw (2006), and Oxford (2006). A good number of these papers were revised and published in books and journals.[2]

During this period, she was teaching—and inspiring—students at the DIT; writing the program notes for the annual Bach cantata series at St. Ann's (appropriately named) Church, Dawson Street, Dublin; and generally encouraging others in their research. One of the projects to which she devoted much insight, energy, and promotion was in setting up an Institute for Baroque Studies at the DIT, focusing on the music of Bach and combining musicology with performance practice. Regrettably the project did not receive the initial funding she had hoped, and it never happened, though she never gave up on the idea. But her personal library of Bach and baroque music literature now forms a significant part of the library of the DIT Conservatory of Music in Rathmines: the "Anne Leahy Library Collection."

Of all the meetings and conferences in which she participated in recent years, five stand out. The International Bach Symposium sponsored by the University of Utrecht in the Bach year 2000 was notable in itself, but especially for the way that Anne persuaded leading Bach scholars to join the usual crowd who met together in one of the hotel rooms in the evenings after the sessions to talk, compare notes, and sip single malt scotch. Another occasion was the Ninth Biennial Conference on Baroque Music held at Trinity College, Dublin, also in the Bach year 2000. Anne was a prominent member of the organizing committee, and she worked (with Yo Tomita) to ensure that a significant part of the conference was devoted to papers on Bach.[3]

The American Bach Society meeting in Leipzig in 2006 was particularly important, not only for being the first time the society had met in the Bach city, but for Anne's vision with regard to another Irish Bach conference. She often used to say that she and Yo Tomita represented 100 percent of Bach scholarship in Ireland. In Leipzig she argued that it was about time for another Irish Bach conference. The baroque conference held in the Bach year of 2000 took place in Dublin, Anne's home city, so she was convinced that the next Irish Bach conference should be in Belfast, Yo Tomita's home city. So she got the three of us together in Leipzig, and plans were made for the International Symposium, Understanding Bach's B-minor Mass, which took place in November 2007 at Queen's University, Belfast, Northern Ireland. She was the one who took the initiative in the first instance, and its success was in large measure due to her vision, energy, and drive. All the while she was ill, she expressed the view that she fully intended to participate in Belfast. Sadly, this was not to be.

At the Bach Network UK conference in Oxford in December 2006, Anne responded to one of the papers but was clearly unwell, though she made light of it. The following month, she was to have made a trip to the United States to see friends, to work on the draft of her paper on the American Bach scholar Gerhard Herz,[4] and to discuss with me the revision of her dissertation for publication. She wrote to us to say that she would have to cancel her trip because her doctors wanted her to have some tests. The intensity of the whirl-wind had begun to ebb. Many weeks of treatment ensued, though not once did she complain, and in a few short months the whirlwind became a peaceful breeze and then was stilled.

A short life but a full one, and for those of us who knew her well, totally unforgettable.

★ ★ ★

I not only discussed various aspects of her research while Dr. Leahy was in the late stages of writing her dissertation, but I was also external examiner for her doctoral defense in Utrecht in November 2002. Based on this knowledge of her research, I encouraged her to think about its publication. Thus, during the following few years, as her teaching and other professional commitments permitted, we discussed how the manuscript should be revised for publication. In particular she was committed to restructuring the main chapters and to presenting some of the material in a different way. But she was never granted the time to put this into effect. Since to some extent I knew what she intended to do, I did consider the possibility of undertaking such substantial revision myself. However, for various reasons I decided against such a course of action. There was the danger of disturbing her distinctive style, which I did not want to do, so I decided to leave the structure and content of the chapters substantially as they were originally written.

Dr. Leahy was able to rewrite significant portions of the introduction, and I have conflated two versions into one. The final chapter of the dissertation was basically a summary of the chapters without much reflection on the significance of the "Leipzig" chorale preludes as a whole, or any discussion of a number of questions arising from the manuscript P271, such as the relationship between the six trio sonatas (BWV 525–530) and the Canonic Variations (BWV 769a), which are also included in the manuscript. In the computer files she created to work on for the chapters of the book, she did not include the dissertation's conclusion. It therefore seems certain that she intended to write a new concluding chapter that would address the broader issues relating to the collection. This would have included a discussion of whether or not the Canonic Variations on *Vom Himmel hoch* (BWV 769a)—which interrupt the sequence of the chorale preludes, appearing before *Vor deinem Thron* (BWV 668) in P271—were intended to be included as part of the collection. In the draft of the revised introduction, she signals that this issue would be discussed in the chapters that followed. Clearly this would have been included in the new final chapter that was never written.

Apart from the conflation of the two versions of the introduction, I have kept my editorial intrusions to a minimum, only making significant changes where Dr. Leahy had discussed with me the kind of revisions she wanted to make. Of course, had she lived long enough to complete this work of rewriting, it would have been a different book. Nevertheless, it remains an extremely thoughtful and useful piece of work that will inform, stimulate, and influence all who have an interest in this collection of Bach's organ chorale preludes.

★ ★ ★

Perhaps some comment on the methodology pursued in this study is needed here, since on the one hand this is something that Dr. Leahy intended to expand on in the introduction, and on the other, there has been some hesitancy about interpreting compositional details from the perspective of external, nonmusical contexts. For example, Dr. Leahy contributed an essay on Bach's vocal and organ settings of *Nun komm der Heiden Heiland* to the Festschrift issued in my honor.[5] In a review of the Festschrift, David Yearsley, while commending "Leahy's intuitive sense [that] provides a useful starting point for contemplating Bach's richly inventive confrontation with the same text and melody across different genres," nevertheless registers unease. He writes, "I often read such theologically informed exegesis of Bach's music cautiously, since I lack confidence in a hermeneutics that so easily deciphers the significance of musical passages by rough-and-ready analogy."[6] Such caution is necessary because it is so easy to read into music meanings that are subjective responses rather than objective observations, and such responses inform us more about the interpreter and less about the interpreted, as John Butt demonstrates in his parody of theological interpretation as applied to the opening chorus of the St. Matthew Passion.[7] But caution and unease do not mean that such investigations are invalid for musicological inquiry. The problem is that too many theological interpretations of Bach's music are made without a significant grasp of music theory, and too many musical analyses of Bach's music are made without reference to the liturgical and theological contexts within which and for which the music was originally composed. Opera cannot be discussed only from the point of view of its music. For example, the music of Mozart's *Magic Flute* will be misunderstood if it is explored without reference to the ideals of

Enlightenment philosophy, the beliefs and practices of Freemasonry, or later eighteenth-century criticism of Roman Catholicism. Similarly, Bach's vocal and organ music cannot be fully understood apart from the liturgical practices and theological beliefs that were then current in Lutheran tradition.

Bach's four-part chorales have formed the basis of teaching music theory for generations. Students are taught to hone their analytical skills to be able to recognize the voice-leading and harmonic progressions of these superlative examples. In exercises of phenomenology rather than epistemology, they learn how to describe what Bach has composed but not to understand why he chose to use particular harmonic progressions, sometimes quite extravagantly, in situations that in purely musical terms are surprising and unexpected. The problem is that most editions of Bach's four-part chorales are published without texts, yet a majority of these settings can be identified as originating in Bach's cantatas, passions, and oratorios. In their original locations, each of these settings is associated with a particular text, not just a hymn in general but a specific stanza of a hymn. When the specific text is matched to the particular four-part setting, it then becomes abundantly clear why Bach chose to harmonize it the way he did. The harmonization was not a flight of fancy on the part of the composer but rather the portrayal of the meaning of an individual stanza, putting into musical form a distinctive sequence of words.

If the four-part chorales are closely related to individual stanzas of particular hymns, and parallels of such connections between text and music can be found elsewhere in Bach's vocal works, then it is to be expected that in his chorale preludes—organ introductions to congregational singing of the Lutheran hymns—they would also in some way or another reflect the verbal content of those hymns. But chorale preludes are not explicitly linked to specific texts in the same way that four-part chorales and cantata movements are. However, if when analyzing the harmonic language Bach is found to use otherwise inexplicable harmonic or motivic devices, the likelihood is that the composer had in mind a particular stanza rather than the hymn as a whole. The ultimate goal of this study is to attempt to discover the implicit stanzas that Bach most likely focused on when composing and revising the so-called "Leipzig" chorale preludes.

The methodology applied to all the settings in this study is clear and straightforward. First, the hymn text itself is examined, noting its origins, general character, primary concepts, the sections within hymnals it usually appeared in, and the development of thought from stanza to stanza. Second, each chorale prelude is then analyzed purely from a musical point of view, charting its thematic, harmonic, and structural characteristics, especially its compositional peculiarities. Third, the interpretations of other authors are reviewed. Fourth, the stanzas of the associated hymn text are then reexamined to see whether there is one stanza, more than any other, that matches the musical fingerprint of the compositional characteristics of the particular chorale prelude. It is at this last step that not everyone will necessarily agree with the author's findings. But in the last resort, what is important here is not so much her conclusions but the questions she raises and the process she follows. We know from Bach's other works that his compositional decisions were carefully and deliberately considered and executed. This study is similarly a carefully considered attempt to understand something of the background of Bach's compositional choices with regard to his remarkable "Leipzig" chorale preludes.

★ ★ ★

My task as editor has been substantially assisted by the help and support of many of Anne Leahy's colleagues and friends, notably Kerry Houston, Yo Tomita, Siobhán Kilkelly, Ruth Tatlow, Isabella van Elferen, and Joan Lippincott, among others. I am particularly grateful to Derek Moylan who undertook the initial copy editing of most of the manuscript, and especially to Anne's parents, Michael and Gloria Leahy, for their support and commitment to the project.

NOTES

1. *Bach Notes* 8 (Fall 2007): 20–21.
2. For details, see the online Bach Bibliography: http://www.music.qub.ac.uk/tomita/bachbib.
3. Most of the Bach papers were edited by Anne Leahy and Yo Tomita and published as volume 8 of *Irish Musical Studies: Bach Studies from Dublin* (Dublin: Four Courts Press, 2004).
4. Published posthumously: Anne Leahy, "The American Image of Bach from a German Emigré's Perspective: Gerhard Herz and the Modern American Bach Movement," *BACH* 40/1 (2009): 58–79.
5. Anne Leahy, "Bach's Setting of the Hymn Tune '*Nun komm der Heiden Heiland*' in his Cantatas and Organ Works," in *Music and Theology: Essays in Honor of Robin A. Leaver*, ed. Daniel Zager (Lanham, MD: Scarecrow, 2007), 69–101.
6. *Music and Letters* 89 (2008): 616.
7. John Butt, *Bach's Dialogue with Modernity: Perspectives on the Passions* (Cambridge: Cambridge University Press, 2010), 154–156.

Author's Acknowledgments

*T*his study, a revision of my Utrecht University doctoral dissertation, comes about as a result of a lifelong love of the music of J. S. Bach. As an organist and choral singer, I have always prized his music above all others, both as performer and concertgoer.

I am deeply saddened that I must thank my primary doctoral adviser ("promoter" in Dutch), Professor Dr. Kees Vellekoop, posthumously. It was a great shock to hear of his sudden and untimely death in May 2002. I would like to acknowledge with gratitude the support and guidance he gave me while completing this research. "Ar dheis Dé go raibh a anam" [May his soul be on the right hand of God].

I owe a deep debt of gratitude to Professor Dr. Paul Op de Coul who agreed to oversee my work following the death of Professor Vellekoop. Even before this tragic event, he was always friendly and supportive, and for that I am grateful.

It was through the Dutch organist and musicologist Dr. Hans van Nieuwkoop that I was personally introduced to Dr. Albert Clement, who agreed to become my supervisor ("co-promoter" in Dutch). Words cannot sufficiently express the huge debt of gratitude I owe to Dr. Clement. For seven years he guided me through the world of Bach research, showing enormous patience and willingness to impart knowledge in the many discussions we had by telephone, fax, e-mail, and in person.

It was possible for me to complete my research by means of a fellowship awarded by the Research Institute for History and Culture of Utrecht University for the first four months of 2002. I am very grateful to Professor Dr. Wiljan van den Akker (director) and Dr. Frans Ruiter (vice director) who were responsible for helping me in this regard. I would also like to thank Dr.

Martine de Vos (coordinator of graduate studies, Utrecht University) for her support and friendship. Equally, I must thank my colleagues at the DIT Conservatory of Music and Drama, Dublin, who allowed me the freedom to take up this fellowship.

I must mention especially two fellow PhD students who have become dear friends: Isabella van Elferen and Saskia Rolsma. The support and friendship given to me by these two Dutch women enabled me to survive many difficult moments during my stay at Utrecht. I hope we will be lifelong friends.

To the many others who have helped me in so many ways, heartfelt thanks: Mary Adams, Philip Cahill, Brid Grant, Mary Greer, Kerry Houston, Louise van der Kaaden, Siobhán Kilkelly, Michael Marissen, Victor Merriman, Anna Nyurenberg, Yo Tomita, and Klaas Jan de Vries.

Finally, I would like to thank my parents, Michael and Gloria, and my two brothers, Brian and Pat, for their love and support in all that I do.

Introduction

Johan Sebastian Bach's "Leipzig" chorales are to be found along with the six trio sonatas (BWV 525–530) and the Canonic Variations (BWV 769a) in the manuscript P271 of the Staatsbibliothek in Berlin. Bach did not give a title to this important collection of chorale preludes and other organ compositions, though many have subsequently endeavored to supply the lack. The earliest title of the "Leipzig" chorales comes from page 73 of the catalogue of C. P. E. Bach's estate where the manuscript is described as comprising "Sechs Trios mit 2 Clavieren und Pedal und ohngefehr 20 Vorspielen und ausgeführten Chorälen für die Orgel. Von der eigenen Hand des Verfassers." [Six trios for two manuals and pedals and approximately 20 preludes and harmonized chorales for the organ. In the original hand of the composer.] For the first edition of the complete works of J. S. Bach (*Bachgesellschaft*), the editor, Wilhelm Rust, borrowed the title of the Schübler Chorales, giving the chorale preludes from P271 the title "Achtzehn Choräle von verschiedener Art" [Eighteen chorales of various types].[1] Hans Klotz, the editor of this collection for the *Neue Bach-Ausgabe*, gave the title of "Orgelchoräle aus der Leipziger Originalhandschrift" [Organ chorales from the Leipzig Original Manuscript], maintaining Bach's order of P271, placing the Canonic Variations between the first seventeen chorale preludes and the final incomplete BWV 668.[2] Since 1957, when the chorale preludes found in P271 (BWV 651–668) were first published in *NBA*, the issue of whether Bach intended there to be seventeen, eighteen, or more compositions in this collection remains more or less unresolved.

The appellation "Leipzig" is not entirely appropriate. While the manuscript P271 dates from Bach's Leipzig years, most of these chorale preludes were originally composed years earlier in Weimar. As will become clear in the forthcoming discussions, some earlier manifestations of these preludes were only lightly revised in Leipzig, and others were more extensively reworked.

Notwithstanding this anomaly, they continue to be universally referred to as the "Leipzig" chorales, even though there is less agreement on how many Bach intended to collect together: fifteen, seventeen, or eighteen.

To date, any decision regarding Bach's original intentions and the possible purpose of this collection are speculative. Without the emergence of specific documentary evidence, it is difficult to draw definite conclusions. However, the available sources can be examined: that is, the music, the hymn texts, and sources containing information regarding the theological background and context of these hymn texts. By linking these strands, it may be possible to find some answers.

Apart from examining the compositions, musical figures, hymn text, and theological background, it is necessary to highlight Bach's personal and deep involvement in Lutheran theology. It is known from the inventory of his estate at his death that he possessed a substantial theological library, which included the complete works of Martin Luther twice over.[3] In addition to these and other of Luther's works, he owned volumes of the writings of theologians such as August Pfeiffer, Heinrich Müller, and Erdmann Neumeister. This was no passing interest in theology. It represented an interest far beyond the demands of his job as cantor at Leipzig. A conscious interest in theology is reflected in Bach's compositions, especially those having their basis in the texts of the Lutheran chorale.

Each chapter of this book begins with a discussion of the relevant hymn text and its origins. An interesting feature of this collection is the high proportion of Reformation hymns. Twelve hymn tunes are employed by Bach for the eighteen compositions of the "Leipzig" chorales. Four of these are by Luther (1483–1546) (*Komm heiliger Geist, Herre Gott*; *Nun komm der Heiden Heiland*; *Jesus Christus unser Heiland*; and *Komm Gott Schöpfer heiliger Geist*), and two more are by Nicholas Decius (1485–c.1546) (*O Lamm Gottes unschuldig* and *Allein Gott in der Höh sei Ehr*), his direct contemporary and colleague. Another, *An Wasserflüssen Babylon*, is by Wolfgang Dachstein (1487–1533), a student of Luther's, making more than half of the chorale settings from this collection contemporary with Luther. Of the remainder, *Von Gott will ich nicht lassen* by Ludwig Helmbold (1532–1598) also dates from the sixteenth century, with three more dating from the first half of the seventeenth century: *Nun danket alle Gott* by Martin Rinckart (1586–1649), *Vor deinen Thron tret ich* by Bodo von Hodenberg (1604–1650), and *Schmücke dich, o liebe Seele* by Johann Franck (1618–1677). Only one, *Herr Jesu Christ dich zu uns wend*, by Herzog Wilhelm II (1598–1662) of Sachsen-Weimar, was written in the second half of the seventeenth century. It appears that Bach may have had a preference for the older hymns of the Reformation, with those of Luther himself taking up a third of the hymn titles and seven out of the eighteen compositions. In fact, twelve out of eighteen pieces use hymn tunes by Luther and his two contemporaries, Decius and Dachstein.

Some of the hymn texts have *de tempore* functions: two are dedicated to the feast of Pentecost (*Komm heiliger Geist* and *Komm Gott Schöpfer*), one to Advent (*Nun komm der Heiden Heiland*), and one to the Trinity (*Allein Gott in der Höh sei Ehr*). Others have recognizable functions within the liturgy: the pulpit hymn *Herr Jesu Christ, dich zu uns wend*; the *Agnus Dei, O Lamm Gottes unschuldig*; and the Communion hymns *Jesus Christus unser Heiland* and *Schmücke dich, o liebe Seele*. In addition, the Trinitarian hymn *Allein Gott in der Höh sei Ehr* is also the German *Gloria*. Four hymns from the collection remain: *An Wasserflüssen Babylon* is a hymn of penitence, and *Von Gott will ich nicht lassen* one of Christian conduct. *Nun danket alle Gott* was sung at weddings and on many other occasions in the Lutheran liturgy, perhaps most importantly after the singing of the Passion at Good Friday Vespers. The closing hymn of the collection, *Für deinen Thron tret ich*, was normally classified under "Morgenlieder" but actually had the flexibility to be sung at any time of the day. It is also interesting to note that two out of the four hymns of the Ordinary are represented in the *Gloria* and the *Agnus Dei*.

Discussion of the hymn texts is followed by a detailed musical analysis of the composition under discussion. Bach uses many varied styles of writing in this collection. He provides two fantasia-style works in *organo pleno* (BWV 651 and 661); three sarabandes with ornate treatment of the *cantus firmus* (BWV 652, 653, and 654); three trios (BWV 655, 660, and 664); three works each with a highly decorated *cantus firmus* (BWV 659, 662, and 663); a three-*versus* setting (BWV 656); two settings where the *cantus firmus* is presented relatively unadorned in the soprano (BWV 657 and 668); two further compositions in *organo pleno* (BWV 665 and 667); and an almost totally *manualiter* composition that represents an earlier period of Bach's development (BWV 666). In the analyses of these pieces, the main musical features are identified and linked with aspects of the text.

It has been acknowledged by many scholars that the texts of the hymns on which Bach founded his chorale-based works should play an important role in the interpretation of these pieces. Albert Schweitzer was among the first to recognize the potential for text expression in Bach's organ works, and Schweitzer's ideas, although often very subjective, may still be seen as pioneering in the field. It was he who drew to the attention of his organ teacher, Charles-Marie Widor, the significance of the chorale texts. In Widor's preface to the German version of Schweitzer's influential Bach monograph, dated 20 October 1907, he testified to his student's understanding of Bach. Widor had admitted difficulty in comprehending the chorale preludes. Schweitzer pointed out the significance of the text as follows:

> muß Ihnen in den Chorälen vieles dunkel bleiben, da sie sich nur aus den zugehörigen Texten erklären.[4] [many things in the chorales (i.e., chorale preludes) must seem obscure to you, for the reason that they are only explicable by the texts pertaining to them.[5]]

Widor originally asked Schweitzer to write an essay on the chorale preludes for the benefit of French organists, but Schweitzer responded by saying that it was necessary to include the passions and the cantatas in his essay, as the vocal works explained the chorale works and vice versa, hence his full-scale study.[6]

Since Schweitzer's monograph, many authors have written—some overly romantic in style—about the portrayal of text in Bach's chorale preludes. They include Hans Luedtke, Charles Sanford Terry, Harvey Grace, Stainton de B. Taylor, Fritz Dietrich, Rudolf Steglich, and Jacques Chailley, among others.[7] In 1950, Arnold Schmitz broke new ground in his book *Die Bildlichkeit der wortgebundenen Musik Johann Sebastian Bachs*[8] by methodically connecting rhetorical figures in Bach's music with aspects of the related text. This approach in itself was not completely new,[9] but the method of defining these figures marked a significant step forward in the field of Bach interpretation. Schmitz was the first to use rhetorical figures, the so-called "Figurenlehren," in studies of Bach's compositional decisions. Since Schmitz, other writers have looked to the theoretical writings of the baroque to aid their understanding of the composer's approach to composition.

The foundation of the Internationale Arbeitsgemeinschaft für Theologische Bachforschung by Walter Blankenburg and others in 1976 brought together a relatively small group of musicologists and theologians who over the following decades produced a significant body of literature that sought to understand Bach's music within the religious contexts of his time.[10] Bach was a Lutheran who spent most of his professional life serving the various musical needs of Lutheran churches, and his music is inextricably linked to his deep understanding of Lutheran faith and theology. In many respects the Arbeitsgemeinschaft set itself to answer Friedrich Blume's claim at the Bachfest in Mainz in 1962 that Bach may not have been as committed to his Lutheran beliefs as many scholars believed.[11] However, in the last thirty or forty years, considerable work has been done on both Bach's theological library and his musical output in a more contextual approach, and it is clear that while Blume was right to demythologize the often overblown, almost caricature portrayal of Bach as the faithful church musician, he clearly went too far in asserting that Bach was fundamentally nonreligious in the final decades of his life. The Arbeitsgemeinschaft itself was not entirely immune to mythology, as can be seen from some of the writings published under its name or influence,[12] and indeed, it was dissolved because some of its leaders were resistant to the broader religious research of such younger scholars as Michael Marissen, Tanya Kevorkian, and Isabella van Elferen, among others, who have pursued a more multidisciplinary approach, placing Bach's work and music in a much broader cultural context.[13]

Some of the members of the Arbeitsgemeinschaft produced some important and significant studies of individual chorale settings in the "Leipzig" collection. Notable among them is Casper Honders, an influential early member of the Arbeitsgemeinschaft, who set out to study systematically the text of the chorale on which each organ composition was based. This approach, linking the musical style of a composition with one or more specific stanzas of a text, had not been explored in quite this way before.[14] Studying with Honders, Albert Clement applied the methodology to Bach's chorale partitas, to his *Canonic Variations on Vom Himmel hoch*, and to the chorale preludes of *Clavierübung III*.[15] The present study builds on these earlier ones and applies the methodology to the "Leipzig" chorales.

Peter Williams' books on Bach's organ works were at the time of publication groundbreaking volumes and still represent the most comprehensive study of Bach's organ music in general in the English language. Even now, over twenty years later, they contain much valuable information and insight.[16] While Williams leaves many questions unanswered, he recognizes some of the importance of the link between text and music in Bach's chorale-based works. As to date only a few have considered this issue in the English language, Williams' work must be regarded as being of particular significance. In contrast, Russell Stinson's more recent books on the *Orgel-Büchlein* and the "Leipzig" chorales (or "Great Eighteen" as he calls them) do not deal with the issue of text and theology in any way.[17]

To date, only Clement has devoted book-length studies on the text-music relationships in Bach's chorale-based works. Authors such as Harvey Grace, Stainton de B. Taylor, Hermann Keller, and Jacques Chailley have all written books on Bach's organ works,[18] but on the whole they do not go into great detail with regard to possible relationships between text and music, and they do not appear to consistently employ a systematic methodology. Extended articles dating from the early twentieth century, from writers such as Hans Luedtke and Fritz Dietrich, are helpful, but again they do not provide much detail in this regard. In the latter part of the twentieth century, writers such as Casper Honders and Ulrich Meyer have provided insight in a more methodical manner. Peter Williams' work has the added value in that it also surveys most of the important pertinent literature published prior to his research.

Once the origin, authorship, and nature of a text has been established, the most significant part of each chapter explores the interconnections between the text and the main musical attributes of each composition. In many examples, some of these features can be linked to more than one stanza. This may imply that Bach was in fact setting more than one stanza. On the other hand, it may also be possible to connect the setting with a specific stanza by the way that Bach has used a musical technique or characteristic. Parallels are sometimes drawn with others of Bach's compositions, especially vocal movements, where the link between rhetorical figures and aspects of the text is often explicit. When similar texts and musical ideas are paralleled in both vocal and organ works, the analysis is confirmed, and Bach's compositional choices become clearer.

In his recently published facsimile edition of the "Leipzig" chorales, Peter Wollny has examined the contents of the manuscript. Like the *Orgel-Büchlein*, most of the chorale preludes that finally came down to us in manuscript P271 had in fact originated in Weimar, with Bach subsequently revising them at Leipzig. He clearly regarded this as an important collection, as the first fifteen chorale settings are in his own hand (the first thirteen dating from 1739–1742 and the following two from 1746–1747).[19] Of the remaining three compositions, BWV 666–667 are in the hand of Bach's son-in-law Johann Christoph Altnickol, and the final piece is in the hand of an as-yet-unidentified scribe.[20] At various times in his life, Bach assembled chorale-based organ works with unifying themes into collections. At the time that Bach began his autograph score of the "Leipzig" chorales, that is 1739, part 3 of the *Clavierübung* had just been published, and he was also working on the Well-Tempered Clavier, part 2. The only other organ works to be published in his lifetime were the six Schübler Chorales, BWV 645–650, published possibly as late as 1749.[21] It would seem that Bach may have been preparing a fair copy of the chorale preludes from P271 for publication.

The title page of this collection has been left blank, as if Bach had not yet decided on a title. This lack of knowledge regarding Bach's clear purpose for this group of pieces has been an issue for discussion among Bach scholars. There have been many suggestions as to his intentions regarding the collection. Some writers, including Werthemann, Honders, and Leaver, have suggested that these chorale preludes were put together as a collection of *musica sub communione*.[22] Meyer follows Klotz's view that Bach intended the first seventeen pieces as an entity separate from either the Canonic Variations or BWV 668. In his article on the inner unity of the "Siebzehn Choräle," Ulrich Meyer concludes that there is no obvious unifying thread.[23] In a recent dissertation, Evan Scooler has proposed that the eighteen "Leipzig" chorales can be seen as a collection of pieces intended by Bach for the Advent to New Year season.[24] More recently, Leaver has proposed that Bach's inclusion of the Canonic Variations in P271 was intentional and that if the other chorale preludes could have been used in the Advent to New Year season, then clearly variations on a hymn tune related to Christmas were not out of place.[25]

Important questions therefore arise out of Bach's order of the chorale settings in P271, questions that are considered throughout the course of this book:

First, is there a common theme between all settings, or is this manuscript simply reflecting a random choice of chorales placed in a collection together?

Second, is the order of chorale settings important, and could there be a theological significance for Bach's choice of order?

Third, the number of pieces in the collection must also be considered. BWV 668 may or may not be part of the intended collection.

Fourth, the Canonic Variations might also belong in this collection, and this point needs to be considered carefully.[26]

Another issue to be discussed is whether or not these seventeen or eighteen chorale preludes were originally conceived as part of a larger corpus. Like the *Orgel-Büchlein*, the chorale preludes in P271 were written while Bach was at Weimar. Unlike the *Orgel-Büchlein*, Bach does not leave blank pages, nor does he indicate missing settings. The fact that the first thirteen are in Bach's hand and date from an earlier period indicates that perhaps he stopped because he wanted to compose some more settings before inserting the final ones. This was not to be, however, and as other projects took over and ill health plagued him, Bach was perhaps forced to accept that he would not be adding to this collection.

While studying all these compositions, a theological pattern seemed to emerge. As will be demonstrated, in the case of every chorale prelude there appeared to be a link with stanzas that express an eschatological viewpoint. Bach began the Leipzig revisions of these chorale preludes sometime around 1739. In recent years, it has been shown that the Schübler Chorales belong to the last years of Bach's life.[27] In the case of five out of these six chorale preludes, it is possible to study the chorales in their original cantata settings. This provides a useful aid for interpreting the text in relation to the music. Clement has suggested that Bach had an eschatological theme in mind while putting this collection together.[28] In the later years of his life, it would not be surprising to find Bach compiling another collection united by a similar theme. Thus, throughout the course of this book, how Bach may have conveyed an eschatological perspective in his musical setting of each of the hymns will form part of the investigation.

★ ★ ★

The main focus of this study is on the text of the chorales as a source of inspiration for each musical composition. Issues of performance practice are therefore secondary. But understanding these texts and coming to terms with Bach's compositional decisions will hopefully lead to a greater comprehension of his multilayered counterpoint. Further, an assessment of Bach's possible intentions regarding text-music relationships does lead to some conclusions regarding registration and performance issues. These are discussed at the end of each chapter, where appropriate.

Citations from Luther's writings in their original form are taken from the Weimar edition of Luther's works. In most cases, the American edition of Luther's works for the English translation has been used. This explains the somewhat free translation of Luther's original writings in some of the citations. German biblical citations with Luther's comments are taken from *Biblia, Das ist: Die gantze Heilige Schrifft deß Alten und Neuen Testaments . . . von Herrn Doctor Martin Luthers . . .* (Nuremberg: Endter, 1729). Biblical citations in English are from the King James Version of the Bible. Hymn titles and musical compositions are given their modern titles, except for those cases referring to specific sources. The texts of the hymns are given as they appear in the original sources, which explains different spellings of the same word between hymn titles and hymn texts. Translations of cantata texts are those of Melvin Unger, *Handbook to Bach's Sacred Cantata Texts.*[29]

NOTES

1. *BG* xxv/3, 77. The volume was planned for the year 1875 but was not published until 1878.

2. *NBA*, IV/2: BWV 651–667, 3–97; Canonic Variations BWV 769a, 98–112; BWV 668 (incomplete in the manuscript: it appears that a leaf has been lost, which contained the remainder of the composition), 113–114; *KB* IV/2, 13. Klotz maintains that the title of "Achtzehn Choräle von verschiedener Art" is not authentic.

3. For an inventory of Bach's library, see Robin A. Leaver, *Bachs theologische Bibliothek / Bach's Theological Library. Eine kritische Bibliographie / A Critical Bibliography* [Beiträge zur theologischen Bachforschung 1] (Neuhausen-Stuttgart: Hännsler, 1983).

4. Albert Schweitzer, *J. S. Bach* (Leipzig: Breitkopf & Härtel, 1920), vii.

5. Albert Schweitzer, *J. S. Bach*, trans. Ernest Newman (New York: Dover, 1966), 1:vi.

6. Schweitzer, *J. S. Bach* (1920), viii; Schweitzer, *J. S. Bach* (1966), 1:vii.

7. See the bibliography, infra.

8. Arnold Schmitz, *Die Bildlichkeit der wortgebundenen Musik Johann Sebastian Bachs* (Schott: Mainz, 1950; reprinted, Laaber: Laaber Verlag, 1976 and 1980).

9. The modern exploration of baroque "figurenlehre" was begun by Arnold Schering, who invented the term. See Arnold Schering, "Die Lehre von den musikalischen Figuren im 17. und 18. Jahrhundert," *Kirchenmusik Jahrbuch* 21 (1908): 106–114; see also Peter Williams, "Figurenlehre from Monteverdi to Wagner. 1: What is 'Figurenlehre'?" *The Musical Times* 120 (1979): 476–479.

10. See Renate Steiger, ed. *Theologische Bachforschung heute: Dokumentation und Bibliographie der Internationalen Arbeitsgemeinschaft für theologische Bachforschung 1976–1996* (Berlin: Galda & Wilch, 1998).

11. Friedrich Blume, "Umrisse eines neuen Bach-Bildes," *Musica* 16/4 (July–August 1962): 169–176; "Outlines of a New Picture of Bach," *Music & Letters* 44 (1963): 214–227. The lecture and its published form proved controversial, being widely

translated and reprinted, as well as generating an inflamed flurry of writing, both pro and con.

12. See the criticisms of Rebecca Lloyd, "Bach among the Conservatives: The Quest for Theological Truth," PhD diss., King's College, London, 2006.

13. See, for example, Michael Marissen, *Lutheranism, Anti-Judaism, and Bach's St. John Passion* (New York: Oxford University Press, 1998); Michael Marissen, "On the Musically Theological in J. S. Bach's Cantatas," *Lutheran Quarterly* 16 (2002): 48–64; Michael Marissen, "The Character and Sources of the Anti-Judaism in Bach's Cantata 46," *Harvard Theological Review* 96 (2003): 63–99; Tanya Kevorkian, "The Reception of the Cantata during Leipzig Church Services, 1700–1750," *Early Music* 30 (2002): 26–45; Tanya Kevorkian, *Baroque Piety: Religion, Society, and Music in Leipzig, 1650–1750* (Farnham: Ashgate, 2007); Isabella van Elferen, "'Recht bitter und doch süße': Textual and Musical Expression of Mystical Love in German Baroque Meditations of Christ's Passion," *BACH* 35/1 (2004): 1–28; Isabella van Elferen, *Mystical Love in the German Baroque: Theology, Poetry, Music,* Contextual Bach Studies 2 (Lanham, MD: Scarecrow, 2009).

14. Honders' methodology is demonstrated in the following articles: "'Allein Gott in der Höh sei Ehr' BWV 663: Vom Dank zum Trost," *MuG* 4 (1975): 106–110; *Over Bachs Schouder. Een bundel opstellen* (Groningen: Niemeijer, 1985)—especially relevant to this study is the chapter "De 'Siebzehn Choräle': musica sub communione?"; and "Super flumina Babylonis. Bemerkungen zu BWV 653b," *Bulletin Internationale Arbeitsgemeinschaft für Hymnologie* 17 (1989): 53–60.

15. See Albert Clement, "O Jesu, du edle Gabe: Studien zum Verhältnis von Text und Musik in den Choralpartiten und den Kanonischen Veränderungen von Johann Sebastian Bach," PhD diss., University of Utrecht, 1989; Albert Clement, *Der dritte Teil der Clavierübung von Johann Sebastian Bach: Musik, Text, Theologie* (Middelburg: Almares, 1999). See also Albert Clement, "'Sechs Choräle' BWV 645–650 von J. S. Bach und dessen Bedeutung," in *Das Blut Jesu und die Lehre von der Versöhnung im Werk Johann Sebastian Bachs,* ed. Albert Clement [Royal Netherlands Academy of Arts and Sciences: Proceedings of the International Colloquium The Blood of Jesus and the Doctrine of Reconciliation in the Works of Johann Sebastian Bach, Amsterdam, 14–17 September 1993] (Amsterdam: Royal Netherlands Academy of Arts and Sciences, 1995), 285–304.

16. Peter Williams, *The Organ Music of J. S. Bach,* 3 vols. (Cambridge: Cambridge University Press, 1980–1986; 2nd ed. of vols. 1–2, 2003). Some have found Williams' tendency to ask questions but offer few answers somewhat frustrating, such as the harsh review by Wolfgang Stockmeier, *MuK* 69/2 (1999), 111–112, and the more moderate review of Werner Breig, *Mf* 54/1, 76–77.

17. Russell Stinson, *The Orgelbüchlein* (New York: Oxford University Press, 1996); Russell Stinson, *J. S. Bach's Great Eighteen Organ Chorales* (New York: Oxford University Press, 2001).

18. See the bibliography, infra.

19. Wollny, *Die Achtzehn Grossen Orgelchoräle,* xv–xvi.

20. Wollny, *Die Achtzehn Grossen Orgelchoräle,* xv–xvi.

21. Clement, "'Sechs Choräle' BWV 645–650," 287.

22. Helene Werthemann, "Bemerkungen zu Johann Sebastian Bachs Siebzehn Chorälen für Orgel," *MuG* 6 (1968): 154–160; Honders, "'Allein Gott in der Höh sei Ehr' BWV 663"; Robin A. Leaver, CD liner notes, *The Leipzig Chorales of J. S. Bach*, Joan Lippincott organist, Gothic Recordings, G49099, 1998.

23. Ulrich Meyer, "Zur Frage der inneren Einheit von Bachs Siebzehn Chorälen (BWV 651–667)," *BJ* 58 (1972): 63.

24. Evan Scooler, "Function Following Form: J. S. Bach's Changing Conception of the 'Great Eighteen' Organ Preludes," PhD diss., Brandeis University, 2003. Although Scooler's proposals raise interesting questions, he does not really address the theological issues in relation to the "Leipzig" chorales in any particular detail.

25. Robin A. Leaver, "Ms. Bach *P271*, a Unified Collection of Chorale-based Pieces for Organ?" *Bach Notes: The Newsletter of the American Bach Society* 1 (Spring 2004): 1–4.

26. [Ed.: This relationship was not explored in the original dissertation, and Anne Leahy intended to address the issue in this book. Regrettably she was not granted the time to do so and it therefore remains an unfulfilled intention.]

27. Clement, "'Sechs Choräle' BWV 645–650," 285.

28. Clement, "'Sechs Choräle' BWV 645–650," 285–304. In this regard it can be seen that the theses of Scooler (see note 24) and Clement run in parallel, since eschatology is a primary theme of the season of Advent.

29. Melvin Unger, *Handbook to Bach's Sacred Cantata Texts* (Lanham, MD: Scarecrow, 1996).

Komm heiliger Geist, Herre Gott

THE HYMN

The text of *Komm heiliger Geist, Herre Gott* is Luther's translation of the eleventh- or twelfth-century Latin antiphon *Veni, Sancte Spiritus, reple tuorum corda fidelium*.[1] Before the Reformation, it appeared in several single-stanza German translations.[2] Luther was very fond of this hymn, as is recorded in the *Tischreden*: "Den Gesang 'Komm, heiliger Geist' hat der heilige Geist selber von sich gemacht, beyde, Wort und Melodey" [The hymn, "Come Holy Spirit, Lord and God" was composed by the Holy Ghost himself, both words and music.][3] In Luther's version, the original medieval stanza was left almost intact, the text being expanded with two more stanzas to become *Komm heiliger Geist, Herre Gott*.[4] There were some variants of the melody used for this hymn. All the early sources give a simplified version of the plainchant melody of the German sequence, the tune of the Latin antiphon being never used with the German text. The hymn was published in 1524 in the two *Enchiridia* at Erfurt and also in Johann Walter's Wittenberg collection.[5] These publications were regarded as having the proper tune for the hymn. At first it bore the heading "Folget der Gesang *Veni sancte spiritus*, den man singt von dem heiligen Geist, nützlich und gut" [The following hymn *Veni sancte spiritus*, that one sings about the Holy Spirit, useful and good], and later the title was "*Veni sancte spiritus* gebessert durch Martin Luther" [*Veni sancte spiritus* improved by Martin Luther].[6] The text of *Komm heiliger*

Geist, Herre Gott as found in the Weimar hymnbook of 1713, where it is listed as a hymn, "Vom Heil. Pfingst-Fest," is as follows:

1. Komm heiliger Geist/ HERRE GOTT/
   erfüll mit deiner Gnaden gut/
   deiner Gläubigen Hertz/ Muth und Sinn/
   dein brünstig Lieb entzünd in ihn'n.
   O HERR durch deines Lichtes Glantz/
   zu dem Glauben versammlet hast/
   das Volck aus aller Welt Zungen/
   das sey dir HErr zu Lob gesungen/
   Hallel. Halleluja.

1. Come Holy Spirit, Lord God,
   fill with the goodness of your mercy,[7]
   the hearts, minds and spirits of your faithful.
   Ignite your ardent love in them.
   O Lord, through the brilliance of your light,
   into the faith you have gathered
   the peoples of all the world's tongues.
   Let this be sung to your praise.
   Alleluia, alleluia.

2. Du heiliges Licht/ edler Hort/
   laß uns leuchten des Lebens Wort/
   und lehr uns Gott recht erkennen/
   von Hertzen Vater ihn nennen.
   O HErr behüt für fremder Lehr/
   daß wir nicht Meister suchen mehr/
   denn JEsum Christ mit rechten Glauben/
   und ihm aus gantzer Macht vertrauen/
   Hallel. Hallel.

2. You holy light, precious protector,
   let the word of light enlighten us,
   and teach us to truly recognize God,
   and call him Father from our hearts.
   O Lord, guard us from strange teachings
   that we do not seek a master any more,
   so that we believe in Jesus Christ
   and trust him with all our might.
   Alleluia, alleluia.

3. Du heilige Brunst/ süsser Trost/
   nun hilf uns frölich und getrost/
   in deinem Dienst beständig bleiben/
   die Trübsaal uns nicht abtreiben.
   O HERR durch dein Kraft uns bereit/
   und stärck des Fleisches Blödigkeit/
   daß wir hie ritterlich ringen/
   durch Tod und Leben zu dir dringen/
   Hallel. Halleluja.[8]

3. You holy ardor, sweet comfort,
   help us now, glad and comforted
   to remain faithful in your work.
   Do not let sorrows drive us away.
   O Lord, prepare us by your power,
   and strengthen the weakness of the flesh,
   so that we struggle valiantly,
   and press forward to you in life and death.
   Alleluia, alleluia.[9]

Luther's teachings on Pentecost are strongly reflected in the text of *Komm heiliger Geist, Herre Gott*. In his sermon for Pentecost Sunday (1523), Luther explains the work of the Holy Spirit:

> Do schreybt er eyttel fewer flammen yns hertz und macht es lebendig, das es herauß bricht mit fewrigen zungen und thettiger hand und wirtt eyn newer mensch, der do fület, das er gar eyn andern verstand, gemüt und synn gefasst hab dann vor. Szo ist es nun alles lebendig, Lebendig verstandt, liecht, mütt und hertz, das so brunnet und lust hatt zü allem was Gott gefellet. Das ist die rechte unterscheyd zwyschen dem schrifftlichem und geystlichem gesetz Gottis Und do sihet man, was des heyligen geysts werck sey.[10] [There he writes in fiery flame on the heart and makes it alive, causing it to find expression in fiery tongue and active hand; a new man is made, who is conscious of a reason, heart and mind unlike he formerly had.

Everything is now alive: He has a live reason; he has light and courage and a heart which burns with love and delights in whatever pleases God. This is the real difference between the written and spiritual laws of God; and such is the work of the Holy Spirit.[11]]

Luther is describing the Holy Spirit of the New Testament in the above extract. Similarly, the same focus appears to be contained in the *Komm heiliger Geist* hymn text. The descent of the Holy Spirit on the apostles at Pentecost ensures that there is no more fear or struggle, according to Luther. He only comes to those who are in fear, as described in the same sermon as follows:

Darumb wirrt der heylig geyst niemant geben denn eben denen die da stehen ynn betrubnis unnd angst, da schafft das Evangelium nutz und frucht. . . . Denn es muß getzappellt seyn, soll der heylig geyst komen und helffen, Und solls yhm niemant ynn synn nehmen, das es anders werd zugehen. . . . die lieben junger sassen da noch ynn der forcht und erschrecken unnd waren noch ungetrost, war auch noch keyn mütt da. . . . Da der heylig geyst kam, wurden sie getröst und gesterckt unnd voll freude.[12] [Therefore the Holy Spirit is given to none except to those who are in sorrow and fear: in them it produces good fruit. . . . There must be struggling if the Holy Spirit is to abide in the heart, and let no one dare think that it will be otherwise. . . . The dear disciples sat in fear and terror, and still uncomforted and without courage. . . . When the Holy Spirit came they were comforted and strengthened and full of joy.[13]]

Luther is contrasting the written laws associated with the experience of Moses on Mount Sinai with the New Testament feast, which is a time of grace.[14] Renate Steiger clearly outlines the two aspects of Pentecost, pointing out the Old and New Testament elements.[15] These ideas are to be found in Luther's House Postil for the first day of Pentecost, which opens with the following statement:

Audivimus hodie et Evangelium et historiam huius frollichs, heiligen fests, *in quo* beghen *et gratias agimus pro maximo beneficio, quod in terris* erzeigt und da mit uns verlornen menschen uns lassen offenbaren *suum* heilig *verbum e caelo et non simplex verbum, sed* ein unterschiedlich wort gegen dem lege *Mosis, quia hoc die caepit Regnum Christi, per Apostolos* offenbart *coram mundo.*[16] [On this holy and joyful Pentecost Day we celebrate and thank our dear Lord God for the great and timeless gift which he bestowed on earth, when from heaven he revealed to us poor earthlings his holy, precious Word, a Word that is neither common nor ordinary, but is special and stands in sharp contrast to the law of Moses. For it was on this very day that Christ established his kingdom through the apostles, a kingdom that through the gospel is revealed to the whole world.[17]]

Luther emphasizes the festive aspect of Pentecost, stressing the great gift of the Holy Spirit. The fear experienced by the Israelites at Mount Sinai and by the waiting disciples of the New Testament disappears with the descent of the Holy Spirit at Pentecost. This gift of the Spirit, through Christ, is the establishment of the kingdom of Christ through the apostles. Further on in the same sermon Luther describes the feast in more detail:

> *Sed* heute zw tag ist angangen das frolich und selig und liblich reich Christi, das *plenum* ist *fiduciae et securitatis*. Das ist *alia loquela, quae non* yecht homines zwrücke *ut in Sina, non* schreckt, todet und würget, *sed* macht frolich und kecke, *Ut Christus promiserat, quod eis vellet mittere spiritum sanctum, qui non terreret, Sed* keck machen.[18] [But it was on this present Pentecost Day that the joyful, blissful and lovely kingdom of Christ was established, a kingdom filled with joy, courage and certainty. . . . It does just what Christ had promised to his disciples, that he would send to them the Holy Spirit, who would not be a terrifying spook but rather one who comforts, one who would fill them with joy, boldness and courage in the face of every kind of fear.[19]]

The basis of this sermon is the contrast between the terror of the Jews in the Old Testament on Mount Sinai and the grace of the joyful, blissful, and lovely New Testament feast.[20] In Luther's view, the time of Pentecost was a time of grace [Gnadenzeit], and this grace was the work of the Trinitarian God. Luther clearly saw Pentecost as a major feast day, as it was on this day in 1539 that he chose to introduce the Reformation in Leipzig. He preached at the Thomaskirche on Pentecost Sunday, 1539. Unfortunately, this sermon has not survived, but that which he preached the night before at Pleissenburg Castle, Leipzig, is extant.[21]

Each stanza begins with a salutation: the first to "heiliger Geist, Herre Gott," the second to "heiliges Licht, edler Hort," and the third to "heilige Brunst, süsser Trost."[22] All three stanzas can be divided into two halves, with the second half in each case beginning with the address "O Herr." With the first of these, the praise of the Holy Spirit is sung; with the second, the praise of correct learning (the Word); and finally the power of God is invoked.[23] The image of fire and tongues referred to by Luther in his sermon (1523) is found in stanza 1 with the reference to the ignition of love and the tongues of the entire world. Luther also refers to burning with love in the same sermon. It seems clear that Luther incorporates many of the ideas of his Pentecost sermons into the text of *Komm heiliger Geist, Herre Gott*.

Bach's versions of the melody in BWV 651 and 652, as well as those in the harmonized chorales BWV 59/3 (in G) and BWV 226/2 (in B-flat), closely resemble those of 1524 up to phrase 8. Historically, this chorale was transmitted in F or G. In the *NBA* score of BWV 651, mm. 88–89, Hans Klotz replaces the autograph reading of Bach's *cantus firmus* with further notes to the tune's eighth phrase.[24] This section was not altered in the old *Bachgesellschaft* edition. Klotz presumes that mm. 88, 90, and 91 as they appear in P1109 (Penzel Manuscript, source M in *NBA*) are Bach's latest changes, suggesting that the change of the bass note in m. 88 avoids the premature final effect of the semibreve *F* in the pedal.[25] In BWV 651 (mm. 101–103) and BWV 652, Bach uses Johann Walter's conclusion to the *cantus firmus*.[26]

Komm heiliger Geist, Herre Gott was the principal chorale for the three festival days of Pentecost in Saxony and Thuringia.[27] Bach set stanza 1 of this hymn in the cantata *Wer mich liebet, der wird mein Wort halten* (BWV 59), which was composed for the feast of Pentecost, and stanza 3 in the motet *Der Geist hilft unser Schwachheit auf* (BWV 226), although this may not have been meant as part of the original biblical motet.[28] The opening line of this chorale is transformed into a fugue subject in movement 2 of the violin sonata BWV 1005, and Bach also set stanza 3 in a now-lost movement of the cantata *Gott, man lobet dich in der Stille* (BWV 120b) for the two hundredth anniversary of the Augsburg Confession in 1730. A different chorale text was set by Bach to the *Komm heiliger Geist, Herre Gott* melody in the cantata *Er rufet seinen Schafen mit Namen* (BWV 175) for the third day of Pentecost, and he abbreviated the melody as an instrumental obbligato to a vocal duet in movement 5 of the cantata *Erschallet, ihr Lieder, erklinget, ihr Saiten!* (BWV 172), written for the first day of Pentecost.[29]

KOMM HEILIGER GEIST, HERRE GOTT (BWV 651)

Komm heiliger Geist, Herre Gott (BWV 651) is the first chorale prelude to be copied by Bach into P271 and is the opening piece of the collection. It is headed "*Fantasia sup*[*er*] *Kom heiliger Geist. canto fermo in Pedal*" in P271. Bach has also indicated the registration by placing the instruction "*In Organo pleno*" on the left side of the first stave. He has placed the inscription "*J. J.*" (*Jesu Juva*) on the same page, invoking the inspiration of Christ as he begins his project, as was frequently his practice with his cantata scores.

Like most of the settings in this collection, there are two versions: an earlier Weimar one, BWV 651a, and a later Leipzig revision, BWV 651. Of all the compositions in P271, it is the one in which the two versions differ the most. BWV 651a is 48 measures long, while the Leipzig reworking numbers 106 measures. Bach has set less than half of the *cantus firmus* in the earlier piece, while in BWV 651 he sets the entire chorale melody. Lines 2 and 6, as well as lines 3 and 7, are identical, with lines 4 and 8 differing in their ending only. The hymn closes with two four-note alleluias. Hans Klotz has suggested that BWV 651a is not the abridged version of BWV 651 but a work in its own right.[30] Werner Breig has investigated the provenance of the two settings most thoroughly and is convinced that BWV 651 is a later Leipzig revision of BWV 651a.[31] Peter Williams suggests that perhaps BWV 651a is not the original composition and that both versions may be contemporary.[32] Much has been made of the differences and similarities between the two versions; these issues are discussed further in what follows.

The length of the *cantus firmus* and Bach's full use of it in BWV 651 make for a piece of some considerable length. This is an exuberant, tightly knit toccata in *organo pleno* with most of the motivic material being derived from the *cantus firmus*. As with many *organo pleno* chorale settings, the *cantus firmus* appears in the pedal. The upper voices enter imitatively over a pedal *F*, with motivic material clearly stemming from line 1 of the hymn tune, heard in long notes in the pedal from m. 8. This opening motive, which dominates the entire piece, is characterized by arpeggio figures as well as by a syncopated quarter note that appears each time in the second measure of the motivic material. The main modulations are naturally dictated by the hymn tune itself. Yet Bach succeeds in employing some very expressive harmonic touches, even within the confines of the *cantus firmus*.

Following the statement of line 1 of the *cantus firmus* (mm. 8–13), the opening material is heard again, this time in the dominant leading to line 2 at m. 16 and cadencing back to the tonic at m. 20. The following episode (mm. 21–31) introduces an important new *syncopatio* figure, hinted at in m. 22 but becoming significant at m. 26. A double suspension in thirds is heard against the opening arpeggio motive, itself leading to another *syncopatio* at m. 28. Bach had already laid the foundation for the use of such suspensions with the syncopated quarter note in m. 2.

Line 3 of the *cantus firmus* enters in m. 31, with the manual parts above continuing in the pattern of accented dissonance. There is a mere one-measure interlude between the statements of lines 3 and 4 of the *cantus firmus*. An important moment occurs at m. 44, where Bach harmonizes the final *A* of line 4 with an A major chord, thereby launching the second half of the piece. This is followed by the second real episode (mm. 45–52). A *suspiratio* is introduced at m. 46. This episode provides the farthest modulations so far, passing through D minor, F major, A minor, G minor, and back to D and G minor before the entry of line 5 of the *cantus firmus* at m. 52. The accompanying parts continue with the falling suspensions in double thirds first heard beginning at m. 25, as well as utilizing the opening material.

Measures 55–86 correspond with mm. 12–43. Line 8 differs from line 4 in its ending only. At m. 87, the *cantus firmus* leads back to the tonic where it had previously remained on the chord of A major at m. 44. The final section begins at m. 89 leading to the closing alleluias, with the many parallel thirds and sixths providing a triumphant and ecstatic close. At m. 99, Bach skillfully expands the texture to five parts. This increase in the number of parts gives even more prominence to the *syncopatio* figures heard in mm. 98–99. Bach introduces an expressive *a-flat*, which results in a diminished-seventh chord at m. 104.3 as a decisive climax before the final perfect cadence.

Interpretations by Other Authors

The image of the fires of Pentecost has inspired many writers on the subject of *Komm heiliger Geist, Herre Gott* (BWV 651). With the exception of Hans Luedtke, Charles Sanford Terry, Jacques Chailley, and perhaps Peter Williams, no writer makes a connection between a specific stanza and the musical setting in their discussion of this composition.

Albert Schweitzer refers to "feierlicher Pfingstjubel" [festive rejoicing of Pentecost] and "helle Sonne" [bright sun] in relation to BWV 651 in his introduction to the complete works of Bach.[33] In his opinion, the broken chords symbolize the "Feuerzungen" [tongues of fire].[34]

Luedtke sees this setting as portraying stanza 1 in "das Brausen des Pfingstgeistes über die versammelte Gemeinde verkündet" [the heralding of the rushing of the Pentecostal spirit over the assembled community].[35]

Terry considers that the strong statement of the *cantus firmus* and the flickering sixteenth notes seem to paint the text of stanza 2, "He is the verite and the tongues of fire."[36]

Stainton de B. Taylor likens this setting to "a Gothic fanvault which starts from one pillar, yet radiates over a large area without ever losing its connexion with the source."[37] He also suggests that Bach "apparently wishes to suggest the leaping of the 'tongues of fire' around the heads of the apostles."[38]

Hermann Keller finds it significant that Bach begins his collection with Luther's great hymn to the Holy Spirit.[39] Pointing out the virtuoso aspect of the piece, he urges that the Spirit should not evaporate in the technical brilliance.[40]

Chailley sees a relationship with stanza 1 of the text. He refers to the image of light reflected in Bach's setting, specifically citing the word "Glanz" in the context of the final alleluias.[41]

Ulrich Meyer states that the framing function of BWV 651 and BWV 667 in this collection is indisputable, but that any other attempts at finding a cyclical order are not valid.[42] According to him, the tongues of fire are reflected in the head motive and refer to Acts 2:2.[43] Williams considers that,

> A huge continuous fantasia, musically and dogmatically as grand an opening as the prelude to *Clavierübung III*, this setting is easy to see as a response to Pentecost: "And suddenly there came a sound from heaven, as of a rushing mighty wind, and it filled all the house where they were sitting" (Acts 2:2).[44]

Russell Stinson refers to imagery relating to rushing winds and tongues of fire.[45] Most of the attempts to connect text and music in BWV 651 have been limited to a general interpretation of the constant semiquavers as representing the fires of Pentecost. There is more to say about the text-music relationships in this composition; this is the subject of the next section.

Assessment

The three stanzas of *Komm heiliger Geist, Herre Gott* are concerned with different attributes of the Holy Spirit, as described previously. In order to discern the stanza(s) to which Bach is alluding, it is necessary to examine the musical features of *Komm heiliger Geist, Herre Gott* (BWV 651) and investigate how they might relate to the text. As a toccata in *organo pleno*, this composition is characterized by nonstop sixteenth-note movement in an imitative texture, many dissonances and "sighing" motives, and a rapturous closing section. Can these elements lead to one particular stanza of text?

The very authoritative opening motive and its prominent presence throughout BWV 651 may lead one to believe that Bach was immediately establishing a commanding and forceful atmosphere. This mood, maintained for the duration of the entire piece, is enhanced by the addition of other important musical motives. Is the dominance of the thundering sixteenth notes related to one line of text, one stanza, or the entire hymn? How do the "sighing" motives that appear in three different passages relate to the text? Can the frequent use of dissonance relate to the blissful feast of Pentecost?

Some writers have suggested that Bach was depicting the rushing fires of Pentecost, without alluding to the hymn text at all. This seems to imply, therefore, that Bach only interpreted *Komm heiliger Geist, Herre Gott* in a very general way as a Pentecost hymn. Can these writers then say that these specific musical details described above bear no relationship to the text?

Examining the possibilities that Bach may have considered, it appears unlikely that he was portraying the text of stanza 3. Stanzas 1 and 2 have much in common. The concept of light is important to both stanzas, as is faith and the strong, powerful nature of the Holy Spirit. Stanza 3 portrays the Holy Spirit as "süsser Trost," and the dominant theme here is one of comfort. Although there are words in stanza 3 such as "frölich," "beständig," and "ritterlich ringen," which could be linked to the musical setting, the opening line, "Du heilige Brunst/ süsser Trost," does not seem appropriate to the toccata style. On many occasions when Bach refers to "süss," he writes in a very specific style, often incorporating the sweet sound of parallel thirds and sixths.[46]

It may be that the *plenum* registration and the toccata style are related to the text. Conceivably, these characteristics could relate to either stanza 1 or stanza 2. It is possible to link key words such as "Herre Gott," "Gläubigen," "entzünd," "brünstig," and "lichtes Glantz" (stanza 1) or "Licht," "Hort," "leuchten," and "glauben" (stanza 2) to this musical style. Bach may be portraying both stanzas 1 and 2 here, or he may be being more specific. Stanza 2 starts with "Du heiliges Licht, edler Hort." The reference to light is certainly relevant to Pentecost and the *plenum* setting, but stanza 1 also contains a reference to light in the fifth line of the text. The music for line 5 of the *cantus firmus* is identical to line 1, apart from the first note. This allows Bach to bring about a return of the opening music for the second half of the piece. Therefore lines 1 and 5 of the *cantus firmus* receive similar musical treatment. This might imply that these lines had analogous meanings. Here lines 1 and 5 of stanzas 1 and 2 are compared:

Stanza 1	*Stanza 2*
Komm heiliger Geist/ Herre Gott/	Du heiliges Licht/ Herre Gott/
O Herr durch deines Lichtes Glantz	O Herr behüt für fremder Lehr

It seems that lines 1 and 5 for stanza 1 are more suited to the musical setting than those of stanza 2. It may be that the reference to light in stanza 1 and its treatment with the opening motive then negates the need to depict stanza 2, which would also portray this word in the same way. Lines 1 and 5 of stanza 2 do not appear to have a common link, not enough to give them a similar musical setting.

One of the striking features of this setting is the constant reworking of the opening motive, perhaps highlighting the first line of text in a special way. As the opening piece of the collection, it might stand to reason that Bach would invoke "heiliger Geist/ Herre Gott" of stanza 1.

The opening of BWV 651 could certainly be seen as a fitting portrayal of line 1 of stanza 2 also. The corresponding musical setting of line 5, however, is not so easily understood. There are no obvious reasons to link the notion of protection from strange teaching to this music, nor does this line of text have any striking common ground with the opening line. As there seems to be a much greater link between lines 1 and 5 of stanza 1, it is more logical that Bach should have chosen this stanza. In stanza 1 there is a reference to the divine power of the Holy Spirit, which is linked to the image of light, portrayed in a corresponding musical fashion. Moreover, primary images for Pentecost contained in stanza 2, such as light and faith, are also included in stanza 1. All of the issues central to the feast of Pentecost can be found in the text of stanza 1, which asks that the Holy Spirit fill the hearts, minds, and spirits of the faithful, igniting his ardent love in them. The line "das Volck aus aller Welt Zungen" is also crucial to the feast of Pentecost. The Spirit brings salvation, and therefore all of humanity is saved, causing the great hymn of praise found in the final line of text before the concluding alleluia. Stanza 2 does not have the powerful theological impact of stanza 1. Additionally, as a chorale prelude in a collection united by an eschatological theme, does stanza 1 not contain more vital elements in this regard? It is striking that Bach chooses to highlight the Holy Spirit in the order of the chorale settings in P271. The first seventeen compositions are placed between the trio sonatas and the Canonic Variations. The seventeenth piece, BWV 667, is also based on a Pentecost hymn by Luther, *Komm Gott Schöpfer heiliger Geist*. The number seventeen has traditionally been associated with the Holy Spirit, and it is possible that Bach is using this symbolism to highlight the role of the Spirit in the salvation of humanity.[47]

After consideration of the above arguments, it seems that the opening stanza of *Komm heiliger Geist, Herre Gott* may be the one that Bach was portraying in BWV 651. Detailed examination of the musical setting may help to confirm this argument.

The opening motive is striking in its rising triadic writing, suggesting strength and power of some sort, perhaps the rushing fires of Pentecost and the Holy Spirit, Lord God. As mentioned above, since this motive dominates the entire composition, Bach may be establishing from m. 1 the authority of the Holy Spirit. This kind of fanfare motive is sometimes used by Bach to express power and great joy.[48] The incessant roar of the sixteenth notes in this *plenum* setting seems to correspond easily to the idea of "Herre Gott" and tongues of fire.

Consistent employment of sixteenth notes is sometimes associated with the Holy Spirit in Bach's music. In addition, he occasionally incorporates the *circulatio* into this kind of writing, as seen in the violin parts of the opening movement of the St. John Passion. In the first movement of the cantata *O ewiges Feuer, o Ursprung der Liebe* (BWV 34), the fires of Pentecost are portrayed in the perpetual sixteenth-note motion. This type of writing is equally suited to line 2 of the text of this cantata, "entzünde die Herzen" [ignite the hearts]. The opening motive of the motet *Der Geist hilft unser Schwachheit auf* (BWV 226) is another example where the Holy Spirit is portrayed in the consistent use of sixteenth notes (see example 1.1).

As in BWV 226, Bach consistently uses sixteenth-note motion through-out BWV 651, perhaps as a means of reminding the listener of the fires of Pentecost.[49] Line 4 of the text of stanza 1 also mentions "entzünd," which, as in BWV 34/1, can be associated with the perpetual sixteenth-note movement. It seems clear, as others have suggested, that Bach is portraying the tongues of fire in this kind of writing in BWV 651. Equally, he could be depicting the tongues of the peoples of the world.

Line 2 of the text, "erfüll mit deiner Gnaden gut," continues with the same motivic development as the opening. At the word "Gnaden," Bach introduces the *syncopatio catachrestica* figure (m. 19.1).[50] In addition, the music modulates toward the subdominant for "gut" (m. 20). How can this seemingly opposite *Affekt* be employed by Bach when the text is clearly about something positive?[51] The theological meaning seems to be at odds with Bach's musical setting. BWV 651 is a joyful and exuberant toccata, and the use of apparently negative aspects such as the *syncopatio* may seem paradoxical. It is possible that in the music Bach is deliberately portraying the opposite of the text.[52]

Following the cadence to F via the subdominant at mm. 19–21, new motives are introduced. Bach begins with the opening motive in the left hand of m. 21, and sixteenth-note motion continues to dominate. In m. 23, Bach introduces a rhythmic motive that returns throughout the piece. This is an eighth-note rest, followed by an eighth note and a quarter note, a motive that is significant in the context of the new "sighing" motive that begins at m. 25.4 (hinted at in m. 21); see example 1.2.

This "sighing" motive (example 1.2) is repeated three times, falling a step each time, always in parallel thirds. Bach does not introduce new motives without a reason. In this passage he seems to be portraying positive and nega-tive ideas through music. Measures 24–25 are centered on G minor leading to D minor, involving minor ninths and some very sharp dissonances (*parrhesia*)

Example 1.1. BWV 226 (mm. 1ff.)

Example 1.2.   BWV 651 (m. 25.4ff.)

such as at m. 25.1, where an *a²* is held above *b-flat¹* in the two upper parts. Just as this passage seems to become resolved, it is followed by the "sighing" motive at m. 25.4. On the last eighth note of m. 27, Bach initiates a *syncopatio* figure, similar to that heard in m. 23, which continues descending a fifth to m. 30, where the music finally cadences to F major with no dissonance at m. 31.1. This passage is striking for its use of *parrhesia* and *syncopatio* in combination with the pleasing sound of double thirds and the positive opening motive. Is it possible that an explanation may be found in the writings of Luther regarding the two sides of the feast of Pentecost?

In his first sermon for Pentecost (*House Postils*, 1534), Luther once more emphasizes the difference between the old and the new Pentecost as follows:

> *In natura potes discernere* freude und traurickeit, leben und tod.[53] [Therefore, I insist that we distinguish between sorrow and joy, between death and life.[54]]

It is possible to relate Bach's use of opposites in BWV 651 to Luther's teachings on Pentecost: the fact that the Spirit comes to those in fear and despair. Although the Pentecost of the New Testament is generally associated with joy and life, Luther repeatedly returns to the theme of fear in his Pentecost sermons. Article 4 (Justification) of the "Apology of the Augsburg Confession" also confirms the idea of fear being associated with the Holy Spirit, describing faith as follows:

> *sed est opus spiritus sancti, quo liberamur a morte, quo eriguntur et vivificantur per-terrefactae mentes.*[55] [It is a work of the Holy Spirit that frees us from death and raises and makes alive terrified minds.[56]]

For Luther and his followers, therefore, the feast of Pentecost has a fearful as well as a joyful side. The point of the new Pentecost is to dispel this fear. Can it be said that Bach's use of figures in this passage is related to Luther's interpretation of the New Testament Pentecost, that the Holy Spirit comes to those in fear and despair? Joy and fear indeed appear to be present in BWV 651: the positive side of Pentecost may be represented in the joyful, exuberant sixteenth notes and the frequent parallel thirds and sixths, while the more fearful aspects are perhaps found in the use of the *syncopatio*, *parrhesia*, and "sighing" motives.

Furthermore, Bach's use of the "sighing" motive can be related to the Holy Spirit. Many of the cantata texts for Pentecost mention the Holy Spirit in this context: for example, in the cantata *Erschallet, ihr Lieder, erklinget, ihr Saiten!* (BWV 172), the text of movement 5 addresses the Holy Spirit as "sanfter Himmelswind" [gentle heavenly wind], asking him, "wehe durch den Herzensgarten!" [waft through this heart's garden!]. The word "seufzen" [sigh] is used by Paul in Romans 8:26 as follows:

> Desselbigen gleichen auch der Geist hilft unsrer Schwachheit auf. Denn wir wissen nicht, was wir beten sollen, wie sichs gebühret, sondern der Geist selbst vertritt uns aufs beste mit unaussprechlichem Seufzen. [Likewise the Spirit also helpeth our infirmities: for we know not what we should pray for as we ought: but the Spirit itself maketh intercession for us with groanings which cannot be uttered.]

Thus the sighs and groanings of the Holy Spirit are associated with ridding humanity of its infirmities. Could Bach's use of the "sighing" motive be related to Paul's description of the Holy Spirit? The Holy Spirit comes to those in fear and despair, and he makes intercession with "groanings which cannot be uttered." This text is also used by Bach in the motet *Der Geist hilft unser Schwachheit auf* (BWV 226). On this occasion, Bach employs the *syncopatio*, perhaps to illustrate the sighings of the Holy Spirit helping those in fear. See example 1.3; this example shows Bach's use of syncopations in relation to the Holy Spirit. It may be possible that the syncopations of BWV 651 could take on a similar meaning to those of BWV 226.

With the entrance of line 3 of the *cantus firmus* at m. 31, Bach continues with syncopations and dissonances in the same vein as before, again employing minor ninth harmonies, passing through G and D minor before finally cadencing to C major in m. 36. Even though the preceding phrase is full of seeming uneasiness, the eventual cadence to C major seems to confirm a more positive atmosphere.

Example 1.3. BWV 226 (mm. 124ff.)

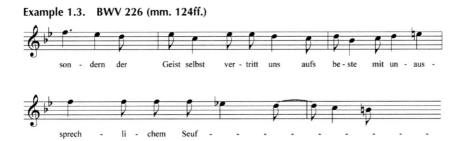

The setting of the following line of text, "dein brünstig Lieb entzünd in ihn'n," appears to be the musical axis of BWV 651. In the earlier Weimar setting, BWV 651a, Bach went to line 8 of the chorale here rather than continuing on with line 4. From m. 43.2 in BWV 651, new material is heard. The concept of "entzünd" seems easy to relate to the overall musical setting. From beginning to end, this piece is filled with fire and power. The cadence from mm. 43–44 is particularly striking, the phrase ending on the dominant of D minor, offering a new starting point for the second half of the piece.

Although the opening motive is heard again halfway through m. 44, Bach ingeniously changes the motivic writing beginning at m. 46, apparently to make a new musical and theological point. In the left hand, a motive is heard that is very similar to that heard at the close of *Von Gott will ich nicht lassen* (BWV 658), where an upbeat eighth note leads to an octave leap (see example 1.4).[57]

The use of this motive is a positive action that can be seen as affirming the power of the Holy Spirit as "Herre Gott" as well as conveying trust and faith in the feast of Pentecost. A *figura suspirans* alternates between the two upper voices above this octave motive. A diminished-seventh chord leads to the dominant of A minor at m. 48, where on the fourth beat of the measure the "sighing" motive in double thirds first heard in m. 25 returns. This time Bach also employs parallel sixths, but the overall *Affekt* is still the same: as before, two seemingly conflicting ideas are present.

Lines 1–4 and 5–8 of this hymn tune resemble each other very strongly, and so Bach uses the same musical material for the corresponding lines of the hymn. What is significant is that the reintroduction of the "sighing" motive at m. 48.4 means that this section offers an extra presentation of this particular motive. It is heard again at m. 68, but it appears that Bach considered it important enough to also place it before the entry of line 5 of the *cantus firmus*.

In line 5, "O Herr durch deines lichtes Glantz," the Holy Spirit is referred to as "Herr" for the second time in stanza 1. This is a very important line of text, as light is also mentioned. This linking of light to faith is a significant theme. Similar concepts are to be found in the text of stanza 7 of *Nun komm der Heiden Heiland* (see the discussion in chapter 8). There seem to be many similarities between BWV 651 and BWV 661. Both are *plenum* settings written in a toccata style with the *cantus firmus* in the pedal. For Luther, light

Example 1.4.   BWV 651 (m. 45.4f.)

and faith were strongly linked, as seen in his sermons for the first Sunday of Advent. Faith and salvation meant being in the light, coming out of darkness as described in the epistle for this Sunday (Romans 13:11–14). Luther's sermon (1522) for that particular Sunday makes this point:

> Gleych wye Christus die ßonn, und das Euangelium der tag ist, ßo ist der glawb das liecht oder sehen und wachen an dißem tag. . . . Nu ist gnug gesagt, das liecht heysse hie den glawben, der vom tag des Euangelii auß der ßonnen Christo ynn unßer hertz leuchtet.[58] [As Christ is the Sun and the Gospel is the day, so faith is the light, or the seeing and watching on that day. . . . Now, as already made plain, the word "light" here carries the thought of "faith." The light of faith, in the Gospel day, shines from Christ the Sun into our hearts.[59]]

The phrase "lichtes Glantz" in stanza 1 has the same melody as "Herre Gott." This was fortunate for Bach, as he could relate the two. The idea of "Lichtes Glantz" and "Herrlichkeit" was already linked by Paul in Hebrews 1:3 as follows:

> Welcher, sintemal Er ist der Glanz seiner Herrlichkeit, und das Ebenbild seines Wesens, und trägt alle Dinge mit seinem kräftigen Wort, und hat gemacht die Reinigung unserer Sünde, durch Sich Selbst, hat Er Sich gesetzt zu der Rechten der Majestät in der Höhe. [Who being the brightness of his glory, and the express image of his person, and upholding all things by the word of his power, when he had by himself purged our sins, sat down on the right hand of the Majesty on high.]

In the above biblical citation, light and divine glory are related to Christ. The letter to the Hebrews is very important as it is here that Jesus is put on an equal footing with the Father, being referred to as God. The Holy Spirit is part of this Godhead, and equally light and divine glory are an important part of his nature. These two aspects appear to be linked musically in BWV 651.

Line 6 of the *cantus firmus* follows, with the text mentioning faith, a keyword for Pentecost, as follows: "zu dem Glauben versammlet hast." As with line 2 of the text, which employed the same music, the certainty expressed by the text does not seem to be reflected in the music. The hymn text asks that the peoples of the world be gathered in faith, but Bach still offers music that turns to G minor by way of a diminished-seventh chord for the word "Glauben," finishing the phrase with a move toward the less positive subdominant side. In m. 63, as in m. 20, Bach even uses a *d-flat*, which causes a diminished-seventh chord, to get back to F. If he really wanted to portray the positive side of the text, would he not have written a more positive cadence? He seems to have wanted to create some kind of uncertainty or feeling of an as-yet-unresolved issue. This notion appears to be confirmed when once again we hear the "sighing" motive beginning at m. 68.4, as first heard at m. 25 with all its attendant preceding dissonant harmony (this time in mm. 67–68).

Line 7 of the *cantus firmus* enters in m. 74. Here the text describes all the peoples of the world gathered together in one faith: "das Volck aus aller Welt Zungen." The tongues of the entire world and the tongues of the flames of Pentecost are depicted in the continuous sixteenth-note movement. There is a feeling that the music is moving toward a climax, and even though this music has been heard before (mm. 31–37), line 7 of the text of stanza 1 seems more appropriate in the context of this particular point of the piece. There is a sense of all the voices of the world uniting in faith in this great *paean* of praise. The consonant intervals of m. 81 lead easily to the entry of line 8 of the *cantus firmus* at m. 82, "das sey dir Herr zu Lob gesungen." The final note of the *cantus firmus* as it appears in P271 is a whole-note *F* tied to a half-note *F*. Hans Klotz seems to have considered that the Penzel manuscript was a more authoritative source than P271.

From m. 89, new material is introduced in an imitative manner leading to the final "Halleluja" beginning at m. 95. From m. 95 to 97, the manual parts have much writing in parallel thirds and sixths, reflecting the joyfulness of the alleluia. In m. 98, Bach reintroduces the "sighing" motive as if to remind his listeners of that part of the message of Pentecost. As he does at the end of the following setting of *Komm heiliger Geist, Herre Gott* in this collection (BWV 652), Bach introduces more voices into the texture, increasing the feeling of ecstasy created by already joyful musical lines. Parallel thirds and sixths remain prominent from m. 100, being present in almost every measure to the end.

From the above investigation of the relationship between text and music in BWV 651, it may become clear why Bach decided to expand the original Weimar version, BWV 651a, of only 48 measures to 106 measures in the later Leipzig version, BWV 651. This is a lengthy hymn stanza of nine lines. To set only four lines of the *cantus firmus* might diminish the importance and relevance of the hymn. It may be that when Bach decided to assemble this collection, he decided that a more substantial interpretation of the text of *Komm heiliger Geist, Herre Gott* was required. Although Bach repeats much of the music in the second half of the piece, due to the similarity between the lines, the second hearing of some of the material adds stature to the piece and may increase the understanding of the text. The climax of the "Hallelujah" section seems to have more meaning following the musical presentation of all preceding eight lines of the *cantus firmus*.

From this discussion it appears that Bach was portraying the text of stanza 1 in BWV 651. In the "Leipzig" chorales, Bach sets *Komm heiliger Geist, Herre Gott* twice. It seems logical that he would somehow set the three stanzas of the hymn over the course of the two compositions. Bach appears to have solved this problem by highlighting the idea of light, referred to in the opening of stanza 2, but also explicitly mentioned in line 5 of stanza 1. In this way he employs an important aspect of stanza 2 in his portrayal of stanza 1 of the hymn. In BWV 652, Bach portrays aspects of Pentecost in a completely different manner from BWV 651, as the discussion in the following section will demonstrate.

KOMM HEILIGER GEIST, HERRE GOTT (BWV 652)

Komm heiliger Geist, Herre Gott (BWV 652) is the longest setting in the "Leipzig" chorales, being 199 measures in total. It is headed "*Komm heiliger Geist. alio modo. à 2 Clav. et Ped.*" in P271. There are two versions of this chorale prelude: an earlier Weimar setting (BWV 652a) and a later Leipzig revision (BWV 652). Bach sets the chorale in triple meter. It has much in common with the two settings that follow: *An Wasserflüssen Babylon* (BWV 653) and *Schmücke dich, o liebe Seele* (BWV 654). The similarities between the three compositions lie in the use of the sarabande meter, the ornamental lines, and the many parallel thirds and sixths. In BWV 652, Bach places the ornamented chorale in the soprano, with the two accompanying parts on a secondary manual supported by a continuo-style bass. The length of the chorale prelude is explained by the long nine-line *cantus firmus*, which Bach quotes in full, and by the fugal expositions that occur between the lines of the chorale. There is less repetition of material than in BWV 651, with Bach repeating only the material for lines 3 and 7.

In the first edition of their book on dance and the music of Bach, Meredith Little and Nathalie Jenne list this chorale prelude as a French gigue.[60] Obviously this is an error as this setting bears many of the hallmarks of the sarabande, such as accented second beats and hemiola rhythms.[61] Bach has included a wide variety of sarabandes in his musical output, some labeled sarabande and others not, of differing time signatures, and some with and some without upbeats.[62] It appears that BWV 652 is a sarabande, as are the following two compositions in P271. In this piece, the fugal entries are all based on the following line of the chorale, entering in the same order of tenor, alto, and bass each time. There is great unity between all four voices, with much of the motivic writing being derived from the *cantus firmus* itself. Almost every cadence in the piece is similar, which also adds to the unity of the composition.

BWV 652 begins with a statement of the fugal subject, which is exactly the same as the first decorated soprano entry that follows at m. 15.3. A fugal exposition follows, with an extra reference to line 1 of the *cantus firmus* in the pedal beginning at m. 19.3. The parallel thirds and sixths that are so much a feature of this piece are heard for the first time at m. 14, being used to very expressive effect in m. 18. Bach elongates the cadence with a tonic pedal at m. 24. The fore-imitation for line 2 of the chorale begins at m. 26. From this point, Bach introduces a countersubject in conjunction with the first entry of each exposition. Lyrical melodic lines are used in tandem with parallel thirds and sixths, and following the entry of the soprano for line 2 of the chorale, the harmony tends toward the subdominant, closing at mm. 39–41 with a plagal cadence in a hemiola rhythm.

Section 3 begins at m. 42.3. Another hemiola, similar to those found in *An Wasserflüssen Babylon* (BWV 653), leads to a cadence at m. 47 with a corresponding cadence at mm. 55–57. The accompanying parts are remarkably expressive with very close thematic relationships between all parts. Bach uses a conventional perfect cadence from m. 63 to 64 but then proceeds to a plagal cadence using the hemiola at m. 64.3.

Section 4 begins at m. 66, and in m. 70 Bach arrives on the dominant of E minor, having used similar harmonies at the same point in BWV 651 (m. 44). There are more passing modulations in this section, leading to the entry of line 4 of the *cantus firmus*, than in any of the previous phrases, touching on the keys of E, B and A minor, D major, and returning to G major via B minor. The entry of the fugal theme at m. 81 is accompanied by dramatic descending lines in tenths in the alto and tenor as the bass rises. With the entry of the *cantus firmus* in the soprano at m. 86, there is more chromatic coloring, passing through A minor and G major to cadence in E minor two measures after the final note of line 4 of the chorale (m. 90.3f.).

Section 5 begins at m. 92. This passage is characterized by gentle syncopations and suspensions as seen at mm. 92, 96, 100, and 102. Following the final note of line 5 of the *cantus firmus*, Bach extends the passage with a further perfect cadence to D at mm. 109f. With the beginning of section 6 at m. 110, he continues the use of syncopations and suspensions. Contrary motion becomes a feature in this passage, especially at mm. 117 and 119. In m. 120, there is a striking use of parallel thirds and sixths in all three accompanying voices. Bach closes this section with a plagal cadence, corresponding to the same point in section 3.

Measures 125–148 correspond to mm. 43–66, being the only musical material that Bach repeats. In the following section, which leads to line 8 of the chorale, Bach uses the *syncopatio catachrestica* to great effect in the pedal in m. 161. In addition, this section features parallel tenths between the two manual parts. With the entrance of the *cantus firmus* at m. 164, the music oscillates between the tonic and subdominant. The final section commences at m. 171.

This is the fore-imitation that leads to the "Hallelujahs." With the entrance of the solo right hand, the writing changes, mainly to sixteenth notes, while also incorporating the *figura corta* to bring this work to a triumphant close.

Interpretations by Other Authors

With the exception of Hans Luedtke and Peter Williams, very few authors have made any specific suggestions regarding the text-music relationships in *Komm heiliger Geist, Herre Gott* (BWV 652).

Albert Schweitzer proposes that BWV 652 suits the festive *Abendmahl* celebration for Pentecost, being appropriate for performance during the distribution of the holy sacrament.[63] In his view, this chorale prelude belongs to the mystical settings in this collection, also mentioning BWV 654 in this context. He refers to the mystery of the Holy Spirit who makes his home in the hearts of believers, combining with elements of the Abendmahl and becoming food for the soul [Seelenspeise].[64]

Luedtke refers to the "affettuoso der Schmucknoten" [*affettuoso* of the ornamental notes] and states that this setting and indeed BWV 651 take up a disproportionate amount of time in a liturgy because of the line-by-line fugal treatment of the *cantus firmus*.[65] In his view, it is probably stanza 3 that Bach is portraying here, referring to this setting as "voller Abendmahlstimmung" [full of the atmosphere of the Abendmahl].[66]

Harvey Grace finds this chorale to be overloaded with ornaments and suggests that one tires of the constant starting of fresh fugal expositions.[67]

Stainton de B. Taylor suggests that in this piece Bach seems to be more concerned with the mystical aspects of the coming of the Holy Spirit.[68]

Ulrich Meyer considers that this setting and *Nun danket alle Gott* (BWV 657) are not up to the standard of the other pieces in the collection.[69] He points out the connection between music and text for the final alleluia, and like many other writers, he comments on Bach's use of the sarabande rhythm.[70]

Williams considers that this setting is more supplicatory in mood than that of BWV 651 and that it is easy to see a connection with the text of stanza 3.[71]

Russell Stinson describes the mood of the coda that begins at m. 187 as transforming from supplication to ecstasy.[72] He deduces that the coda depicts the word "Halleluja" that concludes all three stanzas.[73]

Excursus: The Significance of the Sarabande in Bach's Text-Based Music

Before turning to the issue of text-music relationships in BWV 652, it may be helpful to first consider the possible significance of the sarabande in the text-based works of Bach. The second, third, and fourth settings in the "Leipzig" chorales are sarabandes, that is, *Komm heiliger Geist, Herre Gott* (BWV 652), *An Wasserflüssen Babylon* (BWV 653), and *Schmücke dich, o liebe Seele* (BWV 654). Is there some significance in the fact that these settings all follow each other? Similarities exist between the melody of the first phrase of *Komm heiliger Geist, Herre Gott* and *An Wasserflüssen Babylon*, the first five notes being the same. It is possible that Bach noticed this and, with his concern for cycles in his Leipzig years, placed them one after another. Additionally, Bach may have been emphasizing similar themes from the text of the three hymns and therefore placed them successively in P271.

Bach composed more sarabandes than any other dance type, including many varying types in his output.[74] The sarabandes in the keyboard suites are all labeled as such, but there are also many examples in the vocal works where he utilizes the rhythm without actually calling it a sarabande. In the instrumental suites, the phrasing is very regular, but when he adapts the rhythm to a vocal work, he is not always concerned with regularity of phrasing.

The similarity of compositional approach between BWV 652, 653, and 654 raises the question as to why Bach employed the sarabande for these particular texts, and did that then have a bearing on the fact that they follow each other in P271? Apart from these three chorale preludes, Bach does not use this dance rhythm anywhere else in the collection. The sarabande was regarded as the noblest of the court dances, described by Johann Gottfried Walther as "gravitätisch" [grave] in his *Musicalisches Lexicon*.[75] It may be in the context of studying sarabandes from the vocal music that we can understand Bach's use of it in the organ music.

In the original edition of their book, Little and Jenne give several examples of Bach's use of the sarabande in works where he does not actually use the term.[76] The examples they cite from the sacred vocal works are as follows:[77]

BWV 6/1	"Bleib bei uns"
BWV 27/5	"Gute Nacht"
BWV 75/3	"Mein Jesu soll mein alles sein"
BWV 91/3	"Gott, dem der erdenkeris zu klein"
BWV 96/5	"Bald zur Rechten, bald zur Linken"
BWV 97/7	"Hat er denn beschlosen"
BWV 135/3	"Tröste mir, Jesu mein Gemüte"
BWV 153/8	"Soll ich meinen Lebenslauf"
BWV 188/1	"Ich habe meine Zuversicht"
BWV 244/68	"Wir setzen uns mit Tränen nieder"
BWV 245/19	"Ach mein Sinn"

Further examples are cited by Little and Jenne in the revised edition of their book as follows:[78]

BWV 44/3	"Christen müssen"
BWV 48/1	"Ich elender Mensch"
BWV 57/3	"Ich wünschte"
BWV 77/5	"Ach, es bleibt"
BWV 124/1	"Meinen Jesum"
BWV 125/2	"Ich will"
BWV 245/39	"Ruht wohl"
BWV 249/5	"Seele, deine Specereien"

Examination of some of these movements may help to discern the significance of the sarabande in Bach's text-based works. *Bleib bei uns, denn es will Abend werden* (BWV 6) was first performed on the second Easter day on 2 April 1725.[79] The opening chorus is based on the Gospel for that day: Luke's account of the disciples meeting the risen Christ on the road to Emmaus (Luke 24:13–35).[80] The text of the chorus is taken from verse 29: "Bleib bei uns, denn es will Abend werden und der Tag hat sich geneiget" [Abide with us: for it is toward evening, and the day is far spent]. In eschatological terms, the evening can also be a symbol of ending, and in BWV 6/1 Bach does not seem to be merely providing a literal interpretation of the text. Albert Clement has shown how the organ chorale *Ach bleib bei uns, Herr Jesu Christ* (BWV 649, a transcription of movement 3 of this cantata) has eschatological implications.[81] At the beginning of BWV 6/1, there are twenty-four repeated eighth notes played by violins and viola. This has been used elsewhere by Bach to portray the passing of time, for example, *Liebster Gott, wann werd ich sterben* (BWV 8/1). In using this kind of musical device, involving the number of hours in the day, Bach may be referring to the passing from one life to the next, from life on earth to eternity. The message of the Gospel for the second Easter day shows Christ as the Messiah using the scriptures to explain to the unbelieving disciples who he is and what he has done. The breaking of bread between Christ and the disciples is important, as it places the risen Lord in the context of the Eucharistic banquet.[82] It may be possible to link the use of the sarabande rhythm in BWV 6/1 to eschatological aspects of the text.

The cantata *Wer weiß, wie nahe mir mein Ende?* (BWV 27) was composed for the sixteenth Sunday after Trinity and was first performed on 6 October 1726.[83] This cantata takes its lead from the Gospel of that day: the raising of the young man of Nain from the dead, as told in Luke 7:11–17.[84] All of the cantatas for this Sunday dwell on the individual death of the Christian.[85] The fifth movement, the bass aria "Gute Nacht," is in the rhythm of a sarabande. This particular aria sees the soul bidding farewell to the world using the imagery of night as follows:

Gute Nacht, du Weltgetümmel! / Good night, thou worldly tumult!
Jetzt mach ich mit dir Beschluß; / Now I make an end with thee;
Ich steh schon mit einem Fuß / I stand with one foot already
Bei dem lieben Gott im Himmel. / With (the) dear God in heaven.

This is a significant example as Bach alternates the sarabande rhythm with a more vigorous and energetic sixteenth-note rhythm, depicting the tumult of the earthly world. The musical setting of the third line is characterized by the use of the hemiola, not uncommon in the sarabande.[86] In this case, it might be possible to link the sarabande rhythm to heavenly affairs.

A final example from the cantatas is the soprano aria "Letzte Stunde, brich herein" from the cantata *Der Himmel lacht! Die Erde jubiliert!* (BWV 31). This aria deals with the subject of the final hour, preparing to see the glory of Christ. The text is as follows:

Letzte Stunde brich herein,	Break forth o final hour,
mir die Augen zuzudrücken!	to close my eyes!
Laß mich Jesu Freudenschein	Let me Jesus' ray of gladness
und sein helles Licht erblicken,	and his brilliant light behold,
Laß mich Engeln ähnlich sein.	Let me become like the angels.

This cantata was written for Easter and was first performed on Easter Sunday, 21 April 1715.[87] Against the soprano voice, the violin and viola play the melody of Nicolaus Herman's *Wenn mein Stündlein vorhanden ist.* This hymn was listed as a *de tempore* hymn for Ascension and the sixteenth and twenty-fourth Sundays after Trinity in certain hymnbooks.[88] These last two Sundays were associated with death and the afterlife, and clearly Ascension Day is also linked to eternal life.

Clement has referred to the use of the sarabande in the chorale partita *Sei gegrüsset, Jesu gütig/ O Jesu, du edle Gabe* (BWV 768).[89] In variation 10 of this partita, Bach employs the sarabande rhythm. The text here is of an eschatological nature and therefore has much in common with the texts of the chorales found in P271:

Drauf werd ich, wie mir bereitet	Then I will, as was prepared for me
von den Engelein begleitet/	accompanied by angels,
gehen in dem weissen Kleide/	go in the white cloth,
durch dein Blut zu deiner Freude/	through your blood to your joy,
dein Blut mich von Sünden wäschet/	your blood washes me from sins,
und der Höllen-Gluth auslöschet.[90]	extinguishing the fire of hell.

Clement draws attention to the similarities between the text of Johann Franck's *Schmücke dich, o liebe Seele* and stanza 10 of Johann Böttiger's hymn, posing the question as to whether the soul would be invited to the meal of the Lamb in heaven (Revelation 19:9).[91]

The sarabande rhythm is also to be found in the chorale partita *O Gott, du frommer Gott* (BWV 767.7). Here the text is concerned with the anticipation of the heavenly Jerusalem:

Laß mich an meinem End	Let me at my end
Auff Christi Todt abscheiden.	depart in Christ's death.
Die Seele nim zu dir	Take the soul to you
Hinauff zu deinem Freuden;	Up to your joy;
Dem Leib ein Räumlein gönn	Give the body a little room
Bey seiner Eltern Grab,	By his ancestors' grave,
Auff das er seine Ruh	So that it has its peace
An ihrer Seiten hab.[92]	On their sides.

It seems striking to discover that many of the movements where Bach employs the sarabande rhythm share a common theme—eternity and salvation.[93] The triple meter, associated with heaven in Bach's music, may also be significant.[94] Its meaning in the three sarabandes BWV 652–654 is discussed in the following section and chapters.

Assessment

As seen previously, the only stanza of *Komm heiliger Geist, Herre Gott* that has been associated with BWV 652 is stanza 3. This fact has yet to be proven. An insight into Bach's possible intentions regarding text and music may be achieved by examining the main musical features of BWV 652 and their conceivable correlation to lines of the hymn text. In the preceding discussion of BWV 651, the various aspects of the text of *Komm heiliger Geist, Herre Gott* were highlighted. Stanzas 1 and 2 seem to concentrate on the fires of Pentecost and the dominant and forceful nature of the Holy Spirit, while stanza 3 appears to demonstrate the gentler side of the Spirit, emphasizing his sweet, comforting role that helps humanity strive toward salvation. How can we discover which aspect of the Holy Spirit Bach might be portraying in BWV 652?

Important musical characteristics include the sarabande rhythm, the parallel thirds and sixths, the abundance of ornaments, and the use of the *figura corta*. The above discussion regarding Bach's use of the sarabande rhythm in the text-based works seems to indicate that he employs the sarabande rhythm in an eschatological context. This may be relevant to BWV 652. The Holy Spirit is the bringer of salvation, and therefore any stanza of this hymn could appropriately employ the sarabande rhythm. It is consequently necessary to look for further indications of text-music relationships.

The employment of parallel thirds and sixths can be associated with sweetness and love in Bach's music. An analogy may be drawn with the opening movement of the cantata *Ich freue mich in dir* (BWV 133), where Bach depicts the text "Ach, wie ein süßer Ton" with parallel movement in thirds and sixths in the accompanying violin and the vocal parts.[95] Stanza 1 contains a reference to love, while stanza 3 opens with a salutation to "heilige Brunst/ süsser Trost." The reference in stanza 1 is in the context of the ignition of love, which seems appropriate to the fiery nature of BWV 651. Could this reference to love in stanza 1 be a sufficient reason to suggest that Bach was portraying this love in the parallel thirds and sixths of BWV 652? Parallel motion is present even before the entrance of line 1 of the *cantus firmus* and remains prominent throughout. Is it likely that Bach would use a musical technique in the opening measures of a piece that was not related to the opening line of text? Especially striking are the parallel thirds of the accompaniment of m. 18 (see example 1.5).

The sixth note of the *cantus firmus* occurs at this measure. Examination of line 1 of all stanzas may help to solve the problem. The corresponding words for each stanza at this moment are "Geist," "Licht," and "Brunst," respectively. Are these thirds related to Spirit, light, or ardor? Do the following three syllables help to find an answer to this question "Herre Gott," "edler Hort," or "süsser Trost," respectively? There may be sufficient evidence to now suggest that Bach was portraying the ardor of sweet comfort in the presentation of the opening line of the *cantus firmus* in BWV 652.

The seeming excess of ornaments has been commented on by Harvey Grace, but it is possible that Bach deliberately used this high proportion of ornaments for a theological reason. An explanation for this may be found in Heinrich Müller's first sermon for Pentecost Sunday as follows, where he explains how best the Christian may approach this feast:

> Wisset aber/ die ihr diß Fest recht feyren wollet/ das die Feyer nicht bestehe im Schmuck der Kleider/ nicht in vielen und köstlichen Tractamenten/ nicht in fröligkeit und Wolleben/ nicht im blossen Kirchen-gehen und Predigt-hören. Ach nein/ die Seele muß erbauet und ausgeschmückt seyn zum Tempel des Heil. Geistes.[96] [But know, if you want to celebrate this feast properly, that the fire does not endure in the taste of the clothes, not in many and costly gifts, not in joyousness and good living, not in pure church going and listening to sermons. But no, the soul must be edified and adorned as the temple of the Holy Spirit.]

It is possible that Bach was reflecting Müller's concern that the soul become adorned as the temple of the Holy Spirit in the many ornaments of BWV 652. These ornaments appear to enhance the atmosphere of trust and well-being portrayed in Bach's setting. Equally, the elegant sarabande with its euphonious

Example 1.5.   BWV 652 (m. 18)

parallel motion may best express the sweet and comforting aspect of the Holy Spirit, as opposed to the more powerful and authoritative Spirit of the first two stanzas. This seems to lead to the conclusion that Bach was indeed thinking of stanza 3 when he wrote this piece. Detailed examination of BWV 652 may help to confirm this point.

Throughout BWV 652, the chorale melody is ever present, in the accompanying parts as well as in the solo right-hand line. The melody of line 1 of the *cantus firmus* is clearly expressed in the fore-imitations of mm. 1–15. It seems possible to link the musical language of the accompanying voices of mm. 10–15 to the text "Du heilige Brunst/ süsser Trost." This imagery continues with the entry of the *cantus firmus* at m. 15, and as alluded to above, Bach's employment of parallel thirds at m. 18 seems to be a particularly vivid expression of the word "Brunst." The use of thirds in this measure may also be related to the following two words of text: "süsser Trost."

The countersubject that accompanies the next fugal exposition begins on the second eighth note of m. 27.1. Aspects of the text of this line, "nun hilf uns frölich und getrost," may be illustrated by Bach in his use of thirty-second notes at mm. 36 and 38 and the ornament on the word "frölich." The next section begins at m. 42.3, where the petition of the previous line continues, "in deinem Dienst beständig bleiben." Parallel motion remains a feature of this passage, reflecting perhaps the overall theme of trust and comfort, as well as the petition of the servants of God to remain faithful.

Another request follows: "die Trübsaal uns nicht abtreiben." The presentation of this line of the *cantus firmus* is very expressive, with a long decoration for the word "Trübsaal" (beats 2 and 3 of m. 85), perhaps laying particular emphasis on the sorrows of humanity. This long ornament (see example 1.6) emphasizes the fact that suffering is always long.[97] This highlighting of the word "Trübsaal" continues in a move toward A minor, with minor ninth harmonies in m. 87 and a cadence to E minor for the close of the phrase at mm. 89–91.

In mm. 92–93, Bach introduces a four-note falling chromatic countersubject, incorporating the *syncopatio* in the alto. This line (see example 1.7) is in marked contrast to the positive melodic movement heard in the tenor. In the combination of positive and negative musical *Affekt*, Bach may be commenting on the "Trübsaal" of the previous line while also looking forward to

Example 1.6.   BWV 652
(m. 85)

Example 1.7.   BWV 652 (mm. 92f.)

the more optimistic "O Herr durch dein Kraft uns bereit." The strong rising line of the chorale paraphrase with its decisive modulation to the dominant overcomes the falling chromatic line, which does not appear again in this form. Positive aspects of the text seem to be confirmed in the very assertive cadence to the dominant with its parallel sixths in mm. 108–110. This line of text is very relevant to the theme of stanza 3. For what does the soul ask to be prepared? It is, of course, eternal life and salvation.

At m. 110, a syncopated motive similar to that of m. 92 is heard, but this time without the chromaticism. This may be due to the reference to "stärck" in the following line of text. The paraphrase of the chorale begins in m. 113. In the lower part, an assertive rising arpeggio of G major begins precisely where the word "stärck" occurs. At m. 117, there is dramatic movement in contrary motion where the two manual parts end up two and a half octaves apart. Is it possible that this very strong musical statement is related to the word "stärck"? Bach sometimes depicts weakness or negativity in the use of *catabasis*, but that does not appear to be the case here. The descending pedal line at m. 119 is strengthened by the fact that in this measure there are strong parallel thirds in the accompanying parts, while in m. 120 these parts actually move in parallel motion with the pedal. Although this is a descending line, any possibility of negativity seems to be erased by the very strong parallel lines. With the entry of the *cantus firmus* proper in m. 119, Bach may be once more illustrating the word "stärck" with emphatic writing in thirds and sixths. The weaker end to the phrase with its interrupted cadence could be related to the "Fleisches Blödigkeit," with the music only reaching the tonic at m. 123.

The next line of text, "daß wir hie ritterlich ringen," is preceded by an unremarkable fugal exposition. Bach uses an energetic rhythmic figure of a dotted eighth note followed by two thirty-second notes at m. 143 to help portray the word "ritterlich." This is the same music he used for line 3 of the chorale, but here the dotted rhythm may have more meaning. This figure seems more appropriate to "ritterlich" than "Dienst," which was the corresponding word at line 3.[98]

The following fugal exposition leading to line 8 of the *cantus firmus* is different from that heard after line 3. The countersubject begins after an eighth-note rest, perhaps giving the effect of "dringen." In m. 159, the *cantus firmus* enters in the pedal. This line of text contains the two opposites of "Tod" and "Leben." Once more, it seems possible that Bach is portraying two opposing ideas in the employment of contrasting musical techniques—the *syncopatio catachrestica* and the use of parallel motion. The *syncopatio catachrestica* in m. 161 may be related to the word "Tod," contrasting with the more positive portrayal of "Leben" in the parallel tenths of mm. 159–162. With the entry of the *cantus firmus* in the soprano in m. 164, these opposing ideas are retained by Bach. He uses the *syncopatio catachrestica* in m. 166, perhaps again portraying "Tod," followed by the energetic dotted rhythm heard at m. 142.

Line 8 of the *cantus firmus* is similar to line 4, and it is worth noting the minor changes Bach makes to the presentation of the opening passage of this section. The long ornament that seems to imply the word "Trübsaal" at m. 85 is not used by Bach at the corresponding m. 164 (see example 1.8). Equally, the minor ninth harmonies, also associated with "Trübsaal," are not present in the presentation of line 8. This may lead one to believe that the additions or omissions that Bach made to the presentation of line 8 are indeed related to the text. At m. 167, Bach employs a rhythmic feature of two thirty-second notes, where the corresponding m. 88 has two eighth notes. It is possible that this is related to the urgency of striving toward God in life and death as expressed in the text of line 8.

The fugal exposition that leads to the closing section of this piece could not prepare the listener for the glorious outpouring of ecstatic alleluias. Bach suddenly increases the movement to sixteenth notes with consistent use of the *figura corta*. The positive and ebullient atmosphere is further enhanced by the repeated four-note rising sixteenth-note motive that first appears in m. 187, manifesting itself in many guises right up to the penultimate measure. In addition, Bach chooses to add an extra voice as an accompaniment to this rising motive, making the texture fuller and more powerful. Example 1.9 compares the setting of the word "Hallelujah" in BWV 652 with that of movement 4 of *Christ lag in Todesbanden* (BWV 4), showing a remarkably similar compositional approach.

A motive is introduced in the pedal in m. 187.3 (see example 1.9a), which in Bach's organ works has been associated with great expressions of praise at the power of God, for example, the final stanza of the chorale partita *O Gott, du frommer Gott* (BWV 767), where the text is a glorious outpouring in praise of God. This motive is also to be found in all three accompanying parts of the *Orgel-Büchlein* chorale *Herr Christ, der ein'ge Gottes Sohn oder Herr Gott, nun sei*

Example 1.8.   BWV 652 (mm. 164f.)

Example 1.9a.   BWV 652 (mm. 187f.)

gepreiset (BWV 601) (see example 1.10a), where the former text is headed "Ein Lobsanck von Christo" [a hymn of praise of Christ] in the Erfurt *Enchiridion* of 1524,[99] and the latter as "Ein Gesang nach dem Tische, an stat des Gratias" [a hymn for after meals instead of the *Gracias*] in the Babst hymnbook (Leipzig, 1553).[100] This motive as it appears in BWV 652 is very similar to the "alleluia" motive in movement 6 of the Easter cantata *Christ lag in Todesbanden* (BWV 4) (see example 1.10b).

Following the previous discussion, it is revealing to examine Bach's use of the melody of *Komm heiliger Geist, Herre Gott* in movement 5 of the cantata *Erschallet, ihr Lieder, erklinget, ihr Saiten* (BWV 172). In this duet, four phrases of the chorale melody are presented as an obbligato, while the soprano (soul) and alto (Holy Spirit) sing an amorous duet with the following text:

Soprano:	Soprano:
Komm, laß mich nicht länger warten,	Come, let me wait no longer,
Komm, du sanfter Himmelswind,	Come, thou gentle heavenly wind,
Wehe durch den Herzensgarten!	Waft through this hearts-garden!

Alto:	Alto:
Ich erquicke dich mein Kind.	I will revive thee, my child.

Example 1.9b.   BWV 4.4 (mm. 37f.)

Example 1.10a.   **BWV 601 (beginning)**

Soprano:	Soprano:
Liebste Liebe, die so süße,	Dearest love which (is) so sweet,
Aller Wollust Überfluß,	Of all delight (the) overflowing abundance,
Ich vergeh, wenn ich dich misse.	I shall perish if I do not have thee.

Alto:	Alto:
Nimm von mir den Gnadenkuß.	Accept from me the kiss of grace.

Soprano:	Soprano:
Sei im Glauben mir willkommen,	Be through faith in me made welcome,
Höchste Liebe, komm herein!	Highest love, come in!
Du hast mir das Herz genommen.	Thou hast captured my heart.

Alto:	Alto:
Ich bin dein und du bist mein!	I am thine, and thou art mine!

Example 1.10b.   **BWV 4/6 (mm. 82ff.)**

The text is delivered by soprano and alto in dialogue form in the manner of a love duet. Since stanza 3 of *Komm heiliger Geist* is the stanza that deals with love, it seems likely that Bach was also portraying this stanza in the instrumental obbligato of BWV 172/5. If Bach quotes a chorale melody instrumentally, he usually is sending a theological message in addition to the message of the sung text. This duet from BWV 172 shows the Holy Spirit to be gentle and full of love. Similar sentiments are to be found in stanza 3 of *Komm heiliger Geist, Herre Gott.* Additionally, there are some common musical elements between BWV 172/5 and BWV 652. In the original version of BWV 172/5, and in its first Leipzig version, the obbligato *cantus firmus* was assigned to the oboe d'amore. As Renate Steiger has pointed out, Bach frequently employed this instrument in the context of love.[101] BWV 172/5 is similar in mood to BWV 652. In the later Leipzig version of BWV 172, Bach replaced the oboe d'amore with the organ, thereby making the similarity to BWV 652 even more marked. The longing for heaven can be expressed in BWV 652 and in the obbligato part of the aria in the use of the sesquialtera stop, which Bach described as "vollkommene schöne Sesquialtera."[102]

It is helpful to return to BWV 768/10. Set in the form of a sarabande, it also employs many parallel thirds and sixths. The text of stanza 10 of *O Jesu du edle Gabe* is concerned with the resurrection of mankind, entering eternity accompanied by angels. The longing for eternal happiness is common to both the text of stanza 3 of *Komm heiliger Geist, Herre Gott* and stanza 10 of *O Jesu, du edle Gabe.* It is therefore logical to conclude that there might be many musical elements in common between the two. These common elements are the sarabande rhythm, the parallel thirds and sixths of the accompanying voices, and the presentation of the *cantus firmus* in the uppermost voice.

The common features found in BWV 652 and BWV 768/10 appear to justify the conclusion that Bach may have been depicting similar theological themes. It now seems possible to suggest that Bach is using the sarabande rhythm in BWV 652 in the context of salvation. If he was thinking of stanza 3 when he composed BWV 652, then the sarabande rhythm is eminently suitable to help portray this text.

August Pfeiffer quotes stanza 3 of *Komm heiliger Geist, Herre Gott* in the context of eternal life. In his third "Vorbereitungs-Predigt von der Augsburgischen Confession," he urges the faithful as follows:

> Derowegen sey nur frölich und getrost/ es soll dir im Himmel alles in ewigen Gnaden wohl belohnt werden . . . sey getreu biß in den Todt/ bald/ bald/ ietzt/ ietzt wil ich dir die Krohne des Lebens geben (Apoc. II).[103]
> [Therefore, be just joyful and comforted/ everything will be rewarded to you in everlasting grace in heaven . . . be faithful unto death/ soon/ soon/ now/ now I will give you the crown of life (Revelation 2).]

Following this quotation from Revelation 2:10, Pfeiffer quotes the text of stanza 3 of *Komm heiliger Geist, Herre Gott*. For Pfeiffer, this stanza seems to echo the text of Revelation 2:10. The message of this passage of scripture is to not fear trial and tribulation, as there will be reward in heaven. As such, a composition portraying stanza 3 of *Komm heiliger Geist, Herre Gott* is worthy of inclusion in a collection of chorale preludes united by an eschatological theme.

★ ★ ★

In his two settings of Luther's *Komm heiliger Geist, Herre Gott*, Bach seems to have thoroughly covered all aspects of Pentecost. The thundering perpetual motion of BWV 651 can symbolize the raging fire of Pentecost and the "Herre Gott" aspect of the Holy Spirit who comes to those in fear. Many other subtleties introduced by Bach in BWV 651 seem to reveal the complexity of the feast. The first setting depicts all the powerful aspects of the Holy Spirit. The second portrays the loving and comforting side of his nature, as evidenced by the sweet parallel thirds and sixths, the attractive ornamentation, and the sarabande rhythm. In both cases, the role that the Holy Spirit plays in the salvation of humanity is highlighted. The image of light is an important aspect of BWV 651, corresponding to Luther's concept of light as a representation of faith. In BWV 652, the employment of the sarabande rhythm underlines the eschatological aspect of the feast of Pentecost. In both settings, Bach celebrates the euphoria of the feast in an ecstatic portrayal of the word "Hallelujah" to close each composition.

NOTES

1. Johannes Kulp, *Die Lieder unserer Kirche* [Handbuch zum Evangelischen Kirchengesangbuch, Sonderband], ed. Arno Büchner and Siegfried Fornaçon (Göttingen: Vandenhoeck & Ruprecht, 1958), 162.

2. *WA* 35:165f.; *LW* 53:265.

3. *WA TR* 4:334 (No. 4478); *LW* 53:265. Luther is clearly thinking of the Latin original rather than his own translation.

4. *WA* 35:166; *LW* 53:265. The following information regarding this hymn is based on these sources.

5. For notes on the text, see Philipp Wackernagel, *Das deutsche Kirchenlied von der ältesten Zeit bis zu Anfang des XVII. Jahrhunderts* (Leipzig: Teubner, 1864–1877; reprint, Hildesheim: Olms, 1964), 3:19 (No. 19). For notes on the melody (Erfurt version), see Konrad Ameln, *The Roots of German Hymnody of the Reformation Era* (St. Louis: Concordia, 1984), 21–28, and Zahn 7445a. For the melody as preserved by Johann Walter (Wittenberg), see *WA* 35:511 and Ameln, *The Roots*, 21–28. For Klug's melismatic version (1533/1535), see Ameln, *The Roots*, and Zahn 7445b.

6. Kulp, *Die Lieder unserer Kirche*, 164, and Eduard Emil Koch, *Geschichte des Kirchenlieds und Kirchengesangs der christlichen, insbesondere der deutschen evangelischen Kirche*, 3rd ed. (Stuttgart: Belser, 1866–1876; Hildesheim: Olms, 1973), 8:86.

7. "Gnade" can also mean "grace."

8. *SLG*, 170.

9. Translation based on Mark Bighley, *The Lutheran Chorales in the Organ Works of J. S. Bach* (St. Louis: Concordia, 1986), 163.

10. *WA* 12:570.

11. *Church Postils* 3:277f.

12. *WA* 12:574.

13. *Church Postils* 3:281f.

14. Raymond Brown explains the origins of the feast of Pentecost: "The Feast of Weeks or Pentecost (so called because it was celebrated seven weeks or fifty days after Passover) was a pilgrimage feast when pious Jews came from their homes to the temple or central shrine in Jerusalem . . . an agricultural feast of thanksgiving celebrated in May or June, like the other Jewish feasts it had acquired additional meaning by recalling what God had done for the chosen people in 'salvation history.' The deliverance from Egypt in the middle of the first month (Exodus 12) was commemorated at Passover. In the third month (19:1), and thus about a month and a half later, the Israelites arrived at Sinai; and so Pentecost, occurring at roughly the same interval after Passover, became the commemoration of God's giving the covenant to Israel at Sinai—the moment when Israel was called to be God's own people. In depicting God's appearance at Sinai, Exodus 19 includes thunder and smoke; and the Jewish writer Philo (contemporary with the New Testament) describes angels taking what God said to Moses on the mountaintop and carrying it out on tongues to the people on the plain below. Acts, with its description of the sound of a mighty wind and tongues as of fire, echoes that imagery, and thus presents the Pentecost in Jerusalem as the renewal of God's covenant, once more calling a people to be God's own." Raymond E. Brown, *An Introduction to the New Testament* (New York: Doubleday, 1997), 283f.

15. Renate Steiger, "'Gnadengegenwart.' Johann Sebastian Bachs Pfingstkantate BWV 172 'Erschallet, ihr Lieder, erklinget, ihr Saiten!'" in *Die Quellen Johann Sebastian Bachs. Bachs Musik im Gottesdienst*, ed. Renate Steiger [Internationale Arbeitsgemeinschaft für theologische Bachforschung. Bericht über das Symposium 4.–8. Oktober 1995 in der Internationalen Bachakademie Stuttgart] (Heidelberg: Internationale Arbeitsgemeinschaft für theologische Bachforschung, 1998), 15–57.

16. *WA* 37:399.

17. *House Postils* 2:151 (from the sermon preached in the afternoon at the parish church on Pentecost Day, 1534).

18. *WA* 37:400.

19. *House Postils* 2:152f.

20. See Steiger, "Gnadengegenwart," 16, where she refers to Johann Wolfgang von Goethe's *Reineke Fuchs*, which begins "Pfingsten, das liebliche Fest war gekommen."

21. The sermon preached at Pleissenburg Castle on the occasion of the inauguration of the Reformation in Leipzig, John 14:23–31, 24 May 1539, can be found in

WA 47:772–779 and *LW* 51:303–312. See Robin A. Leaver: "Bach's 'Clavierübung III': Some Historical and Theological Considerations," *Organ Yearbook* 6 (1975): 10.

22. Wilhelm Stapel, *Luthers Lieder und Gedichte* (Stuttgart: Evangelisches Verlagswerk, 1950), 162.

23. Stapel, *Luthers Lieder und Gedichte*, 162.

24. See *NBA* IV/2:11 and *NBA KB* IV/2:65f.

25. See *NBA* IV/2:11 and *NBA KB* IV/2:65f.

26. Alfred Dürr, "Melodievarianten in Johann Sebastian Bachs Kirchenliedbearbeitungen," in *Wolfenbütteler Forschungen 31*, ed. Alfred Dürr and Walther Killy (Wiesbaden: Harrassowitz, 1986), 153 and 158, discusses the different forms of the melody.

27. Günther Stiller, *Johann Sebastian Bach und das Leipziger gottesdienstliche Leben seiner Zeit* (Kassel: Bärenreiter, 1970), 228; English: *Johann Sebastian Bach and Liturgical Life in Leipzig*, trans. Herbert J. A. Bouman, Daniel F. Poellot, and Hilton C. Oswald; ed. Robin A. Leaver (St. Louis: Concordia, 1984), 241; see also Detlef Gojowy, "Kirchenlieder im Umkreis von J. S. Bach." *JbLH* 22 (1978): 108.

28. See Daniel R. Melamed, *J. S. Bach and the German Motet* (Cambridge: Cambridge University Press, 1995), 81–85.

29. For a possible relationship in procedure between BWV 172.5 and BWV 651a, see Werner Brieg, "The 'Great Eighteen' Chorales: Bach's Revisional Process and the Genesis of the Work," in *J. S. Bach as Organist: His Instruments, Music, and Performance Practices*, ed. George Stauffer and Ernest May (Bloomington: Indiana University Press, 1986), 108f.

30. *NBA KB* IV/2:64.

31. Brieg, "The 'Great Eighteen' Chorales," 108.

32. Peter Williams, *The Organ Music of J. S. Bach* (Cambridge: Cambridge University Press, 1980–1986), 2:131. However, the paragraph is omitted from *The Organ Music of J. S. Bach*, 2nd ed. (Cambridge: Cambridge University Press, 2003), 344. Williams makes no reference to the views of Klotz or any other writer on this issue.

33. Harald Schützeichel, ed., *Albert Schweitzer: Die Orgelwerke Johann Sebastian Bachs. Vorworte zu den "Sämtlichen Orgelwerken"* (Hildesheim: Olms, 1995), 247.

34. Schützeichel, *Albert Schweitzer*, 248.

35. Hans Luedtke, "Seb. Bachs Choralvorspiele," *BJ* 15 (1918): 73.

36. Charles Sanford Terry, *Bach's Chorals Part III: The Hymns and Hymn Melodies of the Organ Works* (Cambridge: Cambridge University Press, 1921), 245.

37. Stainton de B. Taylor, *The Chorale Preludes of J. S. Bach* (London: Oxford University Press, 1942), 106.

38. Taylor, *The Chorale Preludes*, 110.

39. Hermann Keller, *Die Orgelwerke Bachs. Ein Beitrag zu ihrer Geschichte, Form, Deutung und Wiedergabe* (Leipzig: Peters, 1948), 181f.; Herman Keller, *The Organ Works of Bach: A Contribution to Their History, Form, Interpretation and Performance*, trans. Helen Hewitt (New York: Peters, 1967), 247.

40. Keller, *The Organ Works*, 247. In Keller's view, the variant BWV 651a may be suitable for service use because of its brevity, and he suggests that this may have been Bach's original intention.

41. Jacques Chailley, *Les Chorals pour Orgue de J.-S. Bach* (Paris: Leduc, 1974), 172.

42. Ulrich Meyer, "Zur Frage der inneren Einheit von Bachs Siebzehn Chorälen (BWV 651–667)," *BJ* 58 (1972): 63.

43. Meyer, "Zur Frage der inneren Einheit," 73. He repeats this opinion in his later study, Ulrich Meyer, "Über J. S. Bachs Orgelchoralkunst," in *Theologische Bach-Studien 1*, ed. Walter Blankenburg and Renate Steiger, [Beiträge zur theologischen Bachforschung 4] (Neuhausen-Stuttgart: Hänssler, 1987), 44.

44. Williams, *The Organ Music of J. S. Bach*, 2nd ed., 342.

45. Russell Stinson, *J. S. Bach's Great Eighteen Chorales* (New York: Oxford University Press, 2001), 75. He also points out that Glenn Gould chose this piece, as recorded by Marie-Claire Alain, for the concluding fireworks scene of the film *Slaughterhouse Five*.

46. An example, discussed later in this chapter, is BWV 133/1.

47. The significance of the order of these pieces and the number seventeen was pointed out by Felix Pachlatko at the meeting of the Internationale Arbeitsgemeinschaft für theologische Bachforschung, Eisenach, March 2002.

48. See, for example, the opening movement of the Pentecost cantata *Erschallet, ihr Lieder, erklinget ihr Saiten!* (BWV 172). Equally, many of the Christmas cantatas contain similar portrayals of joy and celebration; see Albert Clement, *Der dritte Teil der Clavierübung von Johann Sebastian Bach: Musik, Text, Theologie* (Middelburg: Almares, 1999), 130 and 371, n. 64, where he discusses the triadic writing in BWV 678 in theological terms, which might also apply here with BWV 651.

49. See Clement, *Der dritte Teil der Clavierübung*, 26, where he associates sixteenth-note movement in BWV 552/1 with the Holy Spirit; and *Der dritte Teil*, 342f., where he draws similar conclusions from BWV 34/1 and to other writers who associate sixteenth-note movement with the fires of Pentecost.

50. In Johann Gottfried Walther, *Musicalisches Lexicon Oder Musicalische Bibliothec* (Leipzig, 1732), ed. Friederike Ramm (Kassel: Bärenreiter, 2001), 590, the definition is as follows: "*Syncopatio catachrestica*, ist: wenn ein *dissoni*rende Note nicht, wie es sonst die Regel erfordert, durch eine folgende *consoni*rende, die um ein Grad tiefer liegt, aufgelöset wird; sondern sich durch eine andere, fremdere, weitentlegenere, und höhere *Consonanz*, auch wohl gar durch eine abermahlige *Dissonanz*, einen Ausweg suchet" [The *syncopatio catachrestica* occurs when a dissonant note is not resolved according to the rule through a following consonance which lies one step lower but which seeks an evasion through another, foreign, distant, and higher consonance or even through yet another dissonance]; trans. Dietrich Bartel, *Musica Poetica. Musical-Rhetorical Figures in German Baroque Music* (Lincoln: University of Nebraska Press, 1997), 403.

51. If one examines line 2 of the other two stanzas, these are equally positive.

52. Michael Marissen, "On the Musically Theological in J. S. Bach's Church Cantatas," *Lutheran Quarterly* 16 (2002): 48–64, cites many examples where Bach seems to portray the opposite meaning of the text in the music. See further in chapter 2.

53. *WA* 37:403.

54. *House Postils* 2:160.

55. *BSLK*, 183. The Apology was written by Melanchthon but reflects Luther's views.

56. BkC, 139.

57. See further in chapter 7 where the positive aspect of a similar motive in BWV 658 is discussed.

58. *WA* 10¹ᐟ²:11, 12.

59. *Church Postils* 6:17, 19.

60. Meredith Little and Natalie Jenne, *Dance and the Music of J. S. Bach* (Bloomington: Indiana University Press, 1991), 219.

61. This error is corrected in Meredith Little and Natalie Jenne, *Dance and the Music of J. S. Bach*, revised and expanded ed. (Bloomington: Indiana University Press, 2001), 302.

62. Little and Jenne, *Dance and the Music of J. S. Bach* (2001), 302.

63. Schützeichel, *Albert Schweitzer*, 248.

64. Schützeichel, *Albert Schweitzer*, 248.

65. Luedtke, "Seb. Bachs Choralvorspiele," 33f.

66. Luedtke, "Seb. Bachs Choralvorspiele," 73.

67. Harvey Grace, *The Organ Works of Bach* (London: Novello, 1922), 280.

68. Taylor, *The Chorale Preludes of J. S. Bach*, 110.

69. Meyer, "Zur Frage der inneren Einheit," 65.

70. Meyer, "Zur Frage der inneren Einheit," 65.

71. Williams, *The Organ Music of J. S. Bach*, 2:131, but the comment is eliminated from the revision: *The Organ Music of J. S. Bach*, 2nd ed., 345.

72. Stinson, *J. S. Bach's Great Eighteen Chorales*, 77.

73. Stinson, *J. S. Bach's Great Eighteen Chorales*, 77.

74. Little and Jenne, *Dance and the Music of J. S. Bach* (1991), 102.

75. Walther, *Musicalisches Lexicon*, 542.

76. Little and Jenne, *Dance and the Music of J. S. Bach* (1991), 218f.

77. Little and Jenne, *Dance and the Music of J. S. Bach* (1991), 218f.

78. Little and Jenne, *Dance and the Music of J. S. Bach* (2001), 302.

79. *BC* 1:247.

80. Robin A. Leaver, "Bach's Understanding and Use of the Epistles and Gospels of the Church Year," *BACH* 6/4 (1975): 9; Albert Clement, "De orgelkoraalbewerkingen van Joh. Seb. Bach in het kerkelijk jaar," *Het Orgel* 86 (1990): 326.

81. Albert Clement, "'Sechs Choräle' BWV 645–650 von J. S. Bach und dessen Bedeutung," in *Das Blut Jesu und die Lehre von der Versöhnung im Werk Johann Sebastian Bachs*," ed. Albert Clement [Royal Netherlands Academy of Arts and Sciences: Proceedings of the International Colloquium The Blood of Jesus and the Doctrine of Reconciliation in the Works of Johann Sebastian Bach. Amsterdam, 14–17 September 1993] (Amsterdam: Royal Netherlands Academy of Arts and Sciences, 1995), 296f.

82. Brown, *An Introduction to the New Testament*, 261.

83. *BC* 2:585.

84. Leaver, "Bach's Understanding and Use," 9; Clement, "De orgelkoraalbewerkingen van Joh. Seb. Bach in het kerkelijk jaar," 328.

85. BWV 161, 95, 8, and 27.

86. Little and Jenne, *Dance and the Music of J. S. Bach* (1991), 97.

87. *BC* 1:238.

88. Gojowy, "Kirchenlieder im Umkreis von J. S. Bach," 107, 118, 122.

89. Albert Clement, "O Jesu, du edle Gabe: Studien zum Verhältnis von Text und Musik in den Choralpartiten und den Kanonischen Veränderungen von Johann Sebastian Bach," PhD diss., University of Utrecht, 1989, 144.

90. *SLG*, 284.

91. Clement, "O Jesu, du edle Gabe," 145.

92. Albert Fischer and Wilhelm Tümpel, *Das Deutsche Evangelische Kirchenlied des 17. Jahrhunderts* (Gütersloh: Bertelsmann, 1904–1916; reprint, Hildesheim: Olms, 1964), 1:309.

93. In Little and Jenne, *Dance and the Music of J. S. Bach* (1991), there is no reference to text-music relationships in their discussion of the vocal movements in the rhythm of the sarabande. It is very welcome to see a discussion of text in the revised and expanded edition of their book, *Dance and the Music of J. S. Bach* (2001), 239–250. Almost all of the texts they discuss in the context of Bach's use of the sarabande are concerned with death and eternal salvation, although they do not reach a conclusion in this regard, merely stating the facts. More work in the area of Bach's symbolic use of dance rhythms seems to be required, and as such, it is of great interest to read of the symbolic potential of the polonaise in Szymon Paczkowski, "Über die Funktionen der Polonaise und des polnischen Stils am Beispiel der Arie 'Glück und Segen sind bereit' aus der Kantate *Erwünschtes Freudenlicht* BWV 184 von Johann Sebastian Bach," in *Johann Adolf Hasse in seiner Epoche und in der Gegenwart: Studien zur Stil- und Quellenproblematik*, ed. Szymon Paczkowski and Alina Zorawska-Witlowska (Warszawa: Instytut Muzykologii Uniwersytetu Warszawskiego, 2002), 207–224. Paczkowski relates Bach's use of the polonaise to God's royalty and power.

94. An obvious example from the B Minor Mass is the contrast of heaven and earth in the triple time for the *Gloria in excelsis Deo* with the common time *et in terra pax hominibus*.

95. This issue is also discussed in chapter 3.

96. Heinrich Müller, *Evangelische Schluß-Kette / und Kraft-Kern / oder Gründliche Auslegung der gewöhnlichen Sonntags-Evangelien* (Frankfurt am Mayn: Wust, 1672), 437.

97. See the discussion of BWV 682 in Clement, *Der dritte Teil der Clavierübung*, 199, where he refers to the lengthening of the third-last note of the phrase at m. 41 at the word "Leidenszeit" [suffering time], pointing out that with this long note the *mora* or the length of the suffering time is depicted; for another example, see *Der dritte Teil*, 394, n. 111. The long ornament on the word "Trübsaal" in BWV 652 may be interpreted in a corresponding manner.

98. This rhythm is used consistently by Bach throughout movement 3 of the cantata *Es erhub sich ein Streit* (BWV 19). This cantata was for the feast of St. Michael, and the text is concerned with standing before the foe. In the case of this cantata movement, it is possible that this rhythm is associated with the notion of holding firm in battle. In BWV 652, it can be associated with the word "ritterlich" in a similar way.

99. Philipp Wackernagel, *Das deutsche Kirchenlied von der ältesten Zeit bis zu Anfang des XVII. Jahrhunderts* (Leipzig: Teubner, 1864–1877; reprint, Hildesheim: Olms, 1964), 3:46.

100. Wackernagel, *Das deutsche Kirchenlied*, 3:1120.

101. Steiger, "Gnadengegenwart," 54.

102. Hans Klotz, *Studien zu Bachs Registrierkunst* (Wiesbaden: Breitkopf & Härtel, 1985), 51, 93, 97; Clement, "O Jesu, du edle Gabe," 145. This is discussed more fully in chapter 2.

103. August Pfeiffer, *Der wolbewärte / Evangelische / Aug-Apfel / oder / schrifftmässige Erklärung / Der / Augsburgischen / Confession* (Leipzig: Kloß, 1685), 73.

· 2 ·

An Wasserflüssen Babylon

THE HYMN

An Wasserflüssen Babylon is the five-stanza German paraphrase of Psalm 137, *Super Flumina Babylonis*, by Wolfgang Dachstein (1487–1533), who was a student contemporary of Luther's, later becoming an organist and teacher at Strasbourg. It first appeared in 1525 in the third part of Wolf Köpphel's Strasbourg *Kirchenampt*.[1] A number of hymn tunes by himself and his colleague, the cantor Matthias Greiter, were included in this publication. By the 1540s, it had made its way into the major Lutheran hymnbooks of central Germany. As it was a psalm hymn, it was frequently published with an added *Gloria Patri* stanza, as in the Weimar hymnbooks of 1681, 1708, and 1713. Since it is most likely that it was this six-stanza version that Bach knew from the Weimar hymnbook of 1713, this is the text quoted below.

The six-stanza version of *An Wasserflüssen Babylon* was listed in the Weimar hymnbook of 1713 as a *de tempore* hymn for the tenth Sunday after Trinity.[2] As a lament for Jerusalem, Psalm 137 was clearly associated with the Gospel for this Sunday: Luke 19:41–48, where Jesus weeps over Jerusalem, predicting its destruction.[3]

The text of *An Wasserflüssen Babylon* was often grouped with hymns such as Paul Eber's *Wenn wir in höchsten Nöthen* under the heading "Von Creutz, Verfolgung und Anfechtung" [Concerning Cross, Persecution and Trial]. This was the case in the Weimar hymnbooks of 1681, 1708, and 1713. In the *Orgel-Büchlein*, Bach listed the title *An Wasserflüssen Babylon* after that of *Wenn wir in höchsten Nöthen* but left no setting.[4]

Super flumina Babylonis was a psalm for Vespers, and accordingly *An Wasserflüssen Babylon* came to be used at Saturday Vespers in some communities.

37

Occasionally this chorale became the subject of extended instrumental performance, as evidenced by Bach's improvisation on this tune for almost half an hour for the ninety-seven-year-old Jan Adams Reinken at the Hamburg Catharinenkirche in 1720.[5] Reinken himself composed a setting of this chorale, a fantasia of 327 measures. This was an important hymn of penitence for the tenth Sunday after Trinity, and it is probable that it was used as a penitential hymn on other Sundays and weekdays during Bach's lifetime.[6]

The melody was also associated with Paul Gerhardt's text *Ein Lämlein geht und trägt die Schuld*. According to Eduard Emil Koch, the melody held more value than the text.[7] The hymn tune has always been highly valued and referred to as *melodia suavissima*.[8] The text of Psalm 137 deals with the misery of the people of Israel in exile in Babylon. Hence, this psalm has always been seen as a psalm of lament and penitence.[9] Koch classifies it under the heading "Sehnsucht nach Erlösung" [longing for salvation].[10] Casper Honders describes its use as follows:

> und in der Geschichte der christlichen Kirche ist die Identifikation dieses Psalms mit der eigenen, elenden Existenz immer wieder praktiziert worden.[11] [and in the history of the Christian church this Psalm has been always identified with one's personal miserable existence.]

An Wasserflüssen Babylon was normally transmitted in F or G. In BWV 653, the setting is in G. Several important seventeenth-century hymnbooks (such as Schein 1627 and Vopelius 1682) present a chromatic inflection in the chorale's second phrase and its repetition. Bach uses this version in BWV 653, thereby increasing the resemblance between this hymn and the opening phrases of *Komm heiliger Geist, Herre Gott*. In the Weimar hymnbook of 1713, the text of *An Wasserflüssen Babylon* appears as follows:

1. AN Wasserflüssen Babylon/
   da sassen wir mit Schmertzen:
   Als wir gedachten an Zion/
   da weinten wir van Hertzen.
   Wir hiengen auf mit schwerem Muth
   die Harffen und die Orgeln gut/
   an ihre Bäum der Weiden/
   die drinnen find in ihrem Land/
   da musten wir viel Schmach und Schand
   täglich von ihnen leiden.

2. Die uns gefangen hielten lang/
   so hart an selben Orten/
   begehrten von uns einn Gesang/
   mit gar spöttlichen Worten/

1. By the rivers of Babylon
   we sat in sorrow:
   When we remembered Zion
   we wept from our hearts.
   With heavy hearts we hung
   the good harps and instruments
   on the trees of the meadow,
   which are in their land,
   there we much disgrace and shame
   suffered every day.

2. Those who kept us imprisoned long
   and hard in the same place
   demanded a song from us
   with scornful words,

und suchten in der Traurigkeit
ein frölichn Gsang in unserm Leid/
ach lieber thut uns singen/
ein Lob-Gesang/ ein Liedlein schön/
von den Gedichten aus Zion/
das frölich thut erklingen.

3. Wie sollen wir in solchem Zwang/
und elend ietzt vorhanden/
dem HErren singen einn Gesang/
so gar in fremden wLanden:
Jerusalem/ vergeß ich dein/
so wolle GOTT der Rechten mein
vergessen in meinm Leben/
wenn ich nicht dein bleib eingedenck/
mein Zung sich oben angeheng/
und bleib am Rachen kleben.

4. Ja wenn ich nicht mit gantzem Fleiß,
Jerusalem/ dich ehre/
im Anfang deiner Freuden-Preiß
von ietzt und immermehre.
Gedenck der Kinder Edom sehr/
am Tag Jerusalem/ O HErr/
die in ihrr Boßheit sprechen:
Reiß ab/ reiß ab/ zu aller Stund/
vertilg sie gar biß auf den Grund/
den Boden wolln wir brechen.

5. Du schnöde Tochter Babylon/
zerbrochen und zerstöret:
Wohl dem! der dir wird gebn den Lohn/
und dir das wiederkehret/
dein Ubermuth und Schalckheit groß/
und misst dir auch mit solchem Maaß/
wie du uns hast gemessen:
Wohl dem/ der deine Kinder klein
erfaßt und schlägt sie an einn Stein/
damit dein wird vergessen.

6. Ehr sey dem Vater und dem Sohn/
und auch dem heilgen Geiste:
Alls es im Anfang war und nun/
der uns sein Gnade leiste/
daß wir auf diesem Jammerthal/
von Hertzen scheuen überall
der Welt gottloses Leben/

and sought in the sadness
a joyful song in our sorrow,
O! dear one, do sing us
a song of praise, a beautiful little song,
from the poems of Zion,
which sound so joyful.

3. How shall we under such pressure
and in the present misery
sing a song to the Lord
even in a foreign land?
Jerusalem, if I forget you
God will forget my right [hand]
in my life.
If I do not continue to be mindful of you
may my tongue remain fastened above
and stay clinging to the roof of my mouth.

4. If I do not with complete diligence
honor you Jerusalem
in the beginning of your joyful praise
from now and evermore,
think of the children of Edom
on the day of Jerusalem, O Lord,
who in their badness speak,
tear it down, tear it down at any time,
Raze it to the (very) ground,
Let us destroy its foundations.

5. You vile daughter Babylon,
broken and destroyed,
happy the one who will give you recompense,
and returns to you
your wantonness and great guile,
and measures you also with the same measure,
as you have measured us.
Happy the one who your little children,
seize and strike them against a rock,
so that you will be forgotten.

6. Glory be to the Father and to the Son,
and also to the Holy Spirit,
As it was in the beginning and now,
as he renders us his grace,
that we in this vale of tears
from our hearts completely shun
the world of godless life,

und streben nach der neuen Art/	and strive according to the new way,
darzu der Mensch gebildet ward/	so was man created
wer das begehrt/ sprech Amen.[12]	whoever desires that, say Amen.[13]

The biblical text is as follows:

> *Psalm 137.* By the rivers of Babylon, there we sat down, yea, we wept, when we remembered Zion. We hanged our harps upon the willows in the midst thereof. For there they that carried us away captive required of us a song; and they that wasted us required of us mirth, saying, Sing us one of the songs of Zion. How shall we sing the lord's song in a strange land? If I forget thee, O Jerusalem, let my right hand forget her cunning. If I do not remember thee, let my tongue cleave to the roof of my mouth; if I prefer not Jerusalem above my chief joy. Remember, o lord, the children of Edom in the day of Jerusalem; who said, Rase it, rase it, even to the foundation thereof. O daughter of Babylon, who art to be destroyed; happy shall he be, that rewardeth thee as thou hast served us. Happy shall he be, that taketh and dasheth thy little ones against the stones.

As can be seen from these two texts, Dachstein remained very faithful to the original biblical text. In his book *Over Bachs Schouder*, Honders makes the following pertinent comments regarding this hymn:

> Dit lied van smart en lijden, van het wandelen in de vreemdelingschap, van roepen om de Trooster, is vervuld van groot verlangen naar het hemelse Jerusalem.[14] [This hymn of pain and suffering, of wandering in the wilderness, of calling on the Comforter, is filled with great longing for the heavenly Jerusalem.]

In his article on *An Wasserflüssen Babylon* (BWV 653b), Honders also points out the seeming paradox of this Psalm as follows:

> ein Lied von Gefangenschaft und Schmerz, gesungen von denen, die unter einem fremden Joch leben. Daneben auch ein Lied van Organa, von Hymnen und von cantica. Schmerz und Gesang, das Eine und das Andere, schrecklich und herrlich. Geht das zusammen? Kann man singen und Jerusalem vergessen? Spielen und des Geheimnisses Gottes nicht gedenken?[15] [a hymn of imprisonment and pain, sung by those, who live under foreign rule. Beside that, also a hymn of *organa*, hymns and singing. Pain and singing, the one and the other, fearful and wonderful. Does that go together? Can one sing and forget Jerusalem? Play and not think of the mysteries of God?]

Honders is showing how the people of Israel in exile and in great pain are also longing for the heavenly Jerusalem. In the following sections, I will discuss Bach's musical portrayal of this text and try to arrive at possible conclusions regarding text-music relationships.

AN WASSERFLÜSSEN BABYLON (BWV 653)

An Wasserflüssen Babylon (BWV 653) bears the heading "*Am Waßer Flüßen Babylon a 2 Clav. et Pedal*" in P271. Bach has left three versions of this chorale prelude: BWV 653, 653a, and 653b. BWV 653a and 653b were composed at Weimar, while BWV 653 is a later Leipzig revision.[16] BWV 653b is the original five-part version with double pedal, the coloratura *cantus firmus* being presented in the soprano and the left hand providing two lines of accompaniment.[17] BWV 653a is a four-part reworking of BWV 653b. The bass line of BWV 653a is clearly a compromise between the two pedal lines of the original setting. In BWV 653a, the *cantus firmus* is presented in the tenor and is more rhythmically developed than that of BWV 653b. This rhythmic drive is carried even further in BWV 653, the final Leipzig version. According to Hans Klotz, the original version was for Weißenfels and not for Hamburg, as the pedal of the Weißenfels organ had a compass that extended to f^1,[18] while the pedal of the organ at Köthen only extended as far as d^1.[19]

BWV 653 is a ritornello chorale whose material is derived from the first two lines of the *cantus firmus*.[20] The consistent reworking of this ritornello theme is a prominent feature of this movement, with almost every measure derived in some way from the thematic material. The ornamental chorale is presented as a left-hand tenor accompanied by two treble voices and a moving continuo-style pedal line. Two references to the first five notes of the *cantus firmus* are heard in the pedal in the first five measures. Above this, the accompanying parts introduce the ritornello with all the notes of the *cantus firmus* sounding in the treble, while the second voice provides a complementary counterpoint below. The left hand enters in m. 7 with the *cantus firmus*. Bach only alters the original hymn tune once in these two lines: the first *c-natural²* of the second phrase becomes *c-sharp²* as it did in the opening ritornello, to bring about a very brief reference to the dominant. In this composition, the notes of the *cantus firmus* are always clearly discernible throughout, with the ornamentation never obscuring the outlines of the melody. At m. 12.3, the ritornello recommences with a written-out repeat that remains unchanged to

m. 24. At m. 24, the music cadences in the tonic without a reference to the ritornello, as had previously occurred at the corresponding m. 13. Throughout this setting, Bach maintains continuity by consistently using similar cadence structures (for example, mm. 13, 25, and 36).[21]

In the ensuing interlude, a reference to the second phrase of the ritornello is heard in the pedal at m. 27, passing from A minor through D major and back to A minor, before returning to G major for the entry of line 5 of the *cantus firmus* at m. 34. Meanwhile, the treble part also takes up the same part of the ritornello, contributing to the thematic unity that dominates the piece. At m. 33, the ritornello returns in full as heard previously, but this time with a change of accent at mm. 36–37. The ornamental *cantus firmus* enters over a pedal *G* so that the *cantus firmus* is heard solo *en taille*. The ritornello brings the music to the dominant, before modulating to E minor for line 6 of the *cantus firmus* by way of A minor.

Line 6 of the *cantus firmus* begins in E minor but quickly moves to D major. The opening of the ritornello is heard clearly in the lower of the two accompanying parts above the *cantus firmus*. After this, the ritornello recommences in the upper accompanying part, still in the key of D major. The second of the two treble parts introduces a series of suspensions, increasing the harmonic tension and bringing the music to the entry of line 7 of the *cantus firmus* at m. 46, itself at a point of suspension. This phrase passes through A minor to end at m. 50 in the key of E minor. The ritornello is altered at m. 49 to facilitate the move to E minor. In the following interlude, the ritornello is heard in stretto in the two accompanying parts, passing in sequence through A minor and D major before returning to A minor for the entry of line 8 of the *cantus firmus* at m. 56. Here the harmonic tension becomes more intense as the music moves toward D and A minor, only cadencing at the last moment, and even then very briefly, in D major before moving on again toward A minor. Over the ornamental *cantus firmus* the ritornello theme is heard, this time centered on A minor. This statement of the ritornello ends at m. 65, and Bach immediately reintroduces it in stretto above line 9 of the *cantus firmus*. The harmony here is dictated by the *cantus firmus*, which tends toward D minor rather than D major. The cadence at m. 69 ends in D major, while the lower of the two accompanying parts completes the first phrase of the ritornello theme to return to G major.

The final line of the *cantus firmus* enters over a pedal point on G, while the ritornello is heard high above in the top part, commencing at m. 72 and in the second treble part at m. 74. The final note of the *cantus firmus* is held over a moving pedal part, which refers to the opening of the ritornello with a final reference to the theme in the top part at m. 80. In this version, Bach introduces double pedal for the last three measures, with a rising tetrachord which hints at line 2 of the chorale. According to Peter Williams, the descending G major scale in the left hand could be a reference to a setting by Reinken or some other North German composer.[22]

Interpretations by Other Authors

In commenting on the text of *An Wasserflüssen Babylon*, most authors have made observations relating to the lamenting Israelites in exile.

Albert Schweitzer clearly states that both versions by Bach of *An Wasserflüssen Babylon* (BWV 653b and BWV 653) were composed to be played *alternatim* with the stanzas of the sung hymn during the distribution of the holy sacrament.[23]

Hans Luedtke sees the constant reworking of the first two lines of this melody as a means of emphasizing the sorrow of Babylon.[24]

Charles Sanford Terry refers to the atmosphere of languor that makes Bach's setting congruous with stanza 1.[25] He also suggests that the accompaniment represents the ripples of the waters of Babylon.[26]

Stainton de B. Taylor believes that this setting gives the impression of running water, with the embellishments adding an appropriate touch of weary sadness to Bach's setting.[27] He states that without these touches (presumably the ornaments), this would be quite a cheerful piece![28]

Hermann Keller makes the assumption that Bach decided to make the revision a four-part version since double pedal was considered old fashioned by Bach's time.[29]

According to Helene Werthemann, Bach may have been thinking of Paul Gerhardt's passion chorale *Ein Lämlein geht und trägt die Schuld* when he wrote this setting of the melody *An Wasserflüssen Babylon*.[30]

Jacques Chailley refers to the constant repetition of the opening motive, which he suggests serves as a "refrain de complainte" [mournful refrain].[31] As usual with Chailley, he mainly considers the relevance of the first stanza of the hymn. At the end of his discussion, he offers another possible interpretation as follows:

> celle qui, sachant que Sion est toujours présenté comme une "montagne" (c'est en fait une colline qui domine la ville, et sur laquelle était bâti le temple), lui associerait les divers mouvements ascendants, tant de la coda que de la pedale.[32] [that which, knowing that Zion is always presented as a mountain (it is in fact a hill which dominates the town, and on which was built the temple), itself associated with the different ascending motives, up to the coda and the pedal.]

Werner Breig describes the constant reworking of the first two lines of the chorale as a litany-like lament.[33] He sees the use of the sarabande rhythm as representing the affect of mourning, citing the final choruses of the St. John and St. Matthew passions as examples.[34]

Ulrich Meyer comments that this setting achieves the high ideal of inner unity through monothematicism, as in the first *Kyrie* setting, BWV 669, from *Clavierübung III*.[35] According to Meyer, the expression remains neutral in both of these pieces. He shares Werthemann's view that Bach might have been thinking of Gerhardt's passion chorale *Ein Lämlein geht und trägt die Schuld* when he composed BWV 653.[36] This is a little contradictory, since if the expression is neutral, then how can he tell which hymn Bach is depicting?

Casper Honders deals in the main with the five-part, double-pedal version, *An Wasserflüssen Babylon* (BWV 653b). He is concerned with the overall situation of the hymn text: the human (Babylon) can only be saved by God (Zion).[37] Referring to the importance of the constant reworking of the first two phrases of the hymn melody and the relevance to the text, he quotes the first four lines of stanza 1 to support his argument.[38] He states that Dachstein's hymn and Bach's musical setting define the human situation as pitiful, deeply painful, and far removed from an existence safeguarded by the nearness of God. Honders justifies the inclusion of BWV 653 in a collection of *musica sub communione* as follows:

> dann ist auch von daher deutlich, dass wir in den grössten Schmerzen ein gerettetes und geheiligtes Volk sein dürfen, lebend und atmend in der Liturgie der Kirche Christi, dank Gottes gnädiger Zuwendung zu uns allen.[39]
> [then it is also clear, that in the greatest pain, we may be a saved and holy people, living and breathing in the liturgy of the Church of Christ, thanks to God's gracious gift to us all.]

The seemingly deeply melancholic atmosphere of *An Wasserflüssen Babylon* has inspired most writers to concentrate on the painful aspects of the hymn text. In the next section, I will try to ascertain if there are other elements that may have inspired Bach in his portrayal of text in BWV 653.

Assessment

When one begins to investigate text-music relationships in BWV 653, one is immediately struck by the paradox that seems to exist between the text and the musical setting. As reported above, much has been made of the pain-ridden atmosphere of the text of *An Wasserflüssen Babylon*. Examination of Psalm 137 and Dachstein's hymn reveals the depths of despair the Israelites experienced in Babylon. There is not much apparent comfort offered in this gloom-ridden text. How do the angst-laden complaints of the exiled Israelites relate to BWV 653? What theological point is Bach making in his portrayal of this hymn? Can the musical features of this composition lead to any stanza in particular?

As described above, the beauty of the melody of *An Wasserflüssen Babylon* has resulted in its description as *melodia suavissima*.[40] The dominance of this sonorous hymn tune in the accompanying parts as well as in the solo line throughout BWV 653 may be related in some way to the text. Other musical elements include the sarabande rhythm, the ornamental tenor, the employment of parallel thirds and sixths, some use of dissonance and minor tonalities, pedal points, and a double pedal close. Some or all of these features may be related to the text; this is investigated in the following.

An Wasserflüssen Babylon was a *de tempore* hymn for the tenth Sunday after Trinity. Before turning to BWV 653 itself, it is useful to examine the Gospel and some aspects of the cantatas for this Sunday. Close investigation into the Gospel reading for the tenth Sunday after Trinity offers rewarding results. In the Gospel from Luke 19:41–48, Jesus predicts the destruction of Jerusalem by the Romans. Here, God punishes the wayward people for their evil ways. There is a clear link between this extract from Luke's Gospel and Psalm 137, where the Israelites are being punished by God for wrongdoing. The Babylonian captivity is predicted in Ezekiel, beginning at chapter 12:15. Chapters 1 through 23 predict the ruin of Jerusalem. The authority of God is one of the prophet's main issues. He repeatedly states, "Thus saith the Lord GOD." In the closing verses of chapter 11, God states how he will purge Israel from all evil, and that the people of Israel will then keep his laws:

> That they may walk in my statutes, and keep mine ordinances, and do them: and they shall be my people, and I will be their God. But as for them whose heart walketh after the heart of their detestable things and their abominations, I will recompense their way upon their own heads, saith the Lord god. . . . Afterwards the spirit took me up, and brought me in a vision by the Spirit of God into Chaldea, to them of the captivity. So the vision that I had seen went up from me. Then I spake unto them of the captivity all the things that the lord had shewed me.

This passage in turn links to Revelation 21:1–5, where the new heaven and earth replace the devastation of the first heaven and earth.

> And I saw a new heaven and a new earth: for the first heaven and the first earth were passed away; and there was no more sea. And I John saw the holy city, new Jerusalem, coming down from God out of heaven, prepared

as a bride adorned for her husband. And I heard a great voice out of heaven
saying, Behold, the tabernacle of God is with men, and he will dwell with
them, and they shall be his people, and God himself shall be with them, and
be their God. And God shall wipe away all tears from their eyes; and there
shall be no more death, neither sorrow, nor crying, neither shall there be
any more pain: for the former things are passed away. And he that sat upon
the throne said, Behold, I make all things new.

Clearly, Psalm 137, the Gospel reading for the tenth Sunday after Trinity,
much of the writing of the prophet Ezekiel, and chapter 21 of the Book of
Revelation all share a common theme—God punishes wrongdoing, but he
promises salvation in the new Jerusalem, where suffering is no more.

The cantatas for the tenth Sunday after Trinity are also concerned with
the theme of penitence and repentance. They are *Schauet doch und sehet, ob
irgendein Schmerz sei* (BWV 46), *Nimm von uns, Herr, du treuer Gott* (BWV 101),
and *Herr, deine Augen sehen nach dem Glauben* (BWV 102).[41] The first section
of the opening movement of BWV 46 was later parodied by Bach to become
the *Qui tollis* of the *Gloria* of the B Minor Mass. Both share an overall *Affekt* of
pain and pleading. BWV 46/1 takes its text from the Lamentations of Jeremiah
1:12 with the words:

> Schauet doch und sehet, ob irgendein Schmerz sei wie mein Schmerz, der
> mich troffen hat. Denn der Herr hat mich voll Jammers gemacht am Tage
> seines grimmigen Zorns. [Behold, and see if there be any sorrow like unto
> my sorrow, which is done unto me, wherewith the lord hath afflicted me
> in the day of his fierce anger.]

The entire cantata is taken up with the wrath of God at the unrepentant sinner. This theme is also to be found in the text of Psalm 137.

Michael Marissen has pointed out how music and theology sometimes
seem to be at odds in the music of Bach. He cites the alto aria of BWV 46 as
an example. The text refers to tempests of vengeance [Wetter der Rache] for
the sin of humanity, whereas the two recorder parts provide comforting music
in parallel motion.[42] In another paper, Marissen shows how Bach sometimes
provided comfort through the music where it was not present in the text.[43] He
cites as an example the opening aria of the cantata *Meine Seufzer, meine Tränen*
(BWV 13), where Bach goes far beyond the seeming negativity of the text,
offering comfort in the parallel thirds and sixths of the instrumental counterpoint and the triple subdivision of the duple meter.[44] Bach may be employing
similar methods in BWV 653.

I have discussed Bach's use of the sarabande and its possible relevance to
BWV 652 in chapter 1. The use of this rhythm may be relevant to the text-

music relationships in BWV 653. In the vocal works, it seems that Bach uses this rhythm with texts relating to eternal salvation. It is useful to consider one additional aria to those mentioned in chapter 1. Bach's use of the sarabande in an eschatological context is striking in the alto aria "Soll ich mein Lebenslauf" from the cantata *Schau lieber Gott, wie meine Feind* (BWV 153).[45] This cantata was written for the Sunday after New Year and was first performed on 2 January 1724.[46] The entire cantata is taken up with the idea that the Christian must suffer in order to achieve salvation, a theme very close to that of Psalm 137. The text of the aria (movement 8) is as follows:

Soll ich meinen Lebenslauf	If I am to run my lifetime's course
Unter Kreuz und Trübsal führen,	Amidst cross and tribulation
Hört est doch im Himmel auf.	It nevertheless ceases in heaven
Da ist lauter Jubilieren,	There is sheer jubilation
Daselbsten verwechselt mein Jesus das Leiden	At the same place my Jesus transforms suffering
Mit seliger Wonne, mit ewigen Freuden.	Into blessed rapture, into eternal joy.

Melvin P. Unger refers to Revelation 21:1–4 (cited above) with regard to this movement.[47] Ulrich Meyer refers to 1 Peter 4:13 ("But rejoice, inasmuch as ye are partakers of Christ's sufferings; that, when his glory shall be revealed, ye may be glad also with exceeding joy").[48]

Luther's comment on this verse of scripture confirms the value he placed on earthly suffering as follows:

> Zu des Himmels höchsten Freuden werden nur durch tiefe Leiden Gottes Lieblinge verklärt. Durch Leiden zur Herrlichkeit ging's bei Christus, geht's bei seinen Christen.[49] [To Heaven's greatest joy, God's favored ones are glorified only through grievous suffering. As Jesus' path led through suffering to glory, so it is for his Christian (followers).]

The aria text contrasts trials experienced on earth with the jubilation of heaven. Additionally, the cross of Christ is mentioned as a means of transforming suffering into eternal joy. Therefore, it seems that Bach is once more employing the sarabande rhythm to portray an eschatological theme.

In his lectures on the Psalms, Luther does not refer directly to Psalm 137, but he makes many pertinent remarks regarding suffering on earth and eternal reward. He states that truth means that the Christian cannot expect to find peace in this world.[50] Peace will come only above in heaven with Christ. Richard Marius makes the observation that this comment could be the foundation stone for his theology of the cross.[51]

Following the above discussion, I would like to turn to BWV 653 itself and its possible relationship to the theological ideas mentioned above. The prominence given to the melody by Bach, especially the first two lines, beginning in the first measure, gives the piece a warm and hopeful atmosphere. Is this a piece portraying the desolation of the people of Israel, or does Bach somehow portray an element of hope? It is striking what Heinrich Müller writes in his *Evangelische Schluß-Kette* for the fifteenth Sunday after Trinity:

> Ich habe selbst eine Lerche gehabt/ die mir alle Morgen die Melody der beyden herrlichen Kirchen-Gesänge: Aus meines Hertzens Gründe/ und An Wasserflüssen Babylon/ auffs lieblichste vorgesungen. . . . Durch sie lehret uns Gott.[52] [I myself had a lark/ who sang the melodies of the two wonderful church hymns to me in a most lovely way every morning: *Aus meines Hertzens Gründe/* and *An Wasserflüssen Babylon.* . . . Through them [the birds] God teaches us.]

Müller is talking about the beauty of nature, in this case birds, showing that they teach about God's wisdom and power. It is possible that Bach thought this melody was also teaching about the beauty of God's world, and he therefore repeatedly quoted the *incipit* all the way through the piece.

Throughout BWV 653, Bach makes consistent use of the *figura corta*. It is even more prominent in the Leipzig revision than in BWV 653a or 653b. Albert Schweitzer was the first to label this as a "joy motive." He refers to several chorale preludes where the *figura corta* rhythm portrays the joyful feeling of confidence in God's goodness.[53] It is possible that Bach uses this figure to portray the idea that the people of Israel should trust in God's goodness.

The so-called joy motive was sometimes used in the context of the cross of Christ and its paradoxical aspect.[54] In Lutheran theology, eternal life comes by way of the cross of Christ; suffering on earth leads to eternal salvation. This might somehow be linked to Bach's portrayal of *An Wasserflüssen Babylon*. Luther himself wrote on this subject in his *Tisch reden* as follows:

> Darum sollen wir nur fröhlich und zufrieden seyn in Armuth und Trübsal, und gedenken, wir haben einen reichen Herrn, der uns nicht trost- und hülflos lassen kann, und haben also Fried und gut Gewissen. Es gehe, wie der liebe Gott will, so haben sie fried im herzen mit Gott, welchen die Gottlosen nicht haben, wie Jesaias sagt, sondern sind ein wüthend Meer.[55] [Therefore, we should be only happy and glad in destitution and distress, and remember, we have a rich God, who cannot leave us desolate and helpless, and therefore have peace and a good conscience. It happens, as the beloved Lord wants, so they have peace in their hearts with God, which the Godless do not have, as Isaiah says, those without are a raging sea.]

Luther's views are echoed in the theological writings of the seventeenth century. In his *Geistliche Erquick-Stunden*, Heinrich Müller states, "da macht er aus allem Leid grosse Freude" [out of all suffering he makes great joy].[56] In Luther's view, therefore, the suffering of the Israelites was necessary in order for them to achieve salvation. Perhaps Bach is offering the solution to the suffering of the Israelites in his musical portrayal of the text.

As seen from the preceding discussion, the idea of suffering on earth in order to achieve eternal salvation was central to Luther's theology of the cross. It appears that this is also an important aspect of Psalm 137 and its paraphrase, *An Wasserflüssen Babylon*. Further examination of the musical elements of BWV 653 may help to find Bach's possible intentions regarding the text–music relationships of BWV 653.

Bach's use of major and minor tonality throughout BWV 653 is striking. Although he makes much use of minor tonality, in particular in the second half of the piece, he almost always returns to the major within one measure. This could be related to the text. Bach may somehow be trying to provide a musical comfort that the text cannot give. A clear example of this can be seen at mm. 49–50, 55–56, and 59–60. It is possible that Bach is trying to overcome the tribulations of the people of Israel in this musical process. The eventual resolution of minor to major may be a musical indication that the people of Israel will overcome this period of trial.

Dissonance seems to be an important aspect of BWV 653. With the exception of lines 8 and 10 of the chorale, every entry of the *cantus firmus* is marked by a dissonance on the first strong beat. Bach's use of the *syncopatio* as well as the *syncopatio catachrestica* is notable throughout the setting. The use of dissonance increases as the piece progresses. This could be Bach emphasizing the earthly trials of the Israelites in captivity. It may be that in the consistent return to major tonalities and the constant reiteration of the *melodia suavissima*, the overall feeling of hope in salvation is present.

So how can conclusions be drawn regarding the text–music relationships in BWV 653? As reported earlier, several writers have suggested that stanza 1 of the text of *An Wasserflüssen Babylon* is represented in BWV 653. Is it possible to connect this stanza whose text is laden with words such as "Schmertzen," "weinten," "schweren Mut," "Schmach," "Schand," and "Leiden" with Bach's musical setting? Equally, the remaining stanzas all contain references to misery and destruction of some sort.[57] It does not seem plausible to equate the ornamental line accompanied by the pleasing-sounding thirds and sixths with such negative ideas.

In his theology of the cross, Luther repeatedly emphasized that suffering and torment came before eternal salvation. It is conceivable that Bach may have been depicting an overall longing for the heavenly Jerusalem. The music supplies the solution to the problems presented in the text. Honders implies this when he says that the entire setting is filled with a longing for the heavenly Jerusalem.[58] Stanza 4 of the text refers specifically to the heavenly Jerusalem for which the children of Israel long. This particular text is to be found in verse 6 of Psalm 137. Luther's commentary on Psalm 137:6 is helpful in the interpretation of Bach's setting. He states,

> Möchten wir unsere Glieder doch allezeit nur im Dienste des Herrn gebrauchen und das Jerusalem das droben ist (Offenb. 21) unsere höchste Sehnsucht und Freude sein lassen. Wir Kinder des neuen Testaments möchten dieses tiefempfundene Heimwehlied am liebsten mit V.6 schließen.[59] [May we only always use our members in the service of the Lord, and that Jerusalem which is on high may remain our greatest longing and joy. We children of the New Testament may preferably end this deep homesickness hymn with verse 6.]

Luther emphasizes that man's greatest longing is for the heavenly Jerusalem. Bach may be interpreting this in a musical way in his setting of *An Wasserflüssen Babylon*. In the case of BWV 653, the music becomes the theology, itself offering consolation for the sorrow-ridden atmosphere of Babylon expressed in the text. Bach goes beyond the literal meaning of the text of Psalm 137 to offer the ultimate solution to the lamenting Israelites—the hope of eternal salvation. He seems to express, through music, what the text has only implied.[60] It appears to be an overall aspiration to eternal happiness that is portrayed here rather than any stanza in particular. The longing for Zion and the heavenly Jerusalem is to be found in every stanza, and more than anything else it is a feeling of happiness and peacefulness that Bach portrays. Koch's classification of this hymn under the heading "Sehnsucht nach Erlösung" may help to confirm this view.[61] *An Wasserflüssen Babylon* was also important as a Vespers hymn, as noted above. As discussed in chapter 1 in connection with cantata 6, the evening could be regarded literally as the end of the day, or metaphorically as the end of life. Therefore, as a Vespers hymn, *An Wasserflüssen Babylon* could be related to the transition from earthly life to eternal salvation.[62]

The comforting atmosphere is reflected in the many parallel thirds and sixths in the accompanying voices. Similar examples of this kind of writing can be found in BWV 768/10 and in BWV 654. In the former ("O Jesu, du edle Gabe," stanza 10), the text refers to the final coming of man, as he enters eternity in white clothing accompanied by angels.[63] The accompanying parts of BWV 768.10 have many parallel thirds and sixths, which are surely linked to the text.[64] There is a comparable situation in BWV 654 where the text is concerned with the soul adorning itself for the heavenly meal, longing for union with Christ in heaven. The accompanying parts in BWV 653 also have many parallel thirds and sixths. It appears that they may be related to the long-ing for the eternal Jerusalem.[65]

The solo *en taille* melody at mm. 34–36 is worthy of note. The first five notes of line 5 of the chorale are given over a *tasto solo* G. Bach sometimes em-ploys a *tasto solo* when he is portraying peace on earth or eternity, for example in the *et in terra pax* of the B Minor Mass (mm. 113–117) and in No. 21 (mm. 25–30 and 57–60) of the Christmas Oratorio.[66] It is possible that Bach's use of *tasto solo* in this context is related to future eternal peace in Jerusalem. There is another pedal point in mm. 72–75. In the soprano, the opening ritornello is heard based on the opening line, a timely reminder perhaps of the heavenly Jerusalem and eternal salvation. From mm. 77–80, the first line of the chorale is heard outlined in the pedal and repeated in the soprano. At the same time, the final note of the chorale is held for five and a half measures. This very long final note may be connected to the text, in this case to eternal salvation.

The only double pedal of the piece appears in the final two measures, and in this case, the style is completely different from that of the double-pedal ver-sion, BWV 653b. In the upper part, Bach quotes the rising tetrachord, the first four notes of line 5. This complements the final long note of the chorale. Once more, Bach may be looking forward to the final peace of eternal salvation.

Each one of the chorale preludes in the "Leipzig" manuscript is a revi-sion of at least one earlier version composed while Bach was at Weimar. In the case of BWV 653, there are two earlier and quite different versions. The differences between the three settings have been well documented by Werner Breig, and it is not necessary to reproduce the material in detail here.[67] The greatest issue with regard to *An Wasserflüssen Babylon* in the present study is to determine (1) why Bach considered the final version to be the ultimate one, and (2) the significance of this decision concerning the relationship of text and music. Why did Bach revert to four voices from the original five?

Breig offers no solution in relation to text and music but points out that in the 1740s, having completed *Clavierübung III*, Bach must have ap-proached *An Wasserflüssen Babylon* from a different perspective than before. From his experience of contrapuntal writing in *Clavierübung III*, Bach may have wanted a more clearly defined role for each voice. In this case, the final four-part version offers a tighter solution.[68] This seems like a good reason to go from five to four parts. Bach rarely employs double pedal in his chorale settings, the only other case being *Aus tiefer Noth schrei ich zu dir* (BWV 686). In the latter case, double pedal is used in relation to the chorale melody. It may be that Bach used BWV 653b as part of his demonstration of his skills in Hamburg for the aging Reinken.[69] The five-part texture, as well as the double pedal, may have been regarded by the more mature Bach as rather old fashioned.[70] There can be no doubt that Bach regarded BWV 653 as the final version since he copied it into P271 himself. Schweitzer seems to be of the opinion that BWV 653b was an independent setting and comments on how Bach never got around to including it in one of his collections of chorale preludes.[71] An obvious conclusion seems to be that Bach did not include BWV 653b in any of his chorale collections because he considered BWV 653 to be the final version. An important consequence of the change to four parts was that the solo chorale now appeared in the tenor part. This may be significant. Bach sometimes reflected the second person of the Trinity as mediator in the tenor or middle voice.[72] Luther himself refers to the children of the New Testament longing for the heavenly Jerusalem.[73] The only way this salvation can be achieved is through the cross of Christ. Therefore it seems logical to place the *cantus firmus* in the tenor to help portray this New Testament aspect of salvation. This may offer further proof that BWV 653 is in fact Bach's intended final version. If he allowed the *cantus firmus* to remain in the soprano, as in BWV 653b, the soteriological aspect of the text might not be as strong.

With the *cantus firmus* in the tenor as an ornamental part, there could be grounds for associating this kind of writing with the *tierce en taille* style of the French classical school.[74] We know that Bach found the sesquialtera stop to be "vollkommen schon."[75] Bach frequently prescribed the sesquialtera for use in cantatas regarding eternity and death. An obvious example is the opening movement of the cantata *Komm du süße Todesstunde* (BWV 161). This cantata was written for the sixteenth Sunday after Trinity and was first performed on 27 September 1716.[76] Here Bach prescribes the sesquialtera for the organ, on which is played the melody of *Herzlich tut mich verlangen* against the alto's entreaties to sweet death. In the opening chorus of the St. Matthew Passion, Bach prescribes the use of the sesquialtera stop for the organ as it doubles the ripieno sopranos' intonation of *O Lamm Gottes unschuldig*.[77] We could not have a clearer indication from Bach of the association of the sesquialtera stop with the Lamb of God, and therefore with the new Jerusalem. With BWV 653, it would seem to be the logical stop to use.

An important issue to be clarified is whether Bach was indeed thinking of Dachstein's text *An Wasserflüssen Babylon* when he composed BWV 653. There is no evidence to suggest that he had an alternative text in mind. Werthemann's suggestion that Bach may have been thinking of Gerhardt's hymn *Ein Lämlein geht* is too convenient in order to fit BWV 653 into a collection of *musica sub communione*. If Bach had more than one text in mind, he usually indicated it with a double title, as for example in the *Orgel-Büchlein* chorale *Herr Christ der ein'ge Gottessohn oder Herr Gott, nun sei gepreiset* (BWV 601). It has proven more rewarding to explore the eschatological implications of the text of Psalm 137 and Bach's musical setting.

In attempting to find Bach's purpose for creating this collection of chorale preludes, one of the compositions causing difficulty for earlier writers has been *An Wasserflüssen Babylon* (BWV 653). It clearly cannot be regarded as a specific Communion hymn, but when viewed in the broader context of salvation, it is an important setting in this collection. It was common to include hymns of penitence at Communion time in Leipzig, which in combination with the eschatological aspects of this hymn makes it very suitable for performance during the distribution of the holy sacrament.[78] Additionally, a hymn that emphasized longing for the heavenly Jerusalem would not be out of place during the distribution of the sacrament, nor indeed in a collection united by an eschatological theme.

★ ★ ★

It appears that Bach may have been portraying an overall aspiration to the heavenly Jerusalem in BWV 653. The comforting aspect of the music goes way beyond the lamentation expressed in the text. Bach offers comfort to the Israelites, which is not expressed in the text. He does not seem concerned with a literal interpretation, instead concentrating on the eternal consequence thereof. Similarly to BWV 652, the employment of the sarabande rhythm seems to be significant. As outlined in this and the preceding chapter, the sarabande is utilized when Bach is dealing with texts relating to salvation. The pleasing-sounding thirds and sixths and many ornaments may also be related to the aspiration for salvation and for union with Christ in the eternal Jerusalem.

NOTES

1. Eduard Emil Koch, *Geschichte des Kirchenlieds und Kirchengesangs der christlichen, insbesondere der deutschen evangelischen Kirche*, 3rd ed. (Stuttgart: Belser, 1866–1876; Hildesheim: Olms, 1973), 8:526. For notes on the text, see Philipp Wackernagel, *Das deutsche Kirchenlied von der ältesten Zeit bis zu Anfang des XVII. Jahrhunderts* (Leipzig: Teubner, 1864–1877; reprint, Hildesheim: Olms, 1964), 3:98 (No. 135). For notes on the melody, see Zahn 7663.

2. Detlef Gojowy, "Kirchenlieder im Umkreis von J. S. Bach." *JbLH* 22 (1978): 115.

3. Günther Stiller, *Johann Sebastian Bach und das Leipziger gottesdienstliche Leben seiner Zeit* (Kassel: Bärenreiter, 1970), 54: "Am 10. Sonntag nach Trinitatis wurde stets 'in der Vesper-Predigt die Historie der Zerstörung der Stadt Jerusalem gelesen . . . , wobei der Prediger ebenfalls zur Büße und Besserung vermahnet.'" Günther Stiller, *Johann Sebastian Bach and Liturgical Life in Leipzig*, trans. Herbert J. A. Bouman, Daniel F. Poellot, and Hilton C. Oswald; ed. Robin A. Leaver (St. Louis: Concordia, 1984), 64: "On the 10th Sunday after Trinity 'in the Vesper service the history of the

destruction of Jerusalem was read . . . and the preacher also admonished to penitence and improvement.'" See also Koch, *Geschichte des Kirchenlieds und Kirchengesangs*, 8:527.

4. Johann Sebastian Bach, *Orgel-Büchlein BWV 599–644. Faksimile der autographen Partitur*, ed. Heinz-Harald Löhlein (Kassel: Bärenreiter, 1981), 116f.

5. *Dok* 3:84 (No. 666); *NBR* 302; Peter Williams, *The Organ Music of J. S. Bach* (Cambridge: Cambridge University Press, 1980–1986), 3:48f.

6. See Casper Honders, "Super flumina Babylonis. Bemerkungen zu BWV 653b," *Bulletin Internationale Arbeitsgemeinschaft für Hymnologie* 17 (1989): 53.

7. Koch, *Geschichte des Kirchenlieds und Kirchengesangs*, 8:526.

8. Koch, *Geschichte des Kirchenlieds und Kirchengesangs*, 8:528.

9. The concept of human trials and suffering as found in *An Wasserflüssen Babylon* seems to have much in common with the cantata texts that Bach used for the Epiphany season: BWV 3, 13, 32, 58, 123, 153, 154, and 155. In these cantatas, the human soul is struggling through the tribulations of life in an effort to be united with Christ for eternity.

10. Koch, *Geschichte des Kirchenlieds und Kirchengesangs*, 8:526–528.

11. Honders, "Super flumina Babylonis," 53.

12. *SLG*, 356ff.

13. Translation partly based on Mark Bighley, *The Lutheran Chorales in the Organ Works of J. S. Bach* (St. Louis: Concordia, 1986), 36f.

14. Casper Honders, *Over Bachs Schouder. Een bundel opstellen* (Groningen: Niemeijer, 1985), 74.

15. Honders, "Super flumina Babylonis," 53.

16. *NBA KB* IV/2:67.

17. *NBA KB* IV/2:67. Philipp Spitta, *Johann Sebastian Bach*, trans. Clara Bell and J. A. Fuller-Maitland (London: Novello, 1884–1885; reprint, New York: Dover, 1992), 1:616f., suggests the opposite; that is, BWV 653a was the original version. But it seems more likely to be the other way round, as the bass line of BWV 653a is a compromise of the double pedal part of BWV 653b. Additionally, BWV 653 is clearly a revision of BWV 653a, and therefore these two settings were worked on by Bach in succession.

18. *NBA KB* IV/2:68.

19. See Williams, *The Organ Music of J. S. Bach*, 3:128.

20. Russell Stinson, *J. S. Bach's Great Eighteen Chorales* (New York: Oxford University Press, 2001), 15, suggests that it is one of the most complex movements of the "Leipzig" chorales, being at once a *tierce en taille*, a sarabande, a ritornello movement, and an ornamental chorale. He also points out that the origins of this composition may date from the period 1712–1714, the same time that Bach copied out Nicholas de Grigny's *Premier livre d'orgue*. According to Stinson, it is possible that Bach was influenced by de Grigny's *tierce en taille*.

21. Peter Williams, *The Organ Music of J. S. Bach*, 2nd ed. (Cambridge: Cambridge University Press, 2003), 348f.

22. See Williams, *The Organ Music of J. S. Bach*, 2:135, a statement that is weakened in the second edition: Williams, *The Organ Music of J. S. Bach*, 2nd ed., 349.

23. Harald Schützeichel, *Albert Schweitzer: Die Orgelwerke Johann Sebastian Bachs. Vorworte zu den "Sämtlichen Orgelwerken"* (Hildesheim: Olms, 1995), 175, 250.

24. Hans Luedtke, "Seb. Bachs Choralvorspiele," *BJ* 15 (1918): 41.

25. Charles Sanford Terry, *Bach's Chorals Part III: The Hymns and Hymn Melodies of the Organ Works* (Cambridge: Cambridge University Press, 1921), 104.

26. Terry, *Bach's Chorals Part III*, 103.

27. Stainton de B. Taylor, *The Chorale Preludes of J. S. Bach* (London: Oxford University Press, 1942), 107.

28. Taylor, *The Choral Preludes of J. S. Bach*, 107.

29. Hermann Keller, *Die Orgelwerke Bachs. Ein Beitrag zu ihrer Geschichte, Form, Deutung und Wiedergabe* (Leipzig: Peters, 1948), 183; Herman Keller, *The Organ Works of Bach: A Contribution to Their History, Form, Interpretation and Performance*, trans. Helen Hewitt (New York: Peters, 1967), 249.

30. Helene Werthemann, "Bemerkungen zu Johann Sebastian Bachs Siebzehn Chorälen für Orgel," *MuG* 6 (1968): 158.

31. Jacques Chailley, *Les Chorals pour Orgue de J.-S. Bach* (Paris: Leduc, 1974), 70.

32. Chailley, *Les Chorals pour Orgue de J.-S. Bach*, 70.

33. Werner Brieg, "The 'Great Eighteen' Chorales: Bach's Revisional Process and the Genesis of the Work," in *J. S. Bach as Organist: His Instruments, Music, and Performance Practices*, ed. George Stauffer and Ernest May (Bloomington: Indiana University Press, 1986), 111.

34. Brieg, "The 'Great Eighteen' Chorales," 111.

35. Ulrich Meyer, "Über J. S. Bachs Orgelchoralkunst," in *Theologische Bach-Studien 1*, ed. Walter Blankenburg and Renate Steiger, [Beiträge zur theologischen Bachforschung 4] (Neuhausen-Stuttgart: Hänssler, 1987), 42; see also Ulrich Meyer, "Zur Frage der inneren Einheit von Bachs Siebzehn Chorälen (BWV 651–667)," *BJ* 58 (1972): 68.

36. Meyer, "Über J. S. Bachs Orgelchoralkunst," 42.

37. Honders, "Super flumina Babylonis," 57.

38. Honders, "Super flumina Babylonis," 58.

39. Honders, "Super flumina Babylonis," 59.

40. Koch, *Geschichte des Kirchenlieds und Kirchengesangs*, 8:528.

41. *BC* 2:504–507.

42. Michael Marissen, "The Character and Sources of the Anti-Judaism in Bach's Cantata 46," *Harvard Theological Review* 96/1 (2003): 63–99. It is significant that this cantata was written by Bach for the tenth Sunday after Trinity. In BWV 653 and cantata 46, Bach seems to be conveying both elements of the theology relating to this Sunday—God is punishing wrongdoing on the one hand, while on the other hand the Israelites are longing for eternal salvation.

43. Michael Marissen, "On the Musically Theological in J. S. Bach's Church Cantatas," *Lutheran Quarterly* 16 (2002): 50ff.

44. Marissen, "On the Musically Theological," 50ff. During the course of this article, Marissen discusses other works where Bach seems to be contradicting the text in musical terms but may in actual fact be making an even more profound theological observation.

45. Alfred Dürr, *Die Kantaten von Johann Sebastian Bach. Mit ihren Texten* (Kassel: Bärenreiter, 1985), 199, refers to this movement as a minuet. With its consistent emphasis on the second beat of the measure, however, it seems to be more in the style of a sarabande.

46. *BC* 1:135.

47. Melvin P. Unger, *Handbook to Bach's Sacred Cantata Texts. An Interlinear Translation with Reference Guide to Biblical Quotations and Allusions* (Lanham, MD: Scarecrow, 1996), 529.

48. Ulrich Meyer, *Biblical Quotation and Allusion in the Cantata Libretti of Johann Sebastian Bach* (Lanham, MD: Scarecrow, 1997), 20.

49. *Die Bibel oder die ganze heilige Schrift des Alten und Neuen Testaments nach der deutschen Übersetzung Martin Luthers . . . mit erklärenden Anmerkungen* (Stuttgart: Württembergische Bibelanstalt, 1912), New Testament, 363.

50. *WA* 4:17.

51. Richard Marius, *Martin Luther: The Christian between God and Death* (Cambridge, MA: Harvard University Press, 2000), 94.

52. Heinrich Müller, *Geistliche Erquick-Stunden / Oder Dreyhundert Haus- und Tisch-Andachten* (Franckfurt am Mayn: Wust, 1672), 1030; see also Koch, *Geschichte des Kirchenlieds und Kirchengesangs*, 8:527.

53. Albert Schweitzer, *J. S. Bach* (Leipzig: Breitkopf & Hartel, 1920), 459; English: *J. S. Bach*, trans. Ernest Newman (New York: Dover, 1966), 2:66. The chorale preludes he cites are *Wer nur den lieben Gott läßt walten* (BWV 647); *Der Tag, der ist so freudenreich* (BWV 605); *Erschienen ist der herrlich' Tag* (BWV 629); *In dich hab' ich gehoffet* (BWV 640); *Von Gott will ich nicht lassen* (BWV 658); and *Wir danken dir, Herr Jesu Christ* (BWV 623).

54. In the opening chorus of *Jesu, der du meine Seele* (BWV 78), the *figura corta* is consistently used in the context of the cross and suffering of Christ; see Anne Leahy, "The Opening Chorus of Cantata BWV 78, *Jesu, der du meine Seele*: Another Example of Bach's Interest in Matters Soteriological," *BACH* 30/1 (1999): 26–41.

55. *WA TR* 5:230 (No. 5550).

56. Müller, *Geistliche Erquick-Stunden*, No. LXIV, "Vom Ende deß Leidens," 155–157, here 156.

57. "Traurigkeit" and "Leid" (stanza 2); "Elend" (stanza 3); "Boßheit" (stanza 4); "Schnöde Tochter," "zerbrochen," "zerstöret," and "Ubermuth" (stanza 5); "Jammerthal" and "Der Welt gottloses Leben" (stanza 6).

58. Honders, *Over Bachs Schouder*, 74.

59. *Die Bibel . . . nach der deutschen Übersetzung Martin Luthers . . . mit erklärenden Anmerkungen*, Old Testament, 768.

60. See note 44.

61. Koch, *Geschichte des Kirchenlieds und Kirchengesangs*, 8:526–528.

62. See the discussion of the eschatological significance of the passing of time in Robin A. Leaver, "Eschatology, Theology and Music: Death and Beyond in Bach's Vocal Music," in *Irish Musical Studies 8: Bach Studies from Dublin*, ed. Anne Leahy and Yo Tomita (Dublin: Four Courts Press, 2004), 129–147.

63. Albert Clement, "'O Jesu, du edle Gabe': Studien zum Verhältnis von Text und Musik in den Choralpartiten und den Kanonischen Veränderungen von Johann Sebastian Bach," PhD diss., University of Utrecht, 1989, 142.

64. Measures 7, 10, 15, 24, 36, 37, and 39 are examples.

65. Measures 1, 4, 18, 32, 84–86, 99, and 119–122 are examples.

66. See further the discussion of BWV 659 in chapter 8.

67. Werner Brieg, "The 'Great Eighteen' Chorales," 102–120.

68. Werner Brieg, "The 'Great Eighteen' Chorales," 112f.

69. Spitta, *Johann Sebastian Bach*, 1:617.

70. See Schützeichel, *Albert Schweitzer*, 174, where Schweitzer suggests that Bach probably wanted to show the aging Reinken that the younger generation could also write in this highly valued technique of double pedal, even if it was outmoded by 1720.

71. Schweitzer, *J. S. Bach* (1920), 270; *J. S. Bach*, trans. Ernest Newman (1966), 1:293.

72. *Christe, aller Welt Trost* (BWV 670) and *Allein Gott in der Höh sei Ehr* (BWV 663) are examples.

73. *Die Bibel . . . nach der deutschen Übersetzung Martin Luthers . . . mit erklärenden Anmerkungen*, Old Testament, 768.

74. See Stinson, *J. S. Bach's Great Eighteen Chorales*, 79.

75. Clement, "O Jesu, du edle Gabe," 145; Klotz, *Studien zu Bachs Registrierkunst*, 51, 93, 97.

76. *BC* 2:581.

77. *BC* 3:1037.

78. Stiller, *Bach und das Leipziger gottesdienstliche*, 72f.; Stiller, *Bach and Liturgical Life in Leipzig*, 84.

• 3 •

Schmücke dich, o liebe Seele

THE HYMN

*T*he text of *Schmücke dich, o liebe Seele* is by Johann Franck (1618–1677). Stanza 1 and the melody of the hymn were published in 1649 in Johann Crüger's *Geistliche Kirchenmelodien*, with the entire text published in 1653 in Crüger's *Praxis pietatis melica.*[1] The text as it appears in the Weimar hymnbook of 1713 comprises nine stanzas. This Abendmahl hymn contains much imagery relating to the bride/bridegroom theme of the Song of Songs and as such bears a strong relationship to the twentieth Sunday after Trinity. The unification of the soul (bride) with Christ (bridegroom), known as the *unio mystica*, is an important aspect of the hymn text. The *unio mystica* is the unification of the soul with Christ for which all Lutherans longed. It could take place after death in the heavenly Jerusalem. The Abendmahl was a foretaste of this union but was not itself the union.[2] There was a strong Lutheran tradition regarding the love of the soul for Christ, which also had its roots in human love. In his *Himmlischer Liebes-Kuß*, Heinrich Müller writes about the bride/bridegroom theme in relation to Christ and the soul as follows:

> Wie ist eine hertzliche Freude zwischen Braut und Bräutigam? Nicht minder zwischen Christum und der Seele. . . . Wie ein Bräutigam seine Braut/ so schmücket Christus unsere Seele. Sie ist häßlich und ungestalt/ er macht sie schneeweiß. Sie liegt in ihrem Blut/ er reiniget sie durchs Wasserbad im Wort.[3] [How is heartfelt joy between bride and bridegroom? Not less than between Christ and the soul. . . . As a bridegroom adorns his bride, so Christ adorns our souls. It is hateful and ugly; he makes it snow white. It lies in his blood; he cleanses it through a waterbath in words.]

59

Müller compares human love with the love between Christ and the soul, showing how Christ's blood is part of the cleansing process. It is significant that Müller echoes the precise sentiments of Luther's sermons for the twentieth Sunday after Trinity (discussed later). The text of the hymn as found in the Weimar hymnbook of 1713, where it is listed under the heading "Vom H. Abendmahl," is as follows:

1. SChmücke dich/ o liebe Seele!
   laß die dunckle Sünden-Höle/
   komm ans helle Licht gegangen/
   fange herrlich an zu prangen
   denn der HERR voll Heyl und Gnaden/
   will dich itzt zu Gaste laden/
   der den Himmel kan verwalten/
   will itzt Herberg in dir halten.

1. Adorn yourself, o dear Soul,
   leave the dark den of sin,
   come to the bright light,
   begin to shine wonderfully.
   For the Lord, full of salvation and mercy,
   wishes to have you as his guest.
   He who can administer the heavens
   wishes to dwell in you.

2. Eyle/ wie Verlobte pflegen/
   deinem Bräutigam entgegen/
   der da mit dem Gnaden-Hammer
   klopft an deine Hertzens-Kammer:
   Oefn ihn bald die Geistes-Pforten/
   red ihn an mit schönen Worten:
   Komm/ mein liebster laß dich küssen/
   laß mich deiner nicht mehr müssen.

2. Hurry, like fiancées usually do
   to meet your bridegroom,
   who with the hammer of mercy
   knocks at your heart's chamber.
   Quickly open your soul's gate to him,
   speak to him tenderly,
   Come my dearest, let me kiss you,
   let me no longer be without you.

3. Zwar in Kauffung theurer Wahren/
   pflegt man sonst kein Geld zu sparen:
   Aber du wilt für die Gaben
   deiner Huld kein Geld nicht haben/
   weil in allen Bergwercks-Gründen/
   kein solch Kleinod ist zu finden/
   daß die Blut-gefüllte Schalen/
   und diß Manna kan bezahlen.

3. Although in the purchase of expensive goods
   one does not care to save any money:
   But you will for the gift
   of your favor take no money,
   for in all the depths of a mine,
   this treasure cannot be found,
   that the blood-filled bowls
   can be paid with this treasure.

4. Ach wie hungert mein Gemüthe/
   Menschen-Freund nach deiner Güte!
   Ach wie pfleg ich oft mit Thränen
   mich nach dieser Kost zu sehnen!
   Ach wie pfleget mich zu dürsten/
   nach den Tranck des Lebens-Fürsten/
   wünsche stets/ daß mein Gebeine
   mich durch GOtt mit Gott vereine.

4. O how my being hungers
   O friend of man for your goodness!
   O how often I with tears
   habitually long for this food!
   O how I am used to thirsting
   for this drink of the Prince of Life!
   I always wish that my body
   will unite itself to God through God.

5. Beydes Lachen und auch Zittern/
   lässet sich in mir jetzt wittern:
   Das Geheimniß deiner Speise/
   und die unerforschte Weise machet/
   daß ich früh vermercke/

5. Both laughing and trembling
   can be perceived in me.
   The mystery of this food
   and the unexplored manner
   cause me to soon realize

HErr die Grösse deiner Wercke.
Ist auch wohl ein Mensch zu finden/
der dein Allmacht solt ergründen?

the greatness of your work, Lord.
Can anyone be found
who can fathom your omnipotence?

6. Nein/ Vernunft die muß hie weichen/
kan diß Wunder nicht erreichen/
daß diß Brod nie wird verzehret/
ob es gleich viel tausend nehret/
und daß mit dem Saft der Reben/
uns wird Christi Blut gegeben.
O der grossen Heimlichkeiten/
die nur GOttes Geist kan deuten.

6. No, reason must give way here.
It cannot approach this miracle,
that this bread will never be totally consumed
even if it nourishes many thousands,
and that with the juice of grapes
Christ's blood is given to us.
O the great mysteries,
which only the Spirit of God can explain!

7. JEsu meine Lebens-Sonne/
Jesu meine Freud und Wonne/
JEsu du mein gantz Beginnen/
Lebens-Quell und Licht der Sinnen/
hier fall ich zu deinen Füßen/
laß mich würdiglich geniessen
dieser deiner Himmels-Speise/
mir zum Heyl und dir zum Preise.

7. Jesus, sun of my life!
Jesus, my joy and delight!
Jesus, my very beginning!
Fountain of life and light of the mind!
I fall here at your feet.
Let me worthily enjoy,
this your heavenly food,
which is my salvation to your praise.

8. HErr es hat dein treues Lieben
dich vom Himmel abgetrieben/
daß du willig hast dein Leben/
in den Tod für uns gegeben/
und dazu gantz unverdrossen/
HERR/ dein Blut für uns vergossen/
das uns ietzt kan kräftig träncken/
deiner Liebe zu gedencken.

8. Lord, your dear love
forced you from heaven,
so that you willingly
gave your life in death for us,
and besides, completely patiently,
Lord, you shed your blood for us,
which we can now drink vigorously
to remember your love.

9. JEsu/ wahres Brod des Lebens/
hilf/ daß ich doch nicht vergebens/
oder mir vielleicht zum Schaden/
sey zu deinem Tisch geladen!
Laß mich durch diß Seelen-Essen
deine Liebe recht ermessen/
daß ich auch/ wie ietzt auf Erden/
mög ein Gast im Himmel werden.[4]

9. Jesus, true bread of life,
help that I am not in vain
or perhaps to my harm
invited to your table!
Let me through this meal of the soul,
consider your love,
so that I may also, as now on earth
become a guest in heaven.[5]

In his *Tisch des Herrn* (Hamburg, 1722), Erdmann Neumeister writes on the subject of *Schmücke dich, o liebe Seele*, describing the idea of "schmücken" as follows:

Der wahre Seelenschmuck ist Glaube und Liebe zu Jesu, nebst andern heiligen Tugenden.[6] [The true adornment of the soul is faith and love for Jesus, along with other holy virtues.]

During the course of his sermon, he uses words such as "begierig" [desirous] and "verlangen" [longing] in relation to Jesus.[7] The unity between Christ and the soul is explained by him in the context of the final line of stanza 1, "will itzt Herberg in dir halten":

> das heisset/ er will sich mit dir vereinigen, und in dir wohnen: nach seiner Verheissung: Wer mein fleisch isset und trincket mein Blut/ der bleibet in mir/ und ich in ihm. Joh. VI. 56.[8] [that means, he wants to unite himself with you, and live in you: according to his promise: whoever eats my flesh and drinks my blood, lives in me, and I in him. John 6:56.]

Later, Neumeister refers to the bride/bridegroom theme, referring to the Song of Songs and then to the New Testament with regard to the love Christ has for his church (Eph. 5:25 and Gal. 2:20). He returns to the union of the soul and Christ, referring to Christ knocking on the door of the heart to allow him to enter there, as in the Song of Songs 5:2:

> Da ist die Stimme meines Freundes, der anklopfet: thue auf, liebe Freundin, meine Schwester, meine taube, meine Fromme.[9] [It is the voice of my beloved that knocketh, saying: Open to me my sister, my love, my dove, my undefiled.]

The following passage from Revelation 3:20, which so perfectly illustrates the union of Christ as the bridegroom with the soul as bride, is quoted by Neumeister:

> Siehe, ich stehe vor Thür, und klopfe an. So iemand meine Stimme hören wird, und die Thür aufthun, zu dem werde ich eingehen, und das Abendmahl mit ihm halten, und er mit mir.[10] [Behold, I stand at the door and knock: if any man hear my voice, and open the door, I will come in to him, and will sup with him, and he with me.]

Following this quote from Revelation, Neumeister clarifies the situation even further by saying,

> Es werden aber unter solchem Anklopfen gemeynet die innerlichen Bewegungen, die heiligen Gedancken, die hertzlichen Begierden zu Jesu, von Jesu, in Jesu, welche durch sein Wort und seinen heiligen Geist erwecket werden. Ach die lassen sich nicht so sagen und erklären, als selber empfinden und erfahren.[11] [What is meant by such knocking is the inner emotions, the holy thoughts, the heartfelt desire toward Jesus, of Jesus, in Jesus, which are awakened through his Word and his Holy Spirit. But let it not be so much spoken and explained as received and experienced for itself.]

As seen from the above citations, the union of the soul with Christ is repeatedly highlighted by Neumeister in the context of *Schmücke dich, o liebe Seele.*[12] According to him, the union of the soul with Christ was to be an emotional event that was felt and experienced by the believer, not merely spoken about and analyzed. Neumeister emphasizes a theme accentuated by Luther in his sermons for the twentieth Sunday after Trinity—the *unio mystica*. This theme is also the central focus of Franck's hymn and is discussed further in the following sections.

SCHMÜCKE DICH, O LIEBE SEELE (BWV 654)

BWV 654 is headed "*Schmücke dich, o liebe Seele. a 2 Clav. et Pedal*" in P271. As with most of the chorale preludes in this collection, two settings exist: an earlier Weimar version (BWV 654a) and the later Leipzig revision (BWV 654). The only difference between the two is that there is an even higher proportion of ornaments in BWV 654a than in BWV 654. Bach has composed an ornamental chorale prelude with ritornello elements, very similar in style to the two chorale preludes that precede it in P271 (BWV 652 and BWV 653). Many of the features shared between the three settings have been discussed already in chapters 1 and 2. The pedal line of BWV 654 has much in common with the French-style bass line of BWV 653. According to Peter Williams, the long notes of the *cantus firmus* pass into melismatic passages so as to make the chorale virtually unrecognizable.[13] It is not however as unrecognizable as the melismatic treatment given to *Nun komm der Heiden Heiland* in BWV 659.

The hymn comprises eight lines of text in all, with the music for lines 1 and 3, 2 and 4, and 5 and 6 being identical. In addition, lines 2 and 8 are remarkably similar. This allows Bach to maintain continuity by the repetition of motives throughout the piece. In his setting he repeats the music of the first two lines for lines 3 and 4. The composition numbers 129 measures and is one of the longer preludes in the "Leipzig" chorales. Remarkable for the expressive accompanying lines, many of which feature writing in thirds and sixths, it also contains some well-developed part writing. The high proportion of ornaments dominates, adding to the intense and fervent atmosphere. Most of the motivic writing is derived from the *cantus firmus* itself.

The warm and ethereal atmosphere is established immediately in m. 1 where the two accompanying manual parts begin with double trills in sixths. Bach bases the writing on the opening line of the chorale melody with the alto utilizing all the notes of line 1. Ardor and intensity are emphasized in the passing reference to the subdominant in m. 2. The process of adornment is continued in m. 4 with more trills in sixths, followed by expressive interaction between manuals and pedal leading to the first solo entry of the *cantus firmus* in m. 12. The first three notes of the *cantus firmus* are presented in dotted half notes, while the remaining notes of the phrase are lightly ornamented. Again, there is a passing reference to the subdominant, and the music moves from E-flat major to C minor at the cadence in mm. 15–17.

The fore-imitations for line 2 of the chorale are less clearly discernible as being related to the *cantus firmus*, although some of the motivic writing was actually introduced in the first section (for example, see the relationship between m. 7 and m. 19). Harmonic interest is supplied by a cadence to F minor by means of a hemiola (mm. 21–23) before cadencing to B-flat for the entrance of the *cantus firmus* at m. 25. There is a striking descending pedal scale of an octave and a fifth in mm. 25–26, accompanied in the manual parts by rising double thirds. Bach moves toward the flat side for the remainder of the phrase, cadencing in A-flat at the close of the first section (m. 34). This entire section is then repeated.

The fore-imitation for line 5 of the chorale commences at m. 69, the musical material being clearly derived from line 5 of the *cantus firmus*. The rising tetrachord becomes a feature of this section in all of the accompanying parts, including the pedal. This motive is introduced in imitation successively in the alto, tenor, and bass, being subsequently heard in m. 71 in its *rectus* and *inversus* form (bass and alto respectively). Bach successfully combines the lyricism of double thirds and sixths with suspensions on the strong beats of almost every measure throughout this passage. An ideal example of this kind of writing is seen at m. 76 for the entry of line 5 of the *cantus firmus*. There is an expressive move to C minor at m. 77, followed by a passing modulation to G minor before a perfect cadence in B-flat major in mm. 81f.

Since the music for line 6 is identical with line 5, this may be why Bach chose to have an interlude of only one measure between the two sections. Measures 82–88 are based on the motive originally heard at mm. 7 and 19. The importance of this motive is increased by its presentation in sixths in the alto and tenor at m. 84. At m. 85, the bass takes over, while the alto and tenor continue in parallel sixths. The treatment of the right-hand *cantus firmus* becomes more melismatic while the pedal rises a dramatic diminished seventh from A to G-flat[0] at m. 89. In this measure, Bach provides the most vivid and colorful harmony thus far in the piece. He introduces a diminished-seventh chord with an accented dissonance in the right-hand solo part. This is followed on the second beat by a further diminished-seventh chord, leading back to the dominant of B-flat major and onward to E-flat in m. 92.

The following interlude does not involve any fore-imitation of line 7 of the *cantus firmus*. At m. 92, Bach employs a motive that is actually a retrograde of the motive originally heard at m. 7. This is heard in its inversion at m. 95.

The tonality remains centered on F minor from m. 93 to 97, moving toward A-flat for mm. 98f. There is another rising pedal scale of a seventh in mm. 95–97, and a rising scale passage in double thirds leads to the entrance of line 7 of the chorale at m. 100. The F minor tonality is maintained throughout this section to m. 105 where an F major chord leads expressively to B-flat minor, a key far away from the tonic of E-flat major.

The section that leads to the final line of the *cantus firmus* is remarkably expressive. Once again, a rising scale in the pedal, which spans a minor ninth, is utilized and is immediately followed by a falling scale passage. From m. 106 to 111, the tonality remains centered on B-flat minor, changing to B-flat major at m. 112, following a hemiola in mm. 110f. At m. 112, the opening motive is heard once more, this time with trills in double thirds in B-flat major. This passage culminates in the reintroduction of this motive at m. 116, exactly as it was in m. 1. The musical material stays the same as at the beginning to m. 119, where Bach leads to the final phrase of the *cantus firmus* by means of double thirds in the alto and tenor. The *cantus firmus* enters for the last time at m. 120 over double thirds between the alto and pedal. This time the *cantus firmus* is very ornate and skillfully combined with many of the motives previously heard throughout the piece. At the final approach to the tonic in mm. 124–125, a perfect cadence in E-flat is avoided, cadencing instead to the subdominant, A-flat. As the tonic is held in the right-hand solo part, the accompanying voices move through E-flat, back to A-flat, and then lead to a plagal approach to the tonic once more.

Interpretations by Other Authors

Schmücke dich, o liebe Seele (BWV 654) has inspired many poetic descriptions of Bach's compositional art. A well-known statement regarding this piece is that of Robert Schumann, who said that if hope and belief were taken from him, then this piece would renew all once more.[14] It was also allegedly Felix Mendelssohn's favorite piece.[15]

Many writers are in agreement regarding the text-music relationships in BWV 654, and most regard this composition as possessing extraordinary mystical qualities. Philipp Spitta suggests a mental image of subdued, heavenly ecstasy,[16] while Albert Schweitzer also comments on the mystical atmosphere, the bride/bridegroom analogy, and its relevance to the heavenly Abendmahl.[17] Hans Luedtke finds it to be "'unsagbar schön" [indescribably beautiful]. He sees many connections between the text of stanza 1 and this setting and suggests that as the text of line 6 is introduced (he refers to it as line 4: "will dich itzt zu Gaste laden"), the left hand is portraying the text of the final line, "will itzt Herberg in dir halten."[18]

It is interesting that Ulrich Meyer comments on the sarabande rhythm and the overpowering variety of the motivic development, seeing chromatic writing such as that found at mm. 88–90 as being related to the text, although he does not say which stanza.[19] Later on, he refers to the text of stanza 3 as the basic tone of the hymn, reflected in the sarabande rhythm and the expressive sound colors.[20] The text he quotes is "Heilige Lust und tiefes Bangen/ nimmt mein Herze jetzt gefangen." In fact, this stanza was not part of the hymn in Bach's time and is not printed in the Weimar hymnbook of 1713, being only subsequently added in later hymnals. Meyer makes the same assumption in his later article on Bach's chorale settings.[21]

Russell Stinson points out the close correspondence between BWV 654 and the soprano aria "Tief gebückt und voller Reue" from the cantata *Mein Herze schwimmt im Blut* (BWV 199).[22] This aria is in triple time, in E-flat major, and its opening ritornello employs practically the same material as BWV 654. Like others, Stinson suggests that Bach uses ornamentation within the ritornello as a pun on the word "Schmücke." He comments on the similarity of the accompanimental figuration to that of BWV 768/10, which is also a sarabande.[23]

It has not been difficult for most writers to demonstrate the mystical atmosphere of BWV 654. On the whole this has been done in a rather general manner. In the following section, these qualities are explored in detail in an effort to find Bach's possible intentions with regard to text and music.

Assessment

It seems quite clear that Bach is portraying the adornment mentioned in stanza 1 of *Schmücke dich, o liebe Seele* in BWV 654. However, the precise detail of that portrayal needs further investigation. Of primary importance in relation to this text and its setting by Bach is a consideration of Luther's interpretation of the bride/bridegroom relationship and its meaning for Lutherans of the early eighteenth century.

Excursus: Theology Relating to the Twentieth Sunday after Trinity

Important themes for the twentieth Sunday after Trinity included the adornment of the soul as it prepared for eternal life, the *unio mystica*, the bride/bridegroom theme of the Song of Songs and the Abendmahl. *Schmücke dich, o liebe Seele* is strongly associated with this Sunday because of its theological theme.[24] The cantata *Schmücke dich, o liebe Seele* (BWV 180) was composed for the twentieth Sunday after Trinity and was first performed on 22 October 1724.[25] Luther's sermons for this particular Sunday provide an aid to understanding Bach's possible intentions regarding the text-music relationships in BWV 654.

The Gospel reading for this day was Matthew 22:1–14, where Christ tells the parable of the king who had a marriage feast for his son.[26] In the parable, one of the guests does not wear a wedding garment, consequently causing the king to command that his servants cast him out into darkness. This parable is very relevant to *Schmücke dich, o liebe Seele*, where the soul prepares for the marriage feast in heaven. Luther's sermons for this Sunday offer insight into the Lutheran tradition of the relationship of the bride/bridegroom theme with Christ and the soul. In almost all of these sermons, Luther explains this bride/ bridegroom analogy. One of his main arguments with regard to this Gospel is that the guest must come properly dressed to the wedding feast—he who does not is cast out in darkness. Therefore, the soul as bride of Christ must be properly adorned to attend the marriage feast in heaven. In a sermon dating from 1522, Luther explains as follows:

> Zum erstenn ist dye hochtzeit eyn voreynung gotlicher natur mit der menschlichen, unnd wye ein lyeb Christus tzü uns trage, Das wirt yhn dem bilt hye angetzeygt myt der hochtzeytt. Denn es seyn vyl lyebe, aber keyne ist alßo brunstig und hytzig als dye braut lyebe, dye eyne newe brautt tzum breutigam hat. . . . Die liebe hat uns vorgetragen got yn Christo, yn dem das er den vor uns mensch hat lassen werden und voreyniget mit der menschlichenn natur, das wir in dem seinen freuntlichen willen gegen uns spuren und erkennen möchten. Nu wie ein braut den breutigam lieb hat, also hat uns Christus auch lieb und wir widerumb, so wir gleuben und die rechte braut seyn.[27] [First, this marriage feast is a union of the divine nature with the human. And the great love Christ has for us is presented to us in this picture of the wedding feast. For there are many kinds of love, but none is so ardent and fervent as a bride's love, the love a new bride has to her bridegroom, and on the other hand the bridegroom's love to the bride. . . . This true-bride love God presented to us in Christ, in that he allowed him to become man for us and be united with our human nature that we might thus perceive and appreciate his good will toward us. Now, as the bride loves her betrothed, so also does Christ love us; and we on the other hand will love him, if we believe and are the true bride.[28]]

Luther explains the *unio mystica* that takes place at the marriage feast in heaven. In this union, Christ takes on all that is the soul's, and the soul takes on all that is Christ's. Therefore the sins of the soul are taken on by Christ and washed clean in this union by his blood. In the same sermon from 1522, Luther equates the love between Christ and the soul with human love.[29] As with the ideal human love, the union between Christ and the soul is absolute and unconditional. Only then can eternal life be assured. According to Luther, the wedding garment is Christ himself, which is put on by faith as seen in Romans 13:14, "Put ye on the Lord Jesus Christ."[30] Therefore, when the text of stanza 1 of *Schmücke dich, o liebe Seele* asks the soul to adorn itself, it is not merely asking it to be adorned in the physical sense but also in the figurative sense, that it take on Christ in faith, be cleansed by the sacrifice of Christ, and receive salvation. We see this point being made by Luther in his sermon for this same Sunday as follows:

> Aber was thut der breutigam? er ist auch so eckel unnd wil auch nichtt bey yr schlaffenn, sonder ehr schmuckt sie ym vor auffs aller hubste tzü. Wie ghett das tzü? Das lernt Paulus. Er hat vor sie gebenn seynen tzarten leychnam unnd begossenn mit seynem heyligen blut und hat sie gereyniget myt dem badt der widergeburt. Er hat einn badt angerycht, das badt ist dye tauff, do mit wescht er sy, uber das hat er sein wort geben, daran gleubt sie den und durch den glauben wirt sie seynn brautt.[31] [But what does the bridegroom do? He is so fastidious that he will not dwell with his bride until he first adorns her in the highest degree. How is that done? The Apostle Paul teaches us that when he says in Tit. 3:5–6 "He gave his tender body unto death for them and sprinkled them with his holy blood and cleansed them through the washing of regeneration and renewing of the Holy Spirit," he instituted a washing; that washing is baptism, with which he washes her. More than this, he has given to her his word; in that she believes and through her faith she becomes a bride.[32]]

Luther is really emphasizing the redemptive aspect of the heavenly union of the adorned soul with Christ. In the text of stanza 1 of *Schmücke dich, o liebe Seele*, Christ invites the adorned soul to be his guest for the heavenly meal, not only in Communion, but also in heaven itself. This point is also made in Revelation 19:9 as follows:

> Und er sprach zu mir: Selig sind, die zum Abendmahl des Lamms beruffen sind! Und er sprach zu mir: Diß sind warhaftige Wort GOttes. [And he saith unto me, Blessed are they which are called unto the marriage supper of the Lamb. And he saith unto me, These are the true sayings of God.]

True union with Christ in heaven could only come about through death; hence the many writings on the subject of longing for death and consequently heaven.[33]

In his sermons for the twentieth Sunday after Trinity, Luther repeatedly refers to the darkness of the sin of humanity as opposed to the bright light of Christ as follows:

> Und hieraus ist wol zu verstehen, was da hie heisset, das dieser ist on hochzeitlich kleid, nemlich, on den newen schmuck, damit wir Gotte gefallen, welches ist der Glaube an Christum, und also auch on rechte gute wreck. . . . Denn dis Hochzeitlich Kleid mus sein das newe liecht des hertzen, so die erkentnis der grossen gnaden dieses Breutgams und seiner hochzeit in dem hertzen wirket.[34] [And from this it is easy to understand

what is meant by this man's doing without a wedding garment, namely, without the new adornment in which we please God, which is faith in Christ, and therefore also without truly good works. . . . For this wedding garment must be the new light of the heart, kindled in the heart by the knowledge of the graciousness of this bridegroom and his wedding feast.[35]]

Therefore, the soul's adornment is crucial to its participation in the marriage feast of heaven, according to Luther. Without this, the soul will be cast out, as the improperly dressed guest of the parable.[36] Salvation and grace come about through union with Christ in the Abendmahl. This salvation is achieved not only by receiving the Communion but also by acknowledging the commemorative aspect of the sacrament—the fact that Christ died to give humanity salvation. As seen from the above discussion, the love between the soul and Christ was an important topic for the twentieth Sunday after Trinity. The *unio mystica* between Christ and the soul could be prepared for in the Abendmahl, and so *Schmücke dich, o liebe Seele* was an important Abendmahl hymn. Consequently, the sacrifice of Christ also had its role to play in the theology for Trinity 20. This may have great significance for *Schmücke dich, o liebe Seele* (BWV 654), as discussed in what follows.

★ ★ ★

Many elements of BWV 654 indicate the heavenly connection. The number three, as noticed in chapter 1, is frequently related to heaven in Bach's music. The key signature of three flats may be a further heavenly connection. Other musical features of this composition worthy of investigation are the abundance of ornaments, the many parallel thirds and sixths, and the way that Bach handles the tonality of the piece.

It is useful first to examine the opening chorus of the cantata *Schmücke dich, o liebe Seele* (BWV 180). Although the cantata was written after Bach's first version of the chorale prelude (BWV 654a), a study of the cantata movement yields interesting results in demonstrating Bach's interpretation of the hymn text. Bach sets stanza 1 of the hymn as a chorale fantasia in the cantata. Although there are marked differences between the compositional methods of this cantata and BWV 654, there are also some similarities that may help to solve the question of text-music relationships. The idea of heavenly matters and salvation is not far from the surface in BWV 180/1. In the first place, this movement is written in 12/8 meter. Renate Steiger has shown how this time signature is sometimes related to eternal salvation, and this appears to be the case in BWV 180/1.[37]

Secondly, examination of the instrumental writing yields interesting results. As a chorale cantata, BWV 180 belongs in Bach's second Leipzig *Jahrgang* and bears the hallmarks of the mature composer. The string section comprises violins, violas, and continuo, with the three upper string parts playing in unison as a kind of heavenly unity. The remaining instruments are two recorders, an oboe, and an oboe da caccia. Much of the writing for these pairs of instruments is in parallel thirds and sixths. These intervals may be related to the *unio mystica* so clearly expressed in the text of stanza 1. In addition, the oboes may be seen as instruments of love, thus emphasizing the love between the soul and Christ. This kind of writing can be found in many of the cantatas dealing with the topic of love.

The parallel intervals may be seen as a musical representation of an important theological aspect of the hymn text—the *unio mystica*. Parallel thirds and sixths can be associated with sweetness and love. Walter Blankenburg has commented on how the language of human love may also express divine love, thereby suggesting that the means of expressing both human love and divine love through music could also be the same. He refers to m. 6 of the dialogue cantata *Liebster Jesu, mein Verlangen* (BWV 32), written for the first Sunday after Epiphany. Here the soul (soprano) and the Christ (bass) are united musically in parallel motion. Blankenburg describes how the pleasing-sounding thirds are a musical means of expressing unity.[38] Parallel motion frequently depicts love in secular terms in baroque music. Blankenburg comments on the common analogy between human and divine love, stating that the means of portraying both may be the same.[39] Luther refers to the warmth and fervor between a bride and bridegroom,[40] and the love of the soul for Christ may well be reflected in the many parallel thirds and sixths of BWV 654.

BWV 654 has much in common with BWV 768/10. Similarly, this piece is a sarabande, one of the most significant elements being the many thirds and sixths (see example 3.1). In BWV 768/10, the sarabande rhythm and the parallel motion may be related to the text. Stanza 10 of Johannes Böttiger's hymn *O Jesu du edle Gabe* describes the journey of the soul going to heaven. This is a Communion hymn, and stanza 10 also mentions the means of getting to heaven—"dein Blut mich von Sünden wäschet/ und der Höllen-Gluth auslöschet" [Your blood washes me from sin, and conquers hell's power].[41] The soul is dressed in white going to heaven and will be washed clean by the blood

Example 3.1.   BWV 768/10 (mm. 6ff.)

Example 3.2. BWV 654 (mm. 1f.)

of Christ. This is what Luther is also saying in his sermons for the twentieth Sunday after Trinity.

A further example of the cleansing aspect of the blood of Christ is found in the tenor aria of the cantata *Jesu, der du meine Seele* (BWV 78). The devil is washed away by Christ's blood, making the heart of the believer light once more. This movement is for obbligato flute and continuo, and much of the music for flute and voice is in pleasing parallel thirds and sixths. The blood of Christ is common to both BWV 768/10 and BWV 78/3, being in turn linked to the Abendmahl, a commemoration of the sacrifice of Christ.

From the above discussion, it can be seen that the most striking musical features of BWV 654 are the ornaments and the parallel motion. The very arresting opening with trills in parallel sixths (see example 3.2) offers some clue to the interpretation of the text. It may be related to the opening line of one of the nine stanzas. Examination of the text shows that Bach may have been thinking of stanza 1, "Schmücke dich, o liebe Seele"; stanza 5, "Beydes Lachen und auch Zittern"; stanza 7, "Jesu meine Lebens-Sonne"; or stanza 8, "Herr es hat dein treues Lieben," where the trills might represent respectively, adornment, laughing and trembling, the warmth of the soul's love for Jesus, or his for the soul. It is difficult to associate this opening with the texts of any of the remaining stanzas.

Example 3.3. BWV 654 (mm. 88ff.)

Another important aspect of BWV 654 is Bach's presentation of line 6 of the chorale, which incorporates extreme chromatic harmony as well as diatonic movement in thirds and sixths (see example 3.3). It is not easy to relate the musical portrayal of line 6 of the *cantus firmus* to any stanza in particular. What is Bach trying to say here? On the one hand he presents us with writing in agreeable sixths, followed by the most harmonically dissonant (*parrhesia*) measure of the piece (m. 89). It is conceivable that Bach is portraying something that is at once painful and joyful.

The conspicuous presence of ornaments, not only at the opening but throughout the entire composition, could lead one to believe that this aspect of BWV 654 bears a strong implication for the overall understanding of the text-music relationships in this piece. Accordingly, it may be necessary to find a stanza where the employment of ornaments throughout might be justified. In referring to the heavenly marriage feast, Luther speaks of "eternal ornaments" [ewiger schmuck].[42] The repeated references to adornment in Luther's sermons may have inspired Bach to emphasize this aspect of the text.

From the preceding discussion, it seems clear that BWV 654 has many musical features in common with compositions in which the text describes the soul going to heaven and being washed clean by the blood of Christ in order to join in the marriage supper of the Lamb. Should these arguments therefore lead to the text of a stanza containing some or all of these issues? The parallel intervals may be explained as an expression of love and could conceivably be related to any stanza. The parallel intervals, in combination with the ornaments, add a new dimension however, and it seems that this particular unification of musical features could represent the unification of the adorned soul with Christ in heaven. This leads to stanza 1 of *Schmücke dich, o liebe Seele*, as this is the only stanza that clearly describes the adornment of the soul as it prepares to be united with Christ as his guest in heaven. As seen from the preceding quotations from Luther's sermons for the twentieth Sunday after Trinity, this aspect of this Sunday was emphasized repeatedly by him. It does not seem likely that Bach would have ignored such an important theological point. It may be that in BWV 654 Bach was giving a general portrayal of the word "Schmücke" and therefore of the text of stanza 1. No other stanza appears to fit the music more appropriately. Examination of the composition in detail in the context of stanza 1 may provide justification for the suggestion that Bach is portraying this stanza in BWV 654.

In the opening ten measures, Bach establishes the idea of "schmücken," which dominates the entire composition. The entry of the *cantus firmus* at m. 11 begins with three white, unadorned notes for the words "Schmücke dich"— the answer coming in the much more ornate portrayal of "o liebe Seele" (see example 3.4). Bach actually removed ornaments from the second and third

Example 3.4.   BWV 654 (mm. 11ff.)

notes of the *cantus firmus* in his Leipzig revision. Since he rarely seemed to make a revision that was irrelevant, it is possible that Bach wanted to make a point about the process of adornment in his presentation of line 1 of the *cantus firmus*. The request "Schmücke dich" is answered by the ornaments of the second half of the phrase.

The ensuing interlude between lines 1 and 2 of the *cantus firmus* moves toward the darker key of F minor, which may be an advance warning of the text of line 2, "laß die dunckle Sünden-Höle." This "dunckle Sünden-Höle" may also be related to the pedal line of mm. 25–27, which descends an octave and a fifth from c^1 to F. The same music is repeated for the following two lines of text, "Komm ans helle Licht gegangen/ fange herrlich an zu prangen." The atmosphere appears to be appropriate to these words, although there do not seem to be any specific portrayals of details of the text apart from the ongoing portrayal of the word "schmücke."

In m. 76, line 5 of the *cantus firmus* is heard, the text of which is "denn der Herr voll Heyl und Gnaden." "Heyl" and "Gnaden" could be regarded as key words for the twentieth Sunday after Trinity. Christ as Savior washes the soul clean from sin, adorning her for the ultimate feast in heaven. The preparation for this was the Abendmahl, and the redemptive power and grace of the sacrament was very relevant. At the center of all this is Christ's sacrifice.

There is only one measure between the statement of lines 5 and 6 of the *cantus firmus*, its parallel sixths possibly reflecting the word "Gnaden" as well as the union between Christ and the soul, explicit in the text of line 6. There is a marked contrast between the first half of line 6 (mm. 85–88) and the second half (mm. 89–92). In mm. 85–88, the accompaniment is dominated by parallel thirds and sixths, whereas in m. 89, Bach introduces chromatic harmony for the first time of any significance (see example 3.3). An unexpected *g-flat*^{0} in the pedal moves up to *g-natural*^{0}, turning into a diminished-seventh chord at m. 89.3 before resolving more conventionally onto an F major chord, leading to a cadence to E-flat major. It may be that Bach is using this extraordinary chromatic harmony to depict something that is out of the ordinary. The soul strives toward union with Christ in heaven. Bach's use of chromatic harmony at m. 89 for the word "Gast" could be a means of stressing this desire. One final observation in the portrayal of line 6 of the *cantus firmus* is the rising bass line from m. 86 to 89. The soul is invited as a guest to heaven, and therefore this rising bass line might be depicting this aspect of the text.

In m. 99, a rising scale in thirds leads to the entry of line 7 of the *cantus firmus*. As before, this parallel motion can be seen to reflect the mystical union between Christ and the soul. At m. 112, the opening ritornello returns in the dominant and at m. 116 in the tonic. This can serve as a reminder of the overall context of the hymn—the adorned soul going to meet Christ in heaven—and so the glorious thirds and sixths with their double ornaments return. The final line of the text of stanza 1 is very relevant to Neumeister's quotation of Song of Songs 5:2 and Revelation 3:20, where Jesus enters the heart of the believer. The text "will itzt Herberg in dir halten" shows why Bach may have chosen to repeat the opening ritornello material before the entry of the final line of the *cantus firmus*—Jesus dwells in the heart of the believer as he receives the sacrament of the altar. This line of text is very relevant to the theme of stanza 1 of *Schmücke dich, o liebe Seele*. As such, Bach portrays the closing words of this stanza in a florid and vivid fashion.

BWV 654 closes with a calm five-measure coda with subdominant harmonies beneath the long final tonic of the *cantus firmus*. This *Halteton* could possibly be a depiction of the eternal salvation associated so strongly with the Abendmahl, itself an anticipation of the eternal Abendmahl or immortal union with Christ.

Reference has been made in chapters 1 and 2 to the common elements between *Schmücke dich, o liebe Seele* (BWV 654); *Komm heiliger Geist, Herre Gott* (BWV 652); and *An Wasserflüssen Babylon* (BWV 653). In the case of BWV 654, one may also compare variation 10 of BWV 768. BWV 654 is the third of three sarabandes that Bach sets in the "Leipzig" chorales, all three of which appear consecutively in P271, as outlined in chapter 1. In each of the two preceding sarabandes (BWV 652 and 653), the theme of salvation and eternity is relevant. I have found stanza 3 of the hymn *Komm heiliger Geist* to correspond to BWV 652 where the text is concerned with faith in God's (in particular God the Holy Spirit) comfort and protection, but also with the faith that he will prepare weak humans for eternal life. In BWV 653, Bach seems to portray a general longing for the heavenly Jerusalem. In *Komm heiliger Geist, Herre Gott* and *An Wasserflüssen Babylon*, the text is concerned with eternity, but neither hymn mentions the important means of attaining eternity—the Abendmahl—which was a foretaste of heaven on earth, as well as a commemoration of the sacrifice of Christ. Therefore, the order of these three sarabandes is important. BWV 652 talks of striving toward God in life and death, BWV 653 of yearning for the heavenly Jerusalem, although while still struggling on earth, but BWV 654 places the soul as the guest of Jesus in heaven by means of the Abendmahl. This is the final stage of preparation for eternity, and so it is fitting that BWV 654 is the third of the three sarabandes. In order to be the guest of Christ in heaven, the soul must be washed clean of sin, or become "geschmückt." Both Luther and Müller speak of becoming snow white, being washed clean through the blood of Christ, as discussed previously.

As noted earlier, Russell Stinson has pointed out the similarity between the opening of BWV 654 and the aria "Tief gebückt" from the cantata *Meine Herze schwimmt in Blut* (BWV 199). This is indeed true—the bass line is practically identical—but it seems that the bass line itself does not hold any importance with regard to the text and music, merely that it is a normal bass line for a dance, in this case more specifically a sarabande. The significance seems to lie in the use of the sarabande rhythm. The text is as follows:

Tief gebückt und voller Reue	Deeply bent and full of repentance
Lieg ich, liebster Gott, vor dir,	I lie dear God before you,
Ich bekenne meine Schuld,	I recognize my fault,
Aber habe doch Geduld,	But please have patience
Habe doch Geduld mit mir!	Have patience with me!

In the aria, the repentant soul asks God for forgiveness and patience, longing to be free from sin. To be free from sin may be an implicit reference to eternal salvation, where there will be no more sin as believers are united with Christ. Therefore, the sarabande seems significant.

The registration of BWV 654 should portray its heavenly aspect. Therefore, it seems logical to use the "vollkommene schöne Sesquialtera" as described in chapter 2 in relation to *An Wasserflüssen Babylon* (BWV 653).

★ ★ ★

The preceding discussion indicates how an understanding of Luther's writings on the subject of the bride/bridegroom theme is helpful in interpreting the text-music relationships in BWV 654. The abundance of ornaments and the theological significance of the word "schmücken" appear to lead to the text of stanza 1 of *Schmücke dich, o liebe Seele*. The important aspect of the twentieth Sunday after Trinity—the adornment of the soul—dominates Bach's composition in the many ornaments. In returning to the opening music for the closing ritornello, Bach is reiterating the significance of the adorned soul. Union between Christ and the soul, for which all Lutherans long, remains central, symbolized in the many parallel lines which hold a much deeper significance than mere euphonious sounds. Therefore it seems that Bach has conveyed theological issues crucial to the twentieth Sunday after Trinity, and more generally to the Abendmahl, in BWV 654.

NOTES

1. Johannes Kulp, *Die Lieder unserer Kirche* [Handbuch zum Evangelischen Kirchengesangbuch, Sonderband], ed. Arno Büchner and Siegfried Fornaçon (Göttingen: Vandenhoeck & Ruprecht, 1958), 245.

2. For the background, see Isabella van Elferen, *Mystical Love in the German Baroque: Theology, Poetry, Music,* Contextual Bach Studies 2 (Lanham, MD: Scarecrow, 2009).

3. Heinrich Müller, *Himmlischer Liebes-Küß / Oder Übung deß wahren Christenthums / fliessend aus der Erfahrung Göttlicher Liebe* (Franckfurt am Mayn: Wilde, 1669), 235f. "Wasserbad im Wort" is an allusion to baptism.

4. *SLG,* 285ff.

5. Translation based on Mark Bighley, *The Lutheran Chorales in the Organ Works of J. S. Bach* (St. Louis: Concordia, 1986), 209ff.

6. Erdmann Neumeister, *Tisch des Herrn, In LII. Predigten über I. Cor. XI. 23–32. Da zugleich in dem Eingange der selben Unterschiedliche Lieder erkläret worden* (Hamburg: Kißner, 1722), 473.

7. Neumeister, *Tisch des Herrn,* 498.

8. Neumeister, *Tisch des Herrn,* 475.

9. Neumeister, *Tisch des Herrn,* 499.

10. Neumeister, *Tisch des Herrn,* 499. This text was also set very memorably in the Advent cantata *Nun komm der Heiden Heiland* (BWV 61), with the libretto by Neumeister.

11. Neumeister, *Tisch des Herrn,* 499.

12. Detailed discussion of the hymn text may be found in Neumeister, *Tisch des Herrn,* 471–620.

13. See Williams, *The Organ Music of J. S. Bach* (Cambridge: Cambridge University Press, 1980–1986), 2:139; a statement that is simplified to become "its cantus is simpler . . . though disguised by melismas": Williams, *The Organ Music of J. S. Bach,* 2nd ed. (Cambridge: Cambridge University Press, 2003), 352.

14. Harald Schützeichel, ed., *Albert Schweitzer: Die Orgelwerke Johann Sebastian Bachs. Vorworte zu den "Sämtlichen Orgelwerken"* (Hildesheim: Olms, 1995), 250.

15. Schützeichel, *Albert Schweitzer,* 250.

16. Philipp Spitta, *Johann Sebastian Bach,* trans. Clara Bell and J. A. Fuller-Maitland (London: Novello, 1884–1885; reprint, New York: Dover, 1992), 1:617.

17. Schützeichel, *Albert Schweitzer,* 250.

18. Hans Luedtke, "Seb. Bachs Choralvorspiele," *BJ* 15 (1918): 39.

19. Ulrich Meyer, "Zur Frage der inneren Einheit von Bachs Siebzehn Chorälen (BWV 651–667)." *BJ* 58 (1972): 67.

20. Meyer, "Zur Frage der inneren Einheit," 68.

21. Ulrich Meyer, "Über J. S. Bachs Orgelchoralkunst," in *Theologische Bach-Studien 1,* ed. Walter Blankenburg and Renate Steiger, [Beiträge zur theologischen Bachforschung 4] (Neuhausen-Stuttgart: Hänssler, 1987), 42.

22. Russell Stinson, *J. S. Bach's Great Eighteen Chorales* (New York: Oxford University Press, 2001), 14.

23. Stinson, *J. S. Bach's Great Eighteen Chorales,* 80f.

24. Günther Stiller, *Johann Sebastian Bach und das Leipziger gottesdienstliche Leben seiner Zeit* (Kassel: Bärenreiter, 1970), 233; English: *Johann Sebastian Bach and Liturgical Life in Leipzig,* trans. Herbert J. A. Bouman, Daniel F. Poellot, and Hilton C. Oswald; ed. Robin A. Leaver (St. Louis: Concordia, 1984), 248.

25. *BC* 2:637.

26. Robin A. Leaver, "Bach's Understanding and Use of the Epistles and Gospels of the Church Year." *BACH* 6/4 (1975): 8; Albert Clement, "De orgelkoraalbewerkingen van Joh. Seb. Bach in het kerkelijk jaar," *Het Orgel* 86 (1990): 329.

27. *WA* 10^{III}:415f.

28. *Church Postils* 5:231f.

29. "Darumb so die braut spricht: ich binn deyn, du must mich haben, so muß er den meynn ungluck auff sich nemen altzü mal. Alßo sint denn mein sund die ewige gerechtigkeit, mein thot das ewige leben, meyn helle der himmel, den die tzwey, sund und gerechtigkeyt, konnen nicht bey samen stehn, hymmel unnd helle auch nicht, thot und leben auch nicht. . . . also vorschwindt den meyn thot in seinem leben, meine sund yn seyner seligkeyt." *WA* 10^{III}:418. [Therefore the bride says, I am thine, thou must have me; then he must at the same time take all my misfortune upon himself. Thus then are my sins eternal righteousness, my death eternal life, my hell heaven; for these two, sin and righteousness cannot exist together, nor heaven and hell. . . . Therefore my death thus vanishes in his life, my sins in his righteousness and my condemnation in his salvation." *Church Postils* 5:233.

30. *WA* 10^{III}:419; *Church Postils* 5:234.

31. *WA* 10^{III}:417.

32. *Church Postils* 5:233.

33. See Elke Axmacher, "'Ich freue mich auf meinen Tod': Sterben und Tod in Bachs Kantaten aus theologischer Sicht," *Jahrbuch des staatlichen Instituts für Musikforschung Preussischer Kulturbesitz* (1996), 24–40; Alfred Dürr, "'Ich freue mich auf meinen Tod': Sterben und Tod in Bachs Kantaten aus musikwissenschaftlicher Sicht," *Jahrbuch des staatlichen Instituts für Musikforschung Preussischer Kulturbesitz* (1996), 41–51, where the authors discuss the sources relating to the issue of longing for death and the portrayal of this theme in Bach's music.

34. *WA* 22:345.

35. *Church Postils* 5:250.

36. Luther describes how the improperly dressed guest will be cast out in *WA* 52:513 (*House Postils* 3:105).

37. See the numerous examples assembled in Renate Steiger, "'Die Welt ist euch ein Himmelreich.' Zu J. S. Bachs Deutung des Pastoralen." *MuK* 41 (1971): 1–9, 69–79. This issue is discussed in chapters 10 and 11 in relation to *Jesus Christus unser Heiland* (BWV 666) and *Komm Gott Schöpfer heiliger Geist* (BWV 667), both in 12/8 time.

38. Walter Blankenburg, "Mystik in der Musik J. S. Bachs," in *Theologische Bach-Studien 1*, ed. Walter Blankenburg and Renate Steiger, [Beiträge zur theologischen Bachforschung 4] (Neuhausen-Stuttgart: Hänssler, 1987), 57.

39. Blankenburg, "Mystik in der Musik J. S. Bachs," 57.

40. *WA* 22:341; *Church Postils* 5:245.

41. See the discussion in Albert Clement, "'O Jesu, du edle Gabe': Studien zum Verhältnis von Text und Musik in den Choralpartiten und den Kanonischen Veränderungen von Johann Sebastian Bach," PhD diss., University of Utrecht, 1989, 141ff.

42. *WA* 22:337; *Church Postils* 5:240.

• 4 •

Herr Jesu Christ, dich zu uns wend

THE HYMN

Herr Jesu Christ, dich zu uns wend is to be found without mention of an author in *Pensum sacrum* (1648) by Tobias Hauschkonius, and in 1662 in the second edition of the *Lutherischen Handbüchlein* of Johann Niedling of Altenburg.[1] In 1671, Johann Olearius referred to it as the hymn of an unknown author. In Niedling's publication, the hymn bore the title "Frommer Christen Herzen-Seufzerlein und Gnade und Beistand des Heiligen Geistes bei dem Gottesdienst vor den Predigten" [A Pious Christian's Heart-sighs and Grace and Support of the Holy Spirit in the Service before the Sermons]. Initially, the hymn had only three stanzas, with the final stanza appearing in part 1 of *Cantionale Sacrum*, published in Gotha in 1651. The name of Herzog Wilhelm II (1598–1662) of Sachsen-Weimar was first associated with *Herr Jesu Christ, dich zu uns wend* in the Altdorf hymnbook of 1676.[2] In Altenburg, the hymn was sung every week, and by 1714 it was sung in most German churches each Sunday as the usual pulpit hymn sung at the beginning of sermons. The melody first appeared in a *Cantionale Germanicum* from Gochsheim, which was published in 1628, and in the 1648 *Pensum Sacrum*. The melody is related to six Latin odes.

    Herr Jesu Christ, dich zu uns wend was one of four hymns sung every Sunday in Leipzig in Bach's time.[3] Bach has left four settings for organ of this chorale: BWV 709 and 726 from the individually transmitted chorales, BWV 632 from the *Orgel-Büchlein* and BWV 655 from the "Leipzig" chorales. As a pulpit hymn, it was sung in between the preacher's *Exordium* and the main parts of his sermon. Despite its obvious familiarity, Bach does not use this chorale in any of his cantatas. The hymn opens with an invocation to Christ, asking him to send the Holy Spirit who will lead the faithful to truth. This was very relevant to the timing of the hymn within the Lutheran liturgy. The word of God was the most important means of learning for Lutherans, so it was fitting that before the scriptures were heard, Christ and the Holy Spirit would be invoked and asked for guidance. Stanza 2 continues this theme, requesting increased faith, which can only come about through the Holy Spirit. The final line of the text of this stanza asks that the name of Christ be made well known to the Christian. Knowing Christ was the central issue of Luther's theology of the cross, and the combination of this knowledge of Christ and faith led to salvation and everlasting joy. Stanza 3 looks to the end of time, when all Christians will enjoy everlasting happiness, referring to singing with God's host, beholding him face to face (Revelation 4:8 and 22:4). The final stanza is a doxology. Because of its liturgical position within the Abendmahl, this hymn is also relevant to the sacrament of the altar. The text of the hymn as it appears in the Weimar hymnbook of 1713, where it is listed as a hymn for before the sermon, is as follows:

1. HERR JEsu Christ/ dich zu uns wend/
   dein heilgen Geist/ du zu uns send/
   mit Hülf und Gnad er uns regier/
   und uns den Weg zur Wahrheit führ.

1. Turn to us, Lord Jesus Christ,
   send us your Holy Spirit.
   With help and grace he governs us,
   and leads us along the path to truth.

2. Thu auf den Mund zum Lobe dein/
   bereit das Hertz zur Andacht fein/
   den Glauben mehr/ stärck den Verstand/
   daß uns dein Nahm werd wohl bekannt.

2. Open our mouth to your praise,
   prepare our hearts for good meditation.
   Increase our faith, strengthen our understanding
   so that your name will become well known to us.

3. Biß wir singen mit Gottes Heer/
   heilig/ heilig ist Gott der HErr/
   und schauen dich von Angesicht/
   in ewger Freud und selgem Licht.

3. Until we sing together with God's host,
   holy, holy is God the Lord,
   and behold you face to face
   in eternal joy and blessed light.

4. Ehr sey dem Vater und dem Sohn/
   samt heilgen Geist in einem Thron/
   der heiligen Dreyfaltigkeit/
   sey Lob und Preiß in Ewigkeit.[4]

4. Glory be to the Father, and to the Son,
   together with the Holy Ghost in one throne,
   to the Holy Trinity
   be praise and laud eternally.[5]

HERR JESU CHRIST, DICH ZU UNS WEND (BWV 655)

In P271, Bach has placed the heading "*Trio sup[er] Herr Jesu Xst. dich zu uns wend. a 2 Clav. et Pedal.*" Like most of the other settings in this collection, there is an earlier Weimar version, BWV 655a, and a later Leipzig revision, BWV 655. The analogy with BWV 664 *(Trio super: Allein Gott in der Höh sei*

Ehr) is quite clear—two pieces written in a light trio texture. However, apart from the trio writing and the appearance of the *cantus firmus* (or a part thereof) at the close of the piece, these two compositions do not really have much in common.

In BWV 655, the writing for the manual parts is very violinistic and, apart from two incidences of *f-sharp⁰* at mm. 31 and 33, lies completely within the range of the violin. In general the tessitura is very high, with the *c³* appearing eight times in the right hand and twice in the left hand. Motivic material worked out within a ritornello framework is derived from the first line of the *cantus firmus*, with Bach quoting all four lines of the chorale in the pedal from m. 52. The *cantus firmus* consists of four phrases, with lines 1 and 3 modulating to the dominant and lines 2 and 4 being almost identical.

The opening ritornello, which is treated imitatively, bears clear thematic relationship to the first four notes of the *cantus firmus*, as does the pedal motive first heard at m. 2. All of the thematic material is contained in these opening four measures, answered by a further four leading to a cadence in the dominant. Bach makes use of the *circulatio* figure in this section (for example, m. 4.3, right hand) and throughout the piece. At m. 8, the musical material is restated, this time in the dominant with the hands reversed. Halfway through m. 11, this process changes, where Bach embarks on a series of sequences to eventually cadence to D major in m. 15.

Unity is achieved in this setting by the almost constant presence of the ritornello material. As often occurs in movements where Bach uses ritornello structures, the boundaries between ritornello and episodic material may become blurred. At m. 15, the opening material reappears, but this time it is used to modulate, more in the style of an episode. Passing through A minor, the thematic material is then repeated in E minor at mm. 17–20. At m. 22, Bach presents an inversion of the material heard initially at m. 11 in the right hand, leading sequentially to a cadence in B minor at m. 27. The opening ritornello is heard in B minor in mm. 27–30. This is followed by more sequential writing, based initially on a three-sixteenth-note motive followed by a leap, and then on descending scale patterns. The music cadences in D at m. 39.

The ritornello material recommences at m. 39 in the dominant, but this time Bach uses a descending pedal line to accompany the manuals. The introduction of a *c-natural²* at m. 40 results in a return to the tonic, in turn leading to a further flattening to C major at m. 42. From m. 43 to 46, Bach uses the same thematic material as at the beginning, but in the subdominant, extending it by a further measure to cadence in D at m. 48. The motive that appears at m. 48 was first heard at m. 11 in the right hand and in m. 12 in the left hand. This leads to a perfect cadence in G at m. 51.

The final section begins on the second half of m. 51.3. The thematic material is presented imitatively on the manuals followed by the entry of the *cantus firmus* in the pedal at m. 52.3. Line 1 of the *cantus firmus* is accompanied by the opening ritornello material, which brings the tonality to the dominant at m. 55. There is a one-measure link before the entry of line 2 of the chorale at m. 56. The passage from m. 56 to 62, which covers line 2 of the *cantus firmus*, has much writing in parallel thirds and sixths, and the music passes through C major, A minor, and E minor before returning to D in m. 62 for the entry of line 3 of the *cantus firmus*. Measure 63 is noteworthy for its use of broken chords in the manual parts, always followed by an upward leap. The three measures that link the two final phrases of the *cantus firmus* pass the opening motive from hand to hand, first beginning on g^1, then d^2, a^1, e^2, b^1, and finally e^1. Line 4 of the chorale enters at m. 67.3 with the dominant-seventh chord of E minor. Measure 69 is identical to m. 58, while m. 68 is significant for the prominent use of syncopation in the left hand. The final four measures turn back toward the subdominant, ending with a plagal cadence. As he does in BWV 664, Bach also introduces a third voice in the manuals for the final cadence.

Interpretations by Other Authors

In their discussions of BWV 655, many writers allude to the text of stanza 3 of *Herr Jesu Christ, dich zu uns wend*, while others remain more general in their interpretation of the composition. No author writes in detail regarding the text and music in BWV 655, and some of the important musical features have been ignored. These features are considered in the following section in an effort to find Bach's possible intentions in relation to the text and music in BWV 655.

Assessment

Distinctive musical features of *Herr Jesu Christ, dich zu uns wend* (BWV 655) may help to lead to an interpretation of the text-music relationships in this piece. Distinguishing BWV 655 from almost every other chorale trio by Bach is the high tessitura of the right hand, a feature also found on occasion in the left hand. In all, c^3 is heard ten times between both hands.[6] This extreme high note could be considered *hyperbole* and therefore might hold significance for the text.

Other musical features worthy of note include the joyous thirds and sixths, becoming even more prominent toward the end; the emphatic triadic writing of both manuals and pedal; the trio texture; and the delayed entrance of the *cantus firmus*. These musical elements lead to significant links between text and music.

Since the motivic writing in BWV 655 is based almost exclusively on the contours of the opening line of the hymn, it is reasonable to suggest that Bach may have singled this line out for special emphasis. Examination of the opening lines of each stanza may help to discern Bach's possible intentions.

Stanza 1 opens with the line "Herr Jesu Christ/ dich zu uns wend." Christ is asked to turn to humanity, with line 2 of the text providing the explanation of this request, that he send the Holy Spirit. Since in this case the Spirit comes from heaven, one might then expect some descending imagery. There does not seem to be any idea in the opening measures that could lead one to the opening of stanza 1.

Stanza 2 begins, "Thu auf den Mund zum Lobe dein." Here joy is mentioned specifically. It is possible to link the joyful atmosphere of BWV 655 to the joy of this stanza. Similar joy may be interpreted in the opening line of stanza 3, "Biß wir singen mit Gottes Heer," where the faithful look forward to rejoicing with God's angels. There might be a convincing argument that Bach is portraying humanity singing with the angels, as in stanza 3, rather than merely opening their mouths to the praise of God, as in stanza 2. There is also an implication of joy in the opening line of stanza 4, which as a doxology begins by praising God the Father and the Son.

It seems that each stanza of the hymn text can be interpreted as being related to joy, and there can be no doubt that BWV 655 is indeed a joyful setting. Is Bach therefore setting the text of the entire hymn, or is there a single musical element that might link Bach's setting to one stanza in particular? The parallel thirds and sixths, as well as the emphatic triadic writing, could be linked to any stanza of the hymn. However, there is one feature that may be most easily explained in the context of one stanza—that is, the high proportion of appearances of c^3 in this composition. There does not seem to be any part of the text of stanzas 1 or 2 that might lead to an interpretation of this characteristic. This leaves the Trinitarian God of the final stanza, or the rejoicing host of angels in stanza 3. Angels have been portrayed by Bach in high registers in other compositions, and it is possible that Bach is using the same technique here.

One does not have to look very far to find examples of the singing of angels in Bach's music. An obvious example is the setting of the words of Luke 2:14 in the opening movement of the *Gloria in excelsis Deo* of the B Minor Mass. This is the *hymnus angelicus*, the song the angels sang at the birth of Christ. The first section, involving the words "Gloria in excelsis Deo" [Glory to God in the highest], is a riveting triple-metered dance as the angel hosts celebrate the birth of Christ. The angels are represented in their song of glory by the high trumpet and vocal parts. The ensuing line of text, "et in terra pax hominibus bonae voluntatis" [and on earth peace to men who are

God's friends], is portrayed in a musical way initially, in the change to the more temporal time signature of 4/4 and the dropping of the trumpets from the instrumental ensemble. However, although the message is now concerned with peace on earth, hence the 4/4 time signature, it is still the angels who are singing, and this is reflected in the light, fast-moving fugue subject for the text "et in terra pax hominibus bonae voluntatis," which reaches into the higher registers of all five vocal parts. The music progresses to an enormous climax, involving all the instrumental and vocal forces, as the angelic hosts combine in praise of the birth of Christ. This movement was parodied in the Christmas cantata *Gloria in excelsis Deo* (BWV 191), and it seems likely that Bach was portraying the angel hosts in the high running sixteenth-note lines.

Examples reflecting the exuberant outpourings of joy at the birth of Christ can be found in the opening and closing movements of the cantata for the first day of Christmas, *Christen ätzet diesen Tag* (BWV 63). These two movements employ the full instrumental ensemble of no less than four trumpets, as well as three oboes, bassoon, strings, SATB, and continuo. Trumpets were often used by Bach to illustrate heavenly matters.[7] The first trumpet part is very high in both movements, and in the context of a Christmas cantata it seems to be related to the heavenly jubilation at the birth of Christ. The running sixteenth notes of the violins and trumpets reach high above the stave, perhaps reflecting the glory of the heavenly world.

Movement 3 of the cantata *Das neugeborne Kindelein* (BWV 122) is a recitative for soprano accompanied by three flutes. The text is concerned throughout with the song the angel sings to celebrate the salvation of mankind. The accompanying lines lie in the upper registers, again perhaps portraying the heavenly angel song.

An obvious reference to an angel in the organ works comes in the opening variation of the Canonic Variations (BWV 769a/769). Here the angel brings his message from heaven to earth. This descent is represented in the descending lines of the opening motive, a motive that Bach had used many times to illustrate a descending gift from heaven.[8] The joyful song is reflected in the fast-moving sixteenth-note lines.

It is possible to deduce from this discussion that Bach may have been depicting the rejoicing heavenly host in the high tessitura of the manual parts of BWV 655. None of the other stanzas seem to offer an obvious interpretation of this musical characteristic. It may also be appropriate to link the idea of their joyful song to the emphatic triadic writing of BWV 655. In many cantatas by Bach, great joy is celebrated in positive triadic musical motives. This can be seen in the two movements from BWV 63, mentioned previously, as well as in many other examples. The first movement of the cantata *Gelobet seist du, Jesu Christ* (BWV 91) opens with a rising scale that leads into a triadic motive, treated imitatively with seven entries in all. Meanwhile, a chord of G major is held by the two horns and continuo. This kind of opening by Bach does not seem accidental. In the very commanding opening four measures of this cantata, he seems to be consciously sending a positive message of assurance. In this movement, line 4 of the chorale, "des freuet sich der Engel Schar," is portrayed in the running sixteenth-note lines of the accompanying voices and the triadic writing of the instruments (see example 4.1). Following this discussion, it appears that there may be reasons to believe that Bach was thinking of stanza 3 of "Herr Jesu Christ, dich zu uns wend" when he composed BWV 655. The most striking grounds for this suggestion is the high tessitura of the manual parts, combined with the sixteenth-note movement and emphatic triadic writing, which may be related to the rejoicing heavenly host. The compositions cited previously show Bach writing in a similar style in a corresponding context. Other musical characteristics may help to substantiate this proposal.

Before turning to these characteristics, it is helpful to consider the eschatological significance of stanza 3 of *Herr Jesu Christ, dich zu uns wend*. As already noted, there are two references to the book of Revelation. Stanza 3 looks to the end time when humanity will sing with God's host. Line 2 of stanza 3

Example 4.1.   BWV 91/1 (mm. 45ff.)

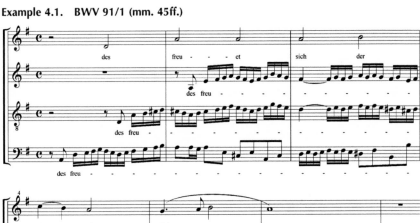

is a reference to Isaiah 6:3 and Revelation 4:8. The stanza from Revelation confirms the eschatological concepts found in stanza 3 of the hymn, as follows:

> Heilig, Heilig, Heilig ist Gott der HErr, der Allmächtige, der da war, und der da ist, und der da kommt. [Holy, holy, holy, lord God Almighty, which was, and is, and is to come.]

Line 3 of this stanza contains a reference to Revelation 22:3–4, as follows:

> und seine Knechte werden Ihm dienen, und sehen sein Angesicht, und sein Name wird an ihren Stirnen seyn [and his servants shall serve him: And they shall see his face; and his name shall be in their foreheads.]

The final line of the text, which refers to everlasting joy and light, serves to further strengthen the eschatological theme. It is therefore not surprising to find this composition in this collection.

It seems pertinent at this point to turn to BWV 655 itself, suggesting how the musical aspects may correspond to the text of stanza 3. The opening manual motive returns as a motto throughout the piece, its buoyant light character maintaining the atmosphere of joy. As discussed before, joy is not exclusive to stanza 3. However, it seems that there is an explicit element of joy mentioned in every line of stanza 3, which is not so in the other stanzas. The light trio texture can especially correspond to the final line of the text, "in ewger Freud und selgem Licht," with its reference to everlasting joy and blessed light.

As shown above, it is possible that Bach's repetition of the opening motive throughout BWV 655 is related to the text. Bach sometimes repeated a melodic idea relating to one line of a chorale in order to emphasize that idea throughout a movement. Examples of this compositional method can be found in the opening chorus of the *Estomihi* cantata *Herr Jesu Christ wahr' Mensch und Gott* (BWV 127). In BWV 127/1, the opening line of the chorale is paraphrased in diminution in the instrumental parts, acting as a motto theme throughout the movement. It is conceivable that Bach is employing this compositional method to emphasize the important theological statement of the opening line, "Herr Jesu Christ, wahr' Mensch und Gott" [Lord Jesus Christ, true man and God]. Bach could be using processes in BWV 655 associating this opening paraphrase of the chorale with the opening line of text, "Biß wir singen mit Gottes Heer." The ten repetitions of c^3 can be termed *hyperbole* and, along with the overall high tessitura, can be seen as linked to "Gottes Heer."

Parallel thirds and sixths may be found in abundance in BWV 655 from m. 40 onward. Writing in parallel thirds or sixths is appropriate for any aspect of the text of stanza 3 of *Herr Jesu Christ, dich zu uns wend*. All of the Christmas cantatas that depict the angel hosts contain glorious writing for voices and instruments in parallel thirds and sixths, so this technique seems to easily correspond to the singing of the angel host. This kind of writing belongs in the realm of the *Sanctus* of the B Minor Mass. Here, the instruments and voices unite in a massive euphonious sound to portray the breathtaking power of the Lord God of Hosts, at times using both thirds and sixths in combination, as the voices sing the threefold *Sanctus* (Heilig, Heilig, Heilig). The words are clearly the same, so the analogy is obvious.[9] The mesmerizing fugue that follows for the words "pleni sunt coeli et terra Gloria" [heaven and earth are full of your glory] continues in the depiction of the whole world—heaven and earth, which must include the angel host—praising the glory of God. At m. 119, there is even a fugal entry for soprano 2 and alto 2 in parallel thirds. Can this be regarded as a justification for the employment of parallel motion in BWV 655? The final two lines of stanza 3 also fit in this context: "und schauen dich von Angesicht, in ewger Freud und selgem Licht." The pleasing-sounding thirds and sixths can also correspond to everlasting joy and blessed light. There will be no more need for light, as this will be provided for by the Lord God and the Lamb. Similar writing is found in movement 2 of *Jesu, der du meine Seele* (BWV 78). In this aria, the text "dein gnädiges Antlitz erfreulich" is set in parallel thirds. The prayer here is that God's countenance will shine on humanity in everlasting blissfulness, and as such it shares a similar context with BWV 655.

The chorale enters in the bass in m. 52 and is heard in its entirety over the course of the remainder of the piece. It seems unusual that Bach would wait until m. 52 to begin the chorale. Herman Keller believed that the omission of the chorale would not be noticed.[10] Everything Bach did in the composition of these chorale preludes seems to have been carefully thought out with all the implications for text and music. The entry of the chorale at this point is certainly not arbitrary or superfluous. If Bach is basing his chorale prelude on a text representing something that will be in the future, then it may be logical to suggest that this is the reason the chorale is not heard immediately at the beginning. Conceivably, the delayed entry of the chorale could represent the end time, with humanity singing the chorale with God's angel host.

Specific musical details are worthy of comment in this passage from m. 52 where the chorale is quoted. As line 2 of the chorale enters in m. 56, the music immediately begins to move in parallel thirds or sixths. This may be related to the text "Heilig, Heilig ist Gott der Herr." Bach would have composed the Weimar setting, BWV 655a, before he composed the *Sanctus* of the B Minor Mass, which was written for Christmas 1724, but the idea of employing parallel thirds and sixths to illustrate the singing of the redeemed in heaven may have already been in his mind during this period.[11]

Line 3 of the chorale enters in m. 62, and in m. 63 a short conversation between the two manual parts is heard, in each case with four sixteenth notes being answered by the same in the other voice (see example 4.2). This may reflect the text "und schauen dich von Angesicht," the conversational aspect of the writing portraying perhaps the idea of two entities looking at each other.[12]

Example 4.2.   BWV 655 (m. 63)

The final line of the chorale enters in m. 67. Theologically this is the climax of stanza 3, and so Bach presents us with a melodic line that rises a minor tenth in m. 68. This kind of positive *anabasis*, stretching heavenward, seems to be a perfect portrayal of "ewgen Freud und selgem Licht"—the higher the music, the greater the light and eternal joy. Bach reiterates this by presenting c^3 three times in the right hand and once in the left hand in the final three measures. This in itself seems very significant—slightly less than half of the total statements of this note heard in BWV 655 are heard in the final three measures. It seems very likely that Bach refers to the heavenly world by using the figure of a *hyperbole* here.

The positioning of BWV 655 within the "Leipzig" chorales could be of significance. Why does Bach start this setting referring to "Biß wir singen"? The text of the preceding chorale setting, *Schmücke dich, o liebe Seele* (BWV 654), ends with "will itzt Herberg in dir halten." In *Schmücke dich, o liebe Seele*, the believing soul wants to find shelter in Christ as he yearns to be united with him in the final Eucharistic banquet in heaven. Therefore, it is very logical that the following setting begins as it does with "biß wir singen," so that Jesus will shelter the believer until all humanity sing together on the final judgment day.

★ ★ ★

I have tried to highlight the principal musical elements of BWV 655 and to link them to the hymn text. These features include the recurrence of the opening motive throughout the composition, the parallel motion, the trio texture, the delayed entrance of the *cantus firmus* in the pedal, and, most of all, the high tessitura of the manual parts, in turn linked to the tenfold repetition of c^3. These characteristics appear to lead to the text of stanza 3, where every line seems appropriate to the musical setting. While the three remaining stanzas can also be linked to specific musical characteristics, there does not seem to be another stanza in which all of the musical elements are so clearly explained. This presents sufficient grounds for suggesting that Bach may have been thinking of the very eschatological stanza 3 when he composed BWV 655.

NOTES

1. Johannes Kulp, *Die Lieder unserer Kirche* [Handbuch zum Evangelischen Kirchengesangbuch, Sonderband], ed. Arno Büchner and Siegfried Fornaçon (Göttingen: Vandenhoeck & Ruprecht, 1958), 203.

2. Kulp, *Die Lieder unserer Kirche*, 203; all the following hymnological information is taken from this source. Eduard Emil Koch, *Geschichte des Kirchenlieds und Kirchengesangs der christlichen, insbesondere der deutschen evangelischen Kirche*, 3rd ed. (Stuttgart: Belser, 1866–1876; Hildesheim: Olms, 1973), 8:149, gives the date of Niedling's *Handbüchlein* as 1638.

3. Günther Stiller, *Johann Sebastian Bach und das Leipziger gottesdienstliche Leben seiner Zeit* (Kassel: Bärenreiter, 1970), 103; English: *Johann Sebastian Bach and Liturgical Life in Leipzig*, trans. Herbert J. A. Bouman, Daniel F. Poellot, and Hilton C. Oswald; ed. Robin A. Leaver (St. Louis: Concordia, 1984), 117.

4. *SLG*, 2.

5. Translation based on Mark Bighley, *The Lutheran Chorales in the Organ Works of J. S. Bach* (St. Louis: Concordia, 1986), 126f.

6. These occur at m. 18 (four times in this measure), m. 43, m. 44, m. 70 (twice), and mm. 71 and 72.

7. A striking example of instrumental writing in a high register in an eschatological context is the final fugal entry that doubles the first soprano in the *Dona nobis pacem* of the B Minor Mass. The trumpet is at the upper end of its range here, and the timing of the entry is perfect on Bach's part, with the high tessitura confirming eternal peace, which is the implication at the end of this monumental work.

8. This motive appears in BWV 172/1, 619, 666, and 667, as well as 769a/769. See the further discussion in chapters 10 and 11, and Anne Leahy, "Bach's Prelude, Fugue and Allegro for Lute (BWV 998): A Trinitarian Statement of Faith?" *Journal of the Society for Musicology in Ireland* 1 (December 2005), 33–51.

9. There is very similar writing in the opening movement of the cantata *Unser Mund sei voll Lachens* (BWV 110) (Christmas Day 1725), where the text "unser Mund sei voll Lachens" is reflected in pleasing triplet writing in sixths and thirds in the voices.

10. Hermann Keller, *Die Orgelwerke Bachs. Ein Beitrag zu ihrer Geschichte, Form, Deutung und Wiedergabe* (Leipzig: Peters, 1948), 184; English: *The Organ Works of Bach: A Contribution to Their History, Form, Interpretation and Performance*, trans. Helen Hewitt (New York: Peters, 1967), 250.

11. Bach employs writing in parallel thirds and sixths in the opening movement of the Ascension oratorio, *Lobet Gott in seinen Reichen* (BWV 11), where voices join in the praise of God in all his kingdoms.

12. This may be similar to the portrayal of "hier und im Himmel oben" in BWV 767/9, where the motives pass from upper to lower registers; see Albert Clement, "'O Jesu, du edle Gabe': Studien zum Verhältnis von Text und Musik in den Choralpartiten und den Kanonischen Veränderungen von Johann Sebastian Bach," PhD diss., University of Utrecht, 1989, 92.

O Lamm Gottes unschuldig

THE HYMN

O Lamm Gottes unschuldig is Nicolaus Decius' (1485–c.1546) paraphrase of the *Agnus Dei* and, along with his paraphrase of the *Gloria, Allein Gott in der Höh sei Her*, is one of the most important and oldest hymns of the Lutheran Church.[1] These two hymns stem from the period of late summer 1522 to early 1523.[2] The *Agnus Dei* originated in the Greek Church, being sung at Matins.[3] Decius originally wrote his German *Agnus Dei* in Low German as *O Lam Godtes unschüldich*. As such, it appeared in 1531 in the Rostock hymnbook and in 1534 in the Magdeburg hymnbook, appearing in High German in Valentin Schumann's Leipzig hymnbook of 1539.[4]

The melody originated with Psalm 45, *Eructavit cor meum*, of the responsary *Regnum mundi* from the *Commune sanctorum* (thirteenth century) and later was associated with the *Sanctus in dominicis adventus et quadragesimae*.[5] The melody of the *Agnus Dei* is merely a variant of the *Sanctus*. The 1542 Erfurt version of the melody was widely used in southern Germany, while in northern Germany the most popular form was that published by Johann Spangenburg in Magdeburg in 1545.[6]

According to Eduard Emil Koch, if Luther had not introduced the *Deutsche Messe* (1526) into the Lutheran Church, *O Lamm Gottes unschuldig* would have remained the true Abendmahl hymn.[7] Also associated with Passion, "O Lamm Gottes unschuldig" is listed in the 1713 Weimar hymnbook as a hymn "Vom Leiden und Sterben JEsu Christi" [Of the suffering and death of Jesus Christ].[8] Clearly Bach considered it thus, as evidenced by its categorization as a Passiontide hymn in the *Orgel-Büchlein*. His employment of this chorale in the opening chorus of the St. Matthew Passion confirms this view.

The text of this opening chorus invites the daughters of Jerusalem to weep, not for Christ but for themselves and for their children (Luke 23:28).[9] Against this, children sing Decius's hymn *O Lamm Gottes unschuldig*. The innocence of the Lamb is contrasted with guilty humanity. Jaroslav Pelikan observes that the German form of the *Agnus Dei* makes explicit what the Latin version had only implied: *O Lamm Gottes unschuldig*.[10] There can be little doubt that, in addition, Bach must have regarded the paraphrase as a hymn for the Ordinary, being an essential part of the Abendmahl liturgy.

Willem Mudde and Helene Werthemann have discussed the question of Bach's interpretation of the purpose of this hymn with regard to BWV 656 in some detail.[11] Werthemann argues that as a setting of a hymn for the Ordinary, *O Lamm Gottes unschuldig* (BWV 656) was a suitable chorale prelude to be played *sub communione*, since this hymn was sung immediately before the faithful received the sacrament of the altar. However, it is also true that many so-called Communion hymns had strong associations with the Passion, for example *Jesus Christus unser Heiland*, stanza 1 of which deals explicitly with the Passion of Christ. Therefore, as a Passion hymn, *O Lamm Gottes unschuldig* was more than suitable as *musica sub communione*.[12] The biblical text on which the hymn is based (John 1:29) has implications of the Passion as follows:

> Des andern Tags sihet Johannes JEsum zu ihm kommen, und spricht: Sihe, das ist GOttes Lamm, welches der Welt Sünde träget. [The next day John seeth Jesus coming unto him, and saith, Behold the Lamb of God, which taketh away the sin of the world.]

In the *Agnus Dei* of the B Minor Mass, Bach seems to interpret the text with the Passion in mind. He chooses the distant key of G minor, the only movement in the Mass in this key, so far removed from either B minor or D major, the two principal keys of the work as a whole. In addition, he uses much chromatic harmony and many cross motives in this movement, clearly reflecting the Passion associations of the text.[13]

The text of the hymn as it appears in the Weimar hymnbook of 1713 is as follows:

1. O Lamm GOttes unschuldig/
   am Stamm des Creutzes geschlachtet:/:
   Allzeit gefunden gedultig/
   wiewohl du warest verachtet/
   all Sünd hast du getragen/
   sonst müsten wir verzagen/
   erbarm dich unser/ O JEsu.

1. O Lamb of God innocently
   slaughtered on the stem of the cross,

   always found patient,
   even though you were despised.
   You have borne all the sins,
   otherwise we would have had to despair,
   have mercy on us, O Jesus.

2. O Lamm GOttes unschuldig/
   am Stamm des Creutzes
   geschlachtet:/:
   Allzeit gefunden gedultig/
   wiewohl du warest verachtet/
   all Sünd hast du getragen/
   sonst müsten wir verzagen/
   erbarm dich unser/ O JEsu.

2. O Lamb of God innocently
   slaughtered on the stem of the cross,

   always found patient,
   even though you were despised.
   You have borne all the sins,
   otherwise we would have had to despair,
   have mercy on us, O Jesus.

3. O Lamm GOttes unschuldig/
   am Stamm des Creutzes
   geschlachtet:/:
   Allzeit gefunden gedultig/
   wiewohl du warest verachtet/
   all Sünd hast du getragen/
   sonst müsten wir verzagen/
   Gib uns dein'n Fried/ O JEsu.[14]

3. O Lamb of God innocently
   slaughtered on the stem of the cross,

   always found patient,
   even though you were despised.
   You have borne all the sins,
   otherwise we would have had to despair,
   grant us your peace, O Jesus.[15]

O LAMM GOTTES UNSCHULDIG (BWV 656)

Bach has left two settings of *O Lamm Gottes unschuldig*, one in the *Orgel-Büchlein* (BWV 618), and one in the "Leipzig" chorales (BWV 656).[16] An earlier Weimar version of BWV 656 exists: BWV 656a. BWV 656 is headed "*O Lamm Gottes unschuldig. 3 versus*" in P271. The main differences between BWV 656a and 656 are that the Weimar version has fewer ornaments, slightly different readings in places, 9/8 for *versus 3* rather than the 9/4 of BWV 656, and in BWV 656a, mm. 64–70 have been omitted for the second repeat. BWV 656 is certainly the more refined version, since the omission of mm. 64–70 in BWV 656a results in a clumsy link to the ensuing entry of the next line of the *cantus firmus* at m. 71.[17]

In *O Lamm Gottes unschuldig* (BWV 656), Bach presents the *cantus firmus* three times in succession, with each section being labeled *versus*. *Versus 1* is also labeled "*manualiter*" in P271, with fore-imitation in the three accompanying parts. The alto begins this process on the tonic, answered by the bass on the dominant, with the tenor adding a countersubject beginning in m. 2. The first phrase of the *cantus firmus* enters in the soprano in m. 10.3 incorporating some ornamentation and a turn toward the subdominant in m. 13.3. This section is repeated for line 2 of the chorale melody. With lines 5–7 of the *cantus firmus*, Bach dispenses with fore-imitation in the accompanying parts and presents the *cantus firmus* immediately in the soprano. The tonality moves at first toward the dominant, closing with a perfect cadence from mm. 42.3–43.1. Following this, the music moves back to the tonic and onward to the relative minor by means of a Neapolitan chord in m. 46. For the final phrase of this *versus*, the tonality passes through E major and B minor before closing on a plagal cadence in the tonic.

The first note of the *cantus firmus* in *versus* 2 enters immediately at m. 55.3 in the alto. Bach adds accompanying parts in the treble and bass, while still omitting the pedal. In this case, the third note of the *cantus firmus* is raised, bringing about a move toward the dominant. The two outer parts present a countersubject with a *suspirans* character. The tonality moves to C-sharp minor in m. 59, with Bach employing the *syncopatio catachrestica* in m. 59.1. There is a return to A major in m. 60, where the tonality remains to m. 70, apart from a brief reference to the dominant in m. 65. This entire section is then repeated. Line 5 of the *cantus firmus* enters in m. 85.3, with Bach marking the entry with the *syncopatio catachrestica*. The tonality passes through C-sharp and F-sharp minor before passing to the dominant, E major. Bach continues with the same countersubject in the two outer parts. There is a brief reference to B minor in m. 92, with line 6 of the chorale closing with a perfect cadence in F-sharp minor. A coloratura link leads to the final phrase of the chorale for m. 93.2–3. In this phrase, the chorale is more ornamental than in any of the previous phrases, and Bach ends this section with a tonic pedal from m. 99 to 103.

For the final *versus* of the chorale, Bach places the *cantus firmus* in the pedal and changes to a triple compound meter of 9/4. Over the pedal, Bach adds a three-part imitative texture, with the voices entering in the order of tenor, alto, soprano. Once more he uses the chromaticized version of the chorale. On this occasion, repeat marks are not used for lines 3 and 4 of the chorale, but instead Bach redistributes the voices, placing them an octave higher and now in a different order (alto, soprano, tenor). This section of *versus 3* ends clearly at m. 122.1. Bach then introduces a new countersubject with the voices entering in the order of tenor, alto, and soprano. The music moves through a circle of fifths, with a perfect cadence to the tonic at m. 127.1. For the entry of line 5 of the *cantus firmus*, the tonality moves to F-sharp minor and once more proceeds through a circle of fifths to cadence on the dominant in m. 131. Following the first three notes of line 6 of the *cantus firmus*, the meter changes to 3/2 in m. 135, where Bach introduces a falling chromatic countersubject. The music comes to rest on the dominant of F-sharp minor at m. 139. The final phrase of the *cantus firmus* commences without any accompaniment at m. 139.3. Against this, Bach places a new countersubject based on a rising and later falling scale passage in the manual parts, closing with a tonic pedal from m. 144 to 152.

Interpretations by Other Authors

Albert Schweitzer writes eloquently about *O Lamm Gottes unschuldig* (BWV 656).[18] He maintains that Bach reproduces only the basic mood of the first two stanzas and goes into detail as to how Bach reflects the text of the final stanza.[19] In his dismissal of *versus* 1 and 2, he misses some of the details of the first two sections. At m. 122, he suggests a representation of a confession of guilt where the voices repeat the text "All Sünd hast du getragen," while in his view, the chromatic motive at m. 135 represents the desperation of "sonst müsten wir verzagen."[20] It is difficult to identify how Bach could be portraying a confession of guilt at m. 122. According to Schweitzer, with "gib uns dein'n Fried" all anxiety is banished, and he compares the writing to the Christmas chorale settings where the voices cry out "Peace on earth." This seems to be a more plausible interpretation. A final observation is made regarding the ascending figures of the penultimate measure, which he sees as representing the heavenly messengers returning to their own kingdom.[21] In his introduction to the collected organ works of Bach, Schweitzer clearly sees *O Lamm Gottes unschuldig* as a Passion hymn. He describes the final angels' song, "gib uns dein'n Fried," as follows: "Was sie einst den Hirten verhießen, ist auf Golgotha erfüllt" [What they once promised the shepherds, is fulfilled on Golgotha].[22]

Hans Luedtke only refers to the word painting of *versus 3*.[23] He regards the lamenting chromatic harmony as depicting "Sonst müsten wir verzagen" and the final line "Gib uns dein'n Fried/ O Jesu" as being represented in the gentle eighth-note movement.[24]

According to Charles Sanford Terry, m. 19 of *versus 3* anticipates the melodic phrase of the line "our sins thou bearest for us."[25] On the entry of the *cantus firmus*, Terry hears in this motive the "increasing urgency of self-accusation" until the words "else had despair reigned o'er us" are heard in the *cantus firmus*. In his view, the chromatic sequences at the 3/2 measure (m. 135) express in poignant harmonies the agony of the Savior's death. Terry gets somewhat carried away with regard to the final phrase of the *cantus firmus*, "grant us thy peace today, O Jesu," where, he states, "the threnody is stilled, and undulating quaver sequences remind us, as Schweitzer comments of the angelic proclamation of 'peace on earth' in some of the Christmas preludes." The final ascending cadence may be pictured—he thinks—as the heavenward flight of the angelic messengers.[26]

Harvey Grace considers that this is one of Bach's most elaborate pieces of program music, stating that since Bach sets the three stanzas of the hymn text, the effect is perhaps too long.[27] Finding some word painting in stanza

3, he suggests that the chromatic scale refers to the Passion, while the diatonic scales of the coda refer to the flights of angels, who are the heralds of peace.[28]

Stainton de B. Taylor considers that BWV 656 is an example of the partita form, three stanzas of the chorale being set in turn. In his opinion, the music mirrors the sense of the hymn without recourse, with the exception of the last stanza, to obvious word painting.[29] Further on he states that it is in stanza 3 that Bach introduces motives for the first time that are descriptive of the words.[30] According to Taylor, at the change to 3/2 time, the chromatic scale passages allude to Christ's suffering on the cross, while thirteen measures from the end, Bach introduces eighth-note scale passages usually employed to represent the flight of angels. Referring to these rising scale passages, he suggests that their purpose here is not very clear. However, in his view they may represent the flight of the Savior's soul to heaven, or the movements of the angelic host supporting him in his last earthly agonies! He finds it significant that the final measure contains a complete rising scale ascending to the highest note of the key.[31]

Hermann Keller refers to the dreamlike quality of *versus 1* and the heroic grandeur of the third, with the second standing between the two like a mediator.[32] He considers that the emotional madrigalesque rest in m. 2 is noteworthy as it teaches us to understand correctly the musical expression of the first stanza.[33] In spite of the luminous key of A major, there is an inexpressibly deep and tender mood reflecting the Passion, according to Keller. This comment is worthy of investigation and will be discussed in the following section. Keller continues by suggesting that there is a sign of the cross in m. 104, while also speculating that the motive in m. 122 depicts the bowed head of the Redeemer and his collapse on the cross.[34] These hypotheses seem to be very subjective and without foundation. In his opinion, the chromaticism of the following measures expresses despair [verzagen], with streams of lamenting voices pouring down. According to Keller, the struggle ends with the final line, where angels carry the spirit to its heavenly peace.[35] This close should not be seen as appeasement [Besänftigung], Keller states, but as a triumph, as in the close of *Valet will ich dir geben* (BWV 735).

Willem Mudde writes on the issue of whether or not Bach used the chorale *O Lamm Gottes unschuldig* as a Passion or Ordinary hymn.[36] He argues that in the organ setting in the "Leipzig" chorales, Bach is setting it as part of the Ordinary as opposed to the setting of the same hymn in the *Orgel-Büchlein* (BWV 618), which according to Mudde is laden with symbolism relating to the Passion. His arguments are that in BWV 656, Bach sets all three stanzas reminiscent of the Latin *Agnus Dei*, it is in A major, and the figuration is happy and playful. Acknowledging the word painting in relation to the final stanza, he also states that given the virtual disappearance of the *Sanctus* and *Agnus Dei* from the liturgy in Leipzig, Rust's conjecture that the "Eighteen Chorales" were written in Leipzig is incorrect.[37]

Hansjürg Leutert states that there is a deep atmosphere of Passion in this setting and considers that the tripartite structure is somehow related to the Trinity.[38] Helene Werthemann refers to Leutert's study and disagrees with him, suggesting instead that perhaps *O Lamm Gottes unschuldig* should be regarded as a hymn for the Ordinary.[39] She points out that Decius's hymn was originally written as a simple *Agnus Dei*, and it was only later that it was increasingly regarded as a Passion hymn. Referring to the *Orgel-Büchlein* and the opening chorus of the St. Matthew Passion, she acknowledges its firmly established position as a Passion hymn. It is not really relevant to discuss the perception of this hymn in the sixteenth century. The fact is that by the eighteenth century it was an accepted Passion hymn. Keller's view of the affective madrigalesque pause is an overinterpretation according to Werthemann. While agreeing with Mudde's view that *O Lamm Gottes unschuldig* is on the one hand a Passion hymn, and on the other a part of the Ordinary, she sees no connection with the Trinity in the tripartite structure of the hymn.[40]

Jacques Chailley regards the first two stanzas more as a formal development than as being descriptive. He sees much word painting in *versus 3*, with Bach depicting the trials of war and the prayer for peace.[41] Stating that the calm atmosphere of the first two lines of *versus 3* portrays the resignation of the Lamb, he suggests that with the entrance of lines 4 and 5 there is a violent interlude making fanfares of war, which justify the final request for peace.[42] In general, Chailley does not make significant comments on the relationship between the text and music.

Ulrich Meyer speculates that the opening four-note motive of *versus 2* is a call to the Lamb of God.[43] He regards the greatest connection between text and music as being in *versus 3*. In his view, the first two of the four motives in this *versus* are striving toward "verzagen" and the expressive descending chromatic fourth, which resolves in the scale passages, depicting "Fried."[44]

Peter Williams disagrees with Leutert's view of BWV 656 that "a deep Passion atmosphere lies over the chorale."[45] He considers the views of Spitta, Schweitzer, Keller, and Leutert to be speculative and refers instead to the graphic depiction, through extreme chromaticism, of the text of the penultimate line, "all Sünd hast du getragen." In his opinion, the last section is clearly less fraught, reflecting the text, which asks for peace.[46]

Russell Stinson considers that *O Lamm Gottes unschuldig* (BWV 656) may be one of the earliest compositions of the collection because of the way Bach depicts the word "verzagen" in the third variation.[47] According to Stinson, this corresponds to Bach's Mühlhausen cantata style with his use of descending chromatic lines depicting grief and the switch from compound to simple triple meter.[48] Later Stinson mentions the final two lines of text of stanza 3 specifically, observing that Bach has set them in a dramatic fashion.[49] Referring to the intense chromaticisms of the penultimate line, Stinson comments on how they miraculously switch to rapid scales for the final line.[50] In his view, the third variation seems inspired, and not merely with regard to text painting, while the first two stanzas seem "conventional and monochromatic, at least in terms of their figuration."[51] Stinson provides an elaborate analysis of this piece but offers no real conclusions regarding text-music relationships.

As seen in this discussion, it is generally assumed that Bach is setting the three stanzas of *O Lamm Gottes unschuldig* in succession. How Bach may have achieved this is the subject of the next section.

Assessment

There are several striking musical characteristics worthy of note in *O Lamm Gottes unschuldig* (BWV 656). Bach presents three successive workings of the *cantus firmus*, each of which he titles *versus*. In *versus 1*, the *cantus firmus* is presented in its entirety in the uppermost voice. In *versus 2* we hear it in the middle voice, and in the final section it appears in the pedal. The register of the *cantus firmus* may be significant to the text. Bach's choice of the time signature of 3/2 may also hold some meaning for text-music relationships. As Bach presents the *cantus firmus* three times, and given that Decius's hymn consists of three stanzas, it may be logical to conclude that Bach was setting the three stanzas of the text in succession. Many writers have written little about the first two sections, concentrating instead on the various aspects of word painting in *versus 3*. I would like to investigate how Bach might be relating text and music in the entire composition.

In *versus 1*, the *cantus firmus* is presented in the soprano. This may or may not have meaning for the text. There may be some relevance to the fact that the *cantus firmus* progresses from the uppermost to the lowest voice during the course of BWV 656.

Before the chorale melody is quoted in full in *versus 1*, its opening line is paraphrased in a three-part contrapuntal texture in mm. 1–9. Since the text of each stanza is identical save for the last line of stanza 3, it seems reasonable to at least assign the opening line of text to the opening line of music. It may be relevant that the first hint of the relative minor comes at m. 15 where the text refers in line 2 to the slaughtering of the Lamb on the cross and in line 4 to the way in which the Lamb was despised. The left-hand *F-sharp* of m. 15.1 is reached by a downward leap of a minor seventh, as if to emphasize the negative aspect of the text at this point. For the text of line 5, the pastoral mood continues but is interrupted by some unexpected harmonic moves in m. 46. The left hand leaps down a major seventh to a *G-natural* in m. 46 onto a seventh chord in third inversion, which proceeds to resolve in an unusual way to a chord of G major. This G major chord becomes the Neapolitan chord in root position of F-sharp minor and moves to the dominant of this key at m. 47.1. This unusual harmonic procedure could be explained by the text at this point, which refers to "verzagen." Bach uses the Neapolitan chord very pointedly in the second *Kyrie* of the B Minor Mass, which in that case seems to be related to the pleading for mercy invoked by the text. It is noteworthy that this is the text that immediately follows in BWV 656: "erbarm dich unser."

Bach continues the pastoral mood for *versus 2*. The *cantus firmus* is presented in the middle part. Now he introduces the *suspirans* figure. The use of this figure helps to emphasize the longing for mercy. In the case of BWV 656, Bach may be using the *figura suspirans* to portray the longing for mercy and eternity implied in the text. In this stanza, there are more obviously positive or joyful elements than in stanza 1. This can be seen in the use of parallel thirds and sixths in mm. 61, 64, and especially mm. 67–69 where the two-part eighth-note movement is an effective portrayal of a happy and joyful atmosphere.

It has been acknowledged by all of the writers mentioned above that there seem to be many links between text and music in *versus 3*. This *versus* may be easier to interpret than the preceding two, and an understanding of the musical elements of *versus 3* can make it easier to interpret the same text in the first two sections.

For *versus 3*, Bach changes the meter to 9/4 time. This is the only place in Bach's chorale settings for organ where he uses this time signature. In the Weimar version of this chorale, BWV 656a, Bach uses 9/8 time at this point. This time signature is used frequently in the cantatas, but not 9/4. It would seem that Bach may have changed the time signature to give section 3 even more status and significance, making it stand out from the other two.

The final *versus* is weightier than the preceding two, as evidenced by the 9/4 time signature and by Bach's writing out of lines 3 and 4, as opposed to an exact repeat. He uses the same basic musical material for lines 3 and 4 but rearranges the voices so that the tessitura is in general higher. This could be a reference to eternal salvation in heaven. As seen in chapter 4, Bach could portray heavenly matters in the high register of an instrument or voice.

Here, as in *versus 2*, Bach employs *d-sharp* as the third note of the *cantus firmus* (m. 104). Where he modulated to C-sharp minor in stanza 2, he now goes to the dominant (E major). Bach increases the amount of parallel thirds and sixths in this *versus*, and in general he seems to be seizing more opportunities for word painting.

In m. 122, Bach introduces a motive that Keller describes as a cross motive. I do not think that this can be regarded as such. The repetition of notes from weak to strong gives a dancing joyful effect, enhanced by the compound triple meter. This becomes even more marked as the number of voices increases, culminating with the entrance of the *cantus firmus* in m. 127.3. Bach may be portraying the joy associated with the Lamb taking away the sin of the world.

The positive atmosphere is maintained up to m. 135 where the time signature returns to 3/2 and the writing becomes very chromatic to represent the word "verzagen." The return to 3/2 gives the effect of slowing down, which along with the chromatic writing creates a very dramatic effect (see example 5.1). Bach has used chromatic writing in many contexts in his vocal and instrumental works. It is frequently related to the Passion, as seen in many movements of the St. Matthew and John passions, as well as in other vocal and organ works.[52] We find Bach using a similar approach in BWV 656. An augmented sixth chord occurs on the second half of beat 3 in m. 136. This is a rare chord for Bach, usually only employed at a very important moment, for example the inverted augmented sixth chord that resolves to the dominant of G at m. 51 of the *Crucifixus* of the B Minor Mass for the text "passus et sepultus est," or the augmented sixth chord at m. 145 of the *Confiteor* of the same work. In the *Crucifixus*, the augmented sixth chord provides the means for the extraordinary move to G major at the end of the movement. Bach's use of this chord in the *Confiteor* comes at the end of the intensely moving passage, where the music slows to *adagio* for the text "et expecto resurrectionem mortuorum" [and I look forward to the resurrection of the dead]. Both texts are clearly related to the salvation of humanity, so it is therefore not surprising that Bach should also use the augmented sixth chord in the final stanza of BWV 656. The text explains

Example 5.1.   BWV 656 (mm. 135.3ff.)

how humanity would have had to despair if Christ had not taken away the sin of the world, and so the implication is that salvation is an issue.

Following the presentation of this penultimate line of text, Bach reaches a chord of C-sharp major at m. 139. This chord would have sounded very unpleasant on the organs of Bach's day.[53] It represents an important moment in BWV 656, providing a link from the tortured despair expressed through the chromatic writing to the much more positive portrayal of the prayer for peace that begins at m. 139.3. In effect, it may be the last reference to the anguish of the preceding section.

The chromaticisms are replaced at m. 140 by scale passages that are mostly diatonic, with the only chromatic inflection being a subdominant implication with an occasional *g-natural*. The peace requested by the text is depicted by an absence of dissonance of any sort on the first beat of each measure of this section. The final *anabasis* of the penultimate measure stresses the feeling of well-being, related no doubt to the peace of eternal salvation.

It may be significant that the final note of the *cantus firmus* in section 3 occurs at m. 144. This number is an important number in the Book of Revelation and is accepted as being related to the concept of salvation. I have referred to the importance of the number 144 in relation to the Lamb of God and salvation in a previous study as follows:

In Revelation 14:1 we see the Lamb of God standing on Mount Zion with 144,000 people, all with his Father's name written on their foreheads. . . . Thus 144 (or 12 × 12) was a symbol of the chosen people; in New Testament terms—the *ecclesia triumphans* (the Church triumphant). In Bach's B Minor Mass the *Et in Spiritum Sanctum* of the *Credo* is 144 bars long. Since that movement speaks of *unam sanctam catholicam et apostolicam ecclesiam* (one holy catholic and apostolic church) the symbolic connection seems clear.[54]

If the number 144 is significant in BWV 656, this might imply that there is a strong eschatological aspect to this composition. This would seem to imply that Bach was considering *O Lamm Gottes unschuldig* as a Passion hymn with all its implications of salvation.

With the *cantus firmus* appearing in the pedal, while the text of *versus 3* is explicitly asking for peace (bringing to mind the words "et in terra pax"), it may now be possible to reach a conclusion as to Bach's choice of register for the *cantus firmus* throughout BWV 656. In order to take away the sin of the world and grant peace to that world as in the final stanza, Christ had to come from heaven to earth. It might therefore be suggested that the progression of the *cantus firmus* from the soprano to the bass depicts the journey of Christ, the Lamb. Bach occasionally seems to attach symbolic significance to the register of a *cantus firmus*. God in heaven can be represented in the soprano, as seen in, for example, *Kyrie, Gott Vater in Ewigkeit* (BWV 669); *Allein Gott in der Höh sei Ehr* (BWV 662); and section 1 of *Komm Gott Schöpfer heiliger Geist* (BWV 667).[55] The role of Christ as mediator is depicted by placing the *cantus firmus* in the tenor as seen in *Allein Gott in der Höh sei Ehr* (BWV 663, BWV 670, BWV 684, and BWV 688).[56] The presence of the Holy Spirit on earth may be represented in the bass voice as seen in the second section of *Komm Gott Schöpfer heiliger Geist* (BWV 667); *Komm heiliger Geist, Herre Gott* (BWV 651); and *Kyrie Gott heiliger Geist* (BWV 671).[57] In the case of BWV 656, Bach does not appear to be making a reference to the different persons of the Trinity but instead may be using the progression of the register of the *cantus firmus* from soprano to bass as a *descensus* portraying Christ's coming from heaven to earth. This image is also represented in the *catabasis* of the *et incarnatus est* of the B Minor Mass.

Before turning to the possible meaning of the 3/2 time signature in BWV 656, it is useful to study its use by Bach in more detail.

Excursus: the Possible Significance of 3/2 Time in Bach's Music

The time signature of 3/2 requires special attention. It is used twice in Bach's "Leipzig" chorales, in BWV 656 and BWV 663. BWV 663 seems to be concerned with Christ and his Passion. Bach also uses this meter in the *Crucifixus* of the B Minor Mass. Nine chorale settings of the *Orgel-Büchlein* are in 3/2 time. Without exception, all of these chorale texts deal with Christ's sacrifice, his conquest of sin and death, and eternal salvation.[58] The same can be said for the other chorale preludes by Bach in this meter.[59] In the cantatas, there are relatively few movements in 3/2 time. A well-known example is movement 2 of *Weinen, Klagen, Sorgen, Zagen!* (BWV 12), from which the *Crucifixus* of the B Minor Mass was derived. The opening movement of the Ascension cantata *Wer da gläubet und getauft wird* (BWV 37) is also in 3/2 time.[60] The text of BWV 37/1 is as follows:

Wer da gläubet und getauft wird,	Whoever believes and baptized is,
der wird selig werden.	he will be saved.

Interestingly, this is a movement in A major. The combination of this key and 3/2 time could have symbolic meaning in a text referring to salvation and eternity. By the time Bach wrote this cantata, he was not inclined to use seemingly old-fashioned features such as the 3/2 meter without specific reason.

Two further examples of texts related to 3/2 meter by Bach may be mentioned here. Although it is generally accepted that the motet *Jesu meine Freude* (BWV 227) dates from Leipzig (probably 1723), it could be that movement 2, and therefore the corresponding movement 10, were composed at

Weimar.[61] The text of movement 2 deals with the eternal future for those who are in Christ:

> Es ist nun nichts, nichts Verdammliches an denen, die in Christo Jesu sind, die nicht nach dem Fleische wandeln, sondern nach dem Geist (Romans 8:1). [There is therefore now no condemnation to them which are in Christ Jesus, who walk not after the flesh, but after the Spirit.]

Movement 10 is concerned with the raising up of mortal bodies by the Spirit as follows:

> So nun der Geist des, der Jesum von den Toten auferwecket hat, in euch wohnet, so wird auch derselbige, der Christum von den Toten auferwecket hat, eure sterblichen Leiber lebendig machen um des willen, daß sein Geist in euch wohnet (Romans 8:11). [But if the Spirit of him that raised up Jesus from the dead dwell in you, he that raised up Christ from the dead shall also quicken your mortal bodies by his Spirit that dwelleth in you.]

The opening section of the motet *Komm, Jesu, komm* (BWV 229) is also in 3/2 time. This motet dates from before 1731/1732.[62] The text corresponding to the 3/2 meter deals with becoming weary of life's journey and longing for salvation as follows:

Komm, Jesu, komm, mein Leib ist müde,	Come, Jesus, come, my body is weary,
die Kraft verschwindt je mehr und mehr.	my strength fails more and more,
Ich sehne mich nach deinem Friede;	I long for your peace;
der saure Weg wird mir zu schwer.	the bitter path is too hard for me.[63]

It seems clear that the motet and cantata texts quoted above are related to salvation and eternal reward. It does not seem to be coincidental that Bach employs the 3/2 meter in each case. It could be that he is deliberately using a time signature to help portray the text. It is noteworthy that the organ works in 3/2 time have similar texts. Additionally, Bach's use of 3/2 time in BWV 656 seems to lend an air of gravity to the setting that would not exist if the composition had been written in quarter-note beats.

As most of the writers mentioned above have suggested, Bach seems to be using more word painting in section 3. It has the same text as the preceding two, with the exception of the final line of text. *Versus* 3 is a fitting musical conclusion to this piece, but perhaps more importantly it also gives the listener the theological conclusion—"Gib uns dein'n Fried/ O Jesu." Since peace is granted because of the Lamb of God, the closing section is the most important one, summing up the meaning of Christ's sacrifice. Peace will be granted, and the implication is that of eternal peace and salvation. The significance of *versus*

3 of BWV 656 may be reflected in the choice of registration. It seems logical to employ a *plenum* registration for this final section which could be preceded by a chorus on a secondary manual.

★ ★ ★

From the observations made in this chapter, some conclusions may be drawn regarding the text and music in BWV 656. Bach is highlighting the reconciliatory nature of the Lamb who came to rescue sinners. With the exception of the chromatic section of *versus 3*, BWV 656 is largely a hopeful and positive setting, concentrating on the soteriological aspect of the hymn text, emphasizing the joy of salvation. Bach achieves this through the bright A major tonality, the use of parallel motion, and the dancing rhythms of *versus 3*, culminating in the expression of eternal peace in the *anabasis* of the closing section. In each section, Bach makes a musico-theological point in relation to "verzagen," but the most poignant portrayal is found in the chromatic harmony of the last section, contrasting strongly with the ebullient 9/4 section that precedes it. Bach regularly employs the *passus duriusculus* in the context of the Passion, and this does not seem to be an exception. Here it may be related to the sacrifice of the Lamb who ensures the eternal peace depicted in the final thirteen measures.

NOTES

1. Johannes Kulp, *Die Lieder unserer Kirche* [Handbuch zum Evangelischen Kirchengesangbuch, Sonderband], ed. Arno Büchner and Siegfried Fornaçon (Göttingen: Vandenhoeck & Ruprecht, 1958), 100f.
2. Kulp, *Die Lieder unserer Kirche*, 100f.
3. Eduard Emil Koch, *Geschichte des Kirchenlieds und Kirchengesangs der christlichen, insbesondere der deutschen evangelischen Kirche*, 3rd ed. (Stuttgart: Belser, 1866–1876; Hildesheim: Olms, 1973), 8:30f.
4. Koch, *Geschichte des Kirchenlieds und Kirchengesangs*, 8:30f.
5. Kulp, *Die Lieder unserer Kirche*, 102.
6. Kulp, *Die Lieder unserer Kirche*, 102.
7. Koch, *Geschichte des Kirchenlieds und Kirchengesangs*, 31.
8. *SLG*, 131f.
9. Jaroslav Pelikan, *Bach among the Theologians* (Philadelphia: Fortress, 1986), 95.
10. Pelikan, *Bach among the Theologians*, 95f.
11. Willem Mudde, "Bachs behandeling van het lied 'O Lamm Gottes unschuldig' in zijn Matthäus-Passion en in zijn Achtzehn Choräle," *Musica sacra: orgaan van de Interdiocesane Kerkmuziekschool en van de Sint-Gregorius-Vereeniging* 62 (1961): 233–241; Helene Werthemann, "Bemerkungen zu Johann Sebastian Bachs Siebzehn Chorälen für Orgel," *MuG* 6 (1968): 154.
12. See previous note.

13. In the *Dona nobis pacem* that follows, Bach presents us with a prayer that asks for peace, but this is more a statement of the realized eschatology of John: the certainty that salvation has already in fact been granted. It is no coincidence either that Bach employs the same music for the *Dona nobis pacem* that he had used in the *Gratias agimus tibi* in the *Gloria*. The words of the *Gratias* give thanks to God for his great glory.

14. *SLG*, 131f.

15. Translation partly based on Mark Bighley, *The Lutheran Chorales in the Organ Works of J. S. Bach* (St. Louis: Concordia, 1986), 191.

16. The setting BWV 1085 may not be by Bach; see *NBA KB* IV/2:23. There is a copy in P802 by Johann Gottfried Walther who attributes the first movement to "J. S. S." [*sic*]. In LM 4983, it is attributed to "Giovan. Sebast. Bach"; see Peter Williams, *The Organ Music of J. S. Bach*, 2nd ed. (Cambridge: Cambridge University Press, 2003), 539f.

17. Williams, *The Organ Music of J. S. Bach*, 2nd ed., 358, suggests that this omission may not have been authorized by Bach.

18. Albert Schweitzer, *J. S. Bach* (Leipzig: Breitkopf & Hartel, 1920), 463; English: *J. S. Bach*, trans. Ernest Newman (New York: Dover, 1966), 2:71.

19. Schweitzer, *J. S. Bach* (1920), 463; *J. S. Bach*, trans. Ernest Newman (1966), 2:71.

20. Schweitzer, *J. S. Bach* (1920), 464; *J. S. Bach*, trans. Ernest Newman (1966), 2: 72.

21. Schweitzer, *J. S. Bach* (1920), 464; *J. S. Bach*, trans. Ernest Newman (1966), 2:72.

22. Harald Schützeichel, *Albert Schweitzer: Die Orgelwerke Johann Sebastian Bachs. Vorworte zu den "Sämtlichen Orgelwerken"* (Hildesheim: Olms, 1995), 252.

23. Hans Luedtke, "Seb. Bachs Choralvorspiele," *BJ* 15 (1918): 43.

24. Luedtke, "Seb. Bachs Choralvorspiele," 43.

25. Charles Sanford Terry, *Bach's Chorals Part III: The Hymns and Hymn Melodies of the Organ Works* (Cambridge: Cambridge University Press, 1921), 283.

26. Terry, *Bach's Chorals Part III*, 284.

27. Harvey Grace, *The Organ Works of Bach* (London: Novello, 1922), 277.

28. Grace, *The Organ Works of Bach*, 277.

29. Stainton de B. Taylor, *The Chorale Preludes of J. S. Bach* (London: Oxford University Press, 1942), 108.

30. Taylor, *The Chorale Preludes of J. S. Bach*, 113.

31. Taylor, *The Chorale Preludes of J. S. Bach*, 113.

32. Hermann Keller, *Die Orgelwerke Bachs. Ein Beitrag zu ihrer Geschichte, Form, Deutung und Wiedergabe* (Leipzig: Peters, 1948), 185; Herman Keller, *The Organ Works of Bach: A Contribution to Their History, Form, Interpretation and Performance*, trans. Helen Hewitt (New York: Peters, 1967), 251.

33. See previous note.

34. Ibid.

35. Ibid.

36. Mudde, "Bachs behandeling van het lied," 233–241.

37. Mudde, "Bachs behandeling van het lied," 233–241. Mudde comments on the tonality of A major, stating that if *O Lamm Gottes unschuldig* were a Passion hymn, then

Bach would not have used this key. It is true that Bach regularly used the key of E minor in connection with the Passion, but portrayal of the Passion does not exclusively belong in the realm of E minor. Although some work has been done in this area, it is perhaps unwise to speculate too much in this regard.

38. Hansjürg Leutert, "Betrachtungen über Bachs Choraltriptychon 'O Lamm Gottes unschuldig' [BWV 656]," *MuG* 21 (1967): 21.

39. Werthemann, "Bemerkungen," 154.

40. Werthemann, "Bemerkungen," 154. Casper Honders, *Over Bachs Schouder. Een bundel opstellen* (Groningen: Niemeijer, 1985), 72 f., also refers to the issue of *O Lamm Gottes unschuldig* as a Passion hymn or as a hymn for the Ordinary. He seems to see it largely as an Abendmahl hymn and agrees with Mudde's views.

41. Jacques Chailley, *Les Chorals pour Orgue de J.-S. Bach* (Paris: Leduc, 1974), 206.

42. Chailley, *Les Chorals pour Orgue*, 206.

43. Ulrich Meyer, "Zur Frage der inneren Einheit von Bachs Siebzehn Chorälen (BWV 651–667)." *BJ* 58 (1972): 70.

44. Meyer, "Zur Frage der inneren Einheit," 70.

45. Williams, *The Organ Music of J. S. Bach*, 2nd ed., 357.

46. Williams, *The Organ Music of J. S. Bach*, 2nd ed., 358.

47. Russell Stinson, *J. S. Bach's Great Eighteen Chorales* (New York: Oxford University Press, 2001), 7.

48. Stinson, *J. S. Bach's Great Eighteen Chorales*, 7. Stinson cites the second movement of the cantata *Gott ist mein König* (BWV 71) and the chorale prelude *Jesus Christus unser Heiland* (BWV 665) as examples of this grief motive.

49. Stinson, *J. S. Bach's Great Eighteen Chorales*, 83.

50. Stinson, *J. S. Bach's Great Eighteen Chorales*, 83.

51. Stinson, *J. S. Bach's Great Eighteen Chorales*, 83.

52. For example, chromatic writing may be found in the two *Kyrie* movements, the *Crucifixus* and *Agnus Dei* of the B Minor Mass, BWV 665 (line 3 of stanza 1, "durch das bitter Leiden sein"), and in BWV 668. In all cases the music seems to be referring either directly to the Passion, asking for mercy, or to the fact that Christ will take away the sin of the world through his Passion.

53. See the discussion of temperament questions in Peter Williams, *The Organ Music of J. S. Bach* (Cambridge: Cambridge University Press, 1980–1986), 3:183–191, especially the footnote on page 189 that refers to the fact that the melody *Allein Gott in der Höh sei Ehr* in A major in the Weißenfels hymnbook (1714) contained a chord of C-sharp major, which in the favorable tuning of a Weimar court organ would be pleasant enough, but in the unequal temperament of village organs would have sounded harsh.

54. Anne Leahy, "The Opening Chorus of Cantata BWV 78, *Jesu, der du meine Seele*. Another Example of Bach's Interest in Matters Soteriological," *BACH* 30/1 (1999): 34f.

55. See Albert Clement, *Der dritte Teil der Clavierübung von Johann Sebastian Bach: Musik, Text, Theologie* (Middelburg: Almares, 1999), 55f. See also the discussions in chapters 9 and 11.

56. See Clement, *Der dritte Teil der Clavierübung*, 62, 229, and 277.

57. Clement, *Der dritte Teil der Clavierübung*, 71. See also note 153, 357f.

58. These compositions are BWV 600, 603, 607, 608, 615, 619, 628, 629, and 630.

59. BWV 724, 729, 704, and the doubtful BWV 1085.

60. Other examples include movements 4 and sections of movement 7 from the cantata *Gott ist mein König* (BWV 71) (1708); movement 4 from the cantata *Der Herr denket an uns* (BWV 196) (1707/1708); and movement 7 from the cantata *Nach dir, Herr, verlanget mich* (BWV 150) (before BWV 71). In the main, these are all early works, and the employment of the 3/2 meter could be seen as being more old-fashioned.

61. See Daniel R. Melamed, *J. S. Bach and the German Motet* (Cambridge: Cambridge University Press, 1995), 85–89.

62. *BC* 3:951; Melamed, *J. S. Bach and the German Motet*, 102. Movements 2 and 10 employ the same music.

63. Translation, CD liner notes to *J. S. Bach Motetten* BWV 225–230, Cantus Cölln, Deutsche Harmonia Mundi, 77368, 1997.

· 6 ·

Nun danket alle Gott

THE HYMN

*T*he text of *Nun danket alle Gott* is by Martin Rinckart (1586–1649) who attended the St. Thomas school in Leipzig and sang under the direction of Cantor Seth Calvisius before studying theology at the university. He then became teacher and cantor at St. Nicholas in Eisleben in 1610 and a year later was ordained deacon of St. Anne's, Eisleben. He became pastor in Erdeborn in 1613, then archdeacon at his hometown of Eilenburg in 1617, where he protected his flock through the devastating Thirty Years' War.[1] Johannes Kulp places the origins of this hymn text at least as early as 1636. It has mistakenly been presumed that this hymn was written for the occasion of the peace of the Thirty Years' War in 1648. *Nun danket alle Gott* probably appeared in the first publication of Rinckart's *Herz-Jesu-Büchlein* in 1636. Unfortunately, this publication is no longer extant, but the second edition, published in 1663, lists this hymn, and it is likely that all hymns in this edition were also in the first. From the preface of Rinckart's *Meißnischer Tränensaat* (1637), it would seem that the manuscript of his *Herz-Jesu-Büchlein* was completed six years before its publication. It is possible, therefore, to date this hymn text to 1630 with reasonable certainty. This was the centenary anniversary of the Augsburg Confession, which was celebrated 25–27 June in Saxony and had special significance for Rinckart. He was the author of plays written for significant commemorations relating to the life and work of Martin Luther. This anniversary of the Augsburg Confession was the most significant thus far. For this he wrote his *Lutherus augustus*, which included four parodies.[2] One of these was on Sirach 50:22–24, which is the first stanza of *Nun danket alle Gott*. It is likely that this hymn was heard for the first time at the celebrations of the centenary of the Augsburg Confession.[3]

Stanza 1 is an outpouring of thanks to God who always has done and will do much good.[4] Stanza 2 continues with the theme of God's goodness. The text goes further to say that he will deliver humanity from all distress both now and forever. This is also a reference to Psalm 25:22, which states, "GOtt erlöse Israel aus aller seiner Noth" [redeem Israel, O God, out of all his troubles]. The idea of salvation and redemption is important in *Nun danket alle Gott*.[5] Stanza 3 is a doxology, with the important reference to Revelation 4:8, "GOtt . . . der da war, und der da ist, und der da kommt" [God . . . which was, and is, and is to come]. Again, there is the implicit reference to salvation. Because of the important eschatological issues in *Nun danket*, it seems clear why Bach would have included a setting of it in the "Leipzig" chorales. This hymn was sung in Leipzig every Good Friday after the performance of the Passion, an added eschatological link given the importance of this feast in the Lutheran calendar.

Rinckart's text appeared in association with Johann Crüger's melody in his *Praxis pietatis melica* of 1647.[6] *Nun danket alle Gott* appears under the section "Dancklieder" in the Weimar hymnbook of 1713, but in actual fact this hymn was used on any occasion of thanksgiving and praise in the Lutheran liturgy.[7] It was regularly sung at weddings.[8] Additionally, *Nun danket alle Gott* was sung in Leipzig at the conclusion of Vespers on Sundays and on festival days each week.[9] Bach harmonized this chorale in BWV 386 and 252 and also used it in the Reformation cantatas BWV 79 and 192. The text of the hymn as it appears in the Weimar hymnbook (1713) is as follows:

1. NUn dancket alle GOTT
   mit Hertzen/ Mund und Händen/
   der grosse Dinge thut
   an uns/ und alle Enden/
   der uns von Mutter-Leib
   und Kindes-Beinen an
   unzehlich viel zu gut/
   und ietzo noch gethan.

1. Let everyone now thank God
   with hearts, mouth and hands,
   who does great things
   for us and all the earth,
   who from our mother's womb
   and our childhood
   did countless good
   continuing to the present.

2. Der ewig-reiche GOTT
   woll uns bey unserm Leben
   ein immer frölichs Hertz
   und edlen Frieden geben/
   und uns in seiner Gnad
   erhalten fort und fort/
   und uns aus aller Noth
   erlösen hier und dort.

2. The eternally rich God
   wants to give us in our lives,
   an ever joyful heart
   and noble peace,
   and in his grace
   continue to keep us
   and from all distress
   deliver now and hereafter.

3. Lob/ Ehr und Preiß sey GOtt/
   dem Vater und dem Sohne/
   und auch dem heilgen Geist/
   im höchsten Himmels-Throne:

3. Praise, glory and honor to God,
   the Father and the Son,
   and also the Holy Ghost,
   in the highest heavens throne,

dem Dreyeinigen GOtt/	the Triune God,
als es uhrsprünglich war/	as he was in the beginning,
und ist und bleiben wird/	and is and will remain,
ietzund und immerdar.[10]	now and for evermore.[11]

NUN DANKET ALLE GOTT (BWV 657)

BWV 657 is headed "*Nun dancket alle Gott. a 2 Clav. et Ped. canto firmo in Soprano*" in P271. It exists also in an earlier Weimar setting: BWV 657a. There is very little difference between the two settings, and according to Hans Klotz, the revision of BWV 657a may have taken place in Weimar.[12] This setting is very much in the style of Buxtehude, with the accompanying parts providing fore-imitation between each phrase of the *cantus firmus*. BWV 657 is in four parts, with the *cantus firmus* presented unadorned in the soprano. In addition to providing a walking bass and fore-imitations, the pedal also states the first two phrases in their entirety.

The fore-imitations are treated in strict imitation, commencing with the alto on the dominant, answered by the tenor, and with a final unadorned entry in the pedal on the dominant. The *cantus firmus* enters in m. 5.3 in the right hand with a perfect cadence to G major in m. 9. The fore-imitation of the second phrase begins in the tenor at m. 9.2, followed by the alto at m. 11.1 and the pedal at m. 12.3. Here the writing differs from that of the first phrase. Bach uses stretto in phrase 1, but in the second the imitative phrases follow each other two measures at a time for six measures. The music passes through E and B minor before cadencing in G major at m. 14. The right hand enters with the second phrase of the *cantus firmus* unadorned at m. 14.3. A bass line rising in semitones from B to e^0 establishes the key of E minor before a plagal cadence in the tonic. This entire section of music is repeated for the third and fourth phrases of the *cantus firmus*.

The fifth phrase of the *cantus firmus* is treated in an imitative fashion commencing at m. 39.2 in the tenor and two beats later by the pedal. The alto enters in m. 41.2, with the final unadorned entry in the right hand occurring at m. 43.3. The music centers around D major for mm. 40–44, with a brief move toward E minor in m. 45 before returning to D major in m. 46, followed by a perfect cadence from m. 46.4 to 47.1. The writing for the sixth phrase is much more condensed, with the fore-imitations entering in stretto in the order of tenor (m. 47.2), bass (m. 47.4), and alto (m. 48.4). The soprano enters with the sixth phrase of the *cantus firmus* in m. 50.3. The music moves through E and B minor in m. 51 before a conclusive move to D major at mm. 52f.

With the seventh phrase, Bach makes a chromatic alteration in the motive used for fore-imitation. The order of entry here is alto (m. 54.2), tenor

(m. 54.4), and bass (m. 56.2). The pedal does not contain the new chromaticisms of the alto and tenor parts. Once more, Bach treats the tenor and alto in a stretto fashion. The right hand enters in m. 57.3 with the seventh phrase of the *cantus firmus*. The chromaticism at m. 55.3 brings about an augmented triad, albeit only for one eighth note, with the chromaticism in the tenor in the following measure helping to establish D major briefly before returning to the tonic in m. 57.1. The music moves to C major with the entry of the *cantus firmus* in m. 57.3 and quickly modulates to A minor for the latter half of the chorale phrase. Once more, Bach uses an expressive augmented chord at m. 59.1, this time in first inversion. There is a perfect cadence to A minor from m. 59.4f.

The fore-imitation for the eighth phrase commences with the alto in m. 61.1, imitated a measure and a half later by the tenor. Bach unusually does not give the pedal any thematic material. The final phrase of the *cantus firmus* is heard in the right hand from m. 65.3 to 68.1. A long tonic pedal note is held in the uppermost voice to the final measure (m. 71). In this phrase the music passes through B minor (m. 62), D major (m. 63), E minor (mm. 63.3f.), and back to D major (m. 64.3) before a perfect cadence to E minor in m. 65.3. The music returns to the tonic key for the third note of the *cantus firmus* at m. 67.3. For the duration of the tonic pedal, Bach makes reference to the subdominant, as was normal for him in such cases. The piece closes with a plagal cadence.

Interpretations by Other Authors

With only one exception, no author on the subject of *Nun danket alle Gott* (BWV 657) associates any particular stanza with Bach's musical setting. In fact, there is very little written about the relationship of the text of the hymn to BWV 657. This seems to indicate that scholars have found it rather problematic to associate any stanza in particular with this composition.

Philipp Spitta regards BWV 657 as flawless, but he does say that the jubilant shout that rises to the clouds is here wanting.[13]

Fritz Dietrich refers to Pachelbel's setting of *Gott hat das Evangelium*, which with its similar rhythms may have provided a model for Bach's setting of *Nun danket alle Gott*.[14]

Stainton de B. Taylor comments on the "joy motives" that play a large part in creating an atmosphere of jubilant thanksgiving. He suggests solemn celebration of a joyful occasion, in which the note of awe is not absent.[15]

Hermann Keller refers to Spitta's characterization and seems to agree with it. He also suggests an intellectuality that has complicated Pachelbel's simple technique.[16]

Jacques Chailley proposes a general idea of the multiplicity of divine benefits but goes on to associate the lines of stanza 1 in turn with the musical setting.[17]

Ulrich Meyer does not relate any specific stanza of the chorale to BWV 657 and describes the imitations as orthodox [schulmäßig].[18]

Peter Williams makes no real comments on any text-music relationships, referring only to the chromatic alteration in the accompaniment of the penultimate line.[19] He regards it as a rare occurrence but does not offer any opinion as to why Bach might have done this.

Russell Stinson finds the counterpoint in this setting to be "extraordinarily busy." He refers to Bach's treatment of the same hymn in the opening chorus of the cantata *Nun danket alle Gott* (BWV 192), though not drawing any conclusions.[20]

It is clear from this review that scholars have not come to any firm conclusions regarding any text-music relationships in BWV 657. This seems to be because they have not found any obvious links between the music and the text. This is the subject of the section that follows.

Assessment

The general atmosphere of the chorale prelude *Nun danket alle Gott* (BWV 657) is one of great joy and jubilation. Bach portrays this with the consistent use of the *figura corta*, the decisive pedal line, the parallel thirds and sixths, and the unadorned presentation of the *cantus firmus* in the soprano. Can any of these musical elements be harnessed to one specific stanza of text with relative certainty?

If one examines the text of *Nun danket alle Gott*, it is possible to identify similar themes within each stanza that could conceivably be given the same musical treatment. Stanza 1 is an outpouring of thanks to God for all things good that have been present at all times from conception to the present day. Stanza 2 praises the eternally rich God who wants to offer peace, protection, and reconciliation. The final stanza sings the praise of the eternal triune God in highest heaven.

Among the musical features that recur consistently throughout the composition, one may find that these elements can be associated with the text of more than one stanza. Elsewhere in this book, it is demonstrated that parallel thirds and sixths can express great joy and jubilation—this is also possible here in the context of any one of the three stanzas.[21] Equally we know that the use of the *figura corta* can express trust in God.[22] Each stanza expresses trust in God in some way or another.

Before turning to the question of specific text–music relationships, it seems helpful to compare BWV 657 with the two cantatas in which Bach uses *Nun danket alle Gott*. The first movement discussed here is BWV 79/3. *Gott der Herr ist Sonn und Schild* (BWV 79) is a Reformation cantata first performed on 31 October 1725.[23] In movement 3, Bach sets stanza 1 of *Nun danket alle Gott* in a straightforward homophonic setting with two obbligato horns punctuated by timpani. The strings, flutes, and oboes follow *colla parte*. This is a straightforward portrayal of praise by Bach.

The cantata *Nun danket alle Gott* (BWV 192) was first performed in autumn 1730, possibly for a wedding or Reformation feast.[24] In BWV 192, Bach sets the three hymn stanzas successively in the three movements. The opening chorus of the cantata is an extended chorale fantasia based on stanza 1 of *Nun danket alle Gott*. There are many musical features in common with BWV 657. Both settings are very festive in character, employing many sixteenth notes, affirming octave leaps, parallel thirds and sixths, and several examples of the *figura corta*. It is useful to examine the opening three measures of BWV 192.1 (see example 6.1). This opening material forms the basis of the ritornello that recurs throughout the movement. It seems clear that the common musical elements of BWV 657 and BWV 192/1 mentioned previously depict the positive text of stanza 1. However, if one continues to study the remaining two movements of BWV 192, it appears that many of these elements are present here too. Therefore, in the case of BWV 657, it does

Example 6.1.   BWV 192/1

not seem possible to merely attribute stanza 1 to Bach's musical setting (see the following discussion).

Stanza 2 of *Nun danket alle Gott* is set in BWV 192/2 as a duet for soprano and bass accompanied by unison flute, oboe, violins, viola, and continuo. Almost like a love duet, it features constant use of the *suspiratio* and many parallel thirds and sixths. Bach introduces features that were not present in the preceding movement, such as the Halteton at m. 8, and many subsequent measures in the instrumental parts. There are also many sustained notes in the vocal parts, almost always for the word "ewig," as well as many examples of the *figura suspirans*.

As *Nun danket alle Gott* was frequently sung at weddings, it was a hymn clearly associated with love. Bach regularly represented the love of the soul for Christ in a duet between soprano and bass, and Luther repeatedly drew the analogy between human and divine love. As shown in chapter 3, the analogy of the bride as soul and the bridegroom as Christ was an integral part of the spiritual writings of the Lutheran tradition. The final line of stanza 2, "erlösen hier und dort," could be an additional explanation as to why Bach set this movement as a duet: Christ is the means of redemption. As the second person of the Trinity, he is often depicted in the duet form, as seen in the *Christe eleison* of the B Minor Mass. The many thirds and sixths found in this movement can easily be seen to allude to such words of the text as "ein fröhlichs Hertz," "edlen Frieden," "Gnad," and a general feeling of well-being.

Stanza 3 of *Nun danket* is set in BWV 192/3. As with the other two movements in this cantata, parallel thirds and sixths abound, this time portraying the "Lob, Ehr und Preiß" to the Trinitarian God on the throne of heaven. Bach also employs the Halteton in this movement (m. 46), which may be related to the eschatological aspect of this stanza—the idea of the eternal God who was there from the beginning, now, and for evermore.

It seems clear from the above discussion of BWV 79/3 and 192 that there are many elements in common between these cantata movements and BWV 657. The same features may sometimes be related to different stanzas, as seen in BWV 192. Bach can use the *figura corta* as an expression of joy and trust in relation to any stanza. Equally, other expressions of joy such as octave leaps, parallel motion, and dancing repeated-note motives are related by Bach to all three stanzas in BWV 192. It does not seem possible to judge that Bach is depicting one stanza more than another in BWV 657, when so many ideas recur both textually and musically. Consequently, it seems that Bach is portraying the entire text of the hymn. Detailed examination of the composition may help to find how Bach seems to do this.

The opening section of the composition from m. 1 to 37 (allowing for the repeat) accounts for the first four lines of the *cantus firmus*. This passage contains most of the features discussed above—many parallel thirds and sixths, the *figura corta*, and the decisive pedal line with many octave leaps. The commanding opening with the melismatic flourish on the fourth note of the *cantus firmus* can be generally interpreted as a motive of confidence, while not portraying any detail specifically. The confident pedal motive from m. 5.4 to 6.2, incorporating the *figura corta*, is also to be found from m. 1.3 to 2.2 in BWV 192. This recurs throughout the composition and is a motive of conviction and affirmation. The music of this opening section could conceivably be portraying the first four lines of any one of the three stanzas.

Following the last note of line 1 of the *cantus firmus* in m. 8, the second line of the hymn tune is heard paraphrased immediately in m. 9. This is accompanied by a decisive I–V–I motive, which is really an extension of the octave leap, the V–I progression emphasizing the positive outpouring of thanks and praise. This kind of writing continues for the duration of the interlude, which leads to the entry of line 2 of the *cantus firmus* in m. 14. In m. 15, the bass motive of mm. 5–6 is heard, once more a depiction of confidence and trust. The rising chromatic line of m. 17 does not seem to have any significance for text-music relationships, as it does not have the meaning that chromaticism has elsewhere in Bach's music, where it frequently is related to the Passion. In m. 19, just before the return to the opening for lines 3 and 4 of the *cantus firmus*, this optimistic flavor is emphasized further by a rising passage in sixths in the two lower manual parts. This *anabasis* offers a very positive *Affekt* and could be related to the second and third lines of the stanza. On this occasion, "ein immer frölichs Hertz" of stanza 2 appears to be the appropriate text. There is a similar *anabasis* in m. 38, leading to the second half of the piece, confirming the overall positive atmosphere.

The similarity in the shape of the opening line and that of line 5 of the chorale enables Bach to use the same motive in the manual part of m. 40 as he did in m. 1. This may serve as a reminder of the opening assertive motive, which now may represent the "Dreyeinigen Gott" of stanza 3. The pedal motive on the last beat and a half of m. 41 is really the same as that of the last beat of m. 5, this theme recurring at regular intervals to remind listeners of the confidence the hymn expresses. It reappears again at m. 43, coinciding with the entry of line 5 of the *cantus firmus*.

In mm. 55 and 59, Bach uses the augmented triad as a dominant to A minor. This is a departure from the more normal harmonic approach of the remainder of the piece. These measures are included in the section that concerns the penultimate line of the hymn, and on examination of the appropriate line in each stanza, it seems that Bach is portraying the line of text of stanza 2 in this case: "und uns aus aller Noth." The word "Noth" has been vividly depicted by Bach in relation to *Allein Gott in der Höh sei Ehr* (BWV 663).[25] It is possible that Bach is emphasizing the same word here. The modulation to A minor can also be seen as a reflection of the distress out of which the believer asks to be delivered. This depiction of "Noth" is different from that found in *Von Gott will ich nicht lassen* (BWV 658), where the text is "und hilft aus aller Noth." In the case of BWV 658, the certainty is already there that God will help us from all distress, but with regard to BWV 657, the believer is asking to be delivered, so there is still an element of uncertainty as expressed by Bach in the augmented chord.

As in BWV 658, BWV 657 has a very long final tonic, lasting four measures. Apart from the final note of line 2 which lasts for six beats, all the other phrases of the *cantus firmus* end with a whole note. To now extend this to last for sixteen beats is a rather large increase in terms of time values. Examination of the final lines of each stanza leads most logically to the final line of the hymn, "ietzund und immerdar." As the final line of the hymn, and as the only final line that refers to eternity so specifically, it seems doubly logical that Bach would portray the eternal aspect of the text in some way. Eternity has been expressed by Bach with the use of pedal notes like this in many compositions.[26]

In all, it is my opinion that Bach sets stanzas from *Nun danket alle Gott* in three compositions: stanza 1 twice (BWV 79/3 and 192/1), stanza 2 once (BWV 192/2), stanza 3 once (BWV 192/3), and all three stanzas in BWV 657. With the exception of BWV 192/2, the *cantus firmus* is set completely unadorned. In the case of the chorale cantatas, this was a normal procedure for the first movement, but it was not the only possibility for the organ works. With regard to BWV 657, it could be that Bach wanted to proclaim the hymn tune without ambiguity. This is what he did in BWV 79/3 at a point where it was not entirely necessary to do so. Perhaps Bach was trying to establish a strong portrayal of the authoritative Trinitarian God. This is the God portrayed implicitly in stanza 1 of *Nun danket alle Gott* and explicitly in the remaining two stanzas. It seems almost as if Bach did not feel it necessary to adorn the *cantus firmus* in any way—its uppermost position being enough to establish supremacy.

★ ★ ★

Many writers seem to have felt that it is unnecessary to try to trace any text-music relationships in BWV 657. This may be due to the fact that there is common ground in all stanzas of the hymn, and therefore it is difficult to pinpoint specific text-music links with precision. All stanzas praise and thank God, and this is reflected in Bach's musical setting. It seems that the musical ideas in BWV 657 cannot be related exclusively to any specific stanza of the hymn. It is clear from examination of BWV 192 that Bach uses many of the features of BWV 657 in all three movements. This seems to indicate that he was indeed thinking of the entire hymn when he composed BWV 657.

NOTES

1. Johannes Kulp, *Die Lieder unserer Kirche* [Handbuch zum Evangelischen Kirchengesangbuch, Sonderband], ed. Arno Büchner and Siegfried Fornaçon (Göttingen: Vandenhoeck & Ruprecht, 1958), 349. The following hymnological information is based on this source.

2. Kulp, *Die Lieder unserer Kirche*, 350.

3. Kulp, *Die Lieder unserer Kirche*, 350.

4. Rinckart also drew on Sirach 39:35 for this stanza.

5. Melvin P. Unger, *Handbook to Bach's Sacred Cantata Texts. An Interlinear Translation with Reference Guide to Biblical Quotations and Allusions* (Lanham, MD: Scarecrow, 1996), 671, gives references to Psalms 28:8–9, 3:8, and 107:1–2 in relation to the text of *Nun danket*.

6. Kulp, *Die Lieder unserer Kirche*, 351.

7. *SLG*, 315. Kulp, *Die Lieder unserer Kirche*, 351, remarks that it was also often sung instead of the *Te Deum*.

8. Günther Stiller, *Johann Sebastian Bach und das Leipziger gottesdienstliche Leben seiner Zeit* (Kassel: Bärenreiter, 1970), 82; English: *Johann Sebastian Bach and Liturgical Life in Leipzig*, trans. Herbert J. A. Bouman, Daniel F. Poellot, and Hilton C. Oswald; ed. Robin A. Leaver (St. Louis: Concordia, 1984), 94.

9. Stiller, *Bach und das Leipziger gottesdienstliche Leben*, 242; Stiller, *Bach and Liturgical Life in Leipzig*, 258.

10. *SLG*, 315.

11. Translation based on Mark Bighley, *The Lutheran Chorales in the Organ Works of J. S. Bach* (St. Louis: Concordia, 1986), 179f.

12. *NBA KB* IV/2:73.

13. Philipp Spitta, *Johann Sebastian Bach*, trans Clara Bell and J. A. Fuller-Maitland (London: Novello, 1884–1885; reprint, New York: Dover, 1992), 1:612.

14. Fritz Dietrich, "J. S. Bachs Orgelchoral und seine geschichtlichen Wurzeln," *BJ* 26 (1929): 61.

15. Stainton de B. Taylor, *The Chorale Preludes of J. S. Bach* (London: Oxford University Press, 1942), 114.

16. Hermann Keller, *Die Orgelwerke Bachs. Ein Beitrag zu ihrer Geschichte, Form, Deutung und Wiedergabe* (Leipzig: Peters, 1948), 186; English: *The Organ Works of Bach: A Contribution to Their History, Form, Interpretation and Performance*, trans. Helen Hewitt (New York: Peters, 1967), 253.

17. Jacques Chailley, *Les Chorals pour Orgue de J.-S. Bach* (Paris: Leduc, 1974), 194f.

18. Ulrich Meyer, "Zur Frage der inneren Einheit von Bachs Siebzehn Chorälen (BWV 651–667)," *BJ* 58 (1972): 69.

19. Peter Williams, *The Organ Music of J. S. Bach*, 2nd ed. (Cambridge: Cambridge University Press, 2003), 359f.

20. Russell Stinson, *J. S. Bach's Great Eighteen Chorales* (New York: Oxford University Press, 2001), 85.

21. See chapter 4.

22. Discussed, for example, in chapters 1 and 7.

23. *BC* 2:779.

24. *BC* 2:789.

25. See the discussion in chapter 9.

26. See the discussion in chapter 1.

• 7 •

Von Gott will ich nicht lassen

THE HYMN

The melody of *Von Gott will ich nicht lassen* appeared with various texts before Ludwig Helmbold (1532–1598) provided the first sacred text in 1563.[1] It was to be found initially in *Recueil de plusieurs chansons divisé en trois parties* in 1557 in Lyon with the following text:

> Une jeune fillette
> de grand' valeur,
> plaisante et joliette,
> de noble coeur,
> outre son gré
> on l'a rendu nonnette,
> ce la poinct ne lui haicte,
> dont vit en grand douleur.[2]

In the Netherlands this melody was also well known, being popular in many love songs. In Germany it first appeared as a hunting song published in 1560 to the following text:

> Einmal tät ich spazieren
> sonderbar allein.
> Was tät mich da verführen?
> ein Weglein, das war klein,
> das saubr und lustig was;
> darin da tät ich finden
> mit meinen schnellen Winden [= Jagdhunden]
> ein Tierlein in dem Gras.[3]

121

Helmbold's text of 1563 is the earliest sacred text. Kulp dates the hymn text to 1563 based on Johann Christoph Olearius's book *Das alte thüringische Lied. Von Gott will ich nicht lassen*, published in Arnstadt in 1719. Olearius refers to the hymn and the year 1563 according to Kulp.[4] The original publication of the hymn is now lost, although the hymn appeared subsequently in many publications between 1569 and 1572.[5]

The hymn text takes its opening line from Psalm 73:23, "dennoch bleibe ich stets an dir; denn du hältst mich bei meiner rechten Hand" [nevertheless I am continually with thee: thou hast holden me by my right hand]. Other texts followed after this, most notably Paul Eber's (1511–1569) New Year hymn *Helft mir Gotts Güte preisen* and Valentin Thilo's (1579–1630) Advent hymn *Mit Ernst, o Menschenkinder.*[6] The melody was published by the French lutenist Jean Baptiste Besard (1567–1625) in his *Thesaurus harmonicus* (1603).[7]

Helmbold wrote this hymn following the descent of the plague upon the town of Erfurt in 1563, hence the hymn's preoccupation with God's protection, death, and salvation. This plague claimed over 4,000 lives, causing many to flee the area. One who took flight with his family was Pankratius Helbich, professor of medicine at Erfurt University. Helmbold had befriended the family, lodging with them for some time. He wrote this text to mark the Helbich family's leave-taking of Erfurt.[8] Helmbold wrote a dedicatory poem to Frau Helbich, heading the hymn text as follows:

> Ein gottfürchtiger und lieblicher Gesang, in den Druck gegeben zu ehren und wohlgefallen der tugendsamen Frauen Reginen Helbechin, Ehegemahl des hochgelehrten Herrn Doctoris Pancratii Helbich, jetziger Zeit Rectoris in der hohen Schul zu Erfurt, meines großgunstigen Herrn, Freunds und Gevatters durch M. Ludwig Helmbold.[9] [A godfearing and loving hymn, published for the praise and pleasure of the virtuous Mrs. Regina Helbech, spouse of the most learned Dr. Pancratus Helbich, currently rector of the high school of Erfurt, my most agreeable master, friend and sponsor by Mr. Ludwig Helmbold.]

The text of the entire hymn is concerned with Christ and salvation. Stanza 1 includes the text "[er] reichet mir seine Hand, den Abend als den Morgen."[10] The reference to evening in the text implies God's presence at the evening of life as well as the literal meaning of the word.[11] The text proceeds to tell of being rescued from sin and disgrace, even from death. It speaks of trust and how Christ has been given to the believer to nourish body and soul in order to save him and bring him to eternity. Stanza 7 shows how the soul will not be lost but led to Abraham's bosom. Eternity is coming and will be full of never-ending joy. The final stanza emphasizes the Trinitarian God and how the Son has fulfilled the will of the Father, with the Spirit ruling with faith and leading the faithful to heaven. The inclusion of this hymn in a collection of chorale preludes relating to salvation seems appropriate. *Von Gott will ich nicht lassen* was listed as a hymn for nine occasions during the church year.[12] The only *de tempore* indication for *Von Gott will ich nicht lassen* is for the third Christmas day, also dedicated to St. John the Evangelist. The Weimar hymnbook of 1713 lists *Von Gott will ich nicht lassen* under the title "Vom Christlichen Leben und Wandel" [of Christian living and conduct], with text as follows:[13]

1. VOn GOtt will ich nicht lassen/
   denn er läßt nicht von mir/
   führt mich auf rechter Strassen/
   da ich sonst irret sehr/
   reichet mir seine Hand/
   den Abend als den Morgen/
   thut er mich wohl versorgen/
   sey/ wo ich woll/ im Land.

1. I will never forsake God,
   for he does not forsake me,
   he leads me on the right path,
   for otherwise I would stray badly.
   He stretches out his hand to me,
   in the evening as in the morning
   he takes good care of me,
   wherever I am in the land.

2. Wenn sich der Menschen hulde
   und Wohlthat all verkehrt/
   so findt sich GOtt gar balde/
   sein Macht und Gnad bewährt/
   und hilft aus aller Noth/
   errett von Sünd und Schanden/
   von Ketten und von Banden/
   und wenns auch wär der Tod.

2. When the favor
   and good deeds of men all turn bad,
   God can soon be found,
   his power and mercy maintained,
   and helps from all distress,
   rescues from sin and shame,
   from chains and bonds
   and even from death.

3. Auf ihn will ich vertrauen
   in meiner schweren Zeit/
   es kan mich nicht gereuen/
   er wendet alles Leid/
   ihm sey es heimgestellt/
   mein Leib/ mein Seel/ mein Leben
   sey Gott dem HERRN ergeben/
   er machs/ wies ihm gefält.

3. I will trust in him
   in my time of trial,
   I cannot regret it,
   for he turns all sorrow away,
   to him be entrusted
   my body, soul and life,
   given to God the Lord,
   He does as it pleases him.

4. Es thut ihm nichts gefallen/
   denn was mir nützlich ist/
   er meynts gut mit uns allen/
   schenckt uns den HErren Christ/
   sein allerliebsten Sohn/
   durch ihn er uns bescheret/
   was Leib und Seel ernehret/
   lobt ihn ins Himmels Thron.

4. Nothing pleases him
   but that which is useful to me.
   He has good intentions for us all,
   sends us the Lord Jesus Christ,
   his dearest Son.
   Through him he gives us
   that which nourishes body and soul.
   Praise him in heaven's throne.

5. Lobt ihn mit Hertz und Munde/
   welchs er uns beydes schenckt/
   das ist ein seelig Stunde/

5. Praise him with heart and mouth,
   both of which we have from him.
   It is a blessed hour,

darinn man sein gedenckt/	in which one thinks of him.
sonst verdirbt alle Zeit/	Otherwise all time is corrupt
die wir zubringn auf Erden/	that we pass here on earth.
wir sollen selig werden/	We are to be saved
und bleibn in Ewigkeit.	and remain in eternity.

6. Auch wenn die Welt vergehet/	6. If the earth passes away
mit ihrem Stoltz und Pracht/	with its pride and splendor,
wedr Ehr noch Gut bestehet/	neither glory nor goods remain,
welchs vor war groß geachtt/	which were highly regarded formerly.
ja wenn wir nach dem Tod/	When after death
tief in die Erd begraben/	we will be buried deep in the earth,
sein Sanft geschlafen haben/	when we have slept,
will uns erwecken GOtt.	God will awaken us.

7. Die Seel bleibt unverlohren/	7. The soul will not be lost,
geführt in Abrahams Schooß/	led to Abraham's bosom,
der Leib wird neu gebohren	the body will be born again,
von allen Sünden loß/	free from all sin,
ganz heilig/ rein und zart/	completely holy, pure and mild,
ein Kind und Erb des HErren/	a child and inheritance of the Lord,
daran muß uns nicht irren	we should not be deceived
des Teufels listig Art.	by the devil's cunning.

8. Darom ob ich schon dulde	8. Therefore if I already even endure
hie Widerwärtigkeit/	wretchedness here,
wie ich auch wohl verschulde/	for which I am indeed responsible,
kömmt doch die Ewigkeit/	eternity is coming soon,
ist aller Freuden voll/	and is full of joy,
dieselb ohn einigs Ende/	which itself is never ending
dieweil ich Christum kenne/	because I know Christ
mir wiederfahren soll.	this shall come to me.

9. Das ist des Vaters Wille/	9. This is the will of the Father
der uns geschaffen hat/	who created us,
sein Sohn hat Guts die Fülle	his Son has gained
erworben und Genad/	fullness and mercy for us.
auch Gott der heilig Geist	God the Holy Spirit also
im Glauben uus [*sic*] regieret	rules us in the faith,
zum Reich der Himmel führet/	and leads us to the kingdom of heaven.
ihm sey Lob/ Ehr und Preiß.[14]	To him be praise, glory and exultation.[15]

VON GOTT WILL ICH NICHT LASSEN (BWV 658)

Von Gott will ich nicht lassen (BWV 658) survives in Bach's hand in P271 with the heading "*Von Gott Will ich [nicht] laßen. canto fermo in Pedal.*" Like most of the chorale settings in P271, Bach has left an earlier Weimar and a later Leipzig revision of this chorale: BWV 658a and BWV 658 respectively. His revisions amount to refinement of the melodic line, with no substantial change in form or content. It is interesting, however, that the "illegal" parallel fifths in m. 30 appear only in the revised version (see the discussion that follows).

This chorale is in the key of F minor, a key rarely employed by Bach in his organ works. When he did use F minor in both his vocal and organ settings, there seems to have been a textual reason. Comparisons may be drawn especially with other chorale-based organ works in this key, the only ones being *Ich ruf zu dir, Herr Jesu Christ* (BWV 639); *Jesus Christus unser Heiland* (BWV 689); and the chorale partita *Christ, der du bist der helle Tag* (BWV 766). Investigation into these organ works will show that the texts of these chorales have much in common with that of *Von Gott will ich nicht lassen*.

BWV 658 is of the paraphrase variety, with the *cantus firmus* appearing in the pedal as a tenor part at eight-foot pitch. If, as some performers do, the *cantus firmus* were to be played at four-foot pitch, the tenor area would be left very bare. When Bach did want a four-foot *cantus firmus*, he generally indicated so, as in the following examples: *Wer nur den lieben Gott läßt walten* (BWV 647) and *Kommst du nun, Jesu, vom Himmel herunter auf Erden* (BWV 650), both from the Schübler Chorales.

One of the most noteworthy elements in this piece is Bach's persistent use of the *figura corta* throughout. There is not one measure where he does not use it. The impact of this figure is visual as well as aural, the printed page giving the impression of much activity and interchange between the parts.

The manual parts provide motivic development arising from the contours of the chorale. The opening right-hand melody is derived from the *cantus firmus*, presenting all the notes from line 1 of the chorale in the first two measures of the piece, with the alto and bass parts also developing this motive. The opening bass motive of a rising minor sixth is developed sequentially between all three accompanying parts in mm. 1–3. Line 1 of the *cantus firmus* enters in the pedal part in m. 4.3. Line 2 of the chorale follows immediately on from this without interruption.

The harmonic writing and the motivic development is much more developed here than in BWV 657. The music passes from F minor through the keys of C minor and A-flat major before returning to F minor in mm. 7.3–8.1. For the remainder of this section, Bach develops the opening bass motive further, with the introduction of a "sighing" motive in m. 9.3 leading to the key of B-flat minor before an expressive return to F minor at m. 10.1. This entire section is repeated.

There is a hint of line 5 of the *cantus firmus* in the soprano part at m. 23.2. The other accompanying parts continue the development of the opening bass motive. Line 5 of the *cantus firmus* enters in the pedal part in m. 24.3. Above this in the soprano, the idea of a falling fourth derived from the chorale is taken over, although this time in a syncopated manner. The tonality passes from F minor through A-flat major and D-flat major before progressing by means of a circle of fifths to E-flat major at m. 29.1. The soprano line clearly outlines line 6 of the *cantus firmus* while still developing the motives of the opening. The final three phrases of the *cantus firmus* are heard consecutively in the pedal from m. 29.3. The tonality passes from A-flat major in m. 30.1, to F minor in m. 30.3, and then to E-flat major in m. 31.1. Unusually, Bach allows parallel fifths to stand in m. 30 between the chorale and the alto on beats 3 and 4. As noted previously, these parallels did not exist in BWV 658a, so it seems that Bach has consciously placed them here.

The penultimate phrase of the *cantus firmus* begins at m. 31.4. The accompanying parts do not make any reference to this phrase but continue to develop the opening motives. The tonality returns to F minor at m. 31.4 before moving to C minor at m. 33.1. The final phrase of the *cantus firmus* enters at m. 33.4. This phrase remains in F minor throughout.

The final four measures of this setting form a remarkably long tonic pedal, over which Bach develops the motivic writing even further. These final four measures are characterized by the marked and consistent use of dissonance (*parrhesia*) and syncopation (*syncopatio*). While employing these negative elements, Bach also adds a more positive touch with the leaping bass octaves in a very characteristic rhythm, forming in fact two completely opposing affects. All is ultimately resolved in the final measure with a welcome chord of F major.

Interpretations by Other Authors

Albert Schweitzer, inspired by the persistent use of the *figura corta* in BWV 658, suggested that Bach was portraying "aller Freuden voll" of stanza 8.[16] Casper Honders suggested that Bach may have been setting stanza 4 of the text. Given that the text refers to the fact that the body and soul are nourished by Christ, who was sent by God the Father, this supports his argument that the "Leipzig" chorales are *musica sub communione*.[17]

Ulrich Meyer also specifically links text and music, suggesting that it is the text of stanzas 6 and 8 that Bach is portraying. He states that Bach often set music that expressed the longing for death and heavenly joy.[18]

Peter Williams refers to the *figura corta* as frequently being used with texts regarding "aufwecken" [wakening]. According to Williams, the final pedal point is the most striking part of the piece, and he concedes that Meyer's view of the repeated *F* being a link to the text of stanza 6 may hold true.[19]

Assessment

Von Gott will ich nicht lassen is a hymn about the protection and mercy of God and how he will provide all believers with eternal life after death. This theme is dealt with in some way in each of the nine stanzas of this hymn. In order to arrive at some conclusions relating to text and music, it is therefore necessary to go to the music to see how the main musical features might be linked to the text of the various stanzas. These features include the constant presence of the *figura corta*, the unusual key of F minor, the use of syncopation and dissonance, the "illegal" parallel fifths in m. 30, and the spectacular coda over a tonic pedal. The various opposing elements of this coda must also be considered—the *parrhesia* of the upper parts, which contrasts with the confident leaping octave motive of the left hand.

It is relatively easy to recognize Bach's portrayal of the confidence of the believing soul in God's goodness in the constant employment of the *figura corta*. This does not necessarily lead to any particular stanza however.

A brief discussion regarding the inclusion of *Von Gott will ich nicht lassen* in a collection of chorale preludes united by an eschatological theme seems appropriate. *Von Gott will ich nicht lassen* was listed as a hymn for nine occasions during the church year.[20] Without exception, all of the epistle readings for these Sundays were concerned with the glory of Christ and eternal life. Salvation is implicit in all of this. If we look at the cantatas written for these Sundays, we find similar themes. Additionally, this hymn was a *de tempore* hymn for the third Christmas day, also dedicated to St. John the Evangelist in the Weimar hymnbook of 1713.[21] Examination of part 3 of the Christmas Oratorio, also written for this day, provides interesting comparisons. The theme of salvation is prominent here also. Therefore, it seems that this hymn is consistently associated with Sundays and feast days on which salvation is a theme. Bach's inclusion of BWV 658 in P271 thus seems logical.

I would like to look carefully at the stanzas that could most conceivably be related to Bach's musical setting. Most of the previously mentioned musical elements can quite easily be seen to be relevant to the text of stanzas 2, 5, 6, 8, or 9. These five stanzas all deal with God's ability to provide humanity with protection in its distress and to guarantee eternal life. In a general way, man's distress is portrayed in the F minor tonality, the frequent dissonances, and the negative elements of the coda. God's protection is invoked by the *figura corta*, the modulations to the major in the second section, and the positive octaves of the coda. The very striking harmonic approach to the coda with the marked use of *parrhesia* must have significance for the text.

It does not seem possible that Bach was portraying the text of stanza 9. The final line of text, "zum Reich der Himmel führet/ ihm sey Lob/ Ehr und Preis," cannot be related to the tortured lines of the closing measures. Similarly, the closing two lines of stanza 8, "dieweil ich Christum kenne/ mir wiederfahren soll," do not seem to correspond to the music and thus negate Schweitzer's view that Bach was portraying stanza 8. The "aller Freuden voll" of line 5 can certainly be regarded in isolation as being related to the *figura corta*, but it is not possible to explain some of the other musical elements in relation to stanza 8. Equally, the music cannot be seen to portray the final two lines of stanza 5, "wir sollen selig werden, und bleibn in Ewigkeit." This leaves stanzas 2 and 6. Stanza 6 could be relevant, as Ulrich Meyer has suggested. Meyer justified his opinion by stating that Bach frequently set music that expressed the longing for death and heavenly joy. This is certainly true and is not a thought original to Meyer, but the argument is not sufficiently strong to make one believe that Bach was portraying either of these stanzas. The text of the final two lines of stanza 6, "sein Sanft geschlafen haben/ will uns erwecken Gott," does not correspond to the musical setting. Peter Williams' view that the leaping octaves in the coda represent "erwecken"[22] is an interpretation offered in isolation, where he does not consider any of the remainder of the text of stanza 6. It is less likely that Bach was portraying only one aspect of the text and more likely that he seized the opportunity to show many details of one stanza as will be shown in the following discussion.

There is one interesting musical element that no writer has hitherto considered with regard to the relationship of text and music in BWV 658: Bach's use of the "illegal" parallel fifths in m. 30 (see example 7.1). These "illegal" fifths occur on the fourth syllable of line 6 of the text. If one examines the text of all the stanzas, there is only one possible stanza where the text at this point would perfectly explain these "forbidden" parallels: stanza 2, mentioning the

Example 7.1.   BWV 658 (m. 30)

word "Sünd" at exactly this place. Bach did not employ them in the earlier Weimar version, BWV 658a. This is the only case in the revisions of these chorales that Bach's modification resulted in a seeming mistake. He apparently did not mind committing this particular sin in the Leipzig revision and may have even enjoyed his little play on words. It seems conclusive, therefore, that Bach intended to portray the text of stanza 2 in BWV 658, committing a compositional "sin" exactly at the point where the text of stanza 2 has the word "sin": "errett von *Sünd* und Schanden" [rescues from *sin* and shame].

The remaining musical elements of BWV 658 will now be considered in detail, using other compositions with similar techniques to illuminate text–music relationships. One of the most striking features of BWV 658 is the consistent employment in every measure of the *figura corta*. Where Bach uses this elsewhere, he usually seems to have just cause, and this composition is no exception. In BWV 658, Bach may be using it to portray confidence in God's goodness in providing salvation for humanity after death. Koch actually categorizes *Von Gott will ich nicht lassen* under the heading "vertrauen auf Gott," as mentioned previously.

It is useful to consider other compositions employing the *figura corta*. In the opening chorus of part 4 of the Christmas Oratorio, Bach employs the *figura corta* as an accompanimental feature to the text "wir wollen dir allein vertrauen." It would seem that Bach's employment of the *figura corta* in this case is directly related to the word "vertrauen."

Mit Fried und Freud ich fahr dahin (BWV 616) is Bach's setting of Luther's paraphrase of the *Nunc Dimittus*, Simeon's song of praise as he departs this life. Bach makes extensive use of the joy motive, or *figura corta*, as he does in BWV 658. In addition, the *figura corta* is often employed in two parts that move in parallel thirds or sixths. Bach is therefore using two musical methods of portraying the joy of the departing Simeon as he enters eternal life. *Mit Fried und Freud* is quoted by Bach in movement 3b of the *Actus Tragicus* (BWV 106). This is an early cantata, written in Mühlhausen, its many theological layers showing Bach's early preoccupation with salvation.[23] In movement 3b, the bass sings "Heute, heute wirst du mit mir" [today, today you will be with me] while the soprano sings stanza 1 of the chorale *Mit Fried und Freud*. Once again Bach uses the *figura corta*, heard in the bass, to accompany Luther's hymn. Bach is reiterating the trust that humanity must have in God's goodness, that God will save those with faith.

Other chorale settings from the *Orgel-Büchlein* that make use of the *figura corta* include *Wenn wir in höchsten Nöten* (BWV 641) and *Wer nur den lieben Gott läßt walten* (BWV 642). In the *Orgel-Büchlein*, Bach originally intended that a setting of *An Wasserflüssen Babylon* would follow *Wenn wir in höchsten Nöten sein* (BWV 641). These are all hymns of penitence, with trust in God for salvation.[24] The setting of *Wer nur den lieben Gott läßt walten* (BWV 647) in the Schübler Chorales also makes use of the *figura corta* to portray the joy of death.[25] Faith in God that he will rescue mankind from sin and shame, chains and bonds, and even death, as stated in the text of stanza 2 of *Von Gott will ich nicht lassen*, is reflected in the ever-present *figura corta*. As shown earlier, Bach used the *figura corta* in many organ works and cantatas to show faith that God would provide salvation at the time of death. As seen in example 7.2, Bach uses the *figura corta* to accompany the word "getrost" [hopeful] in the alto aria of the cantata *Ich freue mich in dir* (BWV 133). In this aria, the Christian rejoices at seeing God face to face at the birth of Christ, exulting in the certainty of eternal salvation. Likewise, in BWV 658, the *figura corta* expresses joy and hope in salvation.

Bach's choice of the key of F minor is unusual. This is the only setting in the "Leipzig" chorales with a key signature of four flats. The only setting in the *Orgel-Büchlein* with four flats is *Ich ruf zu dir, Herr Jesu Christ* (BWV 639). There is only one setting in F minor in *Clavierübung III—Jesus Christus unser Heiland* (BWV 689)—and none in the individually transmitted chorales. The chorale partita *Christ, der du bist der helle Tag* (BWV 766) is also in F minor. All of these chorales share common themes in their texts: *Ich ruf zu dir* deals with issues of death and eternal life; *Jesus Christus unser Heiland* shows how the Passion of Christ and the institution of the Abendmahl provide eternal life;[26] and *Christ, der du bist der helle Tag* is concerned with the protection by God for the believer, with stanza 3 asking specifically for protection from sin and shame. In the case of the latter chorale, stanza 3 is remarkably similar in style to BWV 658. It seems that Bach was consciously using F minor to portray an aspect of the text.[27] F minor would have sounded strange on the unequally tempered organs that Bach played, and therefore Bach must have intended this sound for a particular reason.[28]

One of the other striking elements of BWV 658 is the leaping octave in the left hand of the four-measure coda, contrasting with the dissonance of the upper voices. Before examining this final section of BWV 658, it is useful to

Example 7.2.   BWV 133.2

Ge - trost,   ge-trost,   ge - trost!

examine some organ works employing this motive. In stanza 9 of the chorale partita *O Gott, du frommer Gott* (BWV 767), Bach employs an octave leap in the left hand similar to that of BWV 658.[29] The text here is a doxology to the triune God, praising the three persons of the Trinity in the context of eternity as follows: "Gott Vater! dir sey Preis, hier und im Himmel oben" [God Father to you be praise, here and in heaven above]. Both *O Gott, du frommer Gott* and *Von Gott will ich nicht lassen* invoke the protection of God and deliverance from death. It is not surprising, therefore, to find a bass line similar to that of the closing measures of BWV 658. In BWV 767/9, this octave motive is present throughout much of the piece, confirming the positive side of death from which the soul was awakened in the previous stanza (see example 7.3). A similar interpretation may be applied to the octave leaps in variation 6 in BWV 767, where the issue is also faith and confidence in God.

An equivalent motive can be found in the chorale prelude *Wir danken dir, Herr Jesu Christ, daß du für uns gestorben bist* (BWV 623) (see example 7.4). The text portrays the confidence that God will not abandon the faithful believer but will provide support until eternity is reached by means of the cross. A final example of this kind of octave leap is found in the trio *Allein Gott in der Höh sei Ehr* (BWV 664) (mm. 37–39 and 59–61). Stanza 4 of the hymn *Allein Gott* is relevant to BWV 664 in that this stanza also asks for protection and the turning away of misery and distress. The closing line, "darauf wir uns verlassen," is key to the interpretation of this motive. The believer has absolute trust in the protection of God who will provide eternal salvation. This is the same theme as stanza 2 of *Von Gott will ich nicht lassen*, and so it is not surprising that there are musical elements in common.

The closing chorale of the cantata *Herr, wie du willt, so schicks mit mir* (BWV 73) is stanza 9 of *Von Gott will ich nicht lassen*. This cantata was written for the third Sunday after Epiphany and was first performed on 23 January 1724 in the Nicolaikirche.[30] In this cantata, Bach concentrates on the fact that the believer should place unbiased faith in the Lord, in good times and bad. This theme is very relevant to the hymn *Von Gott will ich nicht lassen*, and therefore it is logical that Bach uses this hymn in BWV 73. In the opening

Example 7.3. BWV 767.9 (mm. 1–2)

Example 7.4.   BWV 623 (mm. 1–3)

movement, a striking recurring feature of the ritornello is the leaping octaves heard in the string part, mostly preceded by an upbeat eighth note. This is identical to the leaping bass part of mm. 36 and 37 of BWV 658. Its prominence in BWV 73/1 and its sudden introduction in BWV 658 may be related. Life and death and God's role in it is the concern in BWV 73/1, as it is in BWV 658. In view of these examples, these octaves could be portraying the passing of time from life to death to eternity.

As appears from this investigation, a number of musical details lead to the conclusion that it was indeed stanza 2 that Bach was portraying in BWV 658. Additionally, this is not unexpected, as, from a theological point of view, stanza 2 is of great eschatological significance. The composition itself will now be examined in detail and the text placed in the context of these musical characteristics.

It is interesting to observe how Bach portrays the opening lines of stanza 2 in his musical setting. The first two lines, "Wenn sich der Menschen Hulde/ und Wohltat all verkehrt," are commented on by Bach in a vivid manner after the statement of the two lines of the *cantus firmus*. The left hand drops to the lowest possible note for the word "verkehrt" in m. 7 (*hyperbole*). Following this, Bach makes extensive use of the *syncopatio catachrestica* as a commentary on the *cantus firmus* just heard. In m. 9 (20), there is a reference to the "sighing" motive for the only time in this piece. This motive is associated in Bach's music with the cross and the sacrifice of Christ, and its presence here is a reminder of the means of salvation for mankind—Christ's struggle with death, so dramatically expressed by Bach in the closing measures of BWV 658. The music of the opening twelve measures is repeated for lines 3 and 4 of the text "so find sich Gott gar balde/ sein Macht und Gnad bewährt." The more positive side of these two lines is reflected in the music after the second-time measure. Here Bach begins to move tentatively toward the major, initiating the more optimistic second section of BWV 658. This may have consequences for relationships between text and music.

The second half of the piece holds interesting clues to aid in interpreting the text. From m. 25, the music turns very confidently toward major tonality.

The first conclusive major cadence in BWV 658 occurs at m. 26 where the music cadences to the relative major of A-flat. This can be directly related to the text of stanza 2, which at this point refers to "und hilft aus aller Noth." God is seen as reacting to the misdeeds of humanity, and the text is now explicit regarding what was implicit in the preceding two lines—salvation will be provided through the mercy and goodness of God—hence the first major cadence of the piece. The optimistic flavor is maintained, as at m. 27.3 the highest note of the piece is reached (*hyperbole*), c^3. Here Bach is clearly commenting on and endorsing the text of the previous line. This measure also has parallel tenths between the two upper parts as well as the rising major sixth *tirata*, all of which add to the very positive affect at this point.

Line 6 of the text continues the theme of the previous line—"errett von Sünd und Schanden"—reaching another high point emotionally in m. 31 with a cadence to E-flat major. Sin and shame are not normally associated with happy major cadences, but it is the fact that believers will be rescued (that is, saved) that is the focus here. Bach inserts a clue relating to the text at this point by deliberately writing parallel fifths between the tenor and alto from beats 2 to 3 of m. 30 on the word "Sünd." This makes sense in stanza 2, but in none of the others. It is particularly significant that these fifths are not present in BWV 658a. The reference to sin may account for the very brief foray into F minor at m. 30.3.

The music predictably turns back toward F minor at m. 32 for the text "von Ketten und von Banden," and therefore Bach's use of F minor in m. 32 and C minor in m. 33 is not surprising. The final line of text, "und wenns auch wär der Tod," leads to the tonic pedal on the word "Tod." There are many remarkable elements in the four-measure coda. The long pedal f^0 may be portraying the long sleep of death. The excruciating harmonic clashes of the two upper voices contrast with the more positive leaping octaves of the bass part. In the upper voices, Bach appears to portray the struggle of Christ with death as he releases mankind from the chains and bonds of sin. Similar conflict is evident in variation 6 of BWV 768.[31] In the latter, the two manual parts move in furious thirty-second notes, portraying being swallowed up in the fires of hell—"Wenn die Höll mich will verschlingen/ und mit ihrem Feuer umringen." Equally, the opening chorus of the cantata *Christ lag in Todesbanden* (BWV 4) depicts the swallowing up of the bands of death in the twisting and tortured vocal lines. In stanza 2 of *Von Gott will ich nicht lassen*, the text refers to the chains and bonds of death in the final two lines, "von Ketten und von Banden," which could account for the kind of twisting musical lines that dominate BWV 658. As well as providing sharp dissonance, Bach also modulates to the flat side—B-flat minor in m. 35, a key associated in the Passions and cantatas with moments of torment and grief. The final release from the chains of death comes in the major triad of the final measure.

★ ★ ★

Von Gott will ich nicht lassen (BWV 658) was composed by Bach with the theme of eternal life in mind. In his musical setting, Bach shows that faith in God for his mercy and protection is essential for eternal salvation. The means of this salvation is Christ's death on the cross. Bach has portrayed the trust of mankind in the *figura corta*, as well as the darker side of salvation—the struggle experienced by Christ as he fought to gain salvation for humanity—depicted by Bach in the dissonances and dark F minor tonality. With these themes in mind, it is clear why Bach should include BWV 658 in a group of chorale preludes such as the "Leipzig" chorales, where an eschatological theme unites all the compositions in the collection.

NOTES

1. Johannes Kulp, *Die Lieder unserer Kirche* [Handbuch zum Evangelischen Kirchengesangbuch, Sonderband], ed. Arno Büchner and Siegfried Fornaçon (Göttingen: Vandenhoeck & Ruprecht, 1958), 441f.

2. Kulp, *Die Lieder unserer Kirche*, 442.

3. Kulp, *Die Lieder unserer Kirche*, 442.

4. Martin Rössler, *Bibliographie der deutschen Liedpredigt* (Nieuwkoop: de Graaf, 1976), 218.

5. Kulp, *Die Lieder unserer Kirche*, 441.

6. Kulp, *Die Lieder unserer Kirche*, 442.

7. Kulp, *Die Lieder unserer Kirche*, 442.

8. Kulp, *Die Lieder unserer Kirche*, 441.

9. Kulp, *Die Lieder unserer Kirche*, 441.

10. *SLG*, 327f.

11. Albert Clement, "'Sechs Choräle' BWV 645–650 von J. S. Bach und dessen Bedeutung," in *Das Blut Jesu und die Lehre von der Versöhnung im Werk Johann Sebastian Bachs*," ed. Albert Clement [Royal Netherlands Academy of Arts and Sciences: Proceedings of the International Colloquium The Blood of Jesus and the Doctrine of Reconciliation in the Works of Johann Sebastian Bach, Amsterdam, 14–17 September 1993] (Amsterdam: Royal Netherlands Academy of Arts and Sciences, 1995), 296.

12. Detlef Gojowy, "Kirchenlieder im Umkreis von J. S. Bach," *JbLH* 22 (1978): 90–123. These occasions were Advent 3; third Christmas day; Sunday after New Year; *Misericordias Domini, Jubilate, Exaudi*; Trinity 7; Trinity 8; and Trinity 14. The Weimar hymnbook of 1713 mentions it for third Christmas day. Eduard Emil Koch, *Geschichte des Kirchenlieds und Kirchengesangs der christlichen, insbesondere der deutschen evangelischen Kirche*, 3rd ed. (Stuttgart: Belser, 1866–1876; Hildesheim: Olms, 1973), 8:365–370, lists it under the category "Vertrauen auf Gott" [Trust in God].

13. *SLG*, 327.

14. *SLG*, 327f.

15. Translation based on Mark Bighley, *The Lutheran Chorales in the Organ Works of J. S. Bach* (St. Louis: Concordia, 1986), 228ff.

16. Harald Schützeichel, *Albert Schweitzer: Die Orgelwerke Johann Sebastian Bachs. Vorworte zu den "Sämtlichen Orgelwerken"* (Hildesheim: Olms, 1995), 253.

17. Casper Honders, *Over Bachs Schouder. Een bundel opstellen* (Groningen: Niemeijer, 1985), 74f.

18. Ulrich Meyer, "Zur Frage der inneren Einheit von Bachs Siebzehn Chorälen (BWV 651–667)" *BJ* 58 (1972): 71.

19. Peter Williams, *The Organ Music of J. S. Bach*, 2nd ed. (Cambridge: Cambridge University Press, 2003), 362.

20. Gojowy, "Kirchenlieder im Umkreis von J. S. Bach," 90–123. These occasions were Advent 3; third Christmas day; Sunday after New Year; *Misericordias Domini, Jubilate, Exaudi*; Trinity 7; Trinity 8; and Trinity 14. The Weimar hymnbook of 1713 mentions it for the third Christmas day. In addition, Bach used *Von Gott will ich nicht lassen* in the cantata *Herr, wie du willt, so schick's mit mir* (BWV 73), for the third Sunday after Epiphany, and in *Ärgre dich, o Seele nicht* (BWV 186a), for the second Sunday of Advent. The melody appears in other cantatas but not Helmbold's text. Bach listed the hymn in the *Orgel-Büchlein* but did not set it.

21. Gojowy, "Kirchenlieder im Umkreis von J. S. Bach," 93.

22. Williams, *The Organ Music of J. S. Bach*, 2nd ed., 362.

23. *BC* 3:897. For a thorough investigation of this cantata, see Eric Chafe, *Tonal Allegory in the Vocal Music of J. S. Bach* (Berkeley: University of California Press, 1991), 91–124. See also Robin A. Leaver: "Eschatology, Theology and Music: Death and Beyond in Bach's Vocal Music," *Irish Musical Studies 8: Bach Studies from Dublin*, ed. Anne Leahy and Yo Tomita (Dublin: Four Courts Press, 2004), 143–146.

24. Luther talked of dying with joy as follows: *Sicut enim Christus per unionem immortalis divinitatis moriendo mortem superavit, ita Christianus per unionem immortalis Christi (que fit per fidem in illum) eciam moriendo mortem superat ac sic Deus diabolum per ipsummet diabolum destruit et alieno oper suum perficet* (*WA* 57[III]:129) [For just as Christ, by reason of his union with immortal divinity, overcame death by dying, so the Christian, by reason of his union with the immortal Christ—which comes about through faith in him—also overcomes death by dying] (*LW* 29:136).

25. Clement, "'Sechs Choräle' BWV 645–650," 287.

26. Clement has suggested that Bach was referring to stanza 2 of *Jesus Christus, unser Heiland* when he composed BWV 689; Albert Clement, *Der dritte Teil der Clavierübung von Johann Sebastian Bach: Musik, Text, Theologie* (Middelburg: Almares, 1999), 287. This stanza refers to the sacrament of the altar in the context of its being a reminder of the cross of Christ that achieved salvation for Christians.

27. Johann Mattheson in *Das Neu-Eröffnete Orchestre* (1713) describes F minor as being used to express "eine gelinde und gelassene, wiewohl dabey tiefe und schwere, mit etwas Verzweiflung vergesellschafte, tödliche Herzens-Angst" [a mild and composed (key) although also deep and heavy, with some associations with despair, deathly heart-felt fear]; cited in Jacobus Kloppers, "Die Interpretation und Wiedergabe der Orgelwerke Bachs: ein Beitrag zur Bestimmung von stilgerechten Prinzipien," PhD diss., Goethe-Universität, Frankfurt am Main, 1965, 135.

Mattheson sometimes exaggerated his ideas, but it is nevertheless noteworthy that there were writings about key characteristics in Bach's lifetime. Wolfgang Auhagen, *Studien zur Tonartencharacteristik in theoretischen Schriften und Kompositionen vom späten 17. bis zum Beginn des 20. Jahrhunderts* (Frankfurt am Main: Lang, 1983) includes an investigation of tonal characteristics in Bach's vocal works but does not delve too deeply into the organ works. Ulrich Meyer, *J .S. Bachs Musik als theonome Kunst* (Wiesbaden: Breitkopf & Härtel, 1979), 76f., writes about the notion of keys and their symbolism as follows: "Die Forschung steht hier vermutlich noch vor vielen Aufgaben" [the research must be directed toward more investigations here]. Eric Chafe, *Tonal Allegory in the Vocal Music of J. S. Bach* (Berkeley: University of California Press, 1991), in a book published more than a decade after Meyer's study, writes extensively about tonal allegory in Bach's vocal works, but as yet there has been no really similar investigation of the significance of keys in the organ works.

28. Although F minor would not have sounded so harsh in the vocal music, nevertheless it seems to have been used by Bach for specific reasons. Chafe, *Tonal Allegory in the Vocal Music of J. S. Bach*, 153, lists cantata movements in F minor and states that "its associations are almost invariably anxiety, tears, tribulation, sin, pain, sorrow, care, suffering and death." The arioso "O Schmerz" (No. 19) from the St. Matthew Passion is an example of one such movement. F minor is the key of greatest suffering in the St. Matthew Passion.

In the St. John Passion, Bach uses the key of F minor for the soprano aria "Zerfließe mein Herz," which talks of the human heart dissolving in tears at the death of Jesus. Another interesting example of an aria in F minor is "Bäche von gesalznen Zähren" from *Ich hatte viel Bekümmernis* (BWV 21). A final example will suffice to demonstrate Bach's use of F minor in the context of man's tribulations in the face of repentance and eternity: the alto aria "Weh der Seele" from the cantata *Herr, deine Augen sehen nach dem Glauben* (BWV 102). This aria is full of affective writing and is striking for its use of the "sighing" motive in the continuo and the dramatic *d-flat* and subsequent *saltus duriusculus* of the oboe in m. 2. All of these elements and the F minor tonality reflect the trials of the Christian as he acknowledges his sin.

29. For a detailed study of this partita, see Albert Clement, "'O Jesu, du edle Gabe': Studien zum Verhältnis von Text und Musik in den Choralpartiten und den Kanonischen Veränderungen von Johann Sebastian Bach," PhD diss., University of Utrecht, 1989, 51–95.

30. *BC* 1:168.

31. See Clement "O Jesu, du edle Gabe," 127ff.

• 8 •

Nun komm der Heiden Heiland

THE HYMN

*T*he text of *Nun komm der Heiden Heiland* is Luther's translation of the fourth-century Latin Advent hymn *Veni redemptor gentium*, attributed to Bishop Ambrose of Milan (334–397).[1] The hymn existed in several German paraphrases before the Reformation, the earliest dating from the twelfth century.[2] The hymn tune was not composed by Ambrosius, nor stanza 8 which was added during the Middle Ages.[3] The earliest source of the melody is a Swiss-Benedictine manuscript dating from 1120. It is possible that it stems from the nearby Benedictine Abbey at St. Gallen, which could perhaps date it as far back as 900.[4] Luther's version was published with the text in 1524 in the Erfurt *Enchiridia* and in Johann Walter's *Geystliche Gesangk Buchleyn* at Wittenberg.[5] It is possible, therefore, that this hymn was written by Luther for Advent 1523.[6] Luther employs a 7.7.7.7 meter, transforming the eight-syllable lines of the original Latin to suit the different metrical pattern. The text of the hymn as it appears in the Weimar hymnbook of 1713, where it is listed under the heading "Von der Menschwerdung JEsu Christi," is as follows:

1. NUn komm der Heyden Heyland/
   der Jungfrauen Kind erkannt/
   des sich wunder' alle Welt/
   GOTT solch Geburt ihm bestellt.

2. Nicht von Manns-Blut noch vom Fleisch/
   allein von dem heilgen Geist/
   ist GOttes Wort wordn ein Mensch/
   und blüht ein Frucht Weibes-Fleisch.

3. Der Jungfrauen Leib schwanger ward/

1. Come now, Savior of the nations,
   Known to be the child of the Virgin,
   All the world marvels that God
   would prepare such a birth for him.

2. Not by the flesh and blood of a man,
   but alone by the Holy Ghost,
   God's word is become human,
   and becomes as the fruit of a woman's flesh.

3. The Virgin's body became with child,

137

doch bleibt Keuschheit rein bewahrt/
leucht herfür manch Tugend schon/
GOtt da war in seinem Thron.

but her chastity was purely preserved.
Many beautiful signs indicated that
God was in his throne.

4. Er gieng aus der Kammer sein/
dem Königlichen Saal so rein/
Gott von Art und Mensch ein Held/
seinn Weg er zu lauffen eilt.

4. He left his chamber,
the royal hall so pure.
God by origin, and man, a champion,
he hurries to run his course.

5. Sein Lauf kam vom Vater her/
und kehrt wieder zum Vater/
fuhr hinunter zu der Höll/
und wieder zu Gottes Stuhl.

5. His course originated with the Father
and returned again to the Father;
went below to hell
and back again to God's seat.

6. Der du bist dem Vater gleich/
führ hinaus den Sieg im Fleisch/
daß dein ewig Gottes Gewalt/
in uns das kranck Fleisch enthalt.

6. You, who are equal to the Father,
take the victory in the flesh
so that your eternal divine power
supports the sick flesh in us.

7. Dein Krippen gläntzt hell und klar/
die Nacht gibt ein neu Licht dar/
tunckel muß nicht kommen drein/
der Glaub bleibt immer im Schein.

7. Your manger shines bright and clear;
the night shines forth a new light.
Darkness must not enter therein.
Faith always remains in the light.

8. Lob sey GOtt dem Vater thon/
lob sey Gott seinm eingen Sohn/
lob sey GOtt dem heilgen Geist/
immer und in Ewigkeit.[7]

8. Praise be to God the Father,
Praise be to God, his only Son,
Praise be to God, the Holy Spirit,
Always and eternally.[8]

Nun komm der Heiden Heiland was the *Hauptlied* or principal hymn for the first Sunday of Advent.[9] The hymn text comprises seven four-line stanzas plus a doxology, concerning itself with Christ's incarnation and the purpose of his life on earth. The opening text, "nun komm" [*veni*], expresses the wish of mankind for Christ's birth on earth. Therefore, this is also a wish for the salvation that comes with the birth of Christ. When Ambrosius (if indeed it is by him) wrote this hymn, the Christian Church did not celebrate Advent as in Bach's day, or indeed today. The observance of Advent as a special time in the church year only began in the fifth and sixth centuries.

The first Sunday of Advent was a special Sunday at Leipzig. It was the first Sunday of the church year, and as such, there were some special liturgical procedures. This Sunday was also linked to Lent as the start of a period of repentance and preparation, in this case for Christmas.[10] Thus a certain paradox existed with the consequent polarity of a festive occasion and a season of repentance and preparation. According to Johannes Kulp, this hymn contains the entire story of salvation.[11] Martin Petzoldt demonstrates how Ambrosius has incorporated the important Christological ideas of the Old and New Testaments into this important Advent hymn.[12]

Stanza 1 speaks directly to Christ, stanzas 2–3 describe the mystery of his birth, and stanzas 4–5 describe the physical process of leaving heaven to carry out his work on earth. Stanza 4 leaves behind the mystical world of the first three stanzas and refers to more earthly matters. Christ leaves the royal hall so pure (stanza 4) to carry out his work on earth. In the last two lines of this stanza, there is a reference to Psalm 19:5–6. The Psalm text refers to the bridegroom leaving his chamber and rejoices as a strong man running a race:

> Er hat die Sonnen eine Hütte in denselben gemacht. Und dieselbe gehet heraus, wie ein Bräutigam aus seiner Kammer, und freuet sich, wie ein Held, zu laufen den Weg. [In them hath he set a tabernacle for the sun, which is as a bridegroom coming out of his chamber, and rejoiceth as a strong man to run a race.]

In the Psalm, the reference is to the sun, which shines to the edge of the heavens. Psalm 19 praises the wonders of God's creation with a special emphasis on light. Light is an important image in the hymn *Nun komm der Heiden Heiland*. In the context of the Psalm, stanza 4 of the hymn could be seen as Christ spreading his light or goodness throughout the world by his incarnation, death, and resurrection. The image of Christ as a bridegroom was a common biblical theme. Luther has commented on this passage from Psalm 19 in his sermon for the first Sunday of Advent:

> Das ist alles von dißem lieblichen anbrechenn des tags, das ist: vom Euangelio gesagt, wilchs die schrifft hoch uund lieblich preysset, denn es macht auch lebendig, frolich, lustig, tettig, unnd bringt alles gutt mit sich. Darumb es auch heyst Euangelium, das ist: eyn lustige bottschafft.[13] [It all refers to the beautiful daybreak of the Gospel. Scripture sublimely exalts the Gospel Day, for it is the source of life, joy, pleasure and energy, and brings all good. Hence the name "Gospel"—joyful news.[14]]

In referring to the beautiful daybreak, Luther is stressing the important Advent theme of light. Stanza 5 refers back to Christ's origin with the Father and his subsequent reunion with him after his life on earth. Stanza 6 is important, as Christ is addressed once more directly as the equal of the Father, claiming his victory. In stanza 7, the light of Christ contrasts with the darkness of evil, representing the triumph of good over evil. The shining bright manger is described in stanza 7. The beliefs of Christianity, which depend on the night when Christ was born, are depicted here in radiant light. Imagery pertaining to light is also contained in the epistle for the first Sunday of Advent (Romans 13:12–14):[15]

> Die Nacht ist vergangen, der Tag aber herbey kommen: So lasset uns ablegen die Werke der Finsternis, und anlegen die Waffen des Lichts. Lasset uns ehrbarlich wandeln, als am Tage, nicht im Fressen und Saufen, nicht im Kammern und Unzucht, nicht in Hader und Neid; Sondern ziehet an den HErrn JEsum Christ, und wartet des Leibes, doch also, daß er nicht geil werde. [The night is far spent, the day is at hand: let us therefore cast off the works of darkness, and let us put on the armor of light. Let us walk honestly as in the day; not in rioting and drunkenness, not in chambering and wantonness, not in strife and envying. But put ye on the Lord Jesus Christ, and make not provision for the flesh, to fulfill the lusts thereof.]

In his sermon for the first Sunday of Advent, Luther equates light with faith and darkness with unbelief:

> drumb sind die wapen des liechts nichts anders denn die werck des glaw- bens. Widderumb, finsternis ist der unglawbe, durch abweßen des Euangeli und Christi, auß menschenleren unnd eygener vornunfft vom teuffell re- girtt; darumb sind die werck der finsterniß, werck des unglawbens.[16] [The armour of light, then, is simply the works of faith. On the other hand, "darkness" is unbelief; it reigns in the absence of the gospel and of Christ, through the instrumentality of the doctrines of men—of human reason— instigated by the devil.[17]]

These statements by Luther are important particularly in the context of stanza 7 of *Nun komm der Heiden Heiland.* Stanza 8 is a doxology.

The traditional, modal form of this melody was commonly used up to the early eighteenth century. Bach often used it in this form: in BWV 36 (movements 6 and 8), in BWV 62 (movements 1 and 6), and in the *Orgel-Büchlein* setting, BWV 599. The melody was mostly transmitted in G or in A dorian. In the second half of the seventeenth century, the Berlin edition of Johannes Crüger's *Praxis pietatis melica* began to present a version of the melody in which the third note of both the first and final phrase was raised chromatically.[18] Nicolaus Bruhns uses the chromatic variant at these two points in his organ setting of the same hymn, as does Bach in BWV 36/2 and 61/1, as well as in BWV 660 and 661.

Nun komm der Heiden Heiland was sung in Leipzig on all four Sundays in Advent and existed in most hymnbooks from around 1600.[19] It is a hymn that preoccupied Bach for much of his working life. He set it in BWV 36, 61, 62, 599, 659, 660, 661, and 699. Very much considered a traditional hymn, *Nun komm der Heiden Heiland* was consistently listed as the *Hauptlied* or main chorale for the first Sunday of Advent and was used by Bach for all three extant cantatas for this Sunday.[20] In BWV 36, Bach sets stanzas 1, 6, and 8; in BWV 61, stanza 1 only; and in BWV 62, stanzas 1 and 8.

Lutheran hymnbooks of the sixteenth and seventeenth centuries consistently begin with *Nun komm der Heiden Heiland*, as does Bach's *Orgel-Büchlein*. However, hymnbooks dating from the end of the seventeenth century began to precede the Advent hymns with hymns suitable for the commencement of worship. The 1681 edition of the Weimar hymnbook followed the older tradition, whereas the later editions followed the later pattern.[21]

NUN KOMM DER HEIDEN HEILAND (BWV 659)

Bach's first setting of *Nun komm der Heiden Heiland* exists in two versions: an earlier Weimar one entitled "*Fantasia*" (BWV 659a) and a later Leipzig revision (BWV 659). The differences lie solely in the ornamental chorale melody. In the later setting, Bach has made the coloratura smoother and more elegant. BWV 659 is headed "*Nun komm der Heÿden Heÿland. a 2 Clav. et Ped.*" in P271 and is of the ornamental chorale type whose origins lie in the chorale settings of Georg Böhm and Dieterich Buxtehude. Neither Böhm nor Buxtehude develop the coloratura *cantus firmus* line to the same extent as Bach, with whom it receives a masterful treatment in the evolution of the ornamental line, as well as in the rich and varied accompanying lines.

In *Nun komm der Heiden Heiland* (BWV 659), continuity is maintained by the ostinato pedal part and the consistent style of melodic writing in both the ornamental *cantus firmus* line and the accompanying manual parts. Between each phrase of the *cantus firmus*, the accompanying parts provide an interlude that on the whole is not related to the *cantus firmus*. The opening *incipit* in the tenor anticipates line 1 of the chorale over a quasi-ostinato-style walking bass. The alto enters two beats after the tenor with a *fuga realis*, or answer. The ornamental *cantus firmus* enters in the soprano at m. 4.2. This voice states clearly the first four notes of the *cantus firmus* (although *f-sharp*[1] instead of *f-natural*[1]).[22] After this, the coloratura is expanded as also happens in BWV 768/1.[23] The ornamental chorale is treated sequentially in m. 5 and the first half of m. 6, which can be termed *climax* or *auxexis*, with a rising *tirata defectiva* to *e-flat*[2] before an elaborate close in G minor.

The final note of the first phrase overlaps with the beginning of the first interlude. The walking ostinato bass resumes with the first phrase of the chorale disguised in the tenor part in m. 8. It is less clear here, however, than in the opening measures. A plagal cadence leads to the presentation of line 2 of the *cantus firmus* which enters at m. 11. Again, only the first four notes can be identified. A threefold sequential passage of the same length as that of the first phrase follows (*climax/auxexis*), rising to g^2, which is the highest note so far. The coloratura continues to climb, reaching c^3, the highest note in the piece, before an elaborate cadence to B-flat major at m. 15.

The walking bass begins again on the second half of m. 16. This interlude lasts for just two measures, with only the slightest hint of the opening notes of line 3 of the chorale in the tenor. The coloratura is marked by even more sequential writing than in the previous phrases. Additionally, the harmonic writing is more daring, with the use of a 9-8 suspension on the first note of the *cantus firmus* at m. 19 giving a very expressive clashing semitone. The opening figure of the phrase is repeated sequentially, outlining the first three notes of the *cantus firmus*. After this, the *cantus firmus* disappears into further sequences in mm. 20 and 21, where there is a reference to the "sighing" motive that falls sequentially to m. 22. This "sighing" motive is heard twice in m. 21. The second time it is heard, the first two sixteenth notes are completely alone without any accompanying parts. This is the only moment in BWV 659 where Bach allows the solo line to be stated unaccompanied. As well as utilizing the "sighing" motive in the ornamental *cantus firmus*, Bach also refers to it in the pedal in m. 21. The entire phrase reaches a climax at m. 22 in an ornamental Neapolitan sixth chord that leads to an inverted cadence in G minor followed by an interrupted cadence to end the third phrase.

The slurred repeated-note motive begins again at m. 23.4 and continues to overlap with the introduction of the final phrase of the chorale. This motive is developed sequentially in both tenor and alto, with the tonality shifting to C minor for this interlude. Measure 28 begins with the walking bass in C minor moving quickly back to G minor. With the exception of some of the accompaniment at the outset of this phrase, this is exactly the same as the opening phrase. Beginning at m. 32, this three-measure coda that pays homage to Buxtehude's setting of the same name also shows the strong influence of Böhm. Improvisatory in character, it is in the main over a tonic pedal, containing for the second time only in this piece the highest note, c^3.

Interpretations by Other Authors

Along with *Schmücke dich, o liebe Seele* (BWV 654), *Nun komm der Heiden Heiland* (BWV 659) has inspired many authors to great poetic heights in their descriptions of this piece. Many have commented on the ethereal and tranquil atmosphere of the composition.

Albert Schweitzer considers that this setting of *Nun komm der Heiden Heiland* points to the mystical elements of the text.[24] He refers to the image of light as follows:

> Es ist eine Musik, die den Hörer in das Dunkel des Advents führt und ihm die Sterne des Himmels verheißungsvoll erstrahlen läßt.[25] [It is music where the listener travels in the darkness of Advent and before him shines the promising star of heaven.]

Hans Luedtke believes that BWV 659 can only refer to stanza 1 of the hymn.[26] For Luedtke, BWV 659 represents waiting for the Savior with great longing: "Der Heyland wird voll Sehnsucht erwartet." He sees a relationship between BWV 659 and the great G minor Fantasy (BWV 542) in their mutual inclination toward melancholy.[27]

Charles Sanford Terry suggests that the three settings of *Nun komm der Heiden Heiland* (BWV 659–661) illustrate the hymn as a whole rather than any particular stanza.[28]

Stainton de B. Taylor describes BWV 659 as having an overall pervading mood of "joyful expectancy." He also refers to the note of poignancy ensured in the sharpening of the fourth note of the chorale melody, with the resulting diminished fourth adding a touch of sadness. In his view, the "leaning" note figures represent mental anguish or penitence, but he also finds the mood to be one of confidence and joy.[29]

Hermann Keller sees the solemn veiling of the chorale melody as being expressive of the impenetrable mystery of the incarnation of God's Son.[30] In his opinion, the work has a fantastic beauty that is never fully perceived, and he regards the three arrangements as belonging together internally.[31]

Jacques Chailley regards only stanza 1 as being relevant to BWV 659.[32] In his view, the first phrase of the ornamental chorale represents pleading with the Savior, with the effect of the supplication being intensified by the rising sequences in mm. 5–6. He suggests that the rising and falling pedal lines represent respectively the prayer to the Savior and the descent of the Savior to earth. Chailley suggests that the perfection of the three-part writing in mm. 8–10 is a reference to the Virgin and that the aura of virginal grace pervades the remainder of the second phrase. According to Chailley, the "sighing" motive first referred to in m. 21 prepares for the fourth phrase, representing Christ carrying the sins of the world. Although the music of the fourth phrase is the same as that of the first, Chailley considers that there is a difference in significance. In his view, the tragic mood of the piece is lessened by the hopeful ascent to *b-flat*^{2}, ending the piece in the joyful anticipation of Christmas.

While not reaching any firm conclusions, Peter Williams proposes many possibilities for notions of imagery in the very varied accompaniment of BWV 659.[33]

Russell Stinson states that the work projects a "deep sense of mysticism quite in keeping with the theme of Christ's incarnation."[34] The absence of the actual chorale melody in the right hand for most of the time could be a depiction of the great mystery of the incarnation, according to Stinson. In conclusion, he comments that Bach may have had the text that concludes the first stanza in mind: "All the world is *amazed* that God gave him such a birth" (Stinson's italics).[35]

Assessment

Most scholars write in general terms about the mystical atmosphere of expectancy in BWV 659. Only Hans Luedtke, Jacques Chailley, and Russell Stinson refer specifically to stanza 1. With three settings of this hymn in one collection, it is logical that Bach would begin with stanza 1, but this must still be proven. Examination of the musical features of BWV 659 may lead to a different stanza of the hymn.

BWV 659 (along with BWV 662) is one of the most ornate chorale preludes in the "Leipzig" chorales. In no other piece in P271 is the *cantus firmus* so disguised in the elaborate passage work of the solo voice. This feature separates it from all other works in this collection. Other striking characteristics include the continuo-style bass, many examples of the *figura corta*, persistent use of the "sighing" motive from m. 21, the ornamental Neapolitan chord at m. 22, and many chromatic inflections throughout the piece. These aspects need to be related to a particular stanza or group of stanzas.

Before turning to the music, it may be helpful to first consider the link between incarnation and atonement in Lutheran theology while also investigating the eschatological significance of *Nun komm der Heiden Heiland*.

Excursus: Incarnation and Passion—The Eschatological Significance of Nun komm der Heiden Heiland

Why should chorale preludes based on *Nun komm der Heiden Heiland* be included in a collection united by an eschatological theme? The link between incarnation and Passion, and therefore salvation, has been shown by many.[36] The saving of mankind begins with the birth of Christ, and therefore his suffering and Passion begin with his birth. This is why a stanza of Paul Gerhardt's *Wie soll ich dich empfangen?* is heard as the first chorale of part 1 of the Christmas

Oratorio. Once again, the contrast of light and dark is found, a theme strongly associated with Advent and Christmas. The sinner asks Christ to set his light beside him: "Oh Jesu, Jesu! Setze mir selbst die Fakkel bei" [Oh Jesu, Jesu! Set thy light beside me]. *Wie soll ich dich empfangen?* was listed as a hymn for the first Sunday of Advent in many hymnbooks, including the Weimar hymnbook of 1713.[37] The first five notes of this chorale melody are heard in the accompaniment at m. 21 of BWV 659. This is also precisely at the moment where Bach introduces the slurred "sighing" motive that has been associated with Passion in many of his works.[38] At the end of the Christmas Oratorio, Bach treats the same chorale in a more upbeat manner, with an orchestration that includes trumpets and timpani. Robin A. Leaver has discussed the link between incarnation and Passion:

> Here Bach links the Incarnation with the Atonement and sees them not as past events but in terms of eschatological completeness. This chorale movement comes at the end of the cycle of six cantatas celebrating the Nativity of Christ and the use of the Passion Chorale melody reminds the hearers that Christ was born to die; but the musical setting, with trumpets and timpani, proclaim eschatological joy in the finished work of Christ.[39]

Thus Advent is clearly associated not only with the birth and Passion of Christ but also with the final coming. Eric Chafe has described the various manifestations of the coming of Christ. He refers to Christ coming in the flesh (past), in the spirit (present), and in judgment at the end of time (future).[40] He continues,

> At Advent and Christmas, therefore, the fulfilment of Old Testament prophecy in the events of the New Testament merged with tropological and eschatological perspectives on those events to articulate the bond between past, present and future in the experience of the believer.[41]

Advent has eschatological significance because it marks a new beginning—the end of one church year and the beginning of another. The broader significance of Advent is that it marks the preparation for the birth of Christ, which itself leads to the salvation of mankind. Part of the epistle of the day (Romans 13:11) also emphasizes this point: "For now is our salvation nearer than when we believed." The use of the word "nun" in "Nun komm der Heiden Heiland" can be interpreted as the "now" of salvation, as seen in the *Nunc dimittus*. In his song of praise, Simeon describes Christ as "ein Licht zu erleuchten die Heiden," thus showing Christ in the context of light as Savior. There is also the sense of using the word "komm" as a prayer or request.[42] The text of the tenor aria in BWV 61 also highlights the idea of coming. The believer invites Christ to his church, giving all true teaching and blessing the altar:

Komm, Jesu, komm zu deiner Kirche	Come, Jesus, come to thy church
und gib ein selig neues Jahr.	and grant a blessed new year,
Befördre deines Namens Ehre,	advance thy name's honor,
erhalte die gesunde Lehre	preserve the sound teaching
und segne Kanzel und Altar!	and bless pulpit and altar.

In his use of this text, Bach appears to be associating the sacrament of the altar with Advent and Christ's coming. These ideas are confirmed in the following bass recitative where the quotation from Revelation 3:20 verifies the eschatological implications:

> Siehe! Ich stehe vor der Tür und klopfe an. So jemand meine Stimme hören wird und die Tür auftun, zu dem werde ich eingehen und das Abendmahl mit ihm halten, und er mit mir. [Behold, I stand at the door, and knock: if any man hear my voice, and open the door, I will come in to him, and will sup with him, and he with me.]

The second movement of BWV 62 also clearly shows the Eucharistic and eschatological significance of Advent and the impending coming of Christ:

Hier werden die Schätze des Himmels entdecket,	Here are the treasures of heaven discovered
hier wird uns ein göttliches Manna bestellt,	here is for us a divine manna appointed
o Wunder!	o wonder!
die Keuschheit wird gar nicht beflecket.	Virginity is not all blemished.

The promise of eternal life is seen in the treasures of heaven and the heavenly manna, which refers to the sacrament of the altar. Once more, Advent and salvation are linked by Bach. This is confirmed in the ensuing recitative for bass where the text refers to saving the fallen ones—"und uns Gefallne zu erkaufen" [and us fallen ones to redeem]. The image of light is also found in this recitative. In the final line of text, Bach uses the *figura corta* for the word "heller." Sometimes Bach uses this figure to portray the joy of salvation that results from the cross.[43] The closing movement of BWV 61 is a setting of the final four lines of Philipp Nicolai's *Wie schön leuchtet der Morgenstern*. The eschatological implications are clear:

Amen, amen!	Amen, amen!
Komm du schöne Freudenkrone,	Come thou beautiful crown of joy,
bleib nicht lange!	tarry not long!
Deiner wart ich mit verlangen.	I wait for thee with yearning.

"Amen, amen" is a reference to Revelation 22:20. Nicolai's hymn in BWV 61 clearly links the birth of Christ and eternal salvation. This is shown musically by Bach in the soaring violin line, with the first violin ending on g^3. *Wie schön leuchtet der Morgenstern* was listed as an Advent hymn in hymnbooks at Eisenach, Leipzig, and Dresden.[44] In his sermon for the third Sunday of Advent (*Evangelisches Praeservativ*), Heinrich Müller quotes the final three lines of *Wie schön leuchtet der Morgenstern*."[45] This is in the context of Christ's depiction throughout the scriptures as one who *will* come. Therefore Bach's inclusion of three settings of Luther's chorale *Nun komm der Heiden Heiland* in a collection united by an eschatological theme seems justified.

Text-Music Relationships

Investigation into the text of *Nun komm der Heiden Heiland* may help to solve the issue of the text-music relationships in BWV 659. Stanza 1 is clearly very important, as it shows Christ as Savior. This aspect of the incarnation was important to Lutherans and it is not stated so clearly in any other stanza. The next four stanzas are also related to the birth of Christ, but no one stanza seems to be as strong as the opening in terms of the significance of Christ's birth. Equally, it does not seem logical that Bach would begin with one of the final three stanzas when he had two more settings to go. It seems reasonable to suggest that from a theological point of view, Bach may logically have chosen to depict stanza 1 in BWV 659. Further investigation of the music may help to establish this point.

It might be helpful to first explore how Bach uses the "sighing" motive in BWV 659. This is very prominent from m. 21. As shown previously, Bach frequently uses this kind of writing in the context of Christ's Passion. The Lutheran link between incarnation and atonement is clear and may help to provide an interpretation of this motive. It may be possible to find a stanza that would justify the use of this figure. The only possibilities seem to be stanza 1 (with the mention of Savior), stanza 5 (with the reference to hell, which could be related to Christ's sacrifice), and stanza 6 (with the reference to victory in the flesh, for the same reasons as stanza 5). The chromatic harmony can be related to these stanzas for the same reasons. It is perhaps possible that Bach is making a point about Christ as Savior in BWV 659 with the "sighing" motive and the chromatic harmony.

Bach uses ornamental lines such as the one found in BWV 659 in many contexts. The hiding of the chorale melody in the solo line could have meaning for the text. Stinson has suggested that this process depicts the mystery of the incarnation. If this is so, then the most obvious stanza seems to be stanza 1. Here incarnation and atonement are most clearly linked.

A closer inspection of Bach's portrayal of the first line of the *cantus firmus* may help. Following the entry of the solo right hand, the first four notes of the chorale melody are heard, after which the remainder of the line disappears into an elaborate melismatic passage where the *cantus firmus* is barely audible. If one examines the opening line of stanza 1, then the text for the first four

notes is "Nun komm der Heyd." It is possible that Bach may be using the subsequent passage work as a deliberate means of emphasizing the text "Heyden
Heyland." There does not seem to be another stanza that would fit in this way.

Following this brief discussion of text and music, it appears that Bach was
portraying the text of stanza 1 in BWV 659. The use of the "sighing" motive
appears to imply this stanza which mentions Christ as Savior. Similarly, the
departure of the melodic line into melismatic passage work after the fourth
note of the *cantus firmus* also seems most appropriate in the context of stanza 1.
Further detailed analysis of this composition may help to establish this point.

Bach's treatment of line 1 of the *cantus firmus*, as outlined above, seems
to be placing special emphasis on the text "Heyden Heyland." It is useful to
note Albert Clement's observations on variation 3 of BWV 769 regarding the
word "Heiland."[46] He refers to Gerd Zacher's suggestion that m. 18 of this
variation is depicting the word "Heiland." Zacher also suggests that the alto
motive in m. 6 on the word "Christ" and in m. 18 on "Heiland" form a cross
symbol with the notes *c-d-c-b-c*. The relative pitches of the notes give the cross:
middle-high-middle-low-middle, thus symbolizing the Greek letter Chi = X
= Christ.[47] Bach uses a similar motive in BWV 659 beginning in m. 5 and
continuing to m. 8 where the solo melody of the first phrase ends. Here, as in
BWV 769.3, the five-note *gruppo* forms a cross symbol as follows:

a
g–g–g
f#

Bach also incorporates the *figura corta* into this motive with the cross symbol in
m. 5. In m. 6, Bach adds the *figura corta* immediately following the *syncopatio*
figure. As suggested above, he could use the *figura corta* in conjunction with
either the *passus duriusculus* or *syncopatio* to illustrate the paradoxical aspect of
Christ's sacrifice. On the one hand, the negative *syncopatio* or *passus duriusculus*
can be related to the cross, while on the other hand the use of the *figura corta*
shows confidence in God's goodness in providing salvation. Bach's use of the
figura corta in combination with a motive incorporating the cross symbol may
have equal significance in BWV 659. In m. 6 of BWV 659, the text refers to
"Heyland" or Savior, and so, by his use of these figures, he may be sending the
listener a definite theological message. Bach uses the cross symbol in relation
to the incarnation in the *et incarnatus est* of the B Minor Mass. This motive is
present in the strings in every measure of this movement. It is also found in
the other settings of *Nun komm der Heiden Heiland* in the "Leipzig" chorales
(BWV 660 and 661).

Similar musical motives are found in the statement of the second phrase of the *cantus firmus*. In m. 14, Bach uses the *gruppo* incorporating the cross symbol and the *figura corta*. It is possible that Bach was thinking of the word "Heyland" as a *locus topicus*. Each phrase of this setting uses the previously mentioned *figura corta* motive in combination with the cross motive. In m. 14, the highest note of the piece, *c³*, is heard. The mood of this section (mm. 9–16) is very positive because of the move toward the relative major, the *anabasis* of the ornamental chorale line, and the reaching of the highest note. The *tirata perfecta* of m. 15 with the subsequent perfect cadence to the relative major confirms the positive *Affekt*.[48] The text at this point is "der Jungfrauen Kind erkannt." The hope of the world lies in this tiny baby, and it is fitting that a positive air pervades this section of the piece.

The third phrase maintains many of the elements of the preceding two phrases while also becoming increasingly expressive. Bach may be expressing the wonder of the world ("des sich wundert alle Welt") through the figure of *auxexis* in the chorale melody at mm. 19 and 20. This figure is used to describe the repetition of a melodic idea a step higher.[49] The use of the *circolo mezzo* within the *auxexis* figure seems to add further intensification. With regard to this figure, Dietrich Bartel quotes Warren Kirkendale as follows:

> As a symbol of perfection, the musical circle has a long tradition of expressing not only circular concepts but also the eternal, infinite and complete, ultimately symbolising God.[50]

The use of the *circolo mezzo* in this context may be appropriate to depict the miracle of the birth of Christ. Bach uses this figure elsewhere in the same context. In the opening movement of *Nun komm der Heiden Heiland* (BWV 61), the words "des sich wundert alle Welt" are depicted in a *circolo mezzo* figure (see example 8.1). The opening movement of *Nun komm der Heiden Heiland* (BWV 62) has circular figures throughout, for example, the first violin part in mm. 3–4, 5–6, and so forth. In this context, the circular figure is combined with the *figura corta* and later on with the two-note slurred motive. This appears to suggest that the recurrence of the *circolo mezzo*, "sighing" motives, and the *figura corta* in Advent cantatas (BWV 61 and 62) and chorale preludes (BWV 659–661) could have symbolic meaning.

Example 8.1.   BWV 61 (mm. 33ff.)

In m. 21 of BWV 659, the slurred sixteenth-note "sighing" motive is introduced. It is heard in combination with the *figura corta* on beats 1 and 2 of this measure, after which it is repeated a step lower for the next two beats. In baroque rhetoric, this was known as *repetitio per gradus*. On the second hearing of this "sighing" motive, the *cantus firmus* is heard completely unaccompanied for the only time in the piece. Bach may be stressing the importance of this motive by presenting it in this way. This figure is significant, as it appears to be related to the cross and the Passion of Christ.[51] At m. 21.3, the "sighing" motive is heard in the pedal, the only time it occurs. Up to this point the bass has been very much a basso continuo, with no change in style. From mm. 21–23, the bass part becomes more static. It may not be a coincidence that this happens just as the "sighing" motive is introduced. The combination of the change in bass style and the unaccompanied *cantus firmus* at m. 21.4 might be related to Christ's Passion. There may be significance to the break in the flow of the bass, with all parts stopping on an elaborate Neapolitan-sixth chord at m. 23. The same combination of Neapolitan harmonies with the "sighing" motive can be found in the *Agnus Dei* of the B Minor Mass. In the case of the *Agnus Dei*, the reference to the cross of Christ is clear: the Lamb of God takes away the sins of the world by his death on the cross (John 1:36).

In BWV 659, the slurred sixteenth-note motive assumes even greater significance in the ensuing interlude. A striking example of the use of this motive occurs in *O Lamm Gottes unschuldig* (BWV 618). Bach combines the slurred "sighing" motive with the *figura corta*. As a Passion hymn, it is no surprise to find this slurred motive. The use of the *figura corta* may imply the joy that Lutherans feel with the salvation that the sacrifice of Christ offers.[52]

In many of Bach's works relating to the birth of Christ, he employs long pedal notes signifying the world standing still at the wonder of the divine birth.[53] While this particular slowing down of the harmonic movement in m. 23 of BWV 659 does not constitute a pedal note, it does create a similar effect.

The slurred "sighing" motive continues, linking the third and fourth phrase of the chorale. The significance of this motive has already been noted above. The final phrase of the chorale is identical to the first. The text of the final phrase, "Gott solch Geburt ihm bestellt," does not seem in itself to be specifically depicted in this phrase. It seems more likely that Bach is referring back to the *locus topicus* of the word "Heyland," as the melody of the final phrase is the same as the first line of the *cantus firmus*. Bach ends BWV 659 with an elaborate three-measure coda, in the main over a tonic pedal, possibly reflecting Buxtehude's setting of the same chorale. The chromaticisms here are perhaps a further reminder of the word "Heyland." Particularly striking is the move from *e-flat*^{2} to *c-sharp*^{2} at m. 33.3. As noted above, this kind of

Neapolitan harmony was frequently used by Bach when there was a reason in the text, such as Passion or suffering.[54]

★ ★ ★

In BWV 659, Bach appears to show how incarnation and atonement are interconnected in Lutheran theology. Even within the context of the joyous anticipation of Christmas, there is a reminder that Christ was born to die, an issue to which Bach returns time and again in his music. Because of this, he seems to be stressing in particular the idea of Christ as Savior, as seen in the cross motives, the chromatic harmony, and the persistent use of the "sighing" motive. Some of these features return in the other two chorale preludes on *Nun komm der Heiden Heiland*, as discussed in the following sections.

NUN KOMM DER HEIDEN HEILAND (BWV 660)

BWV 660 is a trio bearing the heading "*Trio sup[er] Nun komm der Heyden Heÿland. a 2 Clav. et Ped. a due bassi e canto fermo*" in P271. This setting of *Nun komm der Heiden Heiland* exists in three versions: BWV 660a, 660b, and 660.[55] BWV 660a dates from Bach's Weimar period, with BWV 660 being the final revised Leipzig version. An autograph copy of BWV 660a is found at the back of P271. BWV 660b originates from the first quarter of the eighteenth century.[56] BWV 660a and 660 are set as a trio with decorated *cantus firmus* in the soprano, accompanied by two obbligato bass lines. In BWV 660b, the *cantus firmus* is unadorned in the pedal, with the higher of the two bass lines transposed up an octave for the right hand, the original pedal line now in the left hand. There is no autograph manuscript of BWV 660b. A copy exists in P802 by Johann Tobias Krebs. This latter version is unsatisfactory, since the unadorned *cantus firmus* fails to fill the gaps in the counterpoint, and the resulting harmony from transferring the two bass parts to a treble register produces a somewhat clumsy effect.[57] BWV 660a differs from BWV 660 mainly in the coloratura writing of the *cantus firmus*, which is less ornamented. In m. 33 of BWV 660, Bach has altered the left hand. Peter Williams suggests that Bach may have miscopied the last two beats as if their source had a tenor clef.[58] Measure 33.3 of BWV 660 seems a more satisfying musical solution. Other differences lie in the arpeggiation in BWV 660a of the chords in mm. 15 and 42, and in the final major chord of BWV 660a. Williams argues that the chord in m. 15 is in the dominant major, so it is possible that Bach intended that the final tonic chord also be major. He observes how in the autograph of BWV 660, the final measure is very cramped, and that therefore it is possible that a natural sign was omitted in error.[59]

This most unusual setting of *Nun komm der Heiden Heiland* (BWV 660) is unique among Bach's chorale preludes. It is a three-part texture, the uppermost of which is an ornamental working of the *cantus firmus*, with the left hand and pedal forming a strict and often canonic counterpoint below. Both of the lower parts remain within a low tessitura for much of the piece, creating a texture that is rarely found in Bach's writing, least of all in his organ works. According to Albert Schweitzer, this piece was like a contrapuntal exercise from a cantata.[60] Harvey Grace finds this trio to be "one of the most curious of all the chorale preludes."[61] He shares Schweitzer's opinion that it could be an instrumental movement from one of the lost cantatas, or perhaps an arrangement of the Schübler kind.

Roswitha Bruggaier argues that BWV 660a may have been originally composed as a piece with viola da gamba obbligato.[62] The range of the middle line of BWV 660 corresponds to that of the tenor or bass gamba, while the lower line fits the range of the cello. In Bach's organ music, there is no example of the sudden introduction of a chord in one voice of a three-part texture, as appears in mm. 15 and 42 of BWV 660.[63] Bruggaier states that this would not be unusual in the gamba literature.[64] Because of the close position of the two chords, they would be unplayable on the cello, but suitable however for the gamba. According to Bruggaier, the spreading of the two chords in BWV 660 sounds more natural on the gamba than on the organ.[65] While her arguments are illuminating, it is also possible to show the suitability of the writing in BWV 660 for the organ, in particular with the pedal, where the sixteenth notes fall easily into alternate toe patterns. The decorated *cantus firmus*, as it appears here, is not unusual in itself in Bach's organ works. It is possible that BWV 660a was originally a cantata aria for solo soprano, obbligato viola da gamba, and continuo. The thematic relationship between the two lower lines of both BWV 660a and BWV 660 might suggest that the lower line was not merely a continuo but a typical pedal part of a kind found in many of Bach's organ works. Furthermore, there is no existing example of this kind of cello line in Bach's vocal music.[66]

Nun komm der Heiden Heiland (BWV 660) is very compact, concise, and carefully planned. The left hand and pedal contain a mixture of ostinato and ritornello style, with the coloratura *cantus firmus* seeming to be influenced by Böhm. Although the idea of an opening and closing ritornello also exists in the Schübler Chorales, this kind of writing is not to be found elsewhere in Bach's organ works. The use of two bass voices seems to be unprecedented. The two lower parts provide interludes between each statement of the ornamental chorale melody, as well as a six-and-a-half-measure opening and five-measure closing phrase. Although set in a highly ornate fashion, the notes of the chorale melody are clearly discernible throughout.

The left hand begins with a motive derived from the first six notes of the *cantus firmus*. In this setting, Bach is using the chromatic form of the chorale melody that originated in the second half of the seventeenth century.[67] The pedal imitates exactly a half measure later and continues canonically to the end of m. 4. The next two measures are concerned with a falling sequence, coming to rest on the dominant seventh of G minor, before concluding the phrase with a perfect cadence in the tonic key. The right hand enters halfway through m. 6 with the first phrase of the chorale melody. Each note of the hymn tune is present, with the phrase also containing many ornamental notes. The left hand and pedal are for the most part written in strict counterpoint, referring both to the opening motive and the sequential patterns of mm. 4–6. In the passage that follows, Bach continues the sequence he concluded in m. 6, but this time the roles of the left hand and pedal are reversed. The pedal takes the falling sixteenth-note motive and the left hand the eighth notes, bringing the phrase to a perfect cadence in the dominant at m. 15. This interlude uses the same thematic material as the opening phrase, although not in the same order. The motive that opened the piece now appears at the close of this phrase, again with the function of the left hand and pedal reversed.

Measures 15–17 are treated in the manner of a strict canon. The right hand reenters with the chorale melody in m. 17. Again, all the notes of the *cantus firmus* are clearly defined within the decorative melodic line. The accompanying parts use the two motives of the opening phrase, once more in strict counterpoint, the tonality remaining centered on G minor. In the following interlude, Bach moves from G minor to B-flat major. The interlude presents two canonic statements of the opening motive, first in G minor and second in the relative major. The right hand recommences with the *cantus firmus* at m. 24. This is accompanied by the falling sixteenth-note motive in both left hand and pedal, bringing the phrase to a perfect cadence in G minor at m. 27, the highest note, g^2, being reached in m. 26. The beginning of the next interlude overlaps with the close of the preceding phrase, with the left hand reintroducing the opening motive halfway through m. 26. The pedal follows in strict imitation while chromatically altering the d' in m. 27 to an *a-flat'* in order to modulate to the key of C minor. The falling sequence continues from m. 30, reaching a perfect cadence in C minor at m. 33. Measures 30–33 reproduce the music of mm. 4–7, this time in the key of C minor.

The melodic writing of the right hand, which reenters at m. 33, is practically identical to that of the opening phrase of the *cantus firmus*. The accompanying parts differ only in the opening measure of the phrase because of the C minor tonality. The final note of the *cantus firmus* coincides with the beginning of the coda or closing ritornello, which lasts from m. 39 to 42. Measures 39–42 correspond to mm. 12–15, this time being in the tonic key. Below the final eighth-note chord in the left hand, the pedal sounds for a half note.

Interpretations by Other Authors

This most unusual setting of Luther's *Nun komm der Heiden Heiland* has puzzled many writers. Some have dismissed it as strange and incomprehensible, without trying to uncover Bach's possible intentions.

Philipp Spitta refers to this setting as being startlingly reckless and almost unapproachable in the abruptness of its character.[68]

Albert Schweitzer feels sure that this setting is a transcription.[69] He poses the question as to whether or not the second variant, BWV 660b, is the definitive one since it presents the *cantus firmus* unaltered.[70]

According to Hans Luedtke, stanzas 4 and 5 are relevant to this setting.[71] He claims that the first variant, BWV 660a, is the best version, since the *cantus firmus* is here most clearly defined. In his opinion, the heading "a 2 Clav. e pedale" is more suitable than the misleading "a due bassi" of the other two settings.[72] Luedtke feels in particular that the last two lines of stanza 4 of this hymn, "Gott von Art und Mensch ein Held/ sein'n Weg zu laufen er eilt," are most clearly represented in this setting.

Harvey Grace refers to this piece as "one of the most curious of all the chorale preludes."[73] He comments on the diminished fourth, the numerous clashes, the falling sevenths, and the use of bass voices, which produce a piece "so dark in mood as to make it repellent on first acquaintance."[74]

Stainton de B. Taylor refers to this piece as a "gloomy trio."[75] He finds the music to be of a "curiously pessimistic tone, and not among Bach's more inspired efforts, although it mirrors the penitential aspect of the hymn truly enough." He remarks, "yet Bach must have thought highly of it to include it in a collection which numbers so many of his highest flights of technique and imagination."[76]

Hermann Keller is puzzled by the two basses and suggests that they represent Christ's descent into hell.[77]

Ulrich Meyer does not see much connection between the text of this hymn and the musical setting. In an earlier study, he refers to Keller's suggestion that the words "fuhr hinunter zu der Höll" of stanza 5 were represented in the descending basses of the counterpoint, stating that this is the only possible relationship to the text. In his later study he denies any relationship to the text.[78]

Jacques Chailley proposes that Bach does not make specific references to the text in BWV 660 but represents the general idea of supplication to the Savior following his descent on earth.[79] He sees the diminished fourth in the opening motive as a motive of supplication. As with other commentators, he suggests that the descending lines of the two basses represent Christ's descent on earth. In his view, the short final chord portrays God abandoning his only Son.[80]

Helene Werthemann sees a connection between stanza 6 of the hymn and BWV 660.[81] According to her, the use of a coloratura *cantus firmus* usually represents imploring or pleading (cf. BWV 659 and BWV 654), and therefore the words of stanza 5 would not be relevant. She proposes that the use of the bass voices could represent God as the basic fundamental.[82] Werthemann draws a parallel with the *et in unum Dominum* duet from the B minor Mass where the sentiments expressed in the text are exactly the same as those of stanza 6: "et in unum Dominum Jesum Christum consubstantialem Patri" [and in one Lord Jesus Christ, only Son of the Father]. In this duet, the soprano and alto sing in canon throughout.

Peter Williams states that this texture is unique, while in principle suggesting the obbligato lines of a cantata aria or of certain trio sonata textures of the later seventeenth century.[83] Keller's theory that the descending bass represents Christ's descent into hell seems unlikely, according to Williams, and he also disagrees with Chailley's suggestion that the short final chord represents God abandoning his only Son.[84]

As seen from this discussion, this is a composition that raises many questions. Some answers may be found in further investigation into the relationship between text and music, which is the subject of the next section.

Assessment

Various commentators have seen connections between stanzas 4, 5, and 6 and BWV 660, while others have made no connection to the text at all. Closer examination of the musical characteristics of BWV 660 can help to determine with more certainty which stanza Bach may have been depicting.

The most striking musical feature of BWV 660 is the very strict and often canonic imitation between the two accompanying parts. Walter Blankenburg has referred to Bach's use of canon as representing an imitation of God's creative order.[85] In many of Bach's works, he has used this technique to symbolize law and order.[86] Although not a strict canon, BWV 660 contains canonic writing. It is very likely that Bach intended the strict counterpoint to have symbolic meaning, such as the use of canon in the variations on *Vom Himmel hoch da komm ich her* (BWV 769) as referring to Christ fulfilling the will of the Father.[87] Stanzas 4 through 6 of *Nun komm der Heiden Heiland* deal with the Savior's coming to earth to save mankind by his sacrifice and his subsequent return to the Father, thus fulfilling the will of the Father. Thus the canonic writing in BWV 660 may be related to the Son fulfilling the will of the Father.

As shown in the earlier discussion regarding the text of the hymn, stanzas 4 to 6 are concerned with Christ's presence on earth. Christ fulfilled God's law on earth, so it seems reasonable to suggest that the answer to the issues of text–music relationships in BWV 660 may be found in these stanzas. The first three stanzas, being concerned with the actual incarnation and birth, do not seem appropriate in this context. Similarly, there is no apparent reason why Bach might have set stanzas 7 and 8. Stanza 4 shows Christ leaving his heavenly home to do his work on earth. Stanza 5 mentions the Father, which may be a stronger argument for the employment of canon. In stanza 6, Christ is referred to as being equal to the Father. This may be linked to Bach's use of canonic writing. The equality between the Father and the Son may be expressed in the use of two lines imitating strictly at the octave. In this Advent hymn, Christ as Savior is fulfilling the law.

Close examination of the text and its possible relationship to the music seems to be leading to stanza 6. In m. 27.4, Bach writes an *a-flat*⁰ where he had previously written an *a-natural*⁰ in accordance with the *cantus firmus*. It is very likely that this striking alteration is related to the text. It is presented at the start of the interlude that leads to the final line of the stanza. Inspection of the final lines of all stanzas may help to find an answer. The only possibility appears to be the final line of stanza 6: "in uns das kranck Fleisch enthalt." Bach employs a similar "hard leap," or *saltus duriusculus*, for the word "kranken" in BWV 78/2. It therefore seems reasonable to suggest that in the sudden introduction of *a-flat*⁰, Bach is depicting the word "kranck."

It is useful to examine another movement where Bach sets stanza 6 of *Nun komm der Heiden Heiland*: the Advent cantata *Schwingt freudig euch empor* (BWV 36/6).[88] In BWV 36/6, the *cantus firmus* is heard in the tenor accompanied by two oboes d'amore and continuo in strict and often canonic counterpoint. The canonic writing could have a similar meaning to that of BWV 660, that is, portraying Christ as the equal of the Father.

Helene Werthemann's comments on the *et in unum Dominum* from the B Minor Mass are insightful. The Father and Christ are shown as being the same, yet different, in the canonic writing of this movement.[89] Philipp Spitta has also pointed out the significance of canon at the unison in this movement of the B Minor Mass:

> Bach treats the parts in canon on the unison at the beginning of the principal subject each time, not using the canon on the fourth below till the second bar; thus both the unity and the separate existence of the two Persons are brought out. The intention is unmistakable, since the musical scheme allows of the canonic imitation on the fourth below from the very beginning.[90]

For Spitta, Bach deliberately uses canon at the unison to create unity and also to depict independence. Luther's commentary on Psalm 110:1 provides a useful insight into the idea of Christ as equal to the Father as follows:

> Setze dich (spricht er) neben mich auff den hohen stuel, da ich sitze, und sey mir gleich. Denn das heisst er neben jm sitzen, nicht zum füssen, sondern zur rechten, das ist, jnn die selbige Maiestet und gewalt, die da heisst eine Gottliche Gewalt.[91] [Sit next to me on the exalted throne upon which I sit, and be my equal. To sit next to Him—at His right hand, not at His feet—means to possess the very majesty and power that is called divine.[92]]

It is likely that the two canonic voices in BWV 660, both of equal importance, portray the opening line of the text of stanza 6, "Der du bist der Vater gleich." This concept can be linked to Paul's letter to the Philippians 2:6:

> Welcher, ob Er wol in Göttlicher Gestalt war, hielt Ers nicht für einen Raub GOtt gleich seyn. [His state was divine, yet he did not cling to his equality with God.]

Luther comments on this passage in detail:

> Göttliche Gestalt und Gewalt (Gott gleich sein) hatte Christus bei dem Vater von Ewigkeit her . . . im Gehorsam gegen seines Vaters Gegenwillen und aus liebe zu uns erniedrigte er sich selbst sogar bis zum Verbrechertod am Kreuz.[93] [Divine form and power (as one with God) was possessed by Christ with the Father since eternity . . . in fulfilling his father's wishes and out of love for us he humbled himself to a criminal's death on the cross.]

Christ's unity with the Father seen from the Pauline point of view suggests Christ not clinging to his divine state, but humbling himself here on earth as man. Can this be reflected in Bach's use of two independent bass parts that descend to the depths of their ranges at many points throughout BWV 660? The two parts are the same, yet autonomous, precisely what Paul is conveying in his epistle message.

This passage from Philippians is pertinent to the concept of incarnation. These lines are part of a Christological hymn that probably existed before Paul penned his letters to the Philippians.[94] This is also related to the opening of John's Gospel, where John clearly sees Christ as preexisting before the incarnation. Paul does not confirm the preexistence of Christ as God. Was he in the image of God, as Adam was, and chose not to go higher, unlike Adam, thus humbling himself to final abasement on the cross?[95] These concepts undergird stanza 6 of *Nun komm der Heiden Heiland*. Paul directly relates Christ's unity with the Father to his humbling on earth and his death on the cross. Thus it seems reasonable to suggest that the Christological aspect of this stanza is represented in BWV 660. Further examination of the musical aspects of this work may help to confirm this issue.

The opening of BWV 660 may be linked both melodically and texturally to the "Laß ihn kreuzigen" chorus of the St. Matthew Passion. The openings of both pieces are noteworthy for their emphatic use of the cross symbol.[96] It does not seem accidental that the first five notes of the "Laß ihn kreuzigen" chorus (see example 8.2) correspond to the opening five notes of *Nun komm der Heiden Heiland*. Wolfram Syré draws attention to the above connection between the two works. However, he mistakenly says that the "Laß ihn kreuzigen" fugue was the earlier composition.[97] Winfried Zeller refers to the cross symbol as seen in this fugue and makes further references to cantatas and organ works, although not to BWV 660.[98] The first version of this setting, *Nun komm der Heiden Heiland* (BWV 660a), dates from the Weimar period. It is possible that Bach got the idea for the theme of the "Laß ihn kreuzigen" fugue from remembering the opening motive of BWV 660a. Similar crossings can be seen in the bass aria "Komm süßes Kreuz" (No. 57) from the St. Matthew Passion. Here, two bass parts continually cross, the obbligato viola da gamba and the solo bass presenting a texture not unlike that of BWV 660.

As with the "Laß ihn kreuzigen" chorus, the use of the opening motive in BWV 660 results in many cross symbols and suspensions. The use of the interval of the diminished fourth, which results from sharpening the third note of the chorale, helps to support the Christological connection. That this opening motive appears as many as 19 times in BWV 660 suggests its importance and significance for Bach.[99] The tortured suspensions that result from imitation at the unison, as well as the continual crossing of voices, also confirm the Christological connection. The crossing over of voices in cases such as this was known as *metabasis* in baroque rhetoric, usually related to a text.[100] As previously shown, there were many connections in Bach's Advent music with the Passion. Therefore, conceivably, an Advent piece could give a musical indication of this even if the text did not specifically mention it. However, in a case such as BWV 660, where the text seems to be referring directly to Christ's fulfillment of the law, the employment of such techniques appears all the more significant.

Another noteworthy musical feature of BWV 660 is the introduction of a chord at mm. 15 and 42 (see examples 8.3a and 8.3b). The text may provide

Example 8.2.   BWV 244/45b (mm. 1–3)

Example 8.3a. BWV 660
(m. 14.3f.)

a clue for this departure from the trio texture. Examination of movement 4 of the cantata *Christ lag in Todesbanden* (BWV 4) may help to make this clear. In this movement, Bach suddenly introduces chords in the violin part, which up to then had been a single melodic line (see example 8.4). It may be significant that the text at this point is "Gewalt." Normally, when Bach does something unusual, he appears to have a reason related to the text. In this movement, Christ is depicted conquering death and taking away the sin of the world, thereby providing salvation for mankind. His "Gewalt" is very important in this context. This word is equally important in the context of stanza 6 of *Nun komm der Heiden Heiland*, as shown previously. Stanza 6 is addressed to Christ who is equal to the Father and is in possession of "ewig Gottes Gewalt." The importance of this is shown in the reference to Paul above and in Luther's subsequent commentary. Bach may be stressing this issue by the sudden insertion of a chord as in BWV 4/4.[101] There are not many differences between the Weimar setting (BWV 660a) and the Leipzig revision (BWV 660) of *Nun komm der Heiden Heiland*, but it is useful to consider the small changes that Bach did make. In the opening statement of the solo chorale melody, Bach adds more figuration in mm. 8 and 9. For the final eighth note of m. 8, he adds four thirty-second notes as an upbeat to the following note of the chorale

Example 8.3b. BWV 660 (m. 42)

Example 8.4.   BWV 4.4 (mm. 23ff.)

melody *b-flat*[1] (this was known as *tirata mezza*), thus creating the expressive *exclamatio* figure.[102] In m. 9, Bach adds a *circulatio* figure around this *b-flat*, thus emphasizing it even more. "Vater" [Father] being a key word in this phrase, it is not surprising that Bach chooses to highlight it.

The *figura corta* motive appears only twice in the ornamental chorale melody and not at all in the two bass parts. The appearances occur in mm. 8 and 26, and it may be significant that these measures were altered by Bach in his Leipzig revision of the piece. The *figura corta* appears in both versions in m. 8, but not in m. 26 of BWV 660a. At this point, the text of stanza 6 reads, "das dein ewge Gottes Gewalt." As this figure can represent trust in God, the following line of text, "in uns das kranck Fleisch enthalt," may be significant, showing the importance of trust in God for support.[103]

Another significant alteration in m. 26 of BWV 660 is the inversion of the motive on the second beat of the measure. In BWV 660a, the second and third sixteenth notes of the four-sixteenth-note group are an octave lower than in BWV 660. In transposing these two notes up an octave, Bach approaches g^2, the highest note of the piece, by means of a *saltus duriusculus* (in this case an augmented fifth), which in combination with the *figura corta* of the first beat adds great significance to this measure. The eternity of Christ's sacred power is part of the strong message of stanza 6. This eternity exists before and after the other important elements of this stanza, Christ's coming to earth and his subsequent crucifixion and resurrection for man's salvation. Thus we have again the paradoxical elements found so often in Lutheran theology. Directly coinciding with the word "Gottes," Bach uses the *figura corta* followed by the *hyperbole*, but overlaps this with the opening motive to remind the listener of the two elements of his being—his eternal power and his humbling on the cross.

The final difference in the figuration of the solo chorale between BWV 660a and BWV 660 occurs at m. 35. This corresponds to mm. 8 and 9 in the opening phrase. Bach changes the figuration as he did in the opening phrase but without adding the four-note *tirata* figure. Here a *saltus duriusculus* is employed on the word "kranck." As referred to previously, in BWV 78/2, Bach uses a similar "hard interval" for the word "kranken" in mm. 51, 53, and 56.[104] The absence of the *tirata* figure at this point in BWV 660 would lead one to believe that Bach might have deliberately included this figure in the first phrase but not in the final one. The tonality for the entry of line 4 of the *cantus firmus* may be significant. This phrase is melodically the same as the first. Bach begins this phrase in the subdominant key of C minor. Bach may be deliberately going to the flatter key of the subdominant in order to portray the idea of the sick flesh of humanity as expressed in "in uns das kranck Fleisch erhalt." He prepares this tonality in a dramatic way in m. 27 with the unexpected *a-flat⁰*.

The last element of this extraordinary work to be discussed is the short chord and long pedal tonic note in the final measure. A similar moment occurs in the continuo part of the final measure of *Christ lag in Todesbanden* (BWV 4/3), where the continuo sounds a lone *E*. In the case of BWV 4/3, the sin of man and man's weakness is emphasized. The following movement deals with Christ's coming to do away with sin by overcoming death. Likewise, at the end of the *Agnus Dei* of the B Minor Mass, a lone *g⁰* is heard. The unison violins descend a major seventh to *g⁰*, the lowest possible note for the violin, accompanied only by a lone G in the continuo. Once again, the text is related to Christ who takes away the sin of the world, thus providing salvation by his Passion. The victory of Christ over sin and death is relevant to stanza 6 of *Nun komm der Heiden Heiland*, and there could be a link between the lone G that closes BWV 660 and the close of the two movements mentioned above. Christ abases himself to cleanse humanity from sin, leading to eternal life. In his sermon *Von der Betrachtung des heiligen Leidens Christi* (1519) [Of the Meditation on Christ's Holy Passion], Luther recommends the daily contemplation of Christ's Passion. This must be done in the correct way. Luther explains:

> Die bedenckenn das leyden Christi recht, die yhn alßo ansehn, das sie hertzlich darfur erschrecken und yhr gewissen gleych fincket yn eyn vorzagen. Das erschrecken sol da her kummen, das du sihest den gestrengen zorn und unwanckelbarn ernst gottis uber die sund und sundere, das er auch seynem eynigen allerliebsten sun hat nit wollen die sunder loß geben, er thette dan fur sie eynn solche schwere puß, als er spricht durch Jsaiam 53. . . . und wan du recht tieff bedenckst, das gottis sun, die ewige weyßheyt des vatters, selbst leydet, so wirstu wol erschrecken, unnd yhe mehr yhe tieffer.[105] [They contemplate Christ's Passion aright who view it with a terror-stricken heart and a despairing conscience. This terror must be felt

as you witness the stern wrath and the unchanging earnestness with which God looks upon sin and sinners, so much so that he was unwilling to release sinners even for his only and dearest Son without his payment of the severest penalty for them. . . . And if you seriously consider that it is God's very own Son, the eternal wisdom of the Father, who suffers, you will be terrified indeed. The more you think about it the more intensely will you be frightened.[106]]

It is possible that the terror of the cross is being depicted here in the final pedal G of BWV 660. Bach may be stressing the enormity of the task Christ faced in providing salvation for humanity. The fear that Christ felt as he faced his sacrifice, following his Father's will, was very real, as we know from his prayer to God the Father for release in the Garden of Gethsemane the night before he died (Matthew 26:39–42).

★ ★ ★

It seems that Bach was indeed setting stanza 6 of *Nun komm der Heiden Heiland* in BWV 660. Bach's use of strict counterpoint and canon is not surprising in this context. The equality of God the Father and God the Son can be seen in the equality of the two accompanying voices.[107] In coming to earth, Christ does not cling to this equality but follows his Father's will in his crucifixion, thereby fulfilling his law. The law is also reflected in the use of canon. Luther himself commented on the obedience of Christ in Philippians 2. Bach's use of many crossing parts and cross motives is also significant in BWV 660. The introduction of the remarkable chords at mm. 15 and 42 appear to be related to "Gewalt." As in BWV 659, Bach links incarnation and atonement. In the following section I will investigate how Bach may have continued this theme in BWV 661.

NUN KOMM DER HEIDEN HEILAND (BWV 661)

The third setting of *Nun komm der Heiden Heiland* exists in two versions: an earlier Weimar setting (BWV 661a), and a later Leipzig revision (BWV 661). The main differences between the two lie in the use of the *alla breve* time signature in BWV 661 as opposed to the common time of BWV 661a, and the alteration of the final figure of the countersubject in BWV 661. BWV 661 is headed "*Nun komm der Heyden Heÿland. in Organo pleno. canto fermo in Pedal*" in P271. Bach uses a combination of ritornello, fugue, and *cantus firmus* writing in *organo pleno*. The ritornello sections are really a series of fugal expositions, with the interspersing of the *cantus firmus* dictating both the tonal and formal structure of the piece. The penetrating pedal *cantus firmus* is reminiscent of the portrayal of lines 1 and 2 of stanza 1 of *Nun komm der Heiden Heiland* in the first movement of BWV 61.

This setting bears many of the characteristics of the free organ fugues in its melodic writing. The opening ritornello motive is derived from the *cantus firmus* itself, with all of its notes present in the opening fugal theme. As Peter Williams has pointed out, this motive is reminiscent of the *messanza*, one of the *musica ornata* figures listed by such theorists as Johann Georg Ahle (1651–1706) and Wolfgang Casper Printz (1641–1717).[108] This figure is also mentioned by Johann Gottfried Walther in his *Musicalisches Lexicon*.[109] Philipp Spitta remarks on the contrast between the animated and ornate fugal theme and the grandiose calmness of the *cantus firmus*.[110]

In the first section of this piece, the ritornello theme is treated fugally in soprano, alto, and tenor. The soprano enters first with the three-measure theme, with the alto presenting a tonal answer in m. 4. Measures 7–15 provide a link passage to the third fugal entry by way of three two-measure sequences, passing through C minor and B-flat major before returning to G minor. The tenor enters in m. 15 with the theme in the tonic, now with the counter-subject in the alto. The sequences of mm. 7–12 are repeated a fourth higher, followed by two one-measure sequences leading to the second section and the statement of the *cantus firmus*, beginning at m. 24. With the introduction of the *cantus firmus* in the pedal, the texture becomes four part. The beginning of the opening theme can be heard twice in the alto before a full statement follows in the soprano, commencing at m. 28 over the final note of the *cantus firmus*. This time Bach does not alter the notes of the second beat of the fugal theme but continues with a real answer to reach the key of C minor. Several one-measure sequences, passing through C minor and B-flat major, lead back to G minor for the introduction of the second phrase of the *cantus firmus* in the pedal.

The onward movement at the beginning of this third section is intensified by the 4–3 suspension in the alto as the *cantus firmus* enters in the pedal. Above, the tenor states the first measure of the fugal theme, followed two measures later by the alto. It is stated in full by the soprano beginning at m. 42 over the final note of the *cantus firmus*, but this time in the key of B-flat major. At m. 45, the theme is presented in its *inversus* form in the alto, also in B-flat major. Three measures later, the tenor presents the inverted form. Measures 51–54 present an inverted form of mm. 7–10. The tonality passes through F major, G minor, and C minor before returning to B-flat major for the entry of the third phrase of the *cantus firmus* in the pedal. The third phrase of the chorale tune is accompanied by the inverted opening of the fugal theme in the tenor. A full entry in G minor in the same part follows in m. 60, again over the final note of the pedal *cantus firmus*. This section continues, as did the preceding one, with references to the inverted form of the fugal theme in the tenor and soprano, passing through D minor, C minor, and B-flat major before returning to G minor for the final phrase of the *cantus firmus* in the pedal. In the final section, Bach combines the fugal theme in its *rectus* and *inversus* forms, bringing the work to its culmination over a dramatic tonic pedal where both forms of the theme are heard simultaneously in C minor. The alto presents the fugal theme in its *rectus* form one last time before a final close onto the chord of G major.

Interpretations by Other Authors

In their discussions of Bach's organ chorale settings, many authors avoid making any proposals regarding the text and music in BWV 661.

Albert Schweitzer compares this piece to *Komm heiliger Geist, Herre Gott* (BWV 651) and the *Fuga sopra il Magnificat* (BWV 733), suggesting that because of its festive character, Bach may have composed BWV 661 for the first Sunday of Advent.[111]

Hans Luedtke sees a connection between the clarity of this composition and stanza 7 of the hymn.[112]

Stainton de B. Taylor views this as a jubilant setting.[113] He states that Bach "seems intent on a mood of solemn joy in the coming of the Savior, though he makes use of the diminished interval resulting from the sharpening of the third note of the chorale."[114]

Hermann Keller considers this setting to be representative of the hymn of redeemed humanity [Lobpreis der erlösten Menschheit].[115] Therefore, he proposes that it is the text of the final stanza that is relevant here.

Jacques Chailley does not associate the text and music in BWV 661, with the exception of the thirds of mm. 32 and m. 34, which according to him, in Bach's language, evoke the maternal breast and therefore the text of stanza 1.[116] He refers to the descending movement of mm. 70–75 (left hand) and of mm. 75–78 (right hand) as being significant.

Ulrich Meyer agrees with Keller's suggestion that this work is a hymn in praise of the Trinity and therefore reflects stanza 8 of the chorale.[117] He also poses the question, however, as to whether or not the technique of inversion, which is used so freely in BWV 661, is inspired by the text or is merely a contrapuntal exercise.[118] He proposes that, on the other hand, it could reflect the text of stanza 5, "Sein Lauf kam vom Vater her/ und kehrt wieder zum Vater." According to Meyer, BWV 661 is not merely referring to a few phrases of the text but to sentiments already firmly established in the second article of the creed.[119]

Peter Williams suggests that Jesus, as reflected in the Catechism, who "with his splendour and power" protects us "against all enemies," can be depicted here as the Savior in glory.[120]

Most authors are in agreement regarding the festive nature of this piece, even if they do not go into detail regarding text-music relationships. This issue is dealt with in the following section.

Assessment

Since Bach presents three settings of *Nun komm der Heiden Heiland* in succession in this collection, it is possible that he considered them as a minicycle within the larger context of the "Leipzig" chorales. I have already suggested that the texts of stanzas 1 and 6 are relevant to BWV 659 and 660 respectively. It would seem logical that Bach was progressing through the text of the hymn and that in BWV 661 he might consider the text of stanza 7 or 8. Once more, examination of the musical features of BWV 661 may help to find a solution.

Important aspects of BWV 661 are the *organo pleno* indication, the penetrating *cantus firmus*, the fugal treatment, the prominence of inversion, and the change from 4/4 in BWV 661a to 2/2 in BWV 661. Some or all of these features may lead to a particular stanza of the hymn.

In chapter 1, I suggested that the image of light was an important aspect in the portrayal of text in BWV 651. This is mentioned in stanzas 1 and 2 of Luther's *Komm heiliger Geist, Herre Gott*. As such, the *plenum* setting seemed appropriate. In his sermon for the first Sunday of Advent, Luther states that faith is light.[121] It seems reasonable to suggest that Bach's use of the *plenum* setting may have similar meaning here. There is only one stanza of *Nun komm der Heiden Heiland* where faith and light are mentioned: stanza 7. The link between faith, light, and the *plenum* registration may indicate a link with the text of stanza 7. Examination of other musical details may help to illuminate the question.

In BWV 661, Bach replaces the more modern time signature of 4/4 with the slower-moving 2/2 of the *prima prattica*. Bach frequently changed between 4/4 and 2/2. Sometimes copyists were careless about the notation of a time signature. In the cases where there is an autograph score, it would seem that Bach himself may have changed his mind about the meter. There are three instances in the "Leipzig" chorales where he changed the time signature from the earlier Weimar to the Leipzig setting. In BWV 660, the time signature is common time, changed from the earlier indication of cut common time.[122]

The change in BWV 661 may be merely related to performance practice and tempo. This could be considered a more fitting meter for the final setting of this minicycle. By changing the time signature from 4/4 to 2/2, there is a change in the number of accents. In 4/4 time, there are two strong accents per measure, on beats 1 and 3, whereas in 2/2 time there is only one accent on the first beat. If it is indeed the text of stanza 7, then do the words fit in the right place? If one applies the text of the chorale to the bass line of BWV 661a, it seems that the accents are not quite right. The text runs as follows (with accented syllables underlined):

> Dein <u>Krip</u>pen glänzt hell <u>und</u> klar
> <u>Die</u> Nacht gibt ein <u>neu</u> Licht dar
> <u>Tun</u>ckel muß nicht <u>kom</u>men drein
> <u>Der</u> Glaub bleibt <u>im</u>mer im <u>Schein</u>.

If one applies the text of stanza 7 to the bass line of BWV 661, the accents appear more logical.

> Dein <u>Krip</u>pen <u>glänzt</u> hell <u>und</u> <u>klar</u>
> <u>Die</u> Nacht <u>gibt</u> ein <u>neu</u> Licht dar
> Tunckel <u>muß</u> nicht <u>kom</u>men <u>drein</u>
> <u>Der</u> <u>Glaub</u> bleibt <u>im</u>mer <u>im</u> <u>Schein</u>.

Can this test be applied to any of the other stanzas of *Nun komm der Heiden Heiland*? As stated before, it might be reasonable to assert that Bach was depicting either stanza 7 or stanza 8 in BWV 661. If the text of line 1 of stanza 8 is applied with the appropriate accents, the following result is achieved:

> <u>Lob</u> <u>sey</u> GOtt <u>dem</u> Vater <u>thon</u>

This does not seem logical. Neither "Gott" nor "Vater" receives a strong accent, which seems incorrect. Equally, if one looks to the other stanzas of the hymn, reasons can be found why they are not depicted here by Bach. The text of the opening stanza fits very well to the pedal notes. It may even be that Bach was inspired by BWV 661a when he wrote the opening movement of the cantata *Nun komm der Heiden Heiland* (BWV 61), with its equally penetrating *cantus firmus*. However, in the case of BWV 661, it does not seem logical that Bach would return to stanza 1, having set stanzas 1 and 6 in the two previous settings. Additionally, in BWV 61/1, Bach does not maintain this style for the entire movement, treating line 3 in a fugal triple-metered dance and line 4 in a four-part homophonic setting; so the analogy is not completely straightforward. As with the opening line of stanza 8, if one applies the opening lines of each of stanzas 2–6, then weak syllables occur on strong beats, and the result is very unconvincing. With BWV 661a, the first three lines of the *cantus firmus* have weak endings. It is also possible that Bach wanted the music to look clearer, with the *cantus firmus* being given a more emphatic presence.

It appears from the preceding arguments that Bach was setting stanza 7 of *Nun komm der Heiden Heiland* in BWV 661. A closer examination of the music itself may help to establish this possibility.

As with the motivic writing of BWV 660, Bach also uses the cross symbol in BWV 661. In all three settings of *Nun komm der Heiden Heiland*, Bach has introduced the cross motive. This occurs naturally, as it is built into the melodic framework of the first four notes of the chorale. However, the emphatic reference in all three settings to these four notes of the chorale, with its association to the idea of the cross, directly links the crib and Passion as outlined previously. The epistle of the day (Romans 13: 11–14) opens with a reference to salvation:

> Und weil wir solches wissen, nemlich die Zeit, daß die Stunde da ist, aufzustehen vom Schlaf, (sintemal unser Heil jetzt näher ist, denn da wirs gläubten). [And this, knowing the season, that already it is time for you to awake out of sleep: for now is salvation nearer to us than when we first believed.]

The link between light and salvation can be seen in John 8:12.

> Ich bin das Licht der Welt, wer Mir nachfolget, der wird nicht wandeln im Finsternis, sondern wird das Licht des Lebens haben. [I am the Light of the World; anyone who follows me will not be walking in the dark; he will have the light of life.]

Once more, the connection between incarnation and atonement is expressed through Bach's use of the cross symbol in the opening motive of BWV 661, although it is not used in the tortured manner of BWV 660.

For Lutherans, following Christ meant also taking up his cross, and hence the cross symbol is appropriate here. The image of light recurs in the writings of Luther. In his sermon for the first Sunday of Advent on this epistle, he explains the message of Paul:

> "Die nacht ist vorgangen, der tag ist erbey komen." Daß ist eben ßo viel gesagt: als unßer heyll ist nahe; denn Paulus meynett mit dem tag das Euangelium, wilchs ist eyn tag, der die hertzen odder seelen erleucht, darumb weyll der tag anbrochen ist, so ist unser heyl nahe bey unß. . . . Dißen tag macht die aller lieblichst ßonne Jhesus Christus; daher yhn nen-

net Malachias eyne ßonne der gerechtickeyt und spricht c.4: Euch, die yhr furchtet meynen neman, soll auffgehen die ßonne der gerechtickeyt und das heyl unter seynen flugelln; denn alle, die yn Christo glewben, empfahen von yhm die glentz seyner gnade und gerechtickeytt unnd werden selig unter seynen flugelln.[123] ["The night is far spent, and the day is at hand." This is equivalent to saying "salvation is near to us." By the word "day" Paul means the gospel; the Gospel is like the day in that it enlightens the heart or soul. Now, day having broken, salvation is near to us. . . . This Gospel day is produced by the glorious Sun Jesus Christ. Hence Malachi calls him the Sun of Righteousness, saying, "But unto you that fear my name shall the Sun of Righteousness arise with healing in its wings" Mal. 4:2. All believers in Christ receive the light of his grace, and righteousness, and shall rejoice in the shelter of his wings.[124]]

For Luther, light is faith. The text of stanza 7 of *Nun komm der Heiden Heiland* deals with the themes of light and faith. The *cantus firmus* shines brightly through the *organo pleno* texture.

It may be significant to note that the first appearance of the fugal theme in its inversion occurs almost exactly halfway through BWV 661, following the second line of the chorale at m. 45. The text here is "Die Nacht gibt ein neu Licht dar." The contrast between light and dark and good and evil is a common biblical theme. It is possible that Bach was using the contrast of inversion to illustrate this theme. The inversion continues for the statement of the following line of text: "dunkel muß nicht kommen drein." Over the final line of the chorale, the fugal theme is heard in its *rectus* and *inversus* form. They are very forcefully combined in mm. 86–88. Here the words are "Der Glaub bleibt immer im Schein." The implication is that faith and light are synonymous as opposed to the contrast of dark and evil. It seems possible that the element of contrast or opposites as present in BWV 661 has some relevance to Bach's interpretation of the text.[125] The contrast of light and dark was also present in the epistle for the first Sunday of Advent. Faith is the cornerstone of the Lutheran Church, and it is unlikely that Bach would have ignored a reference to it. Faith and light are portrayed in the splendor of the *organo pleno* setting. The dominant feature of BWV 661 is the power of the *plenum*, where clarity and brightness are of paramount importance. Therefore, the text of stanza 7 appears to be relevant here, as it confirms the musical characteristics of the piece.

In Bach's first Advent cantata, *Nun komm der Heiden Heiland* (BWV 61), the theme of light is to be found in the second movement, the tenor recitative. This recitative encapsulates the ideas in the text of stanzas 6 and 7:

Der Heyland ist gekommen,	The Savior has come,
hat unser armes Fleisch	he took our lowly flesh
und Blut an sich genommen	and blood on himself
und nimmt uns zu Blut verwandten an.	and made us kin to him by blood.
O aller höchstes Gut,	O highest good,
was hast du nicht an uns getan?	what have you not done for us?
Was tust du nicht	What do you not still do
noch täglich an den deinen?	daily for your people?
Du kömmst und lässt dein Licht	You come and bring your light
mit vollem Segen scheinen.	With blessed grace upon us.

In this recitative, Bach makes use of the *exclamatio* figure at the word "Licht," thus emphasizing its image. Further emphasis is achieved by the change to arioso for the final two lines of text. Bach repeats the line "du kömmst und lässt dein Licht" three times, adding particular emphasis to the word "Licht."

The image of Christ as not only the Light of the World but also the Star of Jacob is to be found in the Christmas Oratorio. In part 1, the alto recitative, No. 3 contains the text

Nun wird der Stern aus Jacob scheinen,	Now the Star of Jacob will shine
sein Strahl bricht schon hervor.	its beam is already breaking through.

The reference to the Star of David is found in Numbers 24:17:

Ich werde ihn sehen, aber jetzt nicht; ich werde ihn schauen, aber nicht von nahen. Es wird ein Stern aus Jacob aufgehen, und ein Scepter aus Israel aufkommen, und wird zerschmettern die Fürsten der Moabiter, und verstören alle Kinder Seth. [I see him—but not in the present, I behold him—but not close at hand: a star from Jacob takes the leadership, a scepter arises from Israel. It crushes the brows of Moab, the skulls of all the sons of Sheth.]

In his comment on this verse, Luther explains that the Star of David is the Messiah who will be the true King of Israel and will rule in peace and not through war. The image of light in association with the birth of Christ is seen in Matthew 2:2, where the wise men tell of seeing the star in the east. In the third movement of part 1 of the Christmas Oratorio, Bach again uses the *exclamatio* figure to highlight the words "scheinen" and "Strahl." This shows his clear emphasis on words pertaining to light in relation to the incarnation. Part 5 of the Christmas Oratorio deals with the contrast of light and dark in detail. Movement 45 is an alternation of short *turba* chorus sections with alto recitative. The recitative ends with the words

Wohl euch, die ihr dies Licht gesehen,	Happy are you who have seen his light,
es ist zu eurem Heil geschehen.	it was for your salvation.
Mein Heyland du,	My Savior, it is you,
du bist das Licht	you are the light
das auch den Heiden scheinen sollen,	that must shine also on the Gentiles,
und sie kennen dich noch nicht,	and they know you not yet,
als sie dich schon verehren wollen.	as they seek to honor you already.
Wie hell, wie klar,	How bright, how clear,
muß nicht dein Schein,	must not thy light
geliebter Jesu, sein!	O beloved Jesus be!

Once again, Bach highlights the word "Licht" with the use of an *exclamatio* figure. The extent to which part 5 of the Christmas Oratorio is taken up with the theme of light would lead one to believe that Bach might not have ignored an opportunity to also develop this theme in an Advent chorale setting offering similar possibilities with its text. Movement 46 of the Christmas Oratorio is the final stanza of Georg Weissel's hymn *Nun, liebe Seele, nun ist es Zeit*. This stanza deals specifically with the banishing of darkness through the light of Christ, the same theme as we find in the epistle for the first Sunday of Advent. Each line of stanza 7 of *Nun komm der Heiden Heiland* contains a reference to light:

Dein Krippen *glänzt hell und klar*	Your manger shines bright and clear;
Die Nacht gibt ein neu *Licht* dar	the night shows forth a new light.
dunkel muß nicht kommen drein	Darkness must not enter therein.
der Glaub bleibt immer im *Schein*.	Faith always remains in the light.

If stanza 7 is indeed the stanza that Bach is portraying here, then he is setting a stanza containing truths that were very dear to Luther. The representation of faith and light is one of the enduring concepts of the Lutheran church. It may have seemed more logical to Bach to give this setting the 2/2 time signature, thus adding to the gravitas of the musical setting. I have suggested that the technique of inversion represents opposites in BWV 661. Christ has come as a human child, but also as a Savior of the world. The divine and human, good and bad, light and dark seem to be represented in BWV 661 in the consistent use of inversion techniques.

★ ★ ★

Nun komm der Heiden Heiland is one of two hymns set three times by Bach in the "Leipzig" chorales, the other being Nicolaus Decius's *Allein Gott in der Höh sei Ehr*. This in itself shows the importance Bach placed on these two hymns. The use of *Nun komm der Heiden Heiland* in three Advent cantatas (BWV 36, 61, and 62) confirms this significance, as well as the two additional organ settings (BWV 599 and BWV 699). The first Sunday of Advent was important as the opening

Sunday of the church year, and also as it was the last time that concerted music was heard in Leipzig before Christmas. Bach shows the connection between incarnation and atonement in all three settings of *Nun komm der Heiden Heiland* in the "Leipzig" chorales. The Sundays leading up to the first Sunday of Advent concentrated increasingly on eschatology, and this new beginning on the first Sunday of Advent also has important eschatological implications that account for the prominence of the three *Nun komm* settings in the "Leipzig" chorales. Advent heralds the coming of Christ. Christ is also met in death, so the meeting of Christ with humanity can also be understood in a purely eschatological way.

NOTES

1. For Bartel, *Musica Poetica* another similar discussion of Luther's Advent hymn in the works of Bach, see Anne Leahy, "Bach's Setting of the Hymn Tune 'Nun komm der Heiden Heiland' in his Cantatas and Organ Works," in *Music and Theology: Essays in Honor of Robin A. Leaver,* ed. Daniel Zager (Lanham, MD: Scarecrow Press, 2007), 69–101. For the background, see Johannes Kulp, *Die Lieder unserer Kirche* [Handbuch zum Evangelischen Kirchengesangbuch, Sonderband], ed. Arno Büchner and Siegfried Fornaçon (Göttingen: Vandenhoeck & Ruprecht, 1958), 7.

2. *WA* 35:149; Kulp, *Die Lieder unserer Kirche,* 9.

3. Kulp, *Die Lieder unserer Kirche,* 8.

4. Kulp, *Die Lieder unserer Kirche,* 10.

5. Markus Jenny, *Luthers geistliche Lieder und Kirchengesänge. Vollständige Neuedition in Ergänzung zu Band 35 der Weimarer Ausgabe* [Archiv zur Weimarer Ausgabe der Werke Martin Luthers 4] (Cologne: Böhlau, 1985), 72f.

6. *WA* 35:150; *LW* 53:235; Jenny, *Luthers geistliche Lieder,* 72.

7. *SLG,* 2.

8. Translation based on Mark Bighley, *The Lutheran Chorales in the Organ Works of J. S. Bach* (St. Louis: Concordia, 1986), 185ff.

9. Detlef Gojowy, "Kirchenlieder im Umkreis von J. S. Bach," *JbLH* 22 (1978): 90–92, lists *Nun komm der Heiden Heiland* for the first, third, and fourth Sundays of Advent; the 1693 Leipzig hymnal of Gottfried Vopelius lists it as a hymn for all four Sundays of Advent; Günther Stiller, *Johann Sebastian Bach und das Leipziger gottesdienstliche Leben seiner Zeit* (Kassel: Bärenreiter, 1970), 220; English: *Johann Sebastian Bach and Liturgical Life in Leipzig,* trans. Herbert J. A. Bouman, Daniel F. Poellot, and Hilton C. Oswald; ed. Robin A. Leaver (St. Louis: Concordia, 1984), 233.

10. Martin Petzoldt, "Zur Frage der Textvorlagen von BWV 62," *MuK* 60 (1990): 303.

11. Kulp, *Die Lieder unserer Kirche,* 11.

12. Petzoldt, 308. He cites the following biblical sources: Ps. 80:2–3, Isa. 7:14, Ezek. 44:2, Ps. 19, Ps. 45, Matt. 20:28, Luke 2:18, John 1:13–14, Matt. 1:25, John 16:28, 2 Cor. 12:9, Luke 2: 8–12, and 2 Cor. 4:6.

13. *WA* 10$^{1/2}$:10.

14. *Church Postils* 6:17.

15. Robin A. Leaver, "Bach's Understanding and Use of the Epistles and Gospels of the Church Year." *BACH* 6/4 (1975): 8; Albert Clement, "De orgelkoraalbewerkingen van Joh. Seb. Bach in het kerkelijk jaar," *Het Orgel* 86 (1990): 323.

16. *WA* 10$^{1/2}$:12.

17. *Church Postils* 6:19.

18. Clark Kelly, "Johann Sebastian Bach's 'Eighteen' Chorales BWV 651–668: Perspectives on Editions and Hymnology," DMA diss., Eastman School of Music, 1988, 171.

19. Gojowy, "Kirchenlieder im Umkreis von J. S. Bach," 86–89, 90–92.

20. Stiller, *Johann Sebastian Bach und das Leipziger gottesdienstliche Leben*, 220; Stiller, *Johann Sebastian Bach and Liturgical Life in Leipzig*, 233.

21. See Robin A. Leaver, "Bach and Hymnody: The Evidence of the Orgelbüchlein," *Early Music* 13 (1985): 235.

22. Stainton de B. Taylor, *The Chorale Preludes of J. S. Bach* (London: Oxford University Press, 1942), 115, refers to a similar use of an altered note in *Christ lag in Todesbanden* (BWV 625), where the resulting diminished fourth adds a touch of sadness and poignancy. As shown above, two versions of *Nun komm der Heiden Heiland* had come into being during the seventeenth century, with Bach using both the modal and the chromatically altered melody in his various settings. In the autograph of BWV 659, the first phrase of the *cantus firmus* is unaltered in m. 4 while the last phrase is chromaticized (m. 28). Kelly, "Johann Sebastian Bach's 'Eighteen' Chorales," 171–174, points out that while this may have been intentional, with every other preserved movement in which Bach states the complete tune of *Nun komm der Heiden Heiland*, he either alters the *cantus firmus* chromatically in both instances or not at all. It is possible, as Kelly has suggested, that Bach intended the soprano *f-sharp* to occur in m. 4 as well as m. 28. Interestingly, the *f-sharp* is notated in both m. 4 and m. 28 in the existing copies of Bach's early version of this setting (BWV 659a).

23. Fritz Dietrich, "J. S. Bachs Orgelchoral und seine geschichtlichen Wurzeln," *BJ* 26 (1929): 74; see also Albert Clement, "'O Jesu, du edle Gabe': Studien zum Verhältnis von Text und Musik in den Choralpartiten und den Kanonischen Veränderungen von Johann Sebastian Bach," PhD diss., University of Utrecht, 1989, 114 and 250, note 503. In both instances, Bach uses the first few notes of the chorale melody and extends the phrase with melismatic passages. Both cadential figures employ thirty-second notes.

24. Harald Schützeichel, *Albert Schweitzer: Die Orgelwerke Johann Sebastian Bachs. Vorworte zu den "Sämtlichen Orgelwerken"* (Hildesheim: Olms, 1995), 254.

25. Schützeichel, *Albert Schweitzer*, 74.

26. Hans Luedtke, "Seb. Bachs Choralvorspiele," *BJ* 15 (1918): 74.

27. Hans Luedtke, "Seb. Bachs Choralvorspiele," 74.

28. Charles Sanford Terry, *Bach's Chorals Part III: The Hymns and Hymn Melodies of the Organ Works* (Cambridge: Cambridge University Press, 1921), 274.

29. Stainton de B. Taylor, *The Chorale Preludes of J. S. Bach* (London: Oxford University Press, 1942), 115.

30. Hermann Keller, *Die Orgelwerke Bachs. Ein Beitrag zu ihrer Geschichte, Form, Deutung und Wiedergabe* (Leipzig: Peters, 1948), 187; Herman Keller, *The Organ Works of Bach: A Contribution to Their History, Form, Interpretation and Performance*, trans. Helen Hewitt (New York: Peters, 1967), 254.

31. See previous note.

32. Jacques Chailley, *Les Chorals pour Orgue de J.-S. Bach* (Paris: Leduc, 1974), 197ff.

33. Peter Williams, *The Organ Music of J. S. Bach*, 2nd ed. (Cambridge: Cambridge University Press, 2003), 364.

34. Russell Stinson, *J. S. Bach's Great Eighteen Chorales* (New York: Oxford University Press, 2001), 87.

35. Stinson, *J. S. Bach's Great Eighteen Chorales*, 88.

36. Lothar Steiger and Renate Steiger, *Sehet! Wir gehn hinauf gen Jerusalem. Johann Sebastian Bachs Kantaten auf den Sonntag Estomihi* (Göttingen: Vandenhoeck & Ruprecht, 1992), 102; Robin A. Leaver, "Bach's Mature Vocal Works," in *The Cambridge Companion to Bach*, ed. John Butt (Cambridge: Cambridge University Press, 1997), 98f.

37. Gojowy, "Kirchenlieder im Umkreis von J. S. Bach," 90.

38. See the opening movement of cantata *Ich will den Kreuzstab gerne tragen* (BWV 56). This motive is also employed by Bach in m. 4 of the same cantata (bass recitative). Here the motive is associated with the carrying of the cross as in the closing chorus of part 1 of the St. Matthew Passion ("O Mensch bewein dein Sünde groß"). It is also to be found in the *Orgel-Büchlein* setting of the same chorale, BWV 622 (mm. 12 and 21).

39. Robin A. Leaver, "Eschatology, Theology and Music: Death and Beyond in Bach's Vocal Music," in *Irish Musical Studies 8: Bach Studies from Dublin*, ed. Anne Leahy and Yo Tomita (Dublin: Four Courts Press, 2004), 132.

40. Eric Chafe, *Analyzing Bach Cantatas* (New York: Oxford University Press, 2000), 14.

41. Chafe, *Analyzing Bach Cantatas*, 14.

42. There is a link to the close of Revelation 22:20: "Amen, ja komm Herr Jesu."

43. See the discussion in chapter 10.

44. Gojowy, "Kirchenlieder im Umkreis von J. S. Bach," 85–90.

45. Heinrich Müller, *Evangelisches Praeservativ wider den Schaden Josephs / in allen dreyen Ständen* (Franckfurt & Rostock: Wild, 1681), 42.

46. Clement, "O Jesu, du edle Gabe," 194.

47. Clement, "O Jesu, du edle Gabe," 194; see also 263, note 867.

48. The *tirata* was a row of notes of the same duration that ascended or descended by step. The *tirata perfecta* was when these notes spanned an octave. The *tirata* was given text-expressive potential by some writers; see Dietrich Bartel, *Musica Poetica: Musical-Rhetorical Figures in German Baroque Music* (Lincoln: University of Nebraska Press, 1997), 409ff.

49. Bartel, *Musica Poetica*, 209–212.

50. Bartel, *Musica Poetica*, 216; Warren Kirkendale, "*Circulatio*-Tradition. *Maria Lactans*, and Josquin as Musical Orator," *AM* 56 (1984): 69.

51. See the discussion of this motive in relation to BWV 769/3 in Clement, "O Jesu, du edle Gabe," 195.

52. There is a striking use of this motive in the Advent cantata *Bereitet die Wege, bereitet die Bahn!* (BWV 132/5). Here the text refers to the cleansing of the sins of mankind through baptism and the sacrifice of Christ. Phillip Spitta sees this aria as an anticipation of "Erbarme dich" from the St. Matthew Passion. Both arias are in B minor and make extensive use of the *figura corta* motive in the context of the forgiveness of sin; Philipp Spitta, *Johann Sebastian Bach*, trans. Clara Bell and J. A. Fuller-Maitland (London: Novello, 1884–1885; reprint, New York: Dover, 1992), 1:560.

53. For example, mm. 113–117 of the *et in terra pax* from the B minor Mass; mm. 25–30 and 57–60 of "Ehre sei Gott in der Höhe," No. 21 from the Christmas Oratorio; and the opening movement of *Nun komm der Heiden Heiland* (BWV 61). In the latter case, it is precisely at the words "alle Welt" that this pedal note occurs. Regarding the pedal point in No. 21 from the Christmas Oratorio, Blankenburg writes, "Diese Orgelpunkte sollen gewiß die Ruhe des himmlischen Friedens symbolisieren, aber sicherlich nicht nur dies, sondern darüber hinaus den für einen Augenblick eingetretenen Stillstand der Menschheitsgeschichte durch die Erscheinung Gottes in seiner Menschwerdung in Jesus von Nazareth" [This pedal point certainly symbolizes the stillness of heavenly peace, but not only that, also the momentary halting of the history of humanity through the appearance of God made man in Jesus of Nazareth]; Walter Blankenburg, *Das Weihnachts-Oratorium von Johann Sebastian Bach* (Kassel: Bärenreiter, 1982), 69.

54. See the alto aria "Erbarme dich" from the St. Matthew Passion. Here Bach makes much use of Neapolitan harmonies, e.g., mm. 17, 30, 35, and 41.

55. *NBA KB* IV/2:10.

56. *NBA KB* IV/2:76. Klotz argues that BWV 660b is probably a reworking of BWV 660a by a Weimar organist, possibly Johann Tobias Krebs.

57. For further elaboration of this, see *NBA KB* IV/2:76.

58. Williams, *The Organ Music of J. S. Bach*, 2nd ed., 367.

59. It was not unusual to have a final major chord, or indeed to arpeggiate the final chord.

60. Albert Schweitzer, *J. S. Bach*, trans. Ernest Newman (New York: Dover, 1966), 1:292. Rust also suggests this under the title of this trio in the preface to the *BG*, 35:3. Rust arpeggiated the chords in mm. 15 and 42, since he suspected that this voice was originally an obbligato cello part. According to Williams, *The Organ Music of J. S. Bach*, 2nd ed., 366, the lower parts of a cantata aria would rarely compete with one another in this way. Certainly no other models exist of this kind.

61. Harvey Grace, *The Organ Works of Bach* (London: Novello, 1922), 270.

62. Roswitha Bruggaier, "Das Urbild von Johann Sebastian Bachs Choralbearbeitung 'Nun komm der Heiden Heiland' (BWV 660)—eine Komposition mit Viola da Gamba?" *BJ* 73 (1987): 165–168.

63. Bach sometimes added extra voices within a trio texture for the close of a piece, such as in BWV 655 and 664. However, he does not seem to have ever inserted a chord in the middle of a chorale prelude as he does in BWV 660.

64. Bruggaier, "Bachs Choralbearbeitung," 165.

65. Bruggaier, "Bachs Choralbearbeitung," 166.

66. BWV 660a was written while Bach was at Weimar. Alfred Dürr, *Die Kantaten von Johann Sebastian Bach. Mit ihren Texten* (Kassel: Bärenreiter, 1985), 210, notes Bach's occasional preference for the sound of lower instruments. Cantatas originating from around this time include BWV 132, 163, and 155. BWV 163 was written for the twenty-third Sunday after Trinity and contains a bass aria with two obbligato cello parts. BWV 132 was written for the fourth Sunday of Advent, which in 1715 fell on 22 December. The third movement of this cantata is an aria for bass with obbligato cello. BWV 155 includes a duet for alto and tenor with obbligato bassoon. This cantata was written for the second Sunday after Epiphany, which fell on 19 January 1716. Bach also wrote his solo cello suites just after this time in 1720.

67. Kelly, "Johann Sebastian Bach's 'Eighteen' Chorales," 171.

68. Spitta, *Johann Sebastian Bach*, trans. Bell and Fuller-Maitland, 1:618.

69. Schützeichel, *Schweitzer*, 254.

70. Schützeichel, *Schweitzer*, 254.

71. Luedtke, "Seb. Bachs Choralvorspiele," 74.

72. Luedtke, "Seb. Bachs Choralvorspiele," 74.

73. Grace, *The Organ Works of Bach*, 270.

74. Grace, *The Organ Works of Bach*, 271.

75. Taylor, *The Chorale Preludes of J. S. Bach*, 108.

76. Taylor, *The Chorale Preludes of J. S. Bach*, 115.

77. Keller, *Die Orgelwerke Bachs*, 188; Keller, *The Organ Works of Bach*, trans. Hewitt, 255.

78. Ulrich Meyer, "Zur Frage der inneren Einheit von Bachs Siebzehn Chorälen (BWV 651–667)," *BJ* 58 (1972): 73. Ulrich Meyer, "Über J. S. Bachs Orgelchoralkunst," in *Theologische Bach-Studien 1*, ed. Walter Blankenburg and Renate Steiger, [Beiträge zur theologischen Bachforschung 4] (Neuhausen-Stuttgart: Hänssler, 1987), 42, states that there is no relationship between the text and the music of BWV 660. Terry, *Bach's Chorals Part III*, 274, similarly denies any relationship to the text.

79. Chailley, *Les Chorals pour Orgue de J.-S. Bach*, 200.

80. Chailley, *Les Chorals pour Orgue de J.-S. Bach*, 200.

81. Helene Werthemann, "Johann Sebastian Bachs Orgelchoral *Nun komm, der Heiden Heiland, a due bassi e canto fermo*," *MuG* 13/6 (1959): 161–167.

82. Werthemann, "Johann Sebastian Bachs Orgelchoral," 167.

83. Williams, *The Organ Music of J. S. Bach*, 2nd ed., 366.

84. Chailley, *Les Chorals pour Orgue de J.-S. Bach*, 200.

85. Walter Blankenburg, "Die Bedeutung des Kanons in Bachs Werk," *Bachtagung*, 250–258; see also Hans Grüß, "Über die Tradition des Cantus-Firmus-Kanons," *BJ* 71 (1985): 146.

86. *Dies sind die heil'gen zehn Gebot* (BWV 678) and *Vater unser im Himmelreich* (BWV 682) are both canonic pieces in which the canon could refer to the law or to the will of God. In the latter case, Christ is fulfilling the will of the Father. Albert Clement, *Der dritte Teil der Clavierübung von Johann Sebastian Bach: Musik, Text, Theologie* (Middelburg: Almares, 1999), 194, has shown this to be relevant to stanza 4 of this hymn.

87. See, for example, Clement, "O Jesu, du edle Gabe," 179, 185. He cites *O Lamm Gottes unschuldig* BWV 618 and *Christe, du Lamm Gottes* BWV 619 as further examples of canonic treatment reflecting Christ fulfilling the will of the Father.

88. For a more detailed discussion of this cantata in relation to *Nun komm der Heiden Heiland*, see Anne Leahy, "Bach's Setting of the Hymn Tune," 79–85.

89. Werthemann, "Bachs Orgelchoral *Nun komm der Heiden Heiland*," 165.

90. Spitta, *Johann Sebastian Bach*, trans. Bell and Fuller-Maitland, 3:51.

91. *WA* 41:83. I am very grateful to Mary Greer for directing me to this reference.

92. *LW* 13:233.

93. *Die Bibel oder die ganze heilige Schrift des Alten und Neuen Testaments nach der deutschen Übersetzung Martin Luthers . . . mit erklärenden Anmerkungen* (Stuttgart: Württembergische Bibelanstalt, 1912), New Testament, 320.

94. Raymond E. Brown, *An Introduction to the New Testament* (New York: Doubleday, 1997), 491.

95. Brown, *An Introduction to the New Testament*, 492f.

96. One is reminded of the opening of Felice Anerio's (c.1560–1614) four-part motet *Christus factus est* where similar dissonances occur. The opening four notes of the soprano part in the motet correspond to that of *Nun komm der Heiden Heiland*. Anerio sets the alto part with a semitone dissonance against the soprano. Here, Anerio has shaped his soprano line in the sign of the cross at the word *Christus*. There is no evidence that Bach had a copy of Anerio's *Christus factus est* in his collection, but this kind of writing was not uncommon in the Renaissance.

97. Wolfram Syré, "Zur Polarität des Weihnachts- und des Passionsgedankens im Orgelwerk von Johann Sebastian Bach," *MuK* 56 (1981): 17.

98. Winfried Zeller, "Vom Abbild zum Sinnbild: Bach und das Symbol," in *Theologie und Frömmigkeit. Gesammelte Aufsätze I*, ed. Bernd Jaspert [Marburger Theologische Studien 8] (Marburg: Elwert, 1971), 173.

99. This figure appears at mm. 1 (twice), 9, 10 (twice), 15 (twice), 18, 20 (twice), 21, 22, 26, 27, 33, 34, 35, and 36 (twice).

100. Bartel, *Musica Poetica*, 320.

101. This is not the same as the additional voices added at the end of BWV 651, 652, 655, and 664, where it seems to be more associated with exuberant joy.

102. Bartel, *Musica Poetica*, 411.

103. Similar sentiments are expressed in the second movement of *Jesu, der du meine Seele* (BWV 78), where the pleading is not a prayer of misery but an expression of certainty that God will grant the request and be remembered for his mercy. The *figura corta* dominates here to illustrate the trust in God.

104. Renate Steiger, "'Jesu, der du meine Seele' BWV 78," in *Johann Sebastian Bachs Choralkantaten als Choral-Bearbeitungen* [Internationale Arbeitsgemeinschaft für theologische Bachforschung Bulletin 3] (Heidelberg: Internationale Arbeitsgemeinschaft für theologische Bachforschung, 1991), 77.

105. *WA* 2:137.

106. *LW* 42:8f.

107. Werthemann, "Bachs Orgelchoral *Nun komm der Heiden Heiland*," 167, points out that this equality is further emphasized by the switching of the two bass voices at

m. 15. She also notes that in the three cantatas where Bach sets this chorale (BWV 36, 61, and 62), he chooses stanzas 1, 6, and 8 to be quoted directly. This would lead one to believe that Bach considered these particular stanzas to be of special significance.

108. Williams, *The Organ Music of J. S. Bach*, 2nd ed., 368; see also Bartel, *Musica Poetica*, 318.

109. Johann Gottfried Walther, *Musicalisches Lexicon Oder Musicalische Bibliothec* (Leipzig, 1732), ed. Friederike Ramm (Kassel: Bärenreiter, 2001), 401: "*Messanza* ist eine vermengte Figur, so aus vier geschwinden Noten bestehet, welche entweder zum Theil bleiben, und zum Theil sich bewegen, oder theils springen, theils ordentlich gehen. Beym *Praetorio T.3 c.5.* ist *Messanza* oder *Mistichanza* so viel, als ein *Quodlibet*; wenn nemlich aus vielen Motetten und Madrigalien, weltlichen und possierlichen Liedern, eine Halbe oder gantze Zeile Text, sammt den Melodien, herausgenommen, und aus solchen Fleckgen und Stückgen wiederum ein gantzes Lied gemacht wird." [The *messanza* is a mixed figure consisting of four rapid notes of which either some remain stationary while others move or some leap while others move by step. In Praetorius' (*Syntagma*) vol. 3, ch. 5, *messanza* or *mistichanza* is defined as a *quodlibet*: namely when a half or a whole line of text with its melody is taken from a number of motets, madrigals, or secular or lighthearted songs and these portions are fashioned into another song]. See Bartel, *Musica Poetica*, 318f.

110. Spitta, *Johann Sebastian Bach*, trans. Bell and Fuller-Maitland, 1:619.

111. Schützeichel, *Schweitzer*, 255.

112. Luedtke, "Seb. Bachs Choralvorspiele," 74.

113. Taylor, *The Chorale Preludes of J. S. Bach*, 108.

114. Taylor, *The Chorale Preludes of J. S. Bach*, 116.

115. Keller, *Die Orgelwerke Bachs*, 189; Keller, *The Organ Works of Bach*, trans. Hewitt, 255.

116. Chailley, *Les Chorals pour Orgue de J.-S. Bach*, 201.

117. Ulrich Meyer, "Zur Frage der inneren Einheit von Bachs Siebzehn Chorälen," 73.

118. Meyer, "Über J. S. Bachs Orgelchoralkunst," 44.

119. Meyer, "Über J. S. Bachs Orgelchoralkunst," 44.

120. Williams, *The Organ Music of J. S. Bach*, 2nd ed., 369.

121. *WA* $10^{1/2}$:11; *Church Postils* 6:17.

122. In *Herr Jesu Christ, dich zu uns wend* (BWV 655) and *Allein Gott in der Höh sei Ehr* (BWV 664), Bach changed from 2/2 in the Weimar version of both settings to 4/4 in the Leipzig settings.

123. *WA* $10^{1/2}$:8f.

124. *Church Postils* 6:15f.

125. See *NBR*, 19f. The editors discuss Bach's use of inversion in the puzzle canon of 1747: "The canon is an occasional and unpretentious composition, without text, but it reveals to us how strongly Bach felt the change of *Affect* accomplished solely by inversion, trusting the mere indication of a similar contrast in words to tell any able musician the puzzle's solution." The reference is to the puzzle canon, but the implication is that Bach's use of inversion would automatically have been understood as having a relationship to the text.

• 9 •

Allein Gott in der Höh sei Ehr

THE HYMN

$\mathcal{T}$he text of *Allein Gott in der Höh sei Ehr* is Nicolaus Decius's (c.1485–af-ter 1546) German paraphrase of the Latin *Gloria*. The text of the *Gloria* was commonly known as the *hymnus angelicus* because of its derivation from the Christmas story as told in Luke 2:14. This text has been associated with the *Laudamus*, an old church hymn since early Christian times. Luther clearly had a great liking for the angels' song, describing it as follows:

> Denn er ist nicht auff erden gewachsen noch gemacht, Sonder van hymel herunter kommen.[1] [for this hymn did not originate on earth but was brought down from heaven to the earth by the angels.[2]]

The *Gloria* is one of the earliest voices of the Eastern Church, and it was sung in Greek as a morning hymn at Matins. The text of the *Gloria in excelsis* unites the two main components of every Christian hymn, supplication and praise. By the sixth century it had found its way into Western liturgies. It was not originally meant for inclusion in the Mass, being introduced initially as a Christmas hymn, and later as an Easter hymn, only gradually becoming established within the Mass itself.[3] *Allein Gott in der Höh sei Ehr* is one of two German versions of the *Gloria* used in the Lutheran tradition, the second be-ing a setting by Luther, "All Ehr und Lob soll Gottes sein."[4] For the first one hundred years of the Reformation, Luther's version had some currency, but Decius's *Allein Gott* came into virtual universal use.[5] This text, together with Decius's paraphrases of the Latin texts of the *Sanctus* and *Agnus Dei*, are among the oldest hymns of the Reformation. Decius adapted the melody from that of the *Gloria* in the *Missa Tempore Paschali* (Mass 1 *Lux et origino*) of the *Graduale*

179

Romanum. This hymn was originally published in Low German under the title *Aleyne God in der Höge sy eere* in the 1525 Rostock hymnbook, edited by the reformer Joachim Slüter.[6] It appeared in High German in Valintin Schumann's 1539 hymnbook at Leipzig.[7] 1539 was the year that the Reformation was introduced into Leipzig, and two hundred years later, Bach composed three settings of *Allein Gott* for *Clavierübung III.* Both of the above sources list this chorale as *Gloria in excelsis Deo,* a practice that was maintained by later Leipzig editors including Schein (1627) and Vopelius (1682). Johannes Kulp emphasizes that although it was primarily a liturgical hymn, this did not preclude it from being sung at other times.[8]

The hymn comprises four stanzas, with 1 through 3 being written by Decius in 1522, and stanza 4 being added in 1525, probably written by Joachim Slüter, the editor of the hymnal in which it first appeared.[9] *Allein Gott* was listed as a Trinitarian hymn by Georg Christian Schemelli in his hymnbook of 1736. Bach also listed it as such in the proposed contents of the *Orgel-Büchlein.*[10] The doctrine of the Trinity was of fundamental importance to Lutheran theology, and consequently this hymn was regarded as an important pedagogical hymn.[11]

Stanza 1 begins with the song the angels sang at the birth of Christ, highlighting goodwill toward man and peace on earth. This stanza is concerned with the Trinitarian God. Stanza 2 specifically mentions God the Father and focuses on his glory, power, and eternity and the great happiness of mankind. He is praised in a fourfold song of praise, his power being clearly described in the final three lines of stanza 2. The will of the Father is also an important element of this stanza. Stanza 3 deals with God the Son, who has saved humanity by coming to earth. He is hailed as the Lamb of God, and man asks for his mercy. Thus the sentiments of both the *Kyrie* and *Agnus Dei* are incorporated into the *Gloria* hymn. Stanza 4 deals with the Holy Spirit, as well as mentioning once again the Passion and death of Christ, which provides salvation. It is possible that this stanza was added to strengthen the Trinitarian associations of the hymn.[12] This concluding stanza sees the Holy Spirit as Comforter and Paraclete, who is asked to turn away all misery and distress. The Passion of Christ is explicitly mentioned, through which man is released from the devil's power. The redemption of mankind through the Passion and death of Christ was an important aspect of the Lutheran faith, and it is a theme that recurs in the hymn texts of the "Leipzig" chorales. In his writings on the second article of the creed, Luther emphasizes this point:

> Auch stehet das ganze Evangelion, so wir predigen, darauf, daß man diesen Artikel wohl fasse, als an dem alle unser Heil und Seligkeit liegt und so reich und weit ist, daß wir immer gnug daran zu lernen haben.[13] [Indeed the entire Gospel that we preach depends on the proper understanding of this article. Upon it all our salvation and blessedness are based, and it is so rich and broad that we can never learn it fully.[14]]

In his sermon on Luke 2:1–14 for Christmas Day, Luther explains the significance of the Christmas story as told by Luke in relation to this article of the creed:

> In dießem Evangelio ist der artickel des glawbens gegrund, da wyr sagen: Ich glawb ynn Jhesum Christum, der gebornn ist von Marien, der jung-frawen.[15] [In this gospel is the foundation of the article of our faith when we say: "I believe in Jesus Christ, born of the virgin Mary."[16]]

Luther shows how faith in Christ is fundamental to man's understanding of salvation and redemption, and that this faith begins with the small child in the manger.[17] Theologically, faith in the cross was of profound importance for Lutherans. This doctrine is reflected in the fourth article of the Augsburg Confession:

> Weiter wird gelehrt, daß wir Vergebung der Sunde und Gerechtigkeit vor Gott nicht erlangen mogen durch unser Verdienst, Werk und Genugtun, sonder daß wir Vergebung der Sunde bekommen und vor Gott gerecht werden aus Gnaden umb Christus willen durch den Glauben, so wir glauben, daß Christus fur uns gelitten habe und daß uns umb seinen willen die Sunde vergeben, Gerechtigkeit und ewiges Leben geschenkt wird. Dann diesen Glauben will Gott fur Gerechtigkeit vor ihme halten und zurechnen, wie Sant Paul sagt zun Romern am 3. und 4.[18] [Furthermore, it is taught that we cannot obtain forgiveness of sin and righteousness before God through our merit, work, or satisfactions, but that we receive forgiveness of sin and become righteous before God out of grace, for Christ's sake, through faith, when we believe that Christ has suffered for us and that for his sake our sin is forgiven and righteousness and eternal life are given to us. For God will regard and reckon this faith as righteousness in his sight, as Paul says in Romans 3:21–26 and 4:5.[19]]

The following is the text of *Allein Gott in der Höh sei Ehr* as it appears in the Weimar hymnbook of 1713, where it is listed under the heading "Von der H. Dreyfaltigkeit" [concerning the Holy Trinity]:

1. ALlein Gott in der Höh sei Ehr/
   und Danck für seine Gnade:/:
   Darum daß nun und nimmermehr
   uns rühren kan kein Schade.
   Ein Wohlgefalln GOtt an uns hat/
   nun ist groß Fried ohn unterlaß/
   all Fehd hat nun ein Ende.

1. Glory to God alone on high,
   and thanks for his mercy,
   for now and nevermore
   can harm touch us.
   God has goodwill towards us,
   now there is great peace without pause,
   all quarrels now have an end.

2. Wir loben/ preisn/ anbeten dich
   für deine Ehr wir dancken:/:
   Daß du Gott Vater ewiglich
   regierst ohn alles Wancken.
   Gantz ungemessen ist deine Macht/

2. We praise, laud and worship you,
   we give thanks for your glory,
   that you God the Father eternally
   reign without wavering.
   Your power is completely unmeasured,

fort geschicht was dein Will hat bedacht/
wohl uns des feinen HErren.

it does whatever your will considers,
happy we, for our great Lord.

3. O Jesu Christ/ Sohn eingebohrn/
   deines himmlischen Vaters:/:
   Versöhner der'r die warn verlohrn/
   du Stiller unsers Haders/
   Lamm Gottes heilger HErr und Gott/
   nimm an die Bitt von unser Noth/
   erbarm dich unser aller.

3. O Jesu Christ, only begotten Son
   of your heavenly Father,
   reconciler of those who were lost,
   settler of our disputes.
   Lamb of God, holy Lord and God,
   accept the prayer from our distress,
   have mercy on us all.

4. O heiliger Geist du höchtes Gut/
   du allerheilsamster Tröster:/:
   Fürs Teuffels Gwalt fortan behüt/
   die Jesus Christus erlöset/
   durch grosse Marter und bittern Tod/
   abwend all unser Jammer und Noth/
   darauf wir uns verlassen.[20]

4. O Holy Spirit, you highest good,
   you most beneficial comforter,
   guard us henceforth from the devil's power,
   from which Jesus Christ released us
   by his great agony and bitter death,
   turn away all our misery and distress,
   we depend on it.[21]

The melody of this chorale is almost certainly by Decius himself, since he was also known as a musician.[22] The chorale was soon transmitted beyond northern Germany, appearing in England around 1535 with a translation of Decius's paraphrase ("To God the hyghest be glory always") in the *Goostly Psalms*, edited by Myles Coverdale.[23]

Bach uses this melody more than any other chorale: BWV 662, 663, 664, 675, 676, 677, 715, 716 (not included in *NBA* IV/3), and 717; he lists it in the *Orgel-Büchlein*, harmonizes it in BWV 260, and sets it to other texts in cantatas BWV 85, 104, 112, and 128. By the early eighteenth century, as was common with many hymn tunes, variants had crept in, especially with regard to certain notes being chromaticized. In all of his chorale settings, Bach frequently uses variations of the same melody. In his "Leipzig" chorale settings, Bach utilizes versions that closely resemble those from his harmonized chorales BWV 104/6 and BWV 260. The melody was commonly transmitted in G or F. The Weißenfels hymnbook of 1714 published it in A, which was less common.[24] It is only in BWV 663 that Bach bases his *cantus firmus* on a further chromatic variant at mm. 22 and 97.

The Leipzig liturgies allowed for many different permutations regarding the performance of the *Gloria*, be it in Latin or in German. *Allein Gott in der Höh sei Ehr* was one of the four hymns sung by the congregation every Sunday. This hymn had existed since the Reformation for this express purpose.[25] During Bach's tenure at St. Thomas's, the *Gloria* was probably only performed polyphonically on festival days.[26]

Central German hymnbooks most frequently assigned this Trinitarian hymn to the texts "Von der Heiligen Dreyfaltigkeit." Bach lists it in his *Orgel-Büchlein* autograph with the other Trinitarian hymns.[27] Because of its reference to the song of the angels (Luke 2:14) in the opening phrases of the Latin *Gloria*, some Saxon and Thuringian traditions continued to identify the chorale with Christmas. The Dresden hymnbooks of 1676 and 1694 still classified it with the texts "von der Geburt Christi" [concerning the birth of Christ].[28] In the "Leipzig" chorales, *Allein Gott in der Höh sei Ehr* comes immediately after the Advent hymn *Nun komm der Heiden Heiland*. Helene Werthemann suggests that since *Allein Gott* was listed by Schemelli in 1736 as a Trinitarian hymn and also because it was a hymn of praise, the chorale preludes on this hymn in the "Leipzig" chorales could be played *sub communione*.[29]

ALLEIN GOTT IN DER HÖH SEI EHR (BWV 662)

Bach included three very different settings of *Allein Gott in der Höh sei Ehr* in the "Leipzig" chorales. The first (BWV 662) is of the slow ornamental type with the *cantus firmus* in the soprano, one of four chorale settings of this type in the "Leipzig" chorales.[30] It survives in two versions: BWV 662a, which dates from Weimar, and a later Leipzig revision, BWV 662. The latter bears the title "*Allein Gott in der Höh seÿ Ehr. a 2 Clav. et Ped. canto fermo in Sopr.*" and Bach has added the tempo indication of *adagio* under the left-hand stave. This is one of the most elaborate coloratura settings ever written by Bach. Throughout this composition, the coloratura chorale melody is presented in the right hand, accompanied by a two-part left hand with pedal. Although the chorale melody is very ornate, it is clearly discernible throughout, and the piece closes with a unique cadenza-like passage that leads to an elaborate final perfect cadence.

BWV 662 employs the ritornello principle, as do many of Bach's chorale settings in the "Leipzig" chorales and *Clavierübung III*.[31] The opening ritornello theme is presented fugally in the first section of the piece (mm. 1–8). In fact, it is a complete fugal exposition that ceases with the entry of the *cantus firmus*. In addition to the technique of fugue, Bach also employs the well-established process of fore-imitation, since the theme contains all of the notes of line 1 of the *cantus firmus*. This is a technique learned from Dietrich Buxtehude, but here Bach considerably expands the interludes on the accompanying manual, being deliberately more large scale than any of his predecessors. The fugal theme is presented first of all in the tenor, accompanied after less than one measure by the countersubject in the alto. The pedal enters in m. 2 with the first four notes of the countersubject, which itself can be seen as a fugal answer to the first four notes of the *cantus firmus*. The alto takes over the fugal theme in the dominant in m. 3, being this time even more ornate than on the first occasion. The pedal presents an unadorned version of the subject beginning on the last beat of m. 5. This is answered by a further statement of the subject in the alto, with the countersubject in the tenor.

Like *Schmücke dich, o liebe Seele* (BWV 654), this setting of *Allein Gott in der Höh sei Ehr* is highly ornate, even in the accompanying parts. The first phrase of the *cantus firmus* enters in m. 9 over a pedal *A*. Below this intricate line, the accompanying parts combine motivic elements from the opening ritornello, including the fugal theme. A brief half-measure interlude between the first and second lines of the *cantus firmus* establishes the key of F-sharp minor in m. 12. Further motivic development accompanies the second phrase of the *cantus firmus* which leads to an interrupted cadence in the tonic at m. 15. Below this pedal point, the parts continue with their incessant development of the opening ritornello motives, passing through the subdominant before cadencing in the tonic once more. All of this material is repeated for lines 3 and 4 of the chorale.

Bach continues the process of fore-imitation in m. 33. There is a simple and unadorned reference to line 5 of the chorale in the pedal, while the unity of the piece is maintained by the appearance of the fugal theme in the alto part. The material Bach uses in the accompanying voices in mm. 35–37 is also derived from the opening ritornello elements, including a statement of the fugal theme in the pedal. The *cantus firmus* reenters in m. 37 with line 5 of the chorale, cadencing in m. 39 in the key of B minor. In mm. 36–37, a reference to the fugal theme is heard in the tenor, with the ornamental notes written out.

In the ensuing interlude, there is further motivic development, including a reference to the fugal theme in the pedal centered on the subdominant. The *cantus firmus* reenters in m. 41 with line 6 of the chorale. The alto contains the fugal theme, with the pedal alluding to the opening notes of the countersubject. In m. 43, the pedal states the fugal theme leading to F-sharp minor, through B minor and E major, before then returning to A major for the entry of the final phrase of the chorale. This leads to an elaborate close in the tonic at mm. 48–49. A final reference to the fugal theme is made in m. 48 in the pedal. A remarkable coda begins at m. 49 with the three lower parts moving toward the subdominant under a tonic pedal note in the soprano. A cadenza-like passage follows for the solo voice in a very violinistic style, based on a diminished-seventh chord, leading to the final perfect cadence in the tonic.

Interpretations by Other Authors

The presence of three settings of this Trinitarian hymn in the "Leipzig" chorales has prompted many writers to attach great significance to this fact.

Albert Schweitzer suggests that it is very likely that Bach responded to the intonation of the *Gloria* with a chorale on *Allein Gott*.[32] He considers that BWV 662 and 663 have a dreamlike quality, in contrast to the other settings of this hymn which express a more immediate joy.[33]

Hans Luedtke suggests, as he did with the three settings of *Nun komm der Heiden Heiland* (BWV 659–661), that Bach, having composed so many settings of *Allein Gott in der Höh sei Ehr*, may have performed them *alternatim* with the stanzas of the hymn.[34] He sees the text of stanza 3 as being reflected in BWV 662.[35] Because of the connection of this stanza with the crucified Christ, he suggests that the paraphrasing of line 1 of the chorale melody results in a symbol of the cross, which pervades the entire piece.[36] In his view, the free cadential recitative section near the end represents "erbarm dich unser allen," and the final measures are a promise of God's mercy. According to Luedtke, the three settings are representative of the three persons of the Trinitarian God.[37]

Charles Sanford Terry states that Bach invariably uses the melody of *Allein Gott* to express the adoration of the angelic hosts, and in scale passages he pictures the throng of them ascending and descending between earth and heaven.[38] He sees the final thirty-one measures of BWV 662 as being connected to stanza 1 ["on earth is peace restored again, through Jesus Christ our Savior"], with the ascending cadence representing the departing host of angels.[39] The significance of the three settings of the Trinity hymn is also commented on by Terry.[40]

Stainton de B. Taylor regards the three settings of *Allein Gott in der Höh sei Ehr* (BWV 662–664) as paying tribute to the "Holy and undivided Trinity."[41] He claims that "the desire to portray the winging movement of the Angelic Hosts around the Throne in BWV 662 is obvious."[42]

Hermann Keller sees the descending seventh of the advance imitation as bringing heaven down to earth, but he does not consider any other important motives in this setting.[43] He refers to A major as the grail tonality and to the otherworldliness of BWV 662.[44]

Jacques Chailley only considers stanza 1. He sees the three rising notes of the pedal opening as being representative of the glory of God and suggests that the thirds and sixths of mm. 36, 38, 39, and so forth, are proclaiming the peace obtainable through God [Wohlgefalln].[45] According to Chailley, the peace without interruption [ohn Unterlass] is seen in the pervading mood of joy that penetrates the whole piece. With the final section, Chailley suggests that when Bach arrives at the word "Ende," the enormous coda is formed in response to the text, evoking feelings of unrest in the chromatic harmony and the use of augmented seconds. In his opinion, all is resolved in the triumphant final cadence where the minor third becomes major and the chorale finds its end, with the tenor having the final say in the last measure.[46]

Ulrich Meyer agrees with Luedtke and sees the descending opening motive as representing the descent of Christ to earth, therefore reflecting the second half of the hymn text. To support his claim, he states that this symbolism is also portrayed in the *adagio* indication that Bach added to the Leipzig setting of this chorale.[47] In his view, this composition has much in common with *Nun komm der Heiden Heiland* (BWV 659), expressing the benevolence and mercy of God in allowing his Son to come to earth. According to Meyer, this is especially relevant to the words "Versöhner der'r, die warn verlorn."[48]

Peter Williams also connects BWV 659 and BWV 662, although he states that the chorale melody is more recognizable in the latter.[49] Williams is skeptical of both Keller and Meyer, although he does not offer any real interpretation of the text.[50]

Russell Stinson sees the four stanzas of *Allein Gott* as constituting a *paean* to the Trinity and suggests that the three settings in the "Great Eighteen" represent stanzas 2–4. However, he does not clarify his ideas with any detail.[51]

While many writers mention the Trinitarian significance of this hymn, it still remains unclear how Bach fits a hymn of four stanzas into three musical compositions. This is investigated in the following sections.

Assessment

A survey of the literature relating to BWV 662 reveals that there appear to be many conflicting views regarding the text-music relationships in BWV 662. An investigation into the many important musical features of this work may help to reach a conclusion in this regard.

Striking musical elements include the very ornate treatment of the *cantus firmus*, the dominance of the *figura corta*, the many parallel thirds and sixths, the position of the *cantus firmus* in relation to the two other settings, the unadorned statement of line 5 of the *cantus firmus* in the pedal from m. 33, and the rhapsodic unaccompanied melodic line heard just before the close of the piece from mm. 51–52. These characteristics may lead to a particular stanza of the hymn. Additionally, it may be logical to suggest that Bach might have started with stanza 1, given the fact that he set this chorale melody three times in the "Leipzig" chorales. It seems unlikely that he would begin with either stanza 3 or 4.

In many of Bach's chorale preludes, the register of the *cantus firmus* appears to have been significant with regard to text-music relationships.

In these three settings of *Allein Gott in der Höh sei Ehr*, Bach presents the *cantus firmus* first in the top part (BWV 662), second in the middle (BWV 663), and finally in the bass, although only its first two lines (BWV 664). In *Clavierübung III*, Bach takes a similar approach. In the first three chorale preludes, *Kyrie, Gott Vater Ewigkeit* (BWV 669); *Christe aller Welt Trost* (BWV 670); and *Kyrie Gott heiliger Geist* BWV (671), the *cantus firmus* is presented respectively in the soprano, tenor, and bass. In these three settings, Bach represented God the Father in the top part in BWV 669, Christ the mediator in the middle part of BWV 670, and the Holy Spirit in the bass in BWV 671.[52] Albert Clement points out that it is necessary to consider the context of a group of chorale preludes such as these.[53] One cannot automatically assume that the position of a *cantus firmus* has symbolic meaning. Clement goes into great detail regarding the register of the *cantus firmus* in BWV 669–671.[54] It may be possible to apply a similar interpretation to BWV 662–664. Equally, *Allein Gott* being a Trinitarian hymn may have some bearing on the position of the *cantus firmus* in each case.

The Trinitarian aspect of this hymn has been discussed by other authors, and it is helpful to refer to them here. Philipp Spitta discusses this issue as follows:

> And the fact that the chorale "Allein Gott in der Höh sei Ehr" is treated three times has an ecclesiastical and dogmatic reference. For this hymn is sung in praise of the Trinity, to whom also the prayer of the *Kyrie* is addressed; but in the *Kyrie* the three different melodies require as many different treatments, while in "Allein Gott in der Höh sei Ehr" all the verses were to be sung to the same melody.[55]

Spitta is referring to the three settings from *Clavierübung III*, but the same point could be applied to the three settings of *Allein Gott* from the "Leipzig" chorales. In his discussion of the Catechism hymns of *Clavierübung III*, Albert Schweitzer also mentions the Trinitarian character of *Allein Gott* as follows:

> Um das Dogma vollständig zu haben, schickte er diesen fünf Hauptstücken das an die heilige Dreifaltigkeit gerichtete *Kyrie* und *Gloria* des Leipziger Gottesdienstes voraus . . . , das letzte natürlich in drei Versionen.[56] [In order to have the dogma complete, he prefaced these five chief hymns with the *Kyrie* and *Gloria* to the Holy Trinity from the Leipzig service (. . .), this last of course in three versions.[57]]

For Schweitzer, as well as for Spitta, it was natural to have three settings of *Allein Gott in der Höh sei Ehr*. However, as Clement points out, while Bach was clearly referring to the Trinity in his three settings of *Allein Gott*, the fact remains that there are actually four stanzas in this hymn.[58] One must guard against automatically assuming that the first setting (BWV 662) is referring to the Father. The hymn text refers in stanza 1 to the Trinitarian God, in stanza 2 to the Father, in stanza 3 to the Son, and in stanza 4 to the Holy Spirit. Clement also makes the point that the Trinitarian connection with this hymn is unequivocally clear from the hymnbooks of the time, a fact that could not have escaped Bach.[59]

In BWV 662, the *cantus firmus* is presented ornamentally as a right-hand solo. Under normal circumstances, placing the *cantus firmus* in the uppermost position in an isolated chorale prelude might not have significance for the text. It is important to consider BWV 662 within the context of the three settings of *Allein Gott* in the "Leipzig" chorales (BWV 662–664), as mentioned previously. It could be considered significant that Bach places the *cantus firmus* first in the soprano (BWV 662), second in the tenor (BWV 663), and finally in the bass (BWV 664). Since *Allein Gott* was a well-established Trinitarian hymn, in addition to being associated with Christmas and the German *Gloria*, Bach may be making some kind of Trinitarian reference in his three settings of this hymn from the "Leipzig" chorales. It seems reasonable to suggest that the position of the *cantus firmus* in BWV 662 could most logically represent either the Trinitarian God of the first stanza or God the Father of the second stanza. The Trinitarian God, who is in heaven, can easily be portrayed in the uppermost position, but so can God the Father of the second stanza who is also depicted in heaven. It seems less likely that Bach is portraying the second or third persons of the Trinity as portrayed in stanzas 3 and 4.

Throughout BWV 662, the *figura corta* is heard fifty times, enough to be considered extremely significant. This so-called joy motive has been used by Bach in many compositions to indicate confidence in God's goodness and the paradoxical joy associated with the Passion of Christ.[60] It may be possible to find a meaning for its persistent use in the text of the hymn. As a motive of joy and trust in God, it can easily be associated with stanzas 1 and 2, both of which praise the Trinitarian God and God the Father respectively. Bach has used this figure in relation to the joy of salvation in the context of the cross, so it could equally lead to stanza 3 or even stanza 4, which also mentions the Savior. However, is it not more likely that because of the extremely high incidence of this figure in BWV 662, Bach was trying to depict great joy, as expressed in either stanza 1 or stanza 2? Bach may be portraying confidence in God and lack of fear, as expressed in the angels' song, in the use of the *figura corta*. This seems to lead to the text of stanza 1 whose origins lie in the ancient *hymnus angelicus*.

The dominance of parallel thirds and sixths is another striking presence in BWV 662. These parallel intervals are further enhanced by trills in both hands. In *Schmücke dich, o liebe Seele* (BWV 654), trills in parallel thirds and sixths correspond easily to the adorned soul that longs for mystical union with Christ in heaven. It may be possible that in BWV 662 they can also be related to heavenly matters, in this case God in heaven. Words such as "Danck," "Gnade," "Wohlgefalln," and "Fried" (stanza 1); "loben," "preisn," "anbeten," and "wohl" (stanza 2); and perhaps "Tröster" (stanza 4) may be linked with this musical process. There is a generally happy atmosphere in BWV 662. Bach frequently uses parallel thirds and sixths to represent joy and happiness in cantatas, for example the duet for alto and tenor from the cantata *Ein Herz, das seinem Jesum lebend weiß* (BWV 134), written for the third day of Easter 1724.[61] Here the text begins, "Wir danken und preisen dein brünstiges Lieben" [We thank and praise your ardent love].[62] It is perhaps even more rewarding to examine the original secular model for this cantata, *Die Zeit, die Tag und Jahre macht* (BWV 134a), written as a tribute to the princely house of Anhalt-Cöthen for New Year's Day, 1719.[63] In the recitative that precedes the duet between Divine Providence (alto) and Time (tenor), Divine Providence invokes God's glory. The duet deals with striving and conquering, with the closing line as follows: "Es schlägt zum Preise des Höchsten hinaus" [Everything sounds to praise the All-Highest]. Thus Bach here associates praising God on high with parallel thirds and sixths. This may help to lead to the text of stanza 1.

The writing in parallel tenths is at its most pronounced in m. 36, the measure that separates the statement of line 5 of the chorale melody in the pedal with the ornamented statement in the right hand. It appears that Bach considered this line to be important, since he singled it out for special treatment. No other line of the chorale is heard in the pedal in this way. Examination of line 5 of every stanza may help lead to a solution:

> Ein Wohlgefalln GOtt an uns hat (stanza 1).
> Gantz ungemessen ist deine Macht (stanza 2).
> Lamm Gottes heilger HErr und Gott (stanza 3).
> durch grosse Marter und bittern Tod (stanza 4).

It seems reasonable to eliminate stanzas 3 and 4. Since the importance of line 5 is implied by its presence in the pedal from m. 33, it is also logical that this line should be appropriate to the context of the musical features mentioned before. The Lamb of God and "grosse Marter" and "bittern Tod" do not seem to be portrayed in the parallel motion and the constant use of the *figura corta*. It may be possible to link line 5 of stanza 2 with the musical aspects of BWV 662, but it appears more likely that Bach is depicting "ein Wohlgefalln Gott" of stanza 1. God's goodwill is seen in the ever-present *figura corta* and parallel motion.

The final note of the *cantus firmus* is remarkably long in the context of an *adagio* tempo, lasting for two measures. Long notes can have significance for text-music relationships, being sometimes related to eternity. Allied to this long note is the improvisatory solo line that begins at m. 51. Bach sometimes emphasizes important theological moments through the use of unaccompanied recitative-like writing in arias from the cantatas and other vocal works.[64] Investigation into the final lines of all stanzas may help to find a meaning for these two features:

> all Fehd hat nun ein Ende (stanza 1).
> wohl uns des feinen Herren (stanza 2).
> erbarm dich unser aller (stanza 3).
> darauf wir uns verlassen (stanza 4).

The solo writing may best be related to texts relating to salvation, and therefore the closing line of stanza 1 may be most appropriate. The text implies that since all quarrels are at an end, then because of God's mercy, peace will reign eternally. Additionally, it is worth noting how Bach descends a minor tenth at m. 51, counteracting this *catabasis* with a dramatic upward leap of a major thirteenth. This leads to two statements of the *figura corta* in m. 52 before the final perfect cadence that incorporates a rising *tirata defectiva*, itself closing with the *figura corta*. The use of the *figura corta* in the pedal in m. 50, the only place in the entire piece where this occurs, may also be regarded as significant. The general *Affekt* of this final section is remarkably positive, brought about by the sonorous ornamental line, the use of the *figura corta*, and the elaborate perfect cadence. Bach may be depicting the end of all struggles and quarrels in the very positive close to BWV 662, showing the consequence of the end of struggle in the light unaccompanied recitative-like writing. The lengthy final note of the *cantus firmus* can also be related to the eternal aspect of stanza 1: the end of struggle implies the start of eternal life.

It appears that Bach was indeed setting the text of stanza 1 in BWV 662. It is undoubtedly true that when Bach set more than one chorale prelude on the same hymn in a collection, he usually had different stanzas of the hymn in mind. It was not unusual for him to proceed progressively from stanza 1 with the first setting and so on.[65] The evidence seems to point to this stanza. Many of the musical features can find a meaning in the text of the other three stanzas as already discussed, but there is no stanza, apart from stanza 1, that appears to be relevant to all the musical characteristics. Further discussion of BWV 662 may help to show how this is so.

Clement has shown clearly that it is the text of stanza 1 that undergirds *Allein Gott in der Höh sei Ehr* (BWV 675) from *Clavierübung III*.[66] Although BWV 675 and BWV 662 are two very different settings, it is interesting to compare some aspects. BWV 675 displays many obvious Trinitarian features in the triple time signature, the use of triplets, and the original "à 3" indication.[67] There are some common aspects between the two settings, including use of the *figura corta*, crossing of lines, and the prominence afforded to line 5 of the *cantus firmus*.

The heavenly position of the Trinitarian God in the uppermost position of the *cantus firmus* in BWV 662 has been noted above. Perhaps the employment of the key of A major with three sharps can also be regarded as an indication of the Trinity. In BWV 675, Bach also emphasizes line 5 of the text, which itself stems from Luke's Gospel account of the birth of Christ: "Ehre sei Gott in der Höhe und Friede auf Erden *und in den Menschen ein Wohlgefallen!*"[68] God on high, the Trinitarian God, is being praised. Perhaps Bach is deliberately referring back to the angels' message as found in Luke by giving special prominence to line 5 which mentions "Wohlgefalln." Luther himself said that the word "Wohlgefallen" was bad German. He points out that the original Greek is *eudokia*, which means joy and delight and is much more suitable.[69] The unadorned pedal part is accompanied in the manual parts by the *figura corta*. The idea of joy and delight makes the use of the *figura corta* very natural at this point. In general, the constant use of the *figura corta* and the parallel thirds and sixths add a feeling of well-being and comfort to this setting.

In examining the text of stanza 1, it may be important to see this stanza not merely as the angels' song at the birth of Christ, but also to consider its deeper significance. The angels sing the praises of the Trinitarian God, who in his grace has allowed the birth of Christ in order to bring about the end of sin, that humanity may gain salvation. Luther himself gives a detailed commentary on Luke 2:14, the source of the first two lines of text of this hymn, mentioning the redemptive purpose of Christ's birth. In his commentary, he refers to John 3:16, which shows Christ's origins with God. The citation from John is as follows:

> Also hat GOtt die Welt geliebt, daß Er seinen eingebornen Sohn gab, auf daß alle, die an Ihn glauben, nicht verloren werden, sondern das ewige Leben haben. [Yet God loved the world so much that he gave his only Son, so that everyone who believes in him may not be lost, but may have eternal life.]

Here Jesus is proclaiming the purpose for which he has come into this world. Raymond Brown explains this passage:

> Jesus proclaims for the first time the basic Johannine theology of salvific incarnation: He is God's Son come into the world bringing God's own life, so that everyone who believes in him has eternal life and thus is already judged.[70]

Luther's understanding of this passage is similar. He sees Christ as the true Savior and as the only means of eternal life. The expression of God's love in the birth of his Son is the most important of the heavenly things, according to Luther. In his sermon for the afternoon of Christmas Day 1520, Luther repeatedly stresses the fact that Christ is born as Lord and Savior.[71] Thus the message of Christmas has eschatological meaning, and this is most explicitly expressed in stanza 1 of the chorale *Allein Gott in der Höh sei Ehr.*

Keller and Meyer suggest that the opening manual motive may portray Christ's descent to earth. The opening pedal motive (see example 9.1a) may be considered more important. It might be possible to relate this motive to similar melodic patterns in the St. John Passion. The first version of the St. John Passion was written after BWV 662a, in 1724. In this work, Bach develops a cadential formula that was related to the divinity of Christ. The dominant-tonic formula associated with Christ's divine utterance "Ich bin's" is expanded later in the Passion when Christ sings "Du sagst, ich bin ein König" [You say I am a king].[72] It may be that the seeds for this motive were sown in BWV 662a. In BWV 662, Bach uses a cadential formula three times before the entry of the *cantus firmus* in the right hand with the first line of the chorale. He was possibly thinking of the opening text: *Allein Gott in der Höh sei Ehr.* He could also be highlighting the divine heavenly God with this affirmative cadence. This section of the music is also relevant to lines 3 and 4 of the text because of the repeat: "Darum dass nun und nimmermehr uns rühren kann kein Schade." The text is referring to the fact that no harm can come to mankind now or in the future. This is because Christ's incarnation and Passion have achieved eternal salvation for humanity through the mercy and goodness of God in heaven. Therefore, the motive that emphasizes his divine might and power may also be relevant to the text of line 3 of the chorale.

The main differences between BWV 662 and 662a lie in the ornamentation. In BWV 662, Bach indicates the ornamentation more specifically, but as Williams has shown, it is possible that these ornaments would have been taken for granted by the performer, indicated or not.[73] The piece has a high proportion of ornaments, many of them being actually written into the melodic line. Bach seems to indulge in overornamentation when he is dealing with heavenly or divine matters, for example *An Wasserflüssen Babylon* (BWV 653); *Schmücke*

Example 9.1a.   BWV 662 (mm. 2ff.)

Example 9.1b.   BWV 245/2c (m. 2)

dich, o liebe Seele (BWV 654); and *Nun komm der Heiden Heiland* (BWV 659). It may be possible to find a similar context in BWV 662.

There are only two references to the so-called "sighing" motive.[74] These occur at m. 11 (and m. 27) and m. 38. The significance of this motive has been discussed in chapter 8 in connection with *Nun komm der Heiden Heiland* (BWV 659). In the case of BWV 662, Bach could be referring to similar ideas—the saving of the human race through the sacrifice of Christ.

The penultimate line of the chorale enters in m. 41. The text here is "Nun ist groß Fried ohn Unterlass." Apart from the first note of the melody, it is identical to the first and third phrases. Bach chooses to use the motivic material in a different way from his original presentation of this tune. In mm. 41 and 42, he uses the *circolo mezzo* as he did in *Nun komm der Heiden Heiland* (BWV 659). Again it is possible that this has symbolic significance here. The traditional view of the circle as a symbol of perfection may have been in Bach's mind when he used this ornament at this particular point. The text refers to the eternal peace brought about by Christ. The final line of stanza 1 shows the consequence of these events: "all Fehd hat nun ein Ende." Bach makes a few interesting musical comments here. The only place in the entire setting where the accompanying lines cross each other is at m. 46 and m. 47 (see example 9.2). It may be that the crossing of the lines refers to the end of all quarrels, which was itself brought about by the cross—hence the crossing of lines.

Because of the derivation of the opening stanza from the *hymnus angelicus,* Terry has proposed that the descending and ascending angel hosts are represented in BWV 662. Taylor also mentions angels. Bach frequently depicts angels in his music, but as described in chapter 4, this usually involved scalic

Example 9.1c.   BWV 245/18a (mm. 4f.)

Example 9.2.   BWV 662 (mm. 46f.)

passages in sixteenth notes. In the case of BWV 662, the angels' message, rather than the angels themselves, appears to be more important.

★ ★ ★

It appears from the previous discussion that Bach is portraying the text of stanza 1 in BWV 662. Important aspects pointing to this stanza are the emphasis of line 5 in the context of other musical elements such as the *figura corta* and parallel motion. The position of the *cantus firmus* also seems to have a bearing on the stanza chosen by Bach, as does the rhapsodic, recitative-like passage three measures from the end. No other stanza appears to justify the employment of all these elements to the same extent as stanza 1. In the following sections, I will investigate how Bach may have portrayed the remaining stanzas in BWV 663 and 664.

ALLEIN GOTT IN DER HÖH SEI EHR (BWV 663)

This second setting of *Allein Gott* exists in two versions: an earlier Weimar setting (BWV 663a) and a later Leipzig revision (BWV 663). In P271, the latter bears the heading "*Allein Gott in der Höh seÿ Ehr. a 2 Clav. et Ped. canto fermo in Tenore,*" with the indication *cantabile* under the right-hand stave. The only other setting of this type in the "Leipzig" chorales is *An Wasserflüssen Babylon* (BWV 653). BWV 663a differs notationally only slightly from BWV 663.[75] Russell Stinson makes some interesting observations with regard to the verbal instructions, noting that BWV 663 contains more of these than any other setting in the collection.[76] Both versions (BWV 663a and 663) bear the *cantabile* tempo marking. The indication *adagio* appears at the end of the cadenza-like section for the left hand in both settings (m. 96 in BWV 663a and m. 97 in BWV 663). In the earlier version (BWV 663a), the indication *andante* appears at m. 97.2, and in BWV 663 there is no *andante* marking at this point.[77]

   The texture is in four parts, with the ornamental *cantus firmus* in the tenor. A decorated *en taille* melody is unusual for Bach. Chorale preludes with the *cantus firmus* in the tenor are usually less ornate than BWV 663. The opening theme is presented fugally. This theme is derived from the chorale melody, as is the accompanying pedal motive. These motives are constantly reworked throughout the piece to produce a movement that has much in common with the other large fantasia settings in this collection such as BWV 651 and 661. There are many noteworthy features: the flexible 3/2 time signature; the fore-imitation in the pedal of lines 1, 3, 5, and 6 of the chorale; the cadenza passage at m. 95 before the *adagio*; and the division of the *cantus firmus* line between the solo line and the accompaniment.[78]

In the opening fourteen measures, the fugal theme is presented in m. 1 as subject (soprano), in m. 4 as an answer (alto), and in m. 7 as subject (soprano). Over the first seven measures, the pedal provides a walking bass accompaniment, and in m. 9, line 1 of the chorale is heard in the bass. The walking bass resumes at m. 12 (that is, now not related to the *cantus firmus*), bringing the music to a full close at m. 14 with a three-measure pedal point. The *cantus firmus* enters in the tenor at m. 16 in its ornamental form. While this is highly ornate, the notes of the *cantus firmus* are all present. Motives from the opening fugal exposition are employed in the upper parts. In this phrase, the music moves from G major, through C major and A minor, before then settling on a B major chord, the dominant of E minor, for the final note of the *cantus firmus*. Phrase 2 of the *cantus firmus* enters in m. 27 over a rising E minor arpeggio in the pedal. In this phrase, the music returns from E minor through C major to cadence in G major at measure 34. This entire section is then repeated.

From m. 69 to 79, canonic treatment of lines 5 and 6 of the *cantus firmus* is heard between the pedal and the soprano initially, and then between the pedal and alto. The third accompanying part uses mainly motives from the opening fugal material. The phrase passes through A minor to reach E minor for the entry of line 5 of the *cantus firmus* in the tenor at m. 78. This phrase is largely centered on A minor with a perfect cadence in mm. 84–85. In the three-measure interlude between lines 5 and 6, the key of A minor is confirmed with a further cadence, leading to A major, the dominant of D. This phrase progresses to a cadenza-like passage for the solo part at m. 95, in turn leading to an *adagio* at m. 97 for the final three measures of the *cantus firmus*. The ensuing interlude is based at first around the key of E minor, then moving to A minor and G major, with a rising pedal tetrachord in m. 102 and m. 104 respectively. In m. 105, the accompanying manual takes the tenor part, with the *cantus firmus* reentering in m. 106 for the final phrase of the chorale. The solo manual takes two parts at m. 110, a pedal point on *g0* and continuing motivic development in the upper part. A further solo link at m. 113 leads to a cadence in G major and a tenor pedal point of eleven measures beginning at m. 117. An unusual feature of this final section is the rising sixths in the right hand with the *suspirans* accompanying motive.

Interpretations by Other Authors

As with the previous setting of this hymn text, writers refer to the Trinitarian aspect, some using it as an argument for the assignation of a particular stanza. Others refer to the angels' song.

Albert Schweitzer sees the ascension and disappearance of the angels as represented in the ascending cadences.[79] In his description of Bach's musical language, he includes angels as a pictorial theme, stating that charming and flowing motives always enter when angels are mentioned. He argues that whenever Bach is arranging *Allein Gott in der Höh sei Ehr*, he never forgets that the melody is supposed to be the angels' song, and so he sets it in the form of light duets or trios.[80] He also suggests that the *adagio* at m. 97 expresses the words from stanza 1, "Nun ist gross Fried ohn' Unterlass/ all Fehd hat nun ein Ende."[81]

According to Hans Luedtke, the text of stanza 4 is represented in BWV 663. He sees the solo recitative as expressing "abwend all unser jammr," with the intense harmony of the *adagio* that follows representing the word "Noth."[82]

Harvey Grace states that the mood of the piece is kept bright by the "delightfully tuneful treble and alto which lie rather high. The mood darkens for a moment where the tenor part becomes chromatic and rhapsodic, followed by a bar marked *adagio*. Otherwise the music is grace itself, despite its abundance of imitative and canonic writing."[83]

Stainton de B. Taylor refers to the rhapsodic cadenza that leads into a "fine *adagio* closing section, where once again we meet with 'angelic' scale passages, this time symbolizing Jacob's Ladder."[84] The position of the *cantus firmus* in the tenor is justification for interpreting the second person of the Trinity, according to Taylor.[85]

Jacques Chailley only considers stanza 1 of the text. He sees the climbing of an octave in the tenor *cantus firmus* (mm. 16–24) as expressing the words "in der Höh."[86] Chailley claims that the chromaticisms of m. 22 refer not to line 1 of stanza 1, but line 3, which occurs at the same place in the repeat.[87] According to Chailley, m. 27 is also referring to the repeat (line 4). In his view, the remainder of the music after the repeat paraphrases the last three lines of the text. The canon between the bass and soprano, and subsequently between the bass and alto, announces that God has given his peace to mankind. The penultimate line hails the peace without interruption, with Bach here representing the words "ohn Unterlass," while the serenity of G major reflects the word "Fried" of the penultimate line. In his opinion, however, there is a paradox present where Bach signals danger in the interruption of the counterpoint by the use of *ritenuto* and *adagio*, but from m. 99 onward, the peace reappears with the quiet syncopations and rests leading to the return of G major. Chailley sees the parallel sixths of the final five measures as representing the universal peace climbing the heights of more than an octave.[88]

Ulrich Meyer sees the constant *anabasis* as representing the opening of the hymn text. He refers to Bach's work signature *Soli Deo Gloria*, which he claims is expressed here.[89] In his opinion, there is a parallel with the similar setting of the same chorale from *Clavierübung III* (BWV 676).

Casper Honders suggests that in the main, the text of stanza 4 is represented here, with a possible reference to the opening line of stanza 1. He argues his case by fitting the words as they might be sung to the pedal part in mm. 9–12 and mm. 69–72.[90] The *cantabile* indication is most likely to be related to the tempo—the speed should not be too fast or detached,[91] an opinion that coincides with Stinson's cited previously. Honders sees the high point of line 1 of the decorated *cantus firmus* as representing either "Allein Gott in der Höh sei Ehr" or possibly "O heiliger Geist, du *höchstes* gut." According to Honders, the words of stanza 4 seem to fit the best for line 5 of the hymn. His final point is that if the words of stanza 4 are applied to this setting, then in line 6, the sixth syllable of line 6 coincides with the solo recitative-like phrase of two measures that leads to the *adagio* at m. 97. This is referring to the word "Jammer."[92]

Peter Williams agrees with others in the linkage of stanza 1 to BWV 663, while not actually offering any opinions of his own.[93] In his discussion on the settings of *Allein Gott* from *Clavierübung III* (BWV 675–677), Albert Clement refers to BWV 663 and states in a critical remark addressed to Christian Brückner, first that the canon in BWV 663 is conceived in a way quite different from BWV 676, and second that if Bach were relating the use of canon with stanza 3 in BWV 663, this has to be proven in the first place.[94] It is clear that many writers have very different views on the issue of text-music relationships in BWV 663. In the following section, the music and text are examined in an effort to find a solution.

Assessment

Since it appears that Bach may be setting stanza 1 of *Allein Gott* in BWV 662, it might be reasonable to suggest that he is portraying one of the other stanzas in BWV 663. Examination of the text and music may help find an answer to this question.

The most striking musical aspects of BWV 663 include the 3/2 time signature, the use of *anabasis*, the employment of much parallel motion, the *heterolepsis* of m. 30, the canonic treatment of lines 5 and 6 of the chorale, the dramatic unaccompanied solo line of mm. 95–96 with the subsequent slowing to *adagio* in m. 97, and the noteworthy series of rising sixths from m. 123.

In BWV 663, the chorale setting opens with a flowing, positive, rising melodic line. This may be interpreted as an indication of a positive and happy atmosphere. As the opening figure of BWV 663 is clearly derived from line 1 of the chorale, this musical portrayal may also be related to the text of line 1 of one of the stanzas. In this case, examining the opening lines of all the stanzas may help to find a solution. The positive *Affekt* could conceivably be a portrayal of the opening line of stanza 1, "Allein Gott in der Höh sei Ehr," or that of stanza 2, "Wir loben/ preisn/ anbeten dich." The text of stanza 3, which refers to Christ, does not appear to be a likely connection here. The opening of stanza 4, "O heiliger Geist du höchtes Gut," might also be linked to the positive *Affekt*. Since Bach employs the same music for lines 3 and 4 of the chorale as he does for lines 1 and 2, a further clue regarding the positive opening may be found in line 3 of all stanzas. It seems possible to eliminate stanzas 3 and 4 in this regard. It does not seem likely that a reference to "Versöhner," as in stanza 3, or "Teuffels Gwalt," as in stanza 4, would inspire this kind of writing. This leaves "Darum daß nun und nimmermehr" of stanza 1 and "Daß du Gott Vater ewiglich" of stanza 2. Neither of these lines offers an obvious link to the positive musical setting. There is, however, one other aspect of the presentation of line 1(3) of the *cantus firmus* that needs investigation. A striking feature is the long final note of the phrase. As many have noted, Bach frequently employs the Halteton for the word "ewiglich" or "Ewigkeit." It may be possible to link this long final note of the phrase to "ewiglich." Bach also employs a Halteton at the end of the first phrase in BWV 676 (coinciding with the word "ewiglich"). These arguments seem to lead to the text of stanza 2. Further investigations into the music may clarify the situation further.

In m. 30, the highest note of the *cantus firmus* is reached. Here the left hand reaches *a1* and actually crosses over the accompaniment for the only time in the whole piece (see example 9.3). In baroque rhetoric, such crossing was known as *heterolepsis*. Johann Gottfried Walther defines *heterolepsis* as follows:

Example 9.3.   BWV 663 (m. 30)

Heterolepsis. ist, wenn eine Stimme aus einer andern bisweilen einen *Clavem* hinweg nimmet, und den ihrigen unter [?] daß jener beraubten Stimme zukommen läßet: diese *Figur*, als welche sich einer großen Freyheit anmaset, wird mehrentheils *in sola voce*, zu welcher etl. *Instrumenta accompagniren*, gebrauchet.[95] [The *heterolepsis* occurs when one voice takes something from another voice or even another clef and adds to itself that which rightfully belongs to the other voice. This figure, which assumes a great deal of liberty, most frequently occurs in vocal solos accompanied by various instruments.[96]]

Examination of the text of lines 2 and 4 of all stanzas may produce a solution. Possible links to the text may be found in "regierst ohn alles Wancken" (stanza 2) and "deines himmlischen Vaters" (stanza 3). With "reign without wavering," there is a heavenly implication, as there clearly is with the reference to the "heavenly Father" in stanza 3. Since it might be possible to link the portrayal of line 1(3) of the *cantus firmus* with stanza 2, this may be a further indication that Bach is portraying stanza 2 at this point.

Lines 5 and 6 of the chorale are singled out by Bach for canonic treatment. The melody of line 5 is presented first in the pedal from m. 69 and is followed a measure later in the soprano. It is striking that the canon is presented in the two outer voices an octave apart. From m. 73 onward, line 6 of the *cantus firmus* is treated canonically, this time between the bass and alto. Bach sometimes used this process when he wanted to make a specific point in relation to the text. It could have different meaning depending on the context. Examination of lines 5 and 6 of the four stanzas may help find a meaning for the canon. Apart from stanza 2, there does not seem to be an obvious link between the employment of canon and the text. Bach sometimes utilized canon in the context of the will of God.[97] Lines 5 and 6 of stanza 2 are "Gantz ungemessen ist deine Macht/ fort geschicht was dein Will hat bedacht." Clement has shown how Bach illustrates these words in the employment of canon in BWV 676. He points out the many places where Bach uses canon to portray the idea of God's will, the most important probably being Bach's setting of *Vater unser im Himmelreich* (BWV 682) from *Clavierübung III*.[98]

The above argument may show how line 6 of stanza 2 is related to the use of canon. Perhaps a link between line 5 and the canonic process can also be found. The fact that the canon is between the two outside voices for line 5 of the text may also be significant. The text refers to the power of God being completely unmeasured. It is likely that placing the canon between the two outer voices may portray the idea of the power of God being spread from the heavens to the earth, in other words between all possible extremes. Clement has referred to this concept in relation to variation 4 of the Canonic Variations (BWV 769a).[99] In this variation it is in fact an augmentation canon, but the relevant link to BWV 663 is the canon at the octave and the idea of an all-encompassing character in "*alle* Seligkeit."[100] Clement continues this idea in his assessment of BWV 676 as follows:

> Die Textstelle '*ganz ungemessen* ist deine Macht' wird 'in Canone all'ottava' dargestellt, wobei sowohl die Lage in den Außenstimmen als das Kanon-intervall—die ausgemessene Oktave, das den ganzen Tonraum umfassende Intervall, griechisch *diapason*—, auf die allumfassende *potentia Gottes* hin-weisen.[101] [The point in the text 'your might is *completely unmeasured*' is portrayed in a canon at the octave, where its position in the outer voices as well as the canonic interval—the measured octave, whose total interval, the Greek *diapason*—point to the all encompassing *potentia of God*.]

It may be possible to apply a similar interpretation to BWV 663. Clement shows elsewhere how the number eight is associated with baptism and eternity as follows:

> und die Zahl acht wird namentlich mit der ewigen Seligkeit in Verbindung gebracht! Nebenbei sei darauf hingewiesen, daß das achteckige Taufbecken den achten Schöpfungstag bezeichnet, d.h. die mit der Auferstehung Christi beginnende neue Schöpfung, in die der Täufling durch das Taufbad hineingenommen wird. "Acht ist daher die Zahl der Wiedergeburt durch die Taufe, der Auferstehung, des ewigen Lebens."[102] [and the number eight is namely associated with eternal happiness! Moreover it can also be shown, that the octagonal baptismal font portrays the eight days of creation, i.e. with the new creation which begins with the resurrection of Christ, into which the newly baptized is taken. "Eight is the number of rebirth and baptism, of the resurrection, of eternal life."]

The text of lines 5 and 6 of stanza 2 clearly show the eternal side of God the Father. His power is unmeasured, as is eternity. This appears to be further justification for the use of canon at the octave.

Following the canonic treatment of lines 5 and 6 of the chorale (mm. 69–79), the left hand enters in m. 78 with line 5 of the *cantus firmus*. This is treated in a coloratura fashion with many chromatic notes, including *b-flat0* in the context of A minor at m. 83. It may be possible to apply the same interpretation to this line as discussed before, or alternatively to consider that Bach is making a new point regarding text and music. Furthermore, perhaps the dramatic presentation of line 6 that begins at m. 90, leading into a solo recitative-like passage and culminating in slowing to *adagio*, implies the same meaning as that suggested for line 6 above. This section has been the cause of much discussion in the literature. Detailed investigation of the musical elements that make up this passage may help in finding a solution to the issue of text and music at this point in BWV 663.

The striking unaccompanied coloratura line appears to be significant. As shown before, when Bach employs these methods, there is often a strong textual reason. This line incorporates an interval of a diminished third at m. 95. Bach also uses this interval in the *cantus firmus* at m. 22 (55). The diminished third is sometimes used by Bach in relation to supplication and pleading: for example, the fugue subject of the second *Kyrie* of the B Minor Mass. It may be possible to find a meaning for this interval in the text of the hymn. A similar interpretation can be applied to the chromatic notes in the presentation of line 5 of the *cantus firmus* from m. 78. Reexamination of the text of lines 5 and 6 of all stanzas may prove enlightening.

In this context, the text "Lamm Gottes heilger Herr und Gott/ nimm an die Bitt von unser Noth" of stanza 3 or "durch grosse Marter und bittern Tod/ abwend all unser Jammer und Noth" of stanza 4 appears to be the most appropriate. Can a decision be made between these two stanzas? The use of the diminished third at m. 95 may help find an interpretation. As shown previously, Bach uses this interval very pointedly in the second *Kyrie* of the B Minor Mass. In this movement, the *Affekt* is one of pleading for mercy (*Kyrie eleison*). Line 6 of stanza 3 asks the Lamb of God to accept the prayer from the distressed believer. This is a similar context to that of the *Kyrie*. An additional point to be made regarding mm. 95–97 concerns the use of the *figura corta*. This has been used by Bach to portray trust in God. It is significant that Bach incorporates the introduction of the *figura corta* into an ascending scale of a minor tenth, outlining the scale of E minor. This marked use by Bach of *anabasis* and the *figura corta* may also be linked to the text. It may be possible to relate the *figura corta* to Luther's "frölich wechsel."[103] If the use of the diminished third is in some way related to a plea for mercy, then it may be that the *figura corta* is connected with salvation, which is the result of that mercy.

Additional evidence may be found in the slowing to *adagio* at m. 97. This appears to be a very effective portrayal of the word "Noth." There is another connection to the B Minor Mass: this is found at the words "in remissionem peccatorum, et expecto resurrectionem mortuorum" [for the remission of sins and I look for the resurrection of the dead] of the *Confiteor* of the *Credo* of this work. At m. 121 of this movement, Bach suddenly slows to *adagio* and employs extreme chromatic harmony to depict the forgiveness of sin through the sacrifice of Christ that brings mankind to eternal life.[104]

It is useful to refer briefly to Renate Steiger on the issue of Bach's use of the tempo marking *adagio*. She points out the example of BWV 4/3, remarking how even in the very earliest cantatas Bach was making theological points.[105]

In addition, she cites the slowing to *adagio* in the *Actus Tragicus* (BWV 106/2) for the words "in ihm sterben" at m. 41. In this case the harmony changes from diatonic to chromatic with the tempo change, further emphasizing the textual point.[106] She quotes Johann Hermann Schein's heading to the hymn *Ich Hab mein Sach Gott heimgestellt* in his *Cantional* (Leipzig, 1627):

> Wenn sie nun auf den 10. Versicul . . . kommen, da singen sie adagio mit einem sehr langsamen Tactu, weiln in solchen versiculis verba emphatica enthalten, nemlich, "Sterbn ist mein Gwinn."[107] [When you come to stanza 10, then sing *adagio* in a very slow tempo, because the *verba emphatica* is contained in such a stanza, namely, "dying is my gain."]

Steiger uses the opening movement of the cantata *Christus, der ist mein Leben* (BWV 95) as another example of Bach using tempo in an expressive way—the general pause at m. 26 of BWV 95/1, another kind of textual emphasis, again to do with death.[108] In his commentary on BWV 95/1, Alfred Dürr remarks that this kind of expansion of the phrase went back to an old Leipzig tradition.[109] Bach undoubtedly would have been aware of such traditions, and in his use of a tempo change to emphasize text, he was merely carrying on a well-established tradition.

There is a notable change in style from m. 98. The introduction of new musical elements by Bach helps to make the music more positive in *Affekt*. It is very likely that characteristics such as the treatment of the solo line from m. 110, the unaccompanied flourish on the solo manual at m. 113, the marked use of the *figura suspirans* from m. 119, and the remarkable close from m. 123 is related to the text. The very long tonic pedal seems significant. Examination of the final lines of text of all stanzas may be useful in this regard. The texts "all Fehd hat nun ein Ende" (stanza 1), "wohl uns des feinen Herren" (stanza 2), and "erbarm dich unser aller" (stanza 3) might be regarded as equally appropriate. They all fit in with a positive atmosphere. In the context of the tonic pedal, it might be easier to associate the final line of either stanza 1 or stanza 3. In the opening movement of the Advent cantata *Nun komm der Heiden Heiland* (BWV 61), Bach depicts the word "alle" with long pedal notes in the soprano. A similar context may apply here. God's mercy may be portrayed in the *anabasis* in parallel sixths that begins at m. 123. Bach's employment of the *figura suspirans* might also be related to a request for mercy.[110] Mercy for the sin of humanity is provided by Christ in his sacrifice. It appears likely that Bach was portraying lines 5 and 6 of stanza 3 also. The dramatic *anabasis* from m. 123 of a tenth may be related to eternal joy provided by the Lamb of God, who is also the reconciler of those who are lost.

The elongation of the final phrase of the chorale in BWV 663 is noteworthy. Bach chooses not only to add a coda over a held tonic, as was common in his chorale settings, but before this he draws out the close of the phrase considerably. If it is stanza 3 that Bach is portraying here, then the word "aller" covers the final four notes of the phrase, and this lasts for seven measures before reaching the final g^0 in m. 117. Bach may have wanted to give a satisfactorily weighty ending to what after all is a substantial piece. Additionally, this may have been a means of balancing the penultimate phrase, lengthened by the solo improvisatory writing of mm. 95–96. His portrayal of the word "aller" can perhaps be regarded as a universal plea for grace and mercy.

Up to m. 77, where the canon ends, it appears that Bach is setting stanza 2 of *Allein Gott*. However, Bach seems to be portraying the final line of stanza 3 in the closing section of BWV 663. In the preceding discussion it was suggested that lines 5 and 6 of either stanza 3 or 4 might be relevant. It does not seem likely that Bach would portray aspects of three different stanzas in this composition. It is more logical that he was indeed setting lines 5 and 6 of stanza 3. Stanza 4 is concerned mainly with the Holy Spirit. It does not seem feasible that Bach would go from God the Father to the Spirit and then to the Son in the final line. This would not make much sense. Therefore it seems that Bach was combining the important aspects of stanzas 2 and 3 in BWV 663.

At this point it is useful to briefly mention Bach's choice of the time signature of 3/2. In chapter 5, there is a discussion of Bach's use of this meter often in the context of death and eternal salvation.[111] The only place in the B Minor Mass where he employs this time signature is for the *Crucifixus*. The only two pieces in the "Leipzig" chorales in 3/2 time are BWV 663 and *O Lamm Gottes unschuldig* (BWV 656). These two works have Christ's Passion in common. It appears that Bach is portraying elements from stanzas 2 and 3 that represent the Father and the Son. BWV 663 is the central setting of three. Christ is the sacrifice, but God the Father provides salvation—Christ fulfills the law to dispel the Father's wrath, and this may lie behind Bach's apparent choice to refer to stanzas 2 and 3 of *Allein Gott in der Höh sei Ehr* simultaneously.

★ ★ ★

Bach appears to have had in mind stanzas 2 and 3 when composing BWV 663. Many musical elements, such as the positive *Affekt* of the opening, the long note on "ewiglich," and the canon for lines 5 and 6, support the argument in favor of stanza 2. However, it does not seem to be possible to equate the text of lines 5 and 6 of stanza 2 to the solo *cantus firmus* at mm. 95–96 and the subsequent slowing to *adagio*. This musical portrayal leads more logically to the text of stanza 3 and the second person of the Trinity. It is not so easy to equate the first half of the composition to stanza 3, and it appears that Bach was depicting Father and Son in BWV 663. Christ is the means of salvation, but God the Father is the instigator. It remains to be seen whether or not Bach portrayed the other bringer of salvation, the Holy Spirit, in the following composition, BWV 664.

ALLEIN GOTT IN DER HÖH SEI EHR (BWV 664)

Allein Gott in der Höh sei Ehr (BWV 664) is headed "*Trio sup[er] Allein Gott in der Höh seÿ Ehr. a 2 Clav. et Ped.*" in P271. It is one of three trios in the "Leipzig" chorales, the others being *Herr Jesu Christ, dich zu uns wend* (BWV 655) and *Nun komm der Heiden Heiland* (BWV 660). Three versions of this setting exist: a Weimar sketch (BWV 664b), an earlier Weimar version (BWV 664a), and a later Leipzig revision (BWV 664).[112] At the end of BWV 664, Bach has written *SDG* (*Soli Deo Gloria*). The compositional style has much in common with that of the trio sonatas. The relationship to other settings of this chorale (BWV 663 and 676) is also clear.

All motives that appear in the opening measure are derived from the *cantus firmus*. BWV 662 and 663 are characterized by *catabasis* and *anabasis* respectively.[113] In BWV 664, Bach brings the two together in balance and symmetry. This is especially clear in m. 2 where the rising left-hand motive is immediately answered by the falling right-hand motive. The piece is a contrapuntal tour de force with its constant sequences of climax and anticlimax. Throughout, the pedal plays the role of continuo bass, with the first two lines of the *cantus firmus* appearing in the pedal at the end of the piece. Much of the motivic writing in the episodes is derived from the opening fugal material. It seems that the second theme that enters in the left hand at the upbeat to m. 2 is almost more of an additional fugue subject rather than a countersubject. Peter Williams has described this as a "double subject."[114] The two themes are both treated in a strict fugal style. Theme 1 is answered a fourth lower at the upbeat to m. 4, and theme 2 is answered a fifth higher at the upbeat to m. 5.

From m. 1 to 12, the two subjects are heard in the tonic and the dominant, with the opening theme modified in the pedal at m. 10. At the end of m. 12, episode 1 begins. This is clearly related to the opening material in the use of the *rectus* and *inversus* form of the initial left-hand motive. This episode continues to m. 25, passing through the keys of F-sharp minor, B minor, E major, and C-sharp minor before returning to cadence in A major. There is a reference to the pedal theme of m. 10, with certain modifications beginning on the final beat of m. 16. In the second half of m. 25, the tonality moves to D major for an entry of the subject in the left hand. This is answered a measure later in the right hand. A modified pedal answer appears at m. 28, leading to a cadence in the tonic at mm. 31–32 for the beginning of the second episode. This is initially based on the opening left-hand material, but after three measures it moves to a style that is consistent with the trio sonatas. Measures 35–36 bear resemblances to the Venetian manner of violin sonatas, with the broken chords of mm. 37–38 similar to the writing found in BWV 530/1.[115] This episode remains on an *A* pedal for mm. 35–37 before cadencing in F-sharp minor at m. 43. The right-hand motives are heard in both *rectus* and *inversus* forms accompanied in the left hand by a sequence of falling suspensions.

At m. 43, there is a short entry in the submediant minor that leads to episode 3 at m. 46. From m. 49, there is a different approach to the pedal writing, with single quarter notes punctuating the strong beats. This leads to a cadence in m. 56 to D major, which marks the beginning of a passage similar to that of mm. 35–52, this time with the hands reversed. The music cadences to B minor at m. 64. This is followed by a short entry in the supertonic minor in the right hand. Episode 4 commences at m. 67, which is similar to episode 3, but this time with the parts reversed and up a fifth. Measures 50–52 correspond to mm. 70–72. The writing is expanded and moves through a chromatic rising bass back to A major. There is a tonic entry in the right hand at the upbeat to m. 80 followed a measure later by the left-hand answer. This is reversed at the upbeat to m. 83 for a dominant entry in the left hand, answered a measure later by the right hand. In m. 85, the pedal enters with the first two musical phrases of the *cantus firmus*. This leads to a tonic pedal at m. 90, above which the thematic material is developed right through to the final cadence at m. 96.

Interpretations by Other Authors

Many scholars have refrained from discussing the relationship between text and music in BWV 664. Very few have written in any detail about it.

Albert Schweitzer suggests that this composition may be a transcription from a lost Leipzig chorale cantata.[116]

Hans Luedtke sees the first two lines of stanza 1 reflected in BWV 664. According to him, the rejoicing heavenly hosts are joined at the close of this setting by mankind, who are represented in the entry of the *cantus firmus* in the pedal at m. 85.[117] Like many commentators, he draws parallels with the trio *Herr Jesu Christ, dich zu uns wend* (BWV 655).

Jacques Chailley refers to the "fanfares de *Ehre*" [fanfares of praise] in m. 36.[118] In all of his references he seems to be out by a measure, indicating that he counted the upbeat as m. 1. These fanfares actually begin in m. 35. Chailley also refers to m. 94 (in fact m. 95) with its dominant minor ninth harmony as follows:

> une neuvième de dominante mineure à l'assombrissement inattendu, très passager, fait peut-être allusion à la fin du malheur évoqué par le cantique, mais c'est bien dans la gloire triomphante de son élargissement à 5 voix que se clôt le majestueux choral.[119] [an unexpected darkening dominant minor 9th, very transient, perhaps alludes to the end of sadness evoked by the chorale, but it is certainly in the triumphant glory of the expansion to 5 voices that this majestic chorale closes.]

Hermann Keller observes the heavenly hosts soaring up and down in this setting.[120]

Ulrich Meyer considers that the text of stanza 2 is expressed in this setting. According to him, the feeling of unburdened lightness that Bach creates allows us to participate in the songs of the angels.[121] No other author refers to text-music relationships with regard to BWV 664. In the following section, possible interpretations are discussed.

Assessment

In the preceding sections, I have suggested that Bach is portraying the text of stanza 1 in BWV 662 and the text of stanzas 2 and 3 in BWV 663. Since Bach portrays the Trinitarian God in BWV 662, God the Father and the Son in BWV 663, it may be logical to suggest that the Holy Spirit, and therefore stanza 4, would be represented in BWV 664. Examination of the musical elements may lead to some conclusions regarding such text-music relationships.

The most noteworthy musical characteristics of BWV 664 are the trio setting, the A major tonality, the contrapuntal writing, the use of the *circulatio* figure, the almost constant presence of the ritornello material, the characterful writing of the episodes, and the presentation of the first two lines of the *cantus firmus* in the pedal from m. 85.

The opening motive has a joyful ebullient character. It is marked by the use of the *circulatio* as seen at m. 1.3. This figure was sometimes used by Bach in relation to the Holy Spirit as seen in the violin parts of the opening chorus of the St. John Passion and the motet *Der Geist hilft unser Schwachheit auf* (BWV 226). Bach may be referring to the Holy Spirit, and therefore to the text of stanza 4, in the use of this figure. This will be explored further below.

In BWV 664, Bach returns to the heavenly key of A major. I have suggested that the Trinitarian God is depicted in BWV 662 in the same key. Perhaps Bach is making a point about the Trinity here, and if so, he could be pointing to the fact that he is now completing the references by alluding to the Holy Spirit in the final setting. Equally, the technique of the trio might also indicate a connection to the third person of the Trinity.

In this setting, Bach only quotes the first two lines of the chorale melody. Bearing in mind that these two lines are repeated, one can say that Bach quotes the first four lines of the chorale. These are the only specific references to the chorale, but the entire setting is imbued with the melodic contours of line 1 of the chorale in both of the fugal themes. Albert Clement points out the melodic similarities between lines 1, 3, 5, and 6.[122] If one examines the setting from this point of view, it is possible to see that all lines of the chorale are represented here. This setting is positive and joyful in its dancing rhythms

and sparkling melodic writing. This may be related to the life-giving joy of
the Holy Spirit.

In his Pentecost sermons, Luther consistently emphasizes the joy that the
Holy Spirit brings; for example, in a sermon for Pentecost (1534), he writes,

> *Sed Christianus discernat* pfingst *praedicationem, ex qua fieri debent Christiani
> et tales, quales discipuli.*[123] [The new Pentecost and the Holy Spirit produce
> truly joyful Christians, bold and courageous people, just like the apostles
> and disciples (who feared neither the world nor the devil).[124]]

A few pages later in the same sermon, referring to the message of Pentecost,
Luther expands this by saying, "Ist unser freude und trost"[125] [is our comfort
and joy[126]].

It is very likely that Bach was thinking of stanza 4. There can be no
doubt that Bach is portraying great joy, which can be linked to Luther's Pentecost sermons. The life-giving role of the Holy Spirit was stressed by Luther,
and he expounds freely on this issue in *Auf das überchristlich, übergeistlich und
überkünstlich Buch Bocks Emsers zu Leipzig Antwort* (1521) [Answer to the Hy-
perchristian, Hyperspiritual and Hyperlearned Book by Goat Emser in Leipzig
(1521)].[127] The life-giving role of the Holy Spirit is clearly depicted by Bach in
all of his Pentecost cantatas, which are concerned with salvation and the role
that the Holy Spirit plays in revealing the word of God to Christians through
the scriptures.

The thematic material remains consistent right up to m. 35 where Bach
suddenly breaks into material based on broken chords. This is a definite
change from the writing thus far. It seems likely that Bach had a new aspect
of the text in mind, or at least a new angle on it. Measures 35–51 and 56–72
correspond to one another in the use of material with the hands reversed. The
repeated pedal motive (see example 9.4), with its octave leap, is also to be
found in the dramatic coda to *Von Gott will ich nicht lassen* (BWV 658). In the
case of BWV 658, I have suggested that this motive is related to trust in God
and faith that he will rescue humanity from the chains of death.[128] A similar
context may apply here. In this regard, it seems that the text of either stanza
1 or stanza 4 is most appropriate. Stanza 1 expresses trust in God's ability to
provide salvation in a general way. Stanza 4 is more explicit where the text

Example 9.4.   BWV 664 (m. 37)

mentions the Holy Spirit as "allerheilsamster Tröster." Additionally, the text that closes this stanza, "darauf wir uns verlassen," also decisively states this confidence in God's salvation. This may help to prove that Bach was setting stanza 4 in BWV 664.

It may be useful to examine biblical references to the "Tröster." The "Tröster" is mentioned in Isaiah 51:12, where the implication is that it is the Father who is the Comforter: "Ich, ich bin euer Tröster!" [I, even I, am he that comforteth you!] The next references to the "Tröster" are found in the Gospel of John. In John 14:16 and 26, it is the Father who sends the "Tröster":

> Und ich will den Vater bitten, und Er soll euch einen andern Tröster ge-
> ben, daß Er bey euch bleibe ewiglich. . . . Aber der Tröster, der Heilige
> Geist, welchen mein Vater senden wird in meinem Namen, derselbe wirds
> euch alles lehren, und euch erinnern alles deß, das Ich euch gesagt habe.
> [And I will pray the Father, and he shall give you another Comforter, that
> he may abide with you for ever. . . . But the Comforter, which is the
> Holy Ghost, whom the Father will send in my name, he shall teach you all
> things, and bring all things to your remembrance, whatsoever I have said
> unto you.]

The Father sends the Spirit, and subsequently Jesus also sends him, thus stressing the equality between Father and Son. This is also spoken of in Luke 24:49 as follows:

> Und sihe, Ich will auf euch senden die Verheissung meines Vaters. Ihr aber
> solt in der Stadt Jerusalem bleiben, bis daß ihr angethan werdet mit Kraft
> aus der Höhe. [And, behold, I send the promise of my Father upon you:
> but tarry ye in the city of Jerusalem, until ye be endued with power from
> on high.]

Here Jesus is also the one who sends the Spirit. It is therefore clear that each person of the Trinity is very much involved in the feast of Pentecost in equal ways. The Spirit is the final link to salvation: God the Father sends the Son, who then sends the Holy Spirit. Jesus refers to him as the Spirit of truth, and with him there is certainty of salvation. It does not seem likely that Bach would have ignored the Holy Spirit in his three settings of *Allein Gott* in this collection of chorale preludes united by an eschatological theme.

Measures 35–39 form a tonic pedal, with mm. 56–60 being built on a subdominant pedal. The writing from m. 35 to 39 is completely diatonic, and the only chords used are tonic and subdominant. This has an effect similar to a passage such as the *tasto solo* at mm. 113–117 in the opening movement of the *Gloria* of the B Minor Mass. This was inspired by the words "et in terra pax" as the world rejoices at the birth of Christ. Measures 39–43 of BWV 664, which follow this passage, feature a descending scale with trills on every note. This line could conceivably be related to the angels who rejoice at the birth of Christ. Accompanying this descending line is a motive heard in the pedal that I have suggested is associated with great joy in BWV 652. This three-note eighth-note motive, which occurs at m. 39 for the first time, appears at the end of BWV 652 to express the joyful alleluias that close each stanza of *Komm heiliger Geist, Herre Gott*. It may be possible to associate this motive with Christ as Savior. Stanzas 3 and 4 both mention Christ: in stanza 3 he is called the Lamb of God, and in stanza 4 he is referred to as the one who saves humanity through his sacrifice. The reference to "erlöset" in stanza 4 may justify the use of motives that have been associated with the birth of the Savior. Luther repeatedly stresses the fact that Christ was born to take away all misfortunes. This in turn may link to "abwend all unser Jammer und Noth" in stanza 4. In his sermon on the afternoon of Christmas Day 1530, Luther makes exactly this point:

> *Hoc dictum de altera fide, ut non solum credamus filium Mariae, sed qui in sinu virginis iacet, sit noster salvator,* das dichs annhembst *et gratias deo, quod* dich so mit gnaden gemeinet, *quod dederit Salvatorem,* der sol dein sein, *Et* zum *signo misit angelum, qui annunciaret, ut nihil praedicaretur quam quod infans salvator et longe melior quam coelum et terra.* Hunc sollen wir auch also zu erkennen annemen in allen nöten in fur unser Heiland erkennen in anruffen und nicht zweiueln, er werde uns aus allem ungluck erretten. Amen.[129] [What we have said, then, has been about that second faith, which is not only to believe in Mary's Son, but rather that he who lies in the virgin's lap is our Savior, that you accept this and give thanks to God, who so loved you that he gave you a Savior who is yours. And for a sign he sent the angel from heaven to proclaim him, in order that nothing else should be preached except that this child is the Savior and far better than heaven and earth. Him, therefore, we should acknowledge and accept; confess him as our Savior in every need, call upon him, and never doubt that he will save us from all misfortune. Amen.[130]]

Luther shows how even at his birth, Christ's purpose on earth was clear—he came to remove misery and distress. This seems to lead to stanza 4.

The third episode, which begins at m. 46, contains many interesting musical attributes. A short angular motive is heard at m. 46.4 (see example 9.5a). This has the same sort of *Affekt* as the motive used at the opening of BWV 677. Clement has suggested that the opening motive of BWV 677 may be a reference to Christ in the cross form of the opening motive of BWV 677.[131] It may be possible to apply a similar interpretation to this episodic material. This right-hand motive is certainly not one of confidence, in view of the angular character and brevity. The harmonic writing becomes

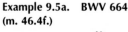

Example 9.5a.   BWV 664
(m. 46.4f.)

much more daring, with Bach introducing minor ninths, from m. 48. In m. 50, Bach introduces an arpeggio eighth-note motive in the left hand (see example 9.5b), which over the course of the next three measures alternates between the hands. From m. 48 to 52 there is a *syncopatio* on the first beat of each measure. Many of these musical features appear to be portraying negative ideas. Bach sometimes uses chromatic harmony, the *syncopatio*, and cross motives in relation to the sacrifice of Christ. Once again, the solution appears to be linked to either stanza 3 or 4. The left-hand motive first heard in m. 49 may help to find an answer. It may be possible to link this to the winged movement of the dove or the Holy Spirit. The idea of protection under the wings was a favorite Old Testament image of Luther's, being a reference to Psalm 91:4f.:

> Er wird dich mit seinen Fittigen decken, und deine Zuversicht wird seyn unter seinen Flügeln, seine Warheit ist Schirm und Schild, Daß du nicht erschrecken müssest vor dem Grauen des Nachts, vor den Pfeilen, die des Tages fliegen. [He shall cover thee with his feathers, and under his wings shalt thou trust: his truth shall be thy shield and buckler. Thou shalt not be afraid for the terror by night; nor for the arrow that flieth by day.]

In addition, the dove was the symbol of the Holy Spirit as seen in John 1:32–34 as follows:

> Und Johannes zeugte, und sprach: Ich sahe, daß der Geist herab fuhr, wie eine Taube vom Himmel, und bleib auf Ihm. Und ich kante Ihn nicht; aber der mich sandte zu taufen mit Wasser, derselbe sprach zu mir: Uber welchen du sehen wirst den Geist her abfahren, und auf Ihm bleiben, derselbige ists, der mit dem Heiligen Geist taufet. Und ich sah es, und zeugte, daß dieser ist GOttes Sohn. [And John bare record, saying, I saw the Spirit descending from heaven like a dove, and it abode upon him. And I knew him not: but he that sent me to baptize with water, the same said unto me,

Example 9.5b.   BWV 664
(m. 49)

upon whom thou shalt see the Spirit descending, and remaining on him, the same is he which baptizeth with the Holy Ghost. And I saw, and bare record that this is the Son of God.]

The idea of protection by the Holy Spirit is found in line 3 of stanza 4.

At m. 53, Bach changes the mood again. Suddenly he is writing in parallel thirds between the two manuals, and the atmosphere becomes much more positive as the harmony becomes diatonic, with a perfect cadence to D major at m. 56. The passage from m. 56 to 72 corresponds to mm. 35–51, with the manual parts reversed. As with the earlier passage, the harmony remains diatonic, this time over a subdominant pedal. Measures 68–72 correspond to mm. 48–52, and therefore the same text-music relationships may apply in these two passages. In the previous section, the atmosphere became more hopeful after m. 53. Similarly, at m. 73, the music becomes more diatonic, with an extra spurt of joy appearing at m. 79 as a *figura corta* and a *circulatio* figure in thirty-second notes lead to an entry in the tonic of the initial fugal subject.

It appears from the preceding discussion that Bach is portraying the text of stanza 4 of *Allein Gott*. As shown above, this hymn was clearly regarded as a Trinitarian hymn, and it is most unlikely that Bach would ignore this fact. If the previous hypothesis is correct, that he is depicting stanza 1 in BWV 662 and stanzas 2 and 3 in BWV 663, then there is not sufficient evidence to assume that he is not depicting stanza 4 in BWV 664. This appears to be the most logical solution.

Measure 80 constitutes a recapitulation of sorts. The *cantus firmus* enters in m. 85 in the pedal. Only lines 1 and 2 are heard, and since these are the same as lines 3 and 4, Bach might be portraying these four lines here. The second line of the *cantus firmus* enters at m. 88 in the pedal. It may be possible to link the high proportion of parallel thirds and sixths with the text. The reappearance of the opening motive can be linked to the Holy Spirit and therefore to the text of line 1, "O heiliger Geist du höchtes Gut." Similarly, the generally high and light texture can be related to the highest good of the Holy Spirit. The return to this material at the close of BWV 664 serves as a reminder of this opening line. The entry of line 2 of the *cantus firmus* in m. 88 is accompanied by much writing in parallel motion. It appears likely that this is a reference to "du allerheilsamster Tröster."

There is a six-and-a-half-measure tonic pedal to close the piece. Bach refers to the rising and falling eighth-note motive of mm. 49–51 and mm. 71–72. He also uses the dissonant minor ninth harmony in m. 93 and m. 95. It is interesting to note the low range of the music in m. 95, given the high tessitura of m. 92 and m. 93. The minor ninth harmony appears in both manual parts. The low tessitura of both parts coupled with the minor ninth harmony could conceivably be a final reference to Christ who turns away all misery and distress.

It is necessary to refer briefly once more to the position of the *cantus firmus* in all three settings. It seems relatively easy to relate the uppermost position of the *cantus firmus* in BWV 662 to the Trinitarian God, and therefore to the text of stanza 1. In BWV 663, the *cantus firmus* appears in the tenor. I have suggested that Bach was portraying the text of stanzas 2 and 3 in this composition. These stanzas deal with the Father and the Son respectively. It is possible to link the reference to the Son to the tenor register of the *cantus firmus*. Bach has represented the second person of the Trinity in this way, for example in BWV 670. However, one cannot automatically presume that a tenor *cantus firmus* is related to the Son. Assuming this without consideration of other factors may have led only to the text of stanza 3 in the context of BWV 663, thereby possibly missing some of the meaning of this work. In BWV 664, two lines of the *cantus firmus* appear at the end of the piece in the pedal. Bach has portrayed the Holy Spirit in the bass in BWV 651, BWV 667 (second section), and BWV 671. The Holy Spirit of the New Testament descends from heaven to earth, and therefore he is depicted in the bass. Stanza 4 refers to the "Tröster," who is the Comforter of the New Testament, so this may be justification for the bass portrayal of the *cantus firmus*. This discussion shows how one must exercise caution in the assignation of voice registers to members of the Trinity. Bach sometimes did follow a pattern of Father, Son, and Holy Spirit in top, middle, and bass voices respectively, but not always, and even when he did, there were often other considerations.

★ ★ ★

In his three settings of the hymn tune *Allein Gott in der Höh sei Ehr* (BWV 662–664), Bach appears to have demonstrated the Trinitarian elements of the hymn. That he saw this hymn as a Trinitarian hymn is evidenced by his three three-part settings of the same hymn in *Clavierübung III*. It seems that in the "Leipzig" chorales he has taken the logical progression of depicting the Trinitarian God first, then God the Father with God the Son second, and finishing with the Holy Spirit, these three settings forming a cycle. In BWV 662, the Trinitarian God in heaven is represented in the uppermost position of the *cantus firmus*. God's mercy is depicted in the parallel motion, many ornaments, and the consistent employment of the *figura corta*. God's goodwill is highlighted in a special way in the unadorned statement of line 5 of the *cantus firmus* in the pedal. The end of all quarrels is portrayed in the lengthy final note of the *cantus firmus*, while the optimistic unaccompanied melismatic passage that follows confirms the hope of eternal salvation expressed in the final line of stanza 1. The positive and happy opening of BWV 663 helps to affirm the praise and thanks of lines 1 and 2 of stanza 2. The use of canon for lines 5 and 6 of the *cantus firmus* corresponds to Bach's use of this process elsewhere as a representation of the will of God. The dramatic unaccompanied passage at m. 95, with the subsequent slowing to *adagio* at m. 97, seems more appropriate to lines 5 and 6 of stanza 3, where the Lamb of God is prayed to by distressed humanity. The representation of two stanzas in BWV 663 solves Bach's problem of how he might portray a four-stanza hymn over three musical settings. In BWV 664, Bach once more depicts the Holy Spirit by perpetual sixteenth-note motion, as he does in BWV 651. The contours of the chorale permeate the entire setting, but only the first two phrases are heard in the pedal at the close of the piece. In this chorale prelude, the jagged lines of some of the episodic writing appear to portray the bitter death of Christ, while the overall positive atmosphere attests to hope in eternal salvation, which the Holy Spirit as the final link from Father and Son may bring.

NOTES

1. *WA* 52:57.

2. *House Postils* 1:143.

3. Johannes Kulp, *Die Lieder unserer Kirche* [Handbuch zum Evangelischen Kirchengesangbuch, Sonderband], ed. Arno Büchner and Siegfried Fornaçon (Göttingen: Vandenhoeck & Ruprecht, 1958), 208.

4. *WA* 35:287ff.; *LW* 53:184.

5. *WA* 35:287ff.; *LW* 53:184.

6. Kulp, *Die Lieder unserer Kirche*, 209; Eduard Emil Koch, *Geschichte des Kirchenlieds und Kirchengesangs der christlichen, insbesondere der deutschen evangelischen Kirche* (Stuttgart: Belser, 1866–1876; Hildesheim: Olms, 1973), 8:106; Philipp Wackernagel, *Das deutsche Kirchenlied von der ältesten Zeit bis zu Anfang des XVII. Jahrhunderts* (Leipzig: Teubner, 1864–1877; reprint, Hildesheim: Olms, 1964), 3:565f. (No. 615); see also the facsimile in Konrad Ameln, *The Roots of German Hymnody of the Reformation Era* (St. Louis: Concordia, 1984), 3.

7. Wackernagel, *Das deutsche Kirchenlied*, 3:566f. (No. 616); facsimile, Ameln, *Roots of German Hymnody*, 4; Zahn 4457. Leaver draws attention to the fact that later Leipzig hymnbooks such as Vopelius (1682) and Wagner (1697) often misattributed the text of *Allein Gott* text to Nicolaus Selnecker, pastor and theologian in Leipzig in the late sixteenth century; see Robin A. Leaver, "Bach's 'Clavierübung III': Some Historical and Theological Considerations," *Organ Yearbook* 6 (1975): 21.

8. Kulp, *Die Lieder unserer Kirche*, 210.

9. Kulp, *Die Lieder unserer Kirche*, 209.

10. Johann Sebastian Bach, *Orgel-Büchlein BWV 599–644. Faksimile der autographen Partitur*, ed. Heinz-Harald Löhlein (Kassel: Bärenreiter, 1981), 64.

11. *BSLK*, 809 (BkC, 512) refers to the Trinity as the highest mystery. Robin A. Leaver writes, "The doctrine of the Trinity was considered by the Lutheran teachers to be not only a touchstone for Christian orthodoxy but a fundamental article of the Christian faith, an article necessary to know for salvation. For to know and worship him aright as a gracious God who through his Spirit seeks and saves sinners for Christ's sake," in "Bach's 'Clavierübung III,'" 20. This Trinitarian doctrine is clearly reflected in the text of *Allein Gott in der Höh sei Ehr*, which was usually included among other Trinitarian hymns in most seventeenth- and eighteenth-century Lutheran hymnals.

12. Casper Honders, *Over Bachs Schouder. Een bundel opstellen* (Groningen: Niemeijer, 1985), 124.

13. *BSLK*, 653.

14. BkC, 415.

15. *WA* 101$^{I/1}$:93.

16. *Church Postils* 1:159.

17. See also the discussion of the links between incarnation and atonement in Lutheran theology in chapter 8.

18. *BSLK*, 56.

19. BkC, 38ff.

20. *SLG*, 183f.

21. Translation based on Mark Bighley, *The Lutheran Chorales in the Organ Works of J. S. Bach* (St. Louis: Concordia, 1986), 34f.

22. Kulp, *Die Lieder unserer Kirche*, 209.

23. Facsimile in Robin A. Leaver, "Die Datierung von Coverdale's *Goostly Psalmes*," *MuK* 51 (1981), 169–171.

24. As mentioned in chapter 5, note 53, the first phrase of *Allein Gott* in the Weißenfels hymnbook closed with a chord of C-sharp major. On most organs in Germany at that time, this would have sounded very unpleasant. It is therefore a key that cannot have been used often; see Peter Williams, *The Organ Music of J. S. Bach* (Cambridge: Cambridge University Press, 1980–1986), 3:189.

25. Günther Stiller, *Johann Sebastian Bach und das Leipziger gottesdienstliche Leben seiner Zeit* (Kassel: Bärenreiter, 1970), 104; English: *Johann Sebastian Bach and Liturgical Life in Leipzig*, trans. Herbert J. A. Bouman, Daniel F. Poellot, and Hilton C. Oswald; ed. Robin A. Leaver (St. Louis: Concordia, 1984), 118.

26. Stiller, *Johann Sebastian Bach und das Leipziger gottesdienstliche Leben seiner Zeit*, 104; *Johann Sebastian Bach and Liturgical Life in Leipzig*, 118.

27. *Allein Gott* is listed between *Gott der Vater wohn uns bei* and *Der du bist drei in Einigkeit*; *Orgel-Büchlein BWV 599–644. Faksimile*, 64. In cantatas BWV 85, 104, and 112 for *Misericordias Domini* (second Sunday after Easter), Bach uses the *Allein Gott* melody with other texts paraphrasing Psalm 23. Cantata BWV 128 for Ascension employs the melody of *Allein Gott* in the opening movement to the text of stanza 1 of *Auf Christi Himmelfahrt allein*, by Joshua Wegelin and Ernst Sonnemann; *BC* 1:311.

28. Clark Kelly, "Johann Sebastian Bach's 'Eighteen' Chorales BWV 651–668: Perspectives on Editions and Hymnology," DMA diss., Eastman School of Music, 1988, 181, points out that "such association of the text with the scriptural history of Jesus'

birth may also account for the occasional designation of 'Allein Gott' as a *de tempore* hymn for the feast of the Visitation."

29. Helene Werthemann, "Bemerkungen zu Johann Sebastian Bachs Siebzehn Chorälen für Orgel," *MuG* 6 (1968): 157. It was not uncommon for hymns of praise to be sung at Communion time for special occasions; see Gerhard Kappner, *Sakrament und Musik* (Gütersloh: Bertelsmann, 1952), 16.

30. The others are *Komm heiliger Geist, Herre Gott* (BWV 652), *Schmücke dich, o liebe Seele* (BWV 654), and *Nun komm der Heiden Heiland* (BWV 659).

31. See Henry J. Eickhoff, "Bach's Chorale Ritornello Forms," *Music Review* 28 (1967): 257–276.

32. Harald Schützeichel, *Albert Schweitzer: Die Orgelwerke Johann Sebastian Bachs. Vorworte zu den "Sämtlichen Orgelwerken"* (Hildesheim: Olms, 1995), 255.

33. Schützeichel, *Albert Schweitzer.*

34. Hans Luedtke, "Seb. Bachs Choralvorspiele," *BJ* 15 (1918): 76.

35. Luedtke, "Seb. Bachs Choralvorspiele," 78.

36. Luedtke, "Seb. Bachs Choralvorspiele," 79.

37. Luedtke, "Seb. Bachs Choralvorspiele," 71.

38. Charles Sanford Terry, *Bach's Chorals Part III: The Hymns and Hymn Melodies of the Organ Works* (Cambridge: Cambridge University Press, 1921), 98.

39. Terry, *Bach's Chorals Part III,* 99.

40. Terry, *Bach's Chorals Part III,* 81.

41. Stainton de B. Taylor, *The Chorale Preludes of J. S. Bach* (London: Oxford University Press, 1942), 108.

42. Taylor, *The Chorale Preludes of J. S. Bach,* 117.

43. Hermann Keller, *Die Orgelwerke Bachs. Ein Beitrag zu ihrer Geschichte, Form, Deutung und Wiedergabe* (Leipzig: Peters, 1948), 189; Herman Keller, *The Organ Works of Bach: A Contribution to Their History, Form, Interpretation and Performance,* trans. Helen Hewitt (New York: Peters, 1967), 256f.

44. See previous note.

45. Jacques Chailley, *Les Chorals pour Orgue de J.-S. Bach* (Paris: Leduc, 1974), 50f.

46. Chailley, *Les Chorals pour Orgue de J.-S. Bach,* 50f.

47. Ulrich Meyer, "In profundis–in excelsis: Zu drei Orgelchorälen J. S. Bachs über 'Allein Gott in der Höh sei Ehr,'" *MuK* 58 (1988): 16.

48. Ulrich Meyer, "Zur Frage der inneren Einheit von Bachs Siebzehn Chorälen (BWV 651–667)," *BJ* 58 (1972): 68.

49. Peter Williams, *The Organ Music of J. S. Bach,* 2nd ed. (Cambridge: Cambridge University Press, 2003), 370f.

50. Williams, *The Organ Music of J. S. Bach,* 2nd ed., 372.

51. Russell Stinson, *J. S. Bach's Great Eighteen Chorales* (New York: Oxford University Press, 2001), 68.

52. Albert Clement, *Der dritte Teil der Clavierübung von Johann Sebastian Bach: Musik, Text, Theologie* (Middelburg: Almares, 1999), 53–56.

53. Clement, *Der dritte Teil der Clavierübung,* 56.

54. Clement, *Der dritte Teil der Clavierübung,* 55f.

55. Philipp Spitta, *Johann Sebastian Bach*, trans. Clara Bell and J. A. Fuller-Maitland (London: Novello, 1884–1885; reprint, New York: Dover, 1992), 3:214.

56. Albert Schweitzer, *J. S. Bach* (Leipzig: Breitkopf & Hartel, 1920), 266.

57. Albert Schweitzer, *J. S. Bach*, trans. Ernest Newman (New York: Dover, 1966), 2:288.

58. Clement, *Der dritte Teil der Clavierübung*, 90.

59. Clement, *Der dritte Teil der Clavierübung*, 91.

60. See similar discussions in chapters 1, 7, 8, and 10.

61. *BC* 1:255.

62. This could equally apply to the many parallel thirds found in *Komm heiliger Geist, Herre Gott* (BWV 652), where the theme is also ardent love.

63. *BC* 4:1467.

64. An example of this is the bass aria BWV 78/6. In this aria, on the final statement of the word "rauben," Bach writes a melismatic, recitative-like passage that leads to the return of the opening ritornello. The text here is "Wenn Christen an dich glauben, wird sie kein Feind in Ewigkeit, aus deinen Händen rauben" [When Christians believe in you, no enemy through all eternity, will steal them out of your hands]. In this case, it appears that Bach is perhaps emphasizing the importance of faith in Christ and his sacrifice. Another notable example in this regard is the final measures of the opening chorus of *Gottes Zeit ist die allerbeste Zeit* (BWV 106), where the soprano sings "Ja komm, Herr Jesu" [Come Lord Jesus] accompanied by a lone pedal note which even disappears for the word "Jesu." In the case of BWV 106/1, the reference is to the final coming, citing the closing text of Revelation. The highly pitched "floating" soprano may be related to the eternal Jerusalem. Bach may be making a similar point in BWV 662.

65. See the comments on Bach's settings of *Allein Gott* in *Clavierübung III* in Clement, *Der dritte Teil der Clavierübung*, 99.

66. Clement, *Der dritte Teil der Clavierübung*, 90–93.

67. Clement, *Der dritte Teil der Clavierübung*, 91f.

68. Clement, *Der dritte Teil der Clavierübung*, 93.

69. *WA* 37:239; *House Postils* 1:141.

70. Raymond E. Brown, *An Introduction to the New Testament* (New York: Doubleday, 1997), 342.

71. *WA* 32:261–270; *LW* 51:209–218.

72. Eric Chafe, *Tonal Allegory in the Vocal Music of J. S. Bach* (Berkeley: University of California Press, 1991), 286; see also Michael Marissen, *Lutheranism, Anti-Judaism, and Bach's St. John Passion* (New York: Oxford University Press, 1998), 13.

73. Williams, *The Organ Music of J. S. Bach*, 2nd ed., 372.

74. This also occurs in the second half of BWV 659.

75. See Williams, *The Organ Music of J. S. Bach*, 2nd ed., 374.

76. Stinson, *J. S. Bach's Great Eighteen Chorales*, 99. Stinson concludes that *andante* is the tempo for the entire piece, save the cadenza, and that Bach is associating *cantabile* with a moderate tempo, having omitted to write *andante* in BWV 663.

77. Stinson, *J. S. Bach's Great Eighteen Chorales*, 99. Stinson suggests that this is Bach's earliest use of the term *cantabile*, one he almost certainly learned from his study of Vivaldi's music, which began c.1713.

78. Stinson, *J. S. Bach's Great Eighteen Chorales*, 99.

79. Schweitzer, *J. S. Bach* (Leipzig), 450; Schweitzer, *J. S. Bach*, trans. Ernest Newman, 2:57.

80. Schweitzer, *J. S. Bach* (Leipzig), 445; Schweitzer, *J. S. Bach*, trans. Ernest Newman, 2:51.

81. Schweitzer, *J. S. Bach* (Leipzig), 462; Schweitzer, *J. S. Bach*, trans. Ernest Newman, 2:70. The same point is repeated in Schützeichel, *Albert Schweitzer*, 256.

82. Luedtke, "Seb. Bachs Choralvorspiele," 81.

83. Harvey Grace, *The Organ Works of Bach* (London: Novello, 1922), 275.

84. Taylor, *The Chorale Preludes of J. S. Bach*, 108f.

85. Taylor, *The Chorale Preludes of J. S. Bach*, 117.

86. Chailley, *Les Chorals pour Orgue de J.-S. Bach*, 52.

87. Chailley, *Les Chorals pour Orgue de J.-S. Bach*, 52.

88. Chailley, *Les Chorals pour Orgue de J.-S. Bach*, 52.

89. Meyer, "In profundis–in excelsis," 16.

90. Honders, *Over Bachs Schouder*, 129f.

91. Honders, *Over Bachs Schouder*, 129.

92. Honders, *Over Bachs Schouder*, 131. Similar arguments are presented in Casper Honders, "'Allein Gott in der Höh sei Her' BWV 663: Vom Dank zum Trost," *MuG* 4 (1975): 106–110.

93. Williams, *The Organ Music of J. S. Bach*, 2nd ed., 373f.

94. Clement, *Der dritte Teil der Clavierübung*, 362, note 58.

95. Johann Gottfried Walther, *Musicalisches Lexicon Oder Musicalische Bibliothec* (Leipzig 1732), ed. Friederike Ramm (Kassel: Bärenreiter, 2001), 155.

96. Dietrich Bartel, *Musica Poetica. Musical-Rhetorical Figures in German Baroque Music* (Lincoln: University of Nebraska Press, 1997), 294.

97. God's will is consistently portrayed by the use of canon in the Epiphany cantatas.

98. Clement, *Der dritte Teil der Clavierübung*, 100f. He also cites cantatas *Alles nur nach Gottes Willen* (BWV 72); *Herr, wie du willt, so schicks mit mir* (BWV 73); and *Was mein Gott will, das gscheh allzeit* (BWV 111), all of which employ canonic writing depicting the will of God.

99. Albert Clement, "'O Jesu, du edle Gabe': Studien zum Verhältnis von Text und Musik in den Choralpartiten und den Kanonischen Veränderungen von Johann Sebastian Bach," PhD diss., University of Utrecht, 1989, 199.

100. Clement, "'O Jesu, du edle Gabe,'" 199.

101. Clement, *Der dritte Teil der Clavierübung*, 101.

102. Clement, "'O Jesu, du edle Gabe,'" 178. The final line is a citation from Gerd Heinz-Mohr, *Lexikon der Symbole: Bilder und Zeichen der christlichen Kunst*, 4th ed. (Düsseldorf: Diederichs, 1976), 311.

103. This is a reference to Luther's essay *Von der Freiheit eines Christenmenschen* [On the Freedom of a Christian] where Luther explains how Christ takes on the sin of the soul in order to provide grace for the soul (*WA* 7:25; *LW* 35:1). The sinner pleads for mercy, symbolized in the chromatic harmony, while the *figura corta* represents the grace of salvation. Christ exchanges the sin of mankind for salvation, and so two opposing musical elements may represent this process.

104. Similar changes in tempo are found in many of the cantatas, for example in BWV 31/3 in the bass aria. Here Bach slows to *adagio* for the words "Der Herr war tot" [the Lord was dead]. There is a similar moment in BWV 4/3 in the tenor aria where Bach slows to *adagio*, this time for the words "Tod's Gestalt" [death's form]. A final example is the indication of *adagio* in the bass recitative of the cantata *O heilges Geist- und Wasserbad* (BWV 165) for the words "hoch heilges Gottes Lamm." It is interesting to note Bach's use of the *figura corta* and parallel sixths in this recitative, related perhaps to the salvation supplied by the Lamb. The soteriological context of the death of Christ seems to be frequently present when Bach suddenly slows the tempo like this.

105. Renate Steiger, ed., *Johann Sebastian Bachs Kantaten zum Thema Tod und Sterben und ihr literarisches Umfeld* (Wiesbaden: Harrassowitz, 2000), 3f.

106. Steiger, *Johann Sebastian Bachs Kantaten*, 4–6.

107. Steiger, *Johann Sebastian Bachs Kantaten*, 9.

108. Steiger, *Johann Sebastian Bachs Kantaten*, 9.

109. Alfred Dürr, *Die Kantaten von Johann Sebastian Bach. Mit ihren Texten* (Kassel: Bärenreiter, 1985), 610.

110. Another fine example of the *suspirans* figure being used in the context of asking for mercy is the first *Kyrie* of the B Minor Mass, for example from m. 109.

111. See page 100.

112. *NBA KB* IV/2:82.

113. See also Meyer, "In profundis–in excelsis," 15.

114. Williams, *The Organ Music of J. S. Bach*, 2nd ed., 375.

115. Williams, *The Organ Music of J. S. Bach*, 2nd ed., 375. See also Fritz Dietrich, "J. S. Bachs Orgelchoral und seine geschichtlichen Wurzeln," *BJ* 26 (1929): 27. Dietrich sees this work, as an Italianate, concertante chorale trio, the fruit of the unification of the two worlds of the seventeenth and eighteenth centuries.

116. Schützeichel, *Albert Schweitzer*, 257.

117. Luedtke, "Seb. Bachs Choralvorspiele," 77.

118. Chailley, *Les Chorals pour Orgue de J.-S. Bach*, 56.

119. Chailley, *Les Chorals pour Orgue de J.-S. Bach*, 56.

120. Keller, *Die Orgelwerke Bachs*, 190; Keller, *The Organ Works of Bach*, trans. Hewitt, 258.

121. Meyer, "In profundis–in excelsis," 16.

122. Clement, *Der dritte Teil der Clavierübung*, 108.

123. *WA* 37:403.

124. *House Postils* 2:160.

125. *WA* 37:404.

126. *House Postils* 2:163.

127. *WA* 7:621–688; *LW* 39:137–224.

128. See chapter 7.

129. *WA* 32:270, following the alternative expanded reading.

130. *LW* 51:218.

131. Clement, *Der dritte Teil der Clavierübung*, 109.

• *10* •

Jesus Christus unser Heiland

THE HYMN

Jesus Christus unser Heiland is Luther's extensive revision of the Latin *cantio*, *Jesus Christus nostra salus*. It appears in the Erfurt *Enchiridia* in 1524 and in Johann Walter's *Geystliche Gesangk Buchleyn* of the same year at Wittenburg.[1] It is also found as a broadsheet, issued without date or place of printing or publication, probably a reprint of an earlier, no longer extant Wittenburg broadsheet.[2] In all of these sources, the hymn bears the heading "Johann Hussens Lied *Jesus Christus nostra salus* vom Abentmal gebessert."[3] It is likely that this hymn did not actually originate with Hus. The attribution of Hus as the author relates to the fact that the first eight stanzas are an acrostic on the name Johannes.[4] It was probably written instead by an archbishop of Prague, Johannes von Jenstein.[5] According to Markus Jenny, it is likely that this melody stems from the Middle Ages, but so far no documentary evidence has been found to support this claim.[6] Hans Joachim Moser suggests that the melody is to be found in 1400 in the circle of the "Monk from Salzburg" (the Benedictine Hermann of Salzburg), associated with the hymn "Reicher Schatz der höchsten Freuden" and the Marian text *Ave virgo maris stella*.[7] But Jenny asserts that this hypothesis has no foundation.[8]

Luther substantially alters the text of the original Latin *cantio*. It seems to be a thorough theological revision with some reference to the *cantio* in stanzas 1, 2, 4, and 6.[9] The earlier text speaks of bread and food. Luther adds wine and drink to this, presenting the sacrament of the altar as "the token of God's love and mercy, which requires no other preparation than faith and no other fruit than love."[10]

219

In his German Mass of 1526, Luther suggested *Jesus Christus unser Heiland* as a chorale to be sung at Communion.[11] It was therefore one of the Catechism hymns. Most of the hymns written by the Wittenberg circle of hymn writers in 1523–1524 are essentially catechetical.[12] Luther was anxious for his followers to learn the word of God not only by listening to sermons but also by singing psalms and hymns based on scripture as follows:

> Also hätte man überall fünf Stück der ganzen christlichen Lehre, die man immerdar treiben soll und von Wort zu Wort fodern und verhören. Denn verlasse Dich nicht drauf, daß das junge Volk alleine aus der Predigt lerne und behalte. Wenn man nu solche Stücke wohl weiß, so kann man darnach auch etliche Psalmen oder Gesänge, so darauf gemacht sind, furlegen zur Zugabe und Stärke desselbigen und also die Jugend in die Schrift bringen und täglich weiter fahren.[13] [Thus we have, in all, five parts covering the whole of Christian teaching, which we should constantly teach and require recitation word for word. For you should not assume that the young people will learn and retain this teaching from sermons alone. When these parts have been well learned, one may assign them also some psalms or some hymns, based on these subjects, to supplement and confirm their knowledge. Thus young people will be led into the Scriptures and make progress every day.[14]]

In schools where the Catechism was regularly taught throughout the week, the singing of Catechism hymns was mandatory. The Saxon Church Order directed that in schools "the children shall be taught with diligence the Catechism and with it the spiritual hymns and psalms of Dr. Luther."[15] Thus the Catechism hymns, and therefore *Jesus Christus unser Heiland*, together rank as an important pedagogical tool in addition to being an aid to worship.

In his 1624 *Tabulatura Nova*, Samuel Scheidt labeled his variations on *Jesus Christus unser Heiland* "*Psalmus sub communione.*"[16] In his first setting of this chorale in the "Leipzig" chorales (BWV 665), Bach gives the indication "*sub communione*" as part of the title. With its reference to the Passion in stanzas 1, 4, and 8, the text was associated with Maundy Thursday in Saxony and Thuringia, and the Weimar and Leipzig hymnbooks frequently listed it for this occasion.[17] *Jesus Christus unser Heiland* was one of the seven most frequently sung Communion hymns and, with Johann Franck's *Schmücke dich, o liebe Seele* and Nicolaus Decius's *O Lamm Gottes unschuldig*, is one of three important Communion hymns in the "Leipzig" chorales.[18]

During the fifteenth century, the melody as Bach knew it was used with the Latin text *Jesus Christus, nostra salus, quod reclamat omnis malus*. The 1524 broadsheet is the earliest known source to combine Luther's adaptation with this tune, which appears there as the lower part (tenor) of a two-voice setting. This tenor is almost identical to the melody as published soon afterward in the Erfurt *Enchiridia* and in Walter's *Geystliche Gesangk Buchleyn* of the same year.[19]

The text of the hymn in the Weimar hymnbook is given under the heading "Vom Heiligen Abendmahl":

1. JEsus Christus unser Heyland/
   der von uns den GOttes Zorn wand/
   durch das bitter Leiden sein/
   half er uns aus der Höllen-Pein.

1. Jesus Christ, our Savior,
   turned God's wrath from us.
   Through his bitter suffering
   He helped us from the pain of hell.

2. Daß wir nimmer des vergessen/
   gab er uns seinn Leib zu essen/
   verborgen im Brod so klein/
   und zu trincken sein Blut im Wein.

2. So that we never forget this,
   he gave us his body to eat,
   hidden in bread so small,
   and his blood to drink in wine.

3. Wer sich zu dem Tisch will machen/
   der hab wohl acht auf sein Sachen/
   wer unwürdig hinzu geht/
   für das Leben den Tod empfäht.

3. Whoever wishes to come to the table
   must well regard his affairs.
   Whoever comes unworthily,
   receives death instead of life.

4. Du solt GOtt dem Vater preisen
   daß er dich so wohl thut speisen/
   und für deine Missethat/
   in den Tod seinn Sohn gegeben hat.

4. You should praise God the Father
   because he feeds you so well,
   and for your sins
   gave his son into death.

5. Du solt gläuben und nicht wancken/
   daß es sey eine Speiß der Krancken/
   den'n ihr Hertz von Sünden schwer/
   und für Angst ist betrübet sehr.

5. You should believe and not doubt
   that it is a food for the sick,
   whose heart is heavy with sins
   and is troubled much through anxiety.

6. Solch groß Gnade und Barmhertzigkeit
   sucht ein Hertz in grosser Arbeit/
   ist dir wohl so bleib davon/
   daß du nicht kriegest bösen Lohn.

6. Such great grace and mercy
   a heart seeks with great effort.
   If you are well, stay away
   so that you do not receive an evil wage.

7. Er spricht selber: Kommt ihr Armen/
   last mich über euch erbarmen/
   kein Artzt ist dem Starcken noth/
   sein Kunst wird an ihm gar ein Spott.

7. He himself says: come you poor ones,
   let me have mercy on you.
   The strong do not need a doctor,
   his art would be wasted on him.

8. Hättst du dir was könt erwerben/
   was dürft ich denn für dich sterben/
   dieser Tisch auch dir nicht gilt/
   so du selber dir helffen wilt.

8. If you could have gained something yourself,
   why would I have needed to die for you?
   This table is also not for you
   if you wish to help yourself.

9. Gläubst du das von Hertzen-Grunde/

   und bekennest mit dem Munde/
   so bist du recht wohl geschickt/
   und die Speiß deine Seel erquickt.

9. If you believe this from the depths of your heart,
   and confess it with your lips,
   you are well fit
   and the food revives your soul.

10. Die Frucht soll auch nicht ausbleiben/   10. The fruit shall also not be wanting,
    deinen Nechsten solt du lieben/   for you should love your neighbor,
    daß er dein geniessen kan/   so that he can benefit of you,
    wie dein GOtt an dir hat gethan.[20]   like your God has done for you.[21]

The text of *Jesus Christus unser Heiland* is concerned with the redemption of humanity that has been gained through the Passion and death of Christ. This is especially addressed in stanza 1. Stanza 2 states that in order to remind believers of this, Christ gave his body to eat and his blood to drink. The redemptive power of the sacrament of the altar was central to Lutheran theology, and it is clearly expressed in the first two stanzas of Luther's hymn. In his Small Catechism, Luther speaks of the benefit of the sacrament of the altar, quoting first the words of Jesus:

> "Nehmet hin, esset, das ist mein Leib, der fur Euch gegeben wird. Solchs tut zu meinem Gedächtnis." Desselbengleichen nahm er auch den Kelch nach dem Abendmahl, danket und gab ihn den und sprach: "Nehmet hin und trinket alle daraus. Dieser Kelch ist das neue Testament in meinem Blut, das fur Euch vergossen wird zur Vergebung der Sunden. Solches tut, sooft Ihr trinkt, zu meinem Gedächtnis."[22] ["Take, eat; this is my body which is given for you. Do this in remembrance of me." In the same way he took also took the cup, after the supper, gave thanks, and gave it to them and said, "take, and drink of it, all of you. This cup is the New Testament in my blood, which is shed for you for the forgiveness of sins. Do this, as often as you drink it, in remembrance of me."[23]]

He continues, explaining the benefits of the sacrament:

> Das zeigen uns diese Wort: "fur Euch gegeben" und "vergossen zur Vergebung der Sunden," nämlich, daß uns im Sakrament Vergebung der Sunde, Leben und Seligkeit durch solche Wort gegeben wird; denn wo Vergebung der Sunde ist, da ist auch Leben und Seligkeit.[24] [The words "given for you" and "shed for you for the forgiveness of sins," show us that forgiveness of sin, life and salvation are given to us in the sacrament through these words, because where there is forgiveness of sin, there is also life and salvation.[25]]

Echoes of Luther's sermons for Palm Sunday and Maundy Thursday are to be heard in each stanza of *Jesus Christus unser Heiland*.[26] In the *House Postil* of 2 April 1534, he states how redemption, justification, and salvation are to be gained solely through Christ's sacrifice.[27] Here Luther is showing that whoever receives Christ in the sacrament will have eternal life. To remind believers of Christ's sacrifice, they receive Communion. Luther demonstrates that the benefit of the crucifixion is mediated to the believer by receiving the body and blood of Christ. The paintings of the Reformation period also reflected these ideals. Calvary was represented in the altarpieces of the period, which immediately connects the cross with the sacrament of the altar. The words of Luther, as found in the section on the Holy Supper in the Large Catechism, correspond closely to the text of *Jesus Christus unser Heiland*.[28] As with many of Luther's hymns, first of all he emphasizes the law, but also the grace of the Gospel. He viewed Christ's words, "Do this . . . in remembrance of me," as a commandment, but he also reiterates the grace to be received from the sacrament:

> Denn da beut er uns an alle den Schatz, so er uns von Himmel bracht hat [. . .] Bist Du beladen und fühlets Dein Schwachheit, so gehe fröhlich hin und lasse Dich erquicken, trösten und stärcken.[29] [For in this sacrament he offers us all the treasure he brought from heaven [. . .] if you are burdened and feel your weakness, go joyfully to the sacrament and let yourself be refreshed, comforted and strengthened.[30]]

In his *Vom Abendmahl Christi, Bekenntnis* [Confession Concerning Christ's Supper] (1528), Luther wrote,

> Aber wir wissen das Christus ein mal fur uns gestorben ist und solch sterben aus teilet er durch predigen, teuffen [geist] lesen, glauben, essen und wie er wil und wo er ist und was er thut.[31] [The passion of Christ occurred but once on the cross. But whom would it benefit if it were not distributed, applied and put to use? And how could it be put to use and distributed except through word and sacrament?[32]]

Here Luther is directly connecting the cross and the sacrament of the altar, a theme to which he repeatedly returned.

Bach's underlinings in his Calov Bible commentary regarding the sacrifice of Christ are notable.[33] For example, he underlines part of Luther's commentary on John 19:34, where the evangelist speaks of the soldier piercing the side of Jesus and the issue of water and blood from the side of the dead body of the Savior.

> Solch groß Wunderwerck am Creutz geschehen/ mit dem verstorbenen Leichnam JESU/ hat der Evangelist Johannes für andern Evangelisten/ nicht ohn Ursach/ noch umbsonst angesetzet. Denn damit hat er nicht allein des blossen Wunderwercks gedencken/ welches am Creutz

geschehen/ sondern auch einen hohen trefflichen Trost uns anzeigen/ und einbilden wollen. Was ist nun/ dz aus des HErrn Jesu Seiten am Creutze zugleich Blut und Wasser fleusset? Antwort: Unser Erlösung ist in dem Wunderwerck verborgen/ wie es S. Johannes selbst deutet und auslegt in seiner 1. Epistel am V. Cap. . . . . <u>Gnade/ Gnade/ vergib/ vergib/ Ablaß/Ablaß/ Vater/ Vater</u>.[34] [This great miracle in the dead body of Jesus on the cross the evangelist John has recorded in his gospel in contrast to the other evangelists, but not without reason or purpose. For in doing so, he not only wanted to call to mind the miracle that occurred on the cross, but he also wanted to show us and impress on us a great and choice source of comfort. But what does this signify, that at the same time blood and water issue from the side of the Lord Jesus on the cross? Answer: our redemption is concealed in this miracle, as St. John himself interprets and explains it in his first epistle, chapter 5:8. . . . <u>Grace! Grace! Forgive! Forgive! Indulgence! Indulgence! Father! Father!</u>[35]]

The words "our redemption is concealed in this miracle" are important here in the context of *Jesus Christus unser Heiland*. The blood of Christ is directly related to the sacrament of the altar and to salvation. The Abendmahl was seen as a foretaste of eternal life by Lutherans. Bach appears to have felt strongly about this issue since he underlined the words of Luther in the Calov commentary. The final underlining regarding the grace that comes with the sacrament shows how he understood the everyday significance of the Abendmahl. Each person takes on the cross of Christ and through faith is forgiven and therefore receives eternal life. Robin A. Leaver sums up the purpose of *Jesus Christus unser Heiland* in his article on the Catechism hymn as follows:

> In time *Jesus Christus unser Heiland* became the primary Communion hymn and also the leading hymn associated with the teaching of the main section of the catechism dealing with the Sacrament of the Altar.[36]

It is illuminating to read Erdmann Neumeister's teaching on this hymn in his *Tisch des HErrn* (Hamburg, 1722). He also highlights the redemptive power of the sacrament of the altar.

> Alle Menschen hätten dadurch in die ewige Verdammnis müßen gestürßet werden, wenn Christus nicht ins Mittel getreten wäre. Darumb heißets auch hier: half er uns aus der Höllen Pein.[37] [All people would have been damned eternally, if Christ did not come as a mediator. Therefore we have here: he helped us from the pain of hell.]

Neumeister continues to relate the hymn to salvation: "Und nun, wodurch vollzog er unsere Erlösung? Durch das bitter Leiden sein"[38] [And now, how did our salvation come to pass? By his bitter suffering]. Neumeister explains stanza 2 of *Jesus Christus unser Heiland*: "Das heißet, er stifftete das Sacrament seines Leibes und Blutes"[39] [That means, he instituted the sacrament of his body and blood]. Neumeister continues his explanation by saying that in order to help the fainthearted and unbelieving who were not present at the time of the death of Christ, Christ instituted the sacrament of the altar so that communicants could experience the death of Christ in the reception of his body and blood in the Holy Supper.[40] He clarifies the word "verborgen" by saying that it could also refer to the hidden mystery of the sacrament.[41] Neumeister quotes Isaiah 45:15 to amplify his proposition: "Fürwahr, Du bist ein verborgen GOtt, du GOtt Israel der Heiland!" [Verily thou art a God that hidest thyself, O God of Israel, the Savior]. It is striking that Neumeister is echoing the words of Luther in his commentary on John 19:34 where he states, "Unser Erlösung ist in dem Wunderwerck verborgen" [Our redemption is concealed in this miracle]. Verse 17 of the same chapter of Isaiah foretells the eternal salvation of mankind:

> Israel aber wird erlöset durch den HErrn, durch eine ewige Erlösung, und wird nicht zu Schanden, noch zu Spott immer und ewiglich. [But Israel shall be saved in the lord with an everlasting salvation: ye shall not be ashamed nor confounded world without end.]

In his comment on this passage, Luther refers to Hebrews 9:12 which speaks of the blood of Christ winning eternal redemption for humanity.[42] Thus the sacrifice of Christ, commemorated in the sacrament of the altar, is once more linked to eternal salvation. According to Neumeister, the inestimable treasure of this salvation was part of the mystery hidden in the bread.[43] He also clearly aligns Passion and Communion when he quotes Paul's account of the Last Supper (1 Cor. 11:26).

> Das geschiet denn, wenn man seine Andacht mit Paßion-und Communion-Gebethen hat, auch solche Lieder singet, die davon handeln.[44] [This happens when one prays using Passion or Communion prayers, or sings hymns in these categories.]

It seems clear that Neumeister's views on the sacrament of the altar were in keeping with Luther's. We know that Bach owned a copy of Neumeister's *Tisch des Herrn* on his death as it was listed in the specification of his library.[45]

Bach uses the melody *Jesus Christus unser Heiland* in its complete form in four works: BWV 363 from the harmonized chorales, BWV 665 and 666 from the "Leipzig" chorales, and BWV 688 from *Clavierübung III*. In each setting, the melody varies slightly. Bach chooses not to employ a widely used variant of this tune in the above settings, where the fourth note was altered chromatically, a version that appears in the hymn collections of Schein (1627) and Vopelius (1682), as well as in the Weißenfels hymnbook of 1714. In his fugue on the chorale in *Clavierübung III* (BWV 689), however, Bach uses the chromatic variant.

JESUS CHRISTUS UNSER HEILAND (BWV 665)

This chorale prelude exists in two versions: an earlier Weimar version (BWV 665a) and a later Leipzig revision (BWV 665). In P271, BWV 665 bears the heading "*Jesus Christus unser Heyland. sub communione. Pedaliter.*" The earlier Weimar setting bears the inscription "*pro organo pleno.*" It is a chorale prelude of the paraphrase type where the treatment of the pedal represents an earlier aspect of Bach's compositional development. The bass voice is sometimes in the manual part and then passes to the pedal. BWV 665 was the last chorale prelude of this collection to be fair copied by Bach.

Jesus Christus unser Heiland (BWV 665) is in four distinct sections with the four phrases of the chorale dictating the structure of the piece. Bach combines the technique of chorale setting with the rhythm of the allemande. In each section, the tenor and alto parts provide fore-imitation with the motives derived from the chorale melody. The pedal enters third in each phrase with an unadorned statement of the chorale. The soprano completes the four-part texture with a more ornate version, extending the cadence with expressive chromatic harmony at the close of each phrase. Only six out of the total fifty-two measures do not contain a reference to the chorale melody.

The musical style of this piece changes from phrase to phrase. A paraphrase of the first phrase of the chorale melody is presented first by the tenor and answered by the alto. This is accompanied by a sixteenth-note countersubject in which the weak eighth note is tied over to the next strong beat (*syncopatio*). In his *Praecepta der musicalischen Composition* (1708), Johann Gottfried Walther assigns the *syncopatio* to the category of the *figurae fundamentales*. He recommends the use of these figures when the text indicates "Härtigheit," or harshness.[46] The first section ends at m. 11. In m. 9, there is an expressive cadence, starting with the half-diminished-seventh chord. This is followed by the extension, consisting of a four-beat codetta as well as a one-and-a-half-measure tonic pedal to close the section. According to Walther, a pedal point brought high pathos to vocal music.[47]

The second phrase is characterized by a leaping bass line. The impact of the leaping bass is intensified by the *exclamatio* of the alto part and the *syncope* of all three voices. The second phrase of the chorale is heard almost unadorned in the tenor, is repeated a fifth higher in the alto, and is presented by the bass as a pedal *cantus firmus*. Following the soprano entry, the section closes with the same sort of intense plagal cadence as before at m. 26.

The third section begins at m. 27 and is remarkably expressive. Bach introduces a dramatic chromatic line that descends a sixth (*passus duriusculus*). This theme is heard equally in its *rectus* and *inversus* forms, with the *inversus* closing in the *figura corta*. For the first time in the piece, the motivic writing is introduced by the soprano, followed by the alto and tenor. The chromatic line is repeated in the soprano and bass at different pitches (*synonymia* or *epizeuxis*). Line 3 of the *cantus firmus* is heard beginning on d^1 in the soprano at m. 30 before the entry proper in the pedal part at m. 33. The soprano repeats it again, starting at m. 35, this time beginning on g^1, as in the pedal. The *anabasis* in the bass at m. 37 leads to the final phrase where its first note is concealed in the final chord of the third phrase at m. 38.1.

In the fourth and final section of this chorale prelude, which begins at m. 38, Bach introduces a rising thirty-second-note figure that dominates the section. Apart from the brief appearance of thirty-second notes in the *figura corta* of the third phrase, this is the first time these note values have been used to such an extent. The final phrase of the chorale is heard in the pedal from m. 44 to 46 and in the soprano from m. 47 to 49. There is a tonic pedal for the final three and a half measures, over which Bach repeats the rising thirty-second-note motive through chromatic sequences before resolving on a chord of E major at m. 52.

There are some small alterations of figuration between BWV 665a and BWV 665. In mm. 28, 31, 34, and 36, Bach has added the *figura corta*, and in mm. 49–50, there is a chromatic alteration.

Interpretations by Other Authors

The dramatic figuration of *Jesus Christus unser Heiland* (BWV 665) has inspired many writers to great lengths in their descriptions of their perceptions of text-music relationships.

Philipp Spitta considers that BWV 665 was one of the grandest and profoundest creations of this most admirable master.[48] He suggests that the first two lines are full of solemn agitation, as though tinged with a memory of the Last Supper, and as yet unaffected by any special considerations. In his view, the chromatic lines that begin at m. 27 represent "das bitter Leiden," and the motive at m. 38 lifts believers triumphantly out of this dejection, culminating in a close full of dignified gravity.[49]

In his introduction to the collected organ works of Bach, Albert Schweitzer states that it is stanza 1 of *Jesus Christus unser Heiland* that Bach is illustrating in BWV 665.[50] He also acknowledges the depiction of each line of the text in turn in his biography of Bach.[51] In referring to the gloomy atmosphere of the opening, he proposes that the great sin of man required the sacrifice of Christ. He associates the bass motive at m. 15 with the rhythm of the accompaniment of the arioso "Erbarm' es Gott" from the St. Matthew Passion, sung when Christ is scourged. According to Schweitzer, the chromatic motive of the third section depicts the "bitter Leiden," relieved by the jubilant thirty-second notes of the final section.[52]

Hans Luedtke agrees with most commentators on this setting, that Bach is portraying stanza 1. He points to the obvious examples of the chromatic harmony of line 3 and the rising motive of line 4.[53] In his opinion, the first phrase represents the "Gut" and "Mildigkeit" of the Savior, while the second phrase produces the image of the crucified Christ.[54] To back up his arguments with regard to the depiction of the crucified Christ, Luedtke cites the alto aria "Sehet! Jesus hat die Hand" from the St. Matthew Passion. According to him, the motive heard first in m. 4 and later in m. 16 on viola II could be seen to represent the outstretched arms of Christ. A similar motive occurs from m. 15 to 25 of BWV 665. He therefore suggests that this motive is related to the cross.

Charles Sanford Terry states that this is one of two chorale preludes—the other being *O Lamm Gottes unschuldig* (BWV 656)—in which Bach illustrates in sequence the lines of text.[55] He claims that for the first thirteen measures Bach's treatment of the *cantus firmus* is inspired by the word "Redeemer." In his view, the bass motive at m. 14 represents the strokes of God's anger, from which the Redeemer's Passion rescued mankind. He agrees with most other writers that the chromatic writing beginning at m. 27 represents "das bitter Leiden" and that the rising motive at m. 38 is one of resurrection, representing man's rescue from the pains of hell.[56]

Harvey Grace sees the carrying of the cross in the counterpoint of line 1.[57] Fritz Dietrich implies that Bach intended to portray the distance between God and man in the jumping motive of line 2, making the analogy of the distance between Adam's fall and salvation through Christ.[58]

Rudolf Steglich also suggests that Bach was basing his setting on stanza 1.[59] He states that there is an instinctive or automatic striving toward the Savior on Bach's part. He refers to the other lines of text in the same manner as previously mentioned writers, pointing out that Bach is expressing musically something that was very personal to him.[60] Steglich comments on line 4 of the text, "half er uns aus der Höllen-Pein":

erlöstes, entlastetes, glückseliges Aufatmen in der endlich erreichten Com-
munio, der Zweieinheit—als ob die befreite Seele ihrem Jesus entgegen-
flöge und er sich ganz ihr zuneigte, in ihr sich verschlösse.[61] [Redemption,
exoneration, blissful release in communion, union with Christ attained at
last—as though the liberated soul has flown to Jesus and He has drawn close
and immersed Himself in her.]

Steglich seems to be describing the Abendmahl as a foretaste of the eternal
Jerusalem.

Stainton de B. Taylor likewise notes Bach's adherence to the text of
stanza 1. He refers to the "scourging" rhythm that Bach used in his Passion
settings, and to the chromatic writing portraying the Savior's suffering.[62] Taylor comments on the motive of resurrection from m. 38 onward, additionally
referring to "a feeling of confidence in the redeeming power of the Savior"
with regard to the closing section.[63]

Hermann Keller is clear in his opinion regarding lines 3 and 4. He sees
line 3 as expressing "das bitter Leiden sein" and line 4 as representing deliverance from the pains of hell [Befreiung aus der Höllenpein].[64]

Jacques Chailley comments on the connection of *Jesus Christus unser Heiland* with Passion as well as with Communion and states that with BWV 665,
as with the settings of *Clavierübung III*, Bach was thinking of the text of stanza
1.[65] He analyzes the setting in relation to the text as follows:

> Le premier vers en effet évoque la Rédemption, le seconde la colère de
> Dieu, le troisième ses souffrances et le dernier la délivrance.[66] [The first line
> in effect evokes salvation, the second the anger of God, the third his suffer-
> ing and the final deliverance.]

He goes through each line in turn with his own description. In his opinion,
the opening line is profoundly expressive, with a brutal change of atmosphere
coming with the seeming confusion of section 2.[67]

Ulrich Meyer similarly suggests that Bach is portraying the text of stanza
1 in BWV 665.[68]

Peter Williams quotes most of the literature without actually making any
firm conclusions of his own.[69] Of the coda he writes, "The motifs thought to
express various images work gradually towards the final pedal point: the big-
gest close so far in the whole collection, perhaps an expression of 'escaping
from the torment of Hell,' even more rhetorical than the comparable endings
of Weimar cantatas such as BWV 161."[70]

Hans Musch has shown how the wrath of God is depicted through
a leaping figure in BWV 688, citing the aria "Warum willst du so zornig

sein" from cantata BWV 101 as an example of Bach depicting the wrath of God.[71]

Russell Stinson also acknowledges the word painting and concludes that it is stanza 1 that is relevant here.[72] All of the above writers mention the text of stanza 1 in their interpretation of BWV 665.

In the following section, the hymn text is investigated to ascertain if there are other possibilities, or if in fact the assertions of these writers may be verified.

Assessment

The investigations of earlier authors seem to lead to the text of stanza 1 of *Jesus Christus unser Heiland*. Before a conclusive opinion may be offered, it is necessary to examine the text of the entire hymn in an effort to see if there are any other possible links between text and music.

Jesus Christus unser Heiland (BWV 665) has many significant musical characteristics. The most obvious is perhaps the dramatic third section (mm. 27–38), which incorporates jagged rising and falling chromatic lines. The sudden introduction of rising thirty-second notes in the fourth section is also worthy of comment. Equally, the use of syncopation in the second section (mm. 14–26) is also striking.

How can the very impressive third section relate to the text? The most likely possibilities may be stanza 1 ("durch das bitter Leiden sein"), stanza 4 ("und für deine Missethat"), and stanza 5 ("den'n ihr Hertz von Sünden schwer"). The Passion of Christ and the sin of mankind were sometimes depicted by Bach in chromatic writing, so it is feasible that he could have been setting one of these three stanzas. None of the other third lines seem appropriate.

It may be that the sudden introduction of rising thirty-second notes is related to the text. The only real possibilities seem to be stanza 1 ("half er uns aus der Höllen-Pein") and perhaps stanza 9 ("und die Speiß deine Seel erquickt"). The syncopations of the second section could possibly be expressing something negative. In this case, conceivable stanzas might be stanza 1 ("der von uns den GOttes Zorn wand"), stanza 5 ("daß es sey eine Speiß der Krancken"), stanza 7 ("last mich über euch erbarmen"), and stanza 8 ("was dürft ich denn für dich sterben").

Common to all connections proposed is the text of stanza 1. It seems logical to conclude that the graphic chromatic lines represent the "bitter Leiden" of Christ, the rising thirty-second notes of the final section the rescue from hell, and the syncopations of the second section the turning of God's wrath from humanity. There does not appear to be such a vivid portrayal of any other stanza. Additionally, this is a very strong stanza theologically, outlining the Lutheran link between Christ's sacrifice, the Abendmahl, and salvation. It does not seem likely that Bach would have ignored a stanza that encapsulates all of Luther's teachings on the Abendmahl. Detailed analysis of BWV 665 may help to confirm this opinion.

The opening phrase of this chorale, with its rising perfect fifth, is in itself a powerful depiction of the opening text "Jesus Christus unser Heyland" (see example 10.1). Bach's task in paraphrasing the melody is made easier by the high quality of his raw material. The tenor clearly states the *cantus firmus* with only a few decorative notes. The accompanying motive at m. 1.3 of the bass uses the "hard" leap or *saltus duriusculus*. This is passed to the other voices on the entry of the *cantus firmus* in the pedal at m. 5.3. It is possible that the use of the *saltus duriusculus* here may be related to the overall context of the hymn. This could be an implied reference to the sacrifice of Christ which provides redemption, commemorated in the sacrament of the altar. The strong opening tenor line can be related to the Savior, while the use of diminished chords and intervals points to his Passion and death. The lower part of the third and fourth beat of m. 1 can visually create a cross sign. This is repeated for the first two beats of m. 2. In the text of stanza 1, the word "Christus" is found, and this motive is used in connection with this word throughout the first section.

Many scholars mentioned above have suggested that the leaping, syncopated bass line of the second section is related to the wrath of God. This in turn might be related to the issue of redemption. God's wrath is turned from humanity because of the actions of Jesus in his death on the cross. This guarantees eternal life. Bach outlines the rising melodic minor scale of E minor in the bass in mm. 15–16. This is repeated in B minor at mm. 18–19. It seems likely that in the *anabasis* of this passage, Bach is aiming at depicting the hope of eternal salvation. The wrath of God is turned away, through the sacrifice of Christ, thereby ensuring salvation for humanity. This is the positive side of God's wrath, as Christ fulfills his law. In the first *Clavierübung III* setting of the same hymn (BWV 688), Bach also uses a leaping figure as seen in the second section of BWV 665, a figuration that has similarities with the aria "Warum willst du so zornig sein" (BWV 101/4), which also depicts the wrath of God.

Example 10.1.   BWV 665 (mm. 1f.)

It appears logical that the chromaticisms of the third section lead to line 3 of stanza 1. The start of the third section may be seen in example 10.2. This kind of chromatic writing has been associated with the Passion of Christ in many of Bach's compositions.[73] The earliest example of this kind of writing can be found in movement 3 of the capriccio *Sopra la lontananza del fratello dilettissimo* (BWV 992) [On the departure (absence) of his most dear brother]. This piece is thought to have been written to commemorate Bach's elder brother Jacob's entrance in 1704 into the service of King Charles XII of Sweden.[74] Movement 3 of this piece is a lament in F minor with twelve variations over a chromatic chaconne bass. Another early example can be found in *Christ lag in Todesbanden* (BWV 4/5). In the movement "Hier ist das rechte Osterlamm," the text refers to the Lamb of God and his sacrifice to achieve the redemption of mankind. A fine example is the opening chorus of *Weinen, Klagen, Sorgen, Zagen!* (BWV 12/2), which was later adapted to become Bach's most supreme example of this kind of writing in the *Crucifixus* of the B Minor Mass. A descending chromatic theme is found in the final movement of *Christen, ätzet diesen Tag* (BWV 63/7), written for Christmas Day in either 1714 or 1715.[75] The chromatic theme occurs on the final two phrases of the text: "Aber niemals nicht geschehn, Das uns Satan möge quälen" [Never may the fiend contrive to reduce us to subjection]. Here the text is referring to the redemption being offered by the birth of Jesus. This kind of writing may seem a little surprising in a Christmas cantata, but in Lutheran theology the way to the cross was through the crib, and references to the Passion are sometimes found in Christmas music.[76]

In m. 28, Bach combines the rising chromatic line with the *figura corta*. Albert Schweitzer was the first to recognize this as a joy motive.[77] There seems to be a paradox here in the combination of the *figura corta* and the *passus duriusculus* representing the Passion and suffering of Jesus. In his sermon *Von der Freiheit eines Christenmenschen* [On the Freedom of a Christian], Luther draws the analogy of the soul as a bride and Christ as the bridegroom. He describes how Christ takes on the sins of the soul so that the soul may have grace, life, and salvation. This is referred to as the "frölich Wechsel" (joyful exchange) by Luther. It seems clear that Luther is showing how there is something joyful in the fact that Christ takes on the sins of the world in his sacrifice in order

Example 10.2.   BWV 665 (mm. 27f.)

to provide eternal salvation.[78] Can this concept be related to Bach's use of the *figura corta* in BWV 665?

There seems to be a paradox in Bach's simultaneous presentation of the *figura corta* and the tragic chromatic line. Bach may be expressing the paradoxical nature of the Passion so frequently encountered in Lutheran sermons and spiritual writings.[79] Bach's use of a joy motive against the *passus duriusculus* may be a foretaste of the redemption gained through the Passion. The important word here is "durch"—*through* Christ's bitter suffering, salvation is assured.

This *figura corta* in m. 28 was added to the Leipzig revision, BWV 665. In BWV 665a, this figure was not present. It may be significant that Bach chose to add it to the later setting of *Jesus Christus unser Heiland*. The use of such figures in Bach's music is usually not accidental. Bach appears to be adding an extra dimension in the Leipzig revision. Another example of this kind of writing can be found in *Jesu, der du meine Seele* (BWV 78/1). This movement is concerned with the redemption gained through the cross. The Passion is depicted in the chromatic descending chaconne theme, which can be heard in 121 of the 144 measures of the movement. Against this, Bach places the *figura corta* in a rising bass motive, perhaps representing the hope that the death of Christ brings, as the text of the chorale later shows. Parallels can be drawn between this movement and BWV 665. Similar comparisons may be made with Bach's use of a stanza from Stockmann's chorale *Jesu Leiden, Pein und Tod* in *Sehet, wir gehn hinauf gen Jerusalem* (BWV 159/5) and in *Himmelskönig sei willkommen* (BWV 182/7). The opening words of the chorale stanza are "Jesu deine Passion ist mir lauter Freude" [Jesus your Passion is great joy for me]. The joy here is seen as a foretaste of heavenly joy.[80] The bass aria "Komm süßes Kreuz" from the St. Matthew Passion is another example of the *figura corta* being used to express the notion of the positive side of the cross, or the hope that the death of Jesus brings. At this point in the St. Matthew Passion, Jesus is setting out to go to Golgotha to be crucified. The French overture dotted rhythm emphasizes the torturous journey, with the dotted sixteenth note always on a low note, suggesting the slow progress up the hill. The use of the *figura corta* is consistent with Bach's use of it elsewhere, always in the context of the paradoxical struggle of the cross.[81] In BWV 665, in addition to using the *figura corta* motive as an expression of hope, Bach also combines a rising diatonic scale with the descending *passus duriusculus* at this point. This becomes a descending major scale on inversion. The contrast between the chromatic and diatonic scale may be Bach's means of confirming Luther's views of the joyful exchange.

It is useful at this point to refer to the puzzle canon that Bach wrote in 1747 for Johann Gottfried Fulde, a student of theology. Bach did not indicate the solution to this canon in the form of written-out music, but he added the inscription *Christus Coronabit Crucigeros* [Christ will Crown the Crossbearers].[82] Once again, the seemingly ambivalent nature of the cross is to be found. The following commentary from the *New Bach Reader* provides an insight:

> This *symbolum* contains a contrast of moods, with its promise that the sad (the top begins with a mournful chromatic descent) shall be happy. Such a contrast of moods, the reader was supposed to conclude, could be expressed in the canon only by contrary motion, and Bach, in his *symbolum* not only hinted in this manner at the principle of solution but also indicated by the three capital C's that the "pivot tone" of the original lines and their inversion was C. The canon is an occasional and unpretentious composition without text, but it reveals to us how strongly Bach felt the change of *Affect* accomplished solely by inversion, trusting the mere indication of a similar contrast in words to tell any able musician the puzzle's solution.[83]

If one considers the use of the descending chromatic line and its many inversions in BWV 665, one could justify a similar interpretation to that of the puzzle canon. The descending chromatic line and its inversion (beginning in m. 27) may represent the cross, while the rising chromatic line or inversion represents the "crown" or joy of the cross.[84] Perhaps Bach is juxtaposing polar opposites in his music to show how the struggle of life leads to eternal happiness.

The rising thirty-second-note motive that is heard throughout the final section of BWV 665 is described by Schweitzer as the expressive motive of resurrection and by Keller as the deliverance from hell.[85] The words here, "half er uns aus der höllen Pein," refer to the consequences of Christ's Passion. Humanity is no longer condemned to hell since the death of Christ has redeemed mankind. A similar motive of rising thirty-second notes is to be found in the opening aria of BWV 145/1, "Ich lebe, mein Herze, zu deinem Ergötzen," possibly first performed on 19 April 1729 on the third Easter day.[86] Here, as in BWV 665, the thirty-second notes are expressing Easter hope and joy.[87]

The *ascensus* thirty-second-note motive is followed by a *circulatio* figure. Although the third phrase has many chromatic notes, the harmony remains relatively simple. In the final section, however, the emotion is intensified by the increased use of chromatic harmony and suspensions. The final phrase of the chorale enters in m. 44 beneath a *figura corta* motive, which is followed by the rising thirty-second-note motive in tenor and alto. A *circulatio* figure leads the music in a downward sequence. This low e^0, in the lowest extremes of the alto part, is heard supported only by the bass G below it (m. 46.3). Here Bach appears to be depicting "der Höllen Pein," since he rarely misses an opportunity to portray the depths of hell in musical terms.[88] In m. 47 of BWV

665, the rising motive is heard simultaneously in both alto and tenor parts. This can be interpreted as a reinforcement of the positive side of Christ's Passion and death. This is the only time where this occurs. The soprano repeats the *cantus firmus* leading to a conclusive close over a tonic pedal (*paragoge*). In mm. 49–50, Bach alters the tenor *c⁰* dotted sixteenth note/eighth note to a chromatic two-eighth-note variant of *c-sharp–natural*. The chromatic alteration makes for a richer harmonic texture while also allowing Bach to combine this motive with the rising thirty-second-note motive, in a final gesture toward the paradoxical cross.

★ ★ ★

Following the above discussion, it is possible to confirm that Bach was portraying the text of stanza 1 in musical terms in his setting BWV 665. The youthfully decisive delineations between sections make this connection between text and tone easy to decipher. This is no facile interpretation of the text. Examination of the theological background to the text of *Jesus Christus unser Heiland* shows once more how well informed Bach was with regard to the texts of the chorales he set.

JESUS CHRISTUS UNSER HEILAND (BWV 666)

This second setting of *Jesus Christus unser Heiland* is headed "*Jesus Christus unser. alio modo*" in P271. It exists in two versions: BWV 666a, an earlier Weimar version, and BWV 666, a later setting, possibly revised in Weimar and not in Leipzig, as with the remainder of this collection.[89] In P271, this setting is in the hand of Johann Christoph Altnickol, Bach's son-in-law. The revised version of BWV 666a (BWV 666) is to be found in sources that also include BWV 665a.[90] In the main, the two settings of BWV 666 are almost identical, with differences of figuration in mm. 19–20, 32, and 33. In the earlier Weimar version, there are some slurs in m. 1 and ornaments at mm. 1.4 and 5.4. All the other notes correspond exactly, with some variation in the layout for the hands. It is clearly a very youthful work, almost completely a *manualiter* setting, with the pedal only entering for a tonic pedal after the final phrase of the chorale has been stated. It is possible that BWV 665 may have been modeled on this setting, given the similarities in structure.

BWV 666 is in 12/8 time and is thirty-eight measures long. Like BWV 665, it is based on the principle of fore-imitation as developed by Dieterich Buxtehude, with clearly defined sections, and as with BWV 665, relatively few measures contain no reference to the chorale. In this case, thirty out of thirty-eight measures contain direct references, with some of the remaining eight referring to motives derived from the chorale.

The opening tenor motive is derived from line 1 of the chorale. This motive is developed in a *fugato* manner by the alto, tenor, and bass parts until the entry of the *cantus firmus* proper in the soprano in m. 6. There is a tonic pedal in mm. 9–10 with a *tirata defectiva* linking the first and second sections. The second section, which begins at m. 11, uses motivic imitation between the alto and bass, with the tenor clearly stating the *cantus firmus*, followed immediately by soprano an octave higher. The third section, beginning at m. 18, follows a similar pattern, but this time the motivic material is in sixteenth notes. The sixteenth-note movement continues in section 4 (from m. 24), but on this occasion the *cantus firmus* is clearly stated four times. It appears first of all in the tenor (m. 24) and is answered a fifth higher in the soprano (m. 27). The bass states the final line of the chorale beginning on *f-sharp*[0] at m. 29.4, answered by the final statement in the soprano beginning on *d*[2] (m. 32). The four-measure coda begins with a rising cadenza-like passage that leads to the entry of the only pedal note in the piece, the tonic *E* in m. 36.

Interpretations by Other Authors

Many commentators have attempted to assign various stanzas of this hymn to this particular setting.

Albert Schweitzer is of the opinion that Bach is portraying the text of stanza 1 in BWV 666.[91]

Hans Luedtke also considers the text of stanza 1 to be relevant.[92] He refers to the gentle 12/8 rhythm being representative of the words "unser Heiland," seeing the setting clearly in two sections, where the second half represents lines 3 and 4 of stanza 1. In his view, the rising thirty-second notes of the final section represent "half uns aus der Höllen Pein."[93]

Charles Sandford Terry suggests that the implication in this particular setting is that Christ delivered humanity out of the pain of hell, since Bach devotes nine measures to an elaboration of phrase 4.[94]

Harvey Grace sees no connection between text and music in this setting, with the exception of the coda, whose *anabasis* and increased animation, he suggests, are symbolic of the resurrection.[95]

Rudolf Steglich tries to prove an elaborate theory linking the penultimate stanza with this setting.[96] To support his case, he uses the fact that the opening four notes of *Jesus Christus unser Heiland* and *Wir glauben an den eingen Gott* are the same and that the penultimate stanza of the former begins "Glaubst du das von Herzensgrunde" [If you believe this from the depths of your heart].

Stainton de B. Taylor dismisses this piece with merely the words "the other setting [BWV 666] is not important."[97] He seems to agree with Terry's statements regarding the final section.[98]

No other authors make any links with text and music in BWV 666.

Assessment

In all other chorales included in the "Leipzig" chorales, where there is more than one setting, Bach appears to set a different stanza. Can this be said with certainty regarding BWV 666? Examination of specific musical details may lead to a particular stanza of the hymn.

The chief musical elements of this composition are the 12/8 meter, the striking motive at m. 18.3, the technique of inversion, the use of parallel thirds and sixths, the sudden increase to sixteenth-note movement from m. 18, the marked *parrhesia* of the closing section, and the extraordinary *anabasis* of three octaves that begins at m. 35.

One of the most important aspects of BWV 666 is the motive heard at m. 18.3. Albert Clement has drawn attention to its use in the opening variation of the Canonic Variations (BWV 769) where the angel brings his message of the good news of the birth of Christ.[99] It is also used by Bach in association with the gift of the Holy Spirit in *Komm Gott Schöpfer heiliger Geist* (BWV 667); in the Pentecost cantata *Erschallet, ihr Lieder, erklinget, ihr Saiten!* (BWV 172); and with the gift of the Lamb of God in *Christe, du Lamm Gottes* (BWV 619). It is possible that there is a stanza of *Jesus Christus unser Heiland* that could offer a similar interpretation. As an Abendmahl hymn, the idea of the gift of the sacrament of the altar is implied in all stanzas. However, it is possible that Bach wanted to refer specifically to the gift of Christ's sacrifice, as in stanza 1, or to the body and blood of the Abendmahl, as in stanza 2. There do not appear to be any other stanzas that specifically warrant the use of this motive.

It is likely that the use of the 12/8 meter has a theological meaning. Renate Steiger has related this meter to the Good Shepherd and the Savior, consequently discovering many movements from cantatas where the 12/8 meter seemed to be used by Bach in the context of salvation.[100] As with the above argument, it is possible that Bach employed this meter as a general means of portraying the salvation ensured by the Abendmahl and the sacrifice of Christ. In this case, stanza 1 seems to be the most fitting one as it mentions Christ as Savior, his sacrifice, and the consequences thereof. No other stanza appears to be as suitable.

The sudden increase to sixteenth-note movement from m. 18 results in a vivid accompaniment to the *cantus firmus*. In BWV 665, the marked increase in movement appears to be related to the final line of text and the promise of eternal salvation. Clearly it can be related to the idea of eternal salvation inherent in stanza 1. It may be equally possible to relate it to the refreshment of the spirit in stanza 9 ("und die Speiß deine Seel erquickt"). The remarkable *anabasis* of mm. 35–36 also appears significant in this regard.

The *parrhesia* that becomes marked at m. 31 is also striking. Bach sometimes uses this kind of writing in the context of something negative. It may be possible to relate it to Christ's "bitter Leiden" of stanza 1. In addition, if one considers this feature in isolation, it is possible that Bach might use *parrhesia* in the context of "Tod" (stanzas 3 and 4), "Sünden" and "Angst" (stanza 5), or "bösen Lohn" (stanza 6).

From this discussion it now seems likely that Bach was once more depicting the text of stanza 1 in BWV 666. If so, it would be an exception, since it was not usual for him to portray the same stanza successively in one collection, but there does not seem to be a convincing explanation for the musical features mentioned above in the context of any other stanza. It may be that Bach decided to depict this stanza in each setting of *Jesus Christus unser Heiland* in this collection, given the theological importance of the stanza. Additionally, since it is very likely that Bach composed BWV 666 before BWV 665, he may have felt drawn to begin with this stanza, so relevant is it to the Lutheran understanding of the Abendmahl.

Albert Clement has made important observations concerning Bach's reception of the Abendmahl.[101] Bach attended church services regularly, but not always. This would imply that for Bach the redemptive power of the Abendmahl was more important than the concept of feeding the soul each Sunday. This emphasizes the importance of the text of stanza 1. In addition, no other stanza of *Jesus Christus unser Heiland* offers such opportunities for expressive text–music associations as stanza 1. It is not easy to relate any of the other stanzas to the musical methods employed by Bach in BWV 666.

In BWV 666, the use of imitative counterpoint seems significant. The first ten measures form the first section, and here Bach employs the techniques of fugal writing. This kind of strict imitation is suitable for line 1 of the text "Jesus Christus unser Heyland." Such counterpoint is related to the law, and Christ came to save humanity to fulfill the law, described in Galatians 4:4 as follows:

> But when the fullness of the time was come, God sent forth his Son, made of a woman, made under the law, to redeem them that were under the law, that we might receive the adoption of sons.

Christ himself makes this point according to Matthew 5:18 as follows:

Think not that I am come to destroy the law, or the prophets: I am not come to destroy, but to fulfill. For verily I say unto you, till heaven and earth pass, one jot or one tittle shall in no wise pass from the law, till all be fulfilled.

The idea of the fulfillment of the law and redemption are clearly theologically linked. Therefore, in the context of Christ as "Heiland," as it happens both here and in Luther's *Nun komm der Heiden Heiland*," it is not surprising to find Bach alluding to law.[102] In his commentary on Galatians, Luther gives an initial explanation of chapter 4:4 as follows:

Observa diligenter, quo modo hic Paulus Christum definiat. Christus, inquit, est filius Dei ac mulieris, qui propter nos peccatores factus est sub legem, ut nos qui sub lege eramus, redimeret. His verbis utrumque complexus est, et personam et officium Christi. Persona constituta est ex divina et humana natura. Id clare indicat, cum dicit: "Misit Deus filium suum, Natum ex muliere." Est igitur Christus verus Deus et verus homo. Officium vero eius his verbis describit: "Factus sub legem, ut eos, qui sub lege," etc.[103] [Mark here how carefully Paul defines Christ. Christ is the Son of God, and of a woman, who, for us sinners, was made under the law, to redeem us who were under the law. In these words he comprehends both the person and the office of Christ. His person consists of his divine and human nature. This he shows when he says: "God sent forth his Son, made of a woman." Christ therefore, is very God, and very man. His office he shows in these words: "Being made under the law, to redeem them that were under the law."[104]]

Luther emphasizes the dual aspect of Christ's nature: the divine and the human. Equally he contrasts law and Gospel.

It seems appropriate to return to the important motive first heard at m. 18.3. The motive that commences in the alto halfway through m. 18 can also be found in the first variation of the Canonic Variations on *Vom Himmel Hoch da komm ich her* (BWV 769); in *Komm Gott Schöpfer heiliger Geist* (BWV 667); and in *Christe, du Lamm Gottes* (BWV 619). This motive also appears in m. 13 of the opening chorus of the Pentecost cantata *Erschallet, ihr Lieder, erklinget, ihr Saiten!* (BWV 172), where the implication is also salvation.[105] It is also found in the opening motive of the *Allegro* of the "Prelude, Fugue and Allegro" (BWV 998) for lute.[106] Wolfram Syré has suggested that the purpose of this motive in BWV 769 and 666 is to link Christmas and Passion.[107] In relation to BWV 769/1, Albert Clement suggests that this is an allusion to the descending angel and also the idea of "edle Gabe" [noble gift].[108] These motives may be seen in examples 10.3a, b, and c. A half measure after this motive is heard for the first time in m. 18 of BWV 666, Bach inverts it in the bass in m. 19. This may be related to the turning away of God's wrath ("der von uns der Gottes Zorn wand"). Here Bach very purposely turns the music in the opposite direction. Additionally, the use of inversion might be similar to that of BWV 661, depicting something contrasting or opposing. This concept can therefore lead to the divine and human aspect of Christ's nature. Equally, Bach may be emphasizing Christ in the image of the Father.

In m. 23, Bach combines the *syncopatio* and the *figura corta*. The *figura corta* is used only in this measure and is heard twice.[109] Against this motive, the motive of m. 18 is heard in its *rectus* and *inversus* form. The *anabasis* that begins halfway through m. 23 continues to span three octaves by m. 24.3. From m. 21 to 24, the third phrase of the chorale is heard: "durch das bitter Leiden sein." As so often happens when Bach refers to the suffering and the cross of Christ, there appears to be a musical paradox. In this case, the *figura corta* and the use of *anabasis* seem to contradict the text. As shown previously, however, this could be related to Luther's "fröhlich Wechsel"—the idea that joy comes through Christ's sacrifice. In m. 24, the *anabasis* of the music, coupled with the writing in tenths and sixths, adds to the feeling of joy created by the use of the sixteenth notes and the *figura corta*. Luther shows in his writings how this joy can be associated with the sacrament and therefore the sacrifice of Christ. The contrasting *syncopatio* is perhaps related to "bitter Leiden."

The sudden increase in notes with the use of sixteenth notes in the figuration can be related to the text. The increase in movement through the use of sixteenth notes has quite a dramatic effect on the listener. With the exception of m. 10, a bridge passage, the music moves in eighth notes to the end of m. 17. Suddenly the writing changes to incorporate notes of half the value for the rest of the piece. There is the joy of the sacrament to be considered, as well as the joy of eternal life promised in the "bitter Leiden" of Christ. A similar technique can be seen in the bass aria "Eilt, ihr angefocht'nen Seelen" from the St. John Passion. In this aria there are sacramental implications. The text refers to running to the cross for spiritual well-being. As has been expressed numerous times in

Example 10.3a.   BWV 619 (mm. 1–3)

Example 10.3b. BWV 769 (mm. 1–2)

this study, there are links between the cross and the Abendmahl, as seen in the altarpieces of Lucas Cranach and in the writings of Luther. Perhaps the running to the cross may be linked with running joyfully to the sacrament. This may be relevant to BWV 666.

In BWV 666, the first three lines of the chorale are heard twice each. Line 4 of the chorale is heard four times. It seems reasonable to suggest that Bach was in some way emphasizing the importance of this line. This would also tie in with Neumeister's explanation of the redemptive power of the Abendmahl, where he states that all people would have been damned eternally were it not for Christ the mediator. For him, this is the explanation of "half er uns aus den Höllen Pein."[110] The Abendmahl is a reminder of the sacrifice of Christ. For many reasons, this section of BWV 666, from m. 24 to the end, is the most striking. First, because of the four-time repetition of the chorale phrase, which is framed on either side by a three-octave *anabasis*. This may be linked to the victory that Christ achieves in his sacrifice on the cross, the release for humanity from eternal damnation. The tonic pedal beginning at m. 36.3 may be related to eternal salvation. A third striking element is the shocking chromatic harmony, which occurs from m. 31, which coincides with the word "Höllen."

Stanza 1 of *Jesus Christus, unser Heiland* has much in common with stanzas 6 and 7 of Johannes Böttiger's hymn "O Jesu, du edle Gabe." In both of these stanzas, the text deals with the extinguishment of the fires of hell through the blood of Christ. Both variations 6 and 7 of BWV 768 end with a tonic pedal. They also make consistent use of the figures of *syncopatio*, *parrhesia*, and *saltus duriusculus*.[111] In BWV 666, these figures also feature, particularly in relation to

Example 10.3c. BWV 666 (mm. 18–19)

the final line of the text. It may be possible to link the use of *parrhesia* and the *saltus duriusculus* from m. 31 to the conquering of hell, as well as to Christ's sacrifice. Here the chorale melody is presented in B minor with a semitone between the first two notes of the phrase, as opposed to a tone. At this point, Bach is using the so-called "hard interval" to produce a negative effect.[112] He further emphasizes this with the *c-natural⁰* on the third beat of m. 30. This leads to the most chromatic measure of all, where the use of the diminished-seventh chord at m. 31.2 is dramatic in its portrayal of the text. In addition to this, a rising *passus duriusculus* is found in the alto part. The negative *Affekt* is reiterated on the final note of the *cantus firmus*. Instead of a conventional perfect cadence to the tonic, Bach turns the harmony away from E minor by use of suspensions and chromaticisms, perhaps to depict the pain of hell one last time. This leads to the final *anabasis* which begins at m. 35, spanning three octaves. It seems logical to conclude that this is related to the sacrifice of Christ, as he finally claims victory.

Renate Steiger has clearly shown the significance of the 12/8 time signature in Bach's cantatas.[113] Traditionally this time signature has had pastoral connotations, used in the context of the Good Shepherd. Steiger refers to John 10:11: "I am the Good Shepherd: the Good Shepherd is one who lays down his life for his sheep." Here Steiger is suggesting that the 12/8 time signature can be interpreted as a symbol of deliverance. According to her, 12/8 is employed by Bach in an eschatological context, where there is reference to eternal salvation and Paradise.[114] Albert Clement finds a direct parallel in variation 7 of BWV 768.[115]

In Lutheran theology, the Abendmahl was understood as a foretaste of eternal salvation. As a Communion hymn, it is therefore not surprising that a setting of *Jesus Christus unser Heiland* should be in 12/8 time. Many of the settings discussed in this section share this same 12/8 time signature: BWV 666, 667, 738, 768/7, and 769/1. In the main, the texts of all these hymns are concerned with human redemption gained through the birth and death of Christ. The connection with the Abendmahl is clear here. The bread of the new covenant is a foretaste of eternal salvation, achieved for mankind through the death of Christ. It seems possible to interpret the 12/8 time signature in eschatological terms in BWV 666. In this context elsewhere, Bach has used the same time signature.

The bass aria "Mache dich, mein Herze, rein," No. 65 in the St. Matthew Passion, is in 12/8 time. The text here can also be understood in the context of the Abendmahl:

Mache dich, mein Herze, rein,	Make thee clean, my heart from sin,
Ich will Jesum selbst begraben,	I want to bury Jesus myself,
Denn er soll nunmehr in mir für und für,	Then he shall in me now and for evermore,
Seine süße Ruhe haben.	Have his sweet rest.
Welt, geh aus, laß Jesum ein!	World, depart; let Jesus in.

This aria occurs after the death of Jesus has taken place. The text speaks of cleansing the human heart from sin and welcoming Jesus for eternity. The Passion and death of Christ are linked here to the Abendmahl, where this event is commemorated, thereby ensuring eternal salvation for humanity. The text of the preceding accompanied recitative confirms this thesis. The consequences of the death of Christ become clear in this recitative.

Am Abend, da es kühle war,	At evening, as it was cool,
Ward Adams Fallen offenbar;	Was Adam's fall made clear;
Am Abend drücket ihn der Heiland nieder.	At evening, too, it weighed the Savior down;
Am Abend kam die Taube wieder	At evening the dove returned
Und trug ein Ölblatt in dem Munde.	And bore the olive leaves in his mouth.
O schöne Zeit! O Abendstunde!	O beauteous time! O evening hour!
Der Frieden schluß ist nun mit Gott gemacht,	Our lasting peace is now with God made sure,
Denn Jesus hat sein Kreuz vollbracht.	For Jesus hath his cross fulfilled.
Sein Leichnam kömmt zur Ruh,	His body comes to rest.
Ach! Liebe Seele, bitte du,	O, loving soul, ask thou it
Geh, lasse die den toten Jesum schenken,	Go, let the dead Jesus be sent,
O heilsames, o köstlichs Angedenken.	O, wondrous gift! A precious, holy burden.

Here, the body of Christ is portrayed as "O heilsames, o köstlichs Angedenken" [Wondrous gift, a precious, holy burden]. In Lutheran terms this must be a reference to the Abendmahl. In his writing on the Abendmahl in the Large Catechism, Luther writes, "Denn da beut er uns an alle den Schatz, so er uns von Himmel bracht hat"[116] [In this sacrament he offers us all the treasure he brought from heaven for us].[117] The idea of Christ in the sacrament of the altar being a priceless treasure or gift was common in Lutheran theology.[118] Neumeister had also referred to this concept in relation to *Jesus Christus unser Heiland*.[119] This may be further justification for the use of the motive at m. 18.4, which seems to be linked to the idea of a gift from heaven as described before. This recitative and aria can be linked to the soprano recitative and aria that occur after the words of institution in the St. Matthew Passion (Nos. 12 and 13). The recitative extols the richness of the gift that Jesus has left for mankind: "Sein Fleisch und Blut, o Kostbarkeit" [His Flesh and Blood, O precious gift!]. The figuration in the soprano aria "Ich will dir mein Herze schenken" is very similar to that of "Mache dich, mein Herze, rein" with the use of the "sighing motive, double oboe obbligato, and the trochaic compound meter.[120] The bass aria No. 65 incorporates the repentance for sin through the cleansing of the heart to receive Jesus and achieve eternal peace. The use of the 12/8 meter in this context can be linked to Bach's use of the same meter in BWV 666.

Bach's use of the key of E minor for both settings is striking. This tonality has been used by Bach in the context of the Passion of Christ in many of his works. Some well-known examples are the opening movement of the

St. Matthew Passion, the *Crucifixus* of the B Minor Mass, and the cantata *Christ lag in Todesbanden* (BWV 4), which although it is an Easter cantata has strong Passion associations. When Bach set the same chorale more than once, he did not always use the same key for every setting; see, for example, the three settings of *Allein Gott in der Höh sei Ehr* (BWV 662–664) and many of the pairs of settings in *Clavierübung III*. Bach may have been making a point in his employment of the key of E minor with *Jesus Christus unser Heiland* (BWV 665–666).

★ ★ ★

At the center of both BWV 665 and 666 seems to be a vivid portrayal of the suffering of Christ and the joyful consequences for mankind. The central chorale settings (BWV 659–666) form an impressive subgroup within the "Leipzig" chorales. The three settings of *Nun komm der Heiden Heiland* (BWV 659–661) represent the start of the church year and Advent, the three settings of the Trinitarian hymn *Allein Gott in der Höh sei Ehr* (BWV 662–664) are also related to Christmas, and these in turn lead to the two settings of the Passion hymn *Jesus Christus, unser Heiland* (BWV 665–666). All of these settings share common themes that are concerned with the birth, Passion, and death of Christ.[121]

NOTES

1. Robin A. Leaver, "Luther's Catechism Hymns 7: Lord's Supper," *Lutheran Quarterly* 12 (1998): 303.
2. Leaver, "Luther's Catechism Hymns 7," 303.
3. Hans Joachim Moser, *Die Melodien der Lutherlieder* (Berlin: Schloessmann, 1935), 42.
4. Markus Jenny, *Luthers geistliche Lieder und Kirchengesänge. Vollständige Neuedition in Ergänzung zu Band 35 der Weimarer Ausgabe* [Archiv zur Weimarer Ausgabe der Werke Martin Luthers 4] (Cologne: Böhlau, 1985), 61; Leaver, "Luther's Catechism Hymns 7," 304.
5. Jenny, *Luthers geistliche Lieder*, 61. For the text of the *cantio*, see Philipp Wackernagel, *Das deutsche Kirchenlied von der ältesten Zeit bis zu Anfang des XVII. Jahrhunderts* (Leipzig: Teubner, 1864–1877; reprint, Hildesheim: Olms, 1964), 1:218 (No. 367).
6. Jenny, *Luthers geistliche Lieder*, 61.
7. Moser, *Die Melodien der Lutherlieder*, 42.
8. Jenny, *Luthers geistliche Lieder*, 61.
9. *WA* 35:143f; *LW* 53:249.
10. *WA* 35:143f; *LW* 53:249.

11. *WA* 19: 99; *LW* 53: 82.

12. Robin A. Leaver, "Luther's Catechism Hymns 1. 'Lord Keep Us Steadfast in Your Word.'" *Lutheran Quarterly* 11 (1997): 398.

13. *BSLK*, 558f.

14. *BkC*, 386.

15. Leaver, "Luther's Catechism Hymns 1," 402f.

16. Samuel Scheidt, *Tabulatura Nova*, vol. 3, ed. Harald Vogel (Wiesbaden: Breitkopf & Härtel, 2001), 158.

17. Detlef Gojowy, "Kirchenlieder im Umkreis von J. S. Bach." *JbLH* 22 (1978): 102.

18. Günther Stiller, *Johann Sebastian Bach und das Leipziger gottesdienstliche Leben seiner Zeit* (Kassel: Bärenreiter, 1970), 114; English: *Johann Sebastian Bach and Liturgical Life in Leipzig*, trans. Herbert J. A. Bouman, Daniel F. Poellot, and Hilton C. Oswald; ed. Robin A. Leaver (St. Louis: Concordia, 1984), 128.

19. The Erfurt melody is Zahn 1576.

20. *SLG*, 275ff.

21. Translation based on Mark Bighley, *The Lutheran Chorales in the Organ Works of J. S. Bach* (St. Louis: Concordia, 1986), 155ff.

22. *BSLK*, 520.

23. *BkC*, 362.

24. *BSLK*, 520.

25. BkC, 362.

26. *WA* 7:689–697; *WA* 12:462–493; *WA* 15:481–509; *WA* 37:344–346.

27. *WA* 37:350 (*House Postils* 1:460).

28. *BSLK*, 707–725; *BkC*, 467–476.

29. *BSLK*, 722, 722.

30. *BkC*, 473f.

31. *WA* 26: 295.

32. *LW* 37: 193.

33. The rediscovery of Bach's Bible commentary, edited largely from Luther's writings by the theologian Abraham Calov (Wittenberg 1681–1682), in the last century has been of enormous importance to Bach scholarship, since it contains marginal comments and underlinings in Bach's hand, confirming his personal interest in and knowledge of theology; see Robin A. Leaver: *J. S. Bach and Scripture: Glosses from the Calov Bible Commentary* (St. Louis: Concordia, 1985), 11.

34. Comment on John 19:34; the underlining is added by Bach.

35. See Leaver, *J. S. Bach and Scripture*, 131, 133.

36. Leaver, "Luther's Catechism Hymns 7," 310.

37. Erdmann Neumeister, *Tisch des Herrn, In LII. Predigten über I. Cor. XI. 23–32. Da zugleich in dem Eingange der selben Unterschiedliche Lieder erkläret worden* (Hamburg: Kißner, 1722), 187.

38. Neumeister, *Tisch des Herrn*, 187.

39. Neumeister, *Tisch des Herrn*, 188.

40. Neumeister, *Tisch des Herrn*, 189.

41. Neumeister, *Tisch des Herrn*, 190.

42. *Die Bibel oder die ganze heilige Schrift des Alten und Neuen Testaments nach der deutschen Übersetzung Martin Luthers . . . mit erklärenden Anmerkungen* (Stuttgart: Württembergische Bibelanstalt, 1912), 878.

43. Neumeister, *Tisch des Herrn*, 187.

44. Neumeister, *Tisch des Herrn*, 276.

45. Robin A. Leaver, *Bachs theologische Bibliothek: eine kritische Bibliographie*, [Beiträge zur theologische Bachforschung 1] (Neuhausen-Stuttgart: Hänssler, 1983), 171–174. Although Neumeister's treatise post-dates Bach's original settings of *Jesus Christus unser Heiland* (BWV 665 and 666), it is instructive to trace the similarities of theological thought.

46. Johann Gottfried Walther, *Praecepta der musicalischen Composition* [MS 1708], ed. Peter Benary (Leipzig: Breitkopf & Härtel, 1955), 258.

47. See Arnold Schmitz, "Die Oratorische Kunst J. S. Bachs. Grundfragen und Grundlagen" [1950], in *Johann Sebastian Bach*, ed. Walter Blankenburg (Darmstadt: Wissenschaftliche Buchgesellschaft, 1970), 82.

48. Philipp Spitta, *Johann Sebastian Bach*, trans. Clara Bell and J. A. Fuller-Maitland (London: Novello, 1884–1885; reprint, New York: Dover, 1992), 1:613.

49. Spitta, *Johann Sebastian Bach*, 1:163

50. Harald Schützeichel, *Albert Schweitzer: Die Orgelwerke Johann Sebastian Bachs. Vorworte zu den "Sämtlichen Orgelwerken"* (Hildesheim: Olms, 1995), 258.

51. Albert Schweitzer, *J. S. Bach* (Leipzig: Breitkopf & Hartel, 1920), 465f.; Albert Schweitzer, *J. S. Bach*, trans. Ernest Newman (New York: Dover, 1966), 2:73f.

52. Schweitzer, *J. S. Bach* (1920), 465f.; Schweitzer, *J. S. Bach* (1966), 2:73f.

53. Hans Luedtke, "Seb. Bachs Choralvorspiele," *BJ* 15 (1918): 43.

54. Luedtke, "Seb. Bachs Choralvorspiele," 43.

55. Charles Sanford Terry, *Bach's Chorals Part III: The Hymns and Hymn Melodies of the Organ Works* (Cambridge: Cambridge University Press, 1921), 234f.

56. Terry, *Bach's Chorals Part III*, 234f.

57. Harvey Grace, *The Organ Works of Bach* (London: Novello, 1922), 279.

58. Fritz Dietrich, "J. S. Bachs Orgelchoral und seine geschichtlichen Wurzeln," *BJ* 26 (1929): 64.

59. Rudolf Steglich, *Johann Sebastian Bach* (Potsdam: Akademische verlagsgesellschaft Athenaion, 1935), 124.

60. Steglich, *Johann Sebastian Bach*, 124.

61. Steglich, *Johann Sebastian Bach*, 124.

62. Stainton de B. Taylor, *The Chorale Preludes of J. S. Bach* (London: Oxford University Press, 1942), 109.

63. Taylor, *The Chorale Preludes of J. S. Bach*, 109.

64. Hermann Keller, *Die Orgelwerke Bachs. Ein Beitrag zu ihrer Geschichte, Form, Deutung und Wiedergabe* (Leipzig: Peters, 1948), 191; Herman Keller, *The Organ Works of Bach: A Contribution to Their History, Form, Interpretation and Performance*, trans. Helen Hewitt (New York: Peters, 1967), 259.

65. Jacques Chailley, *Les Chorals pour Orgue de J.-S. Bach* (Paris: Leduc, 1974), 161.

66. Chailley, *Les Chorals pour Orgue de J.-S. Bach*, 161.

67. Chailley, *Les Chorals pour Orgue de J.-S. Bach*, 161. With regard to the chromatic harmonies of this section, Chailley refers to Olivier Alain's comment "Schumann n'est pas loin" [Schumann is not far].

68. Ulrich Meyer, "Zur Frage der inneren Einheit von Bachs Siebzehn Chorälen (BWV 651–667)," *BJ* 58 (1972): 68.

69. Peter Williams, *The Organ Music of J. S. Bach*, 2nd ed. (Cambridge: Cambridge University Press, 2003), 378.

70. Williams, *The Organ Music of J. S. Bach*, 2nd ed., 378.

71. Hans Musch, "'. . . der von uns den Zorn Gottes wandt . . .' Zu Johann Sebastian Bachs Orgelchoral BWV 688," in *Musica-Scientia et Ars. Eine Festgabe für Peter Förtig zum 60. Geburtstag*, ed. Günther Metz (Frankfurt am Main: n.p., 1995), 91–108.

72. Russell Stinson, *J. S. Bach's Great Eighteen Chorales* (New York: Oxford University Press, 2001), 101.

73. See Walther's comments on the use of dissonance; Johann Gottfried Walther, *Praecepta der musicalischen Composition* [MS 1708], ed. Peter Benary (Leipzig: Breitkopf & Härtel, 1955), 235.

74. Malcolm Boyd, ed., *J. S. Bach*, Oxford Composer Companions (Oxford: Oxford University Press, 1999), 89.

75. *BC* 1:71.

76. This aspect of Christ's birth is dealt with extensively in chapter 8. As referred to there, the opening and closing chorale of the Christmas Oratorio is to the melody of the so-called Passion chorale, primarily associated with Paul Gerhardt's Passion hymn *O Haupt voll Blut und Wunden*, the penultimate stanza of which occurs at a central point in the St. Matthew Passion. Thus this melody is unavoidably associated with the Passion. The use of the *passus duriusculus* can also be seen in many movements of the Passions. One example is the alto aria "Buß und Reu" from the St. Matthew Passion, where the text meditates on the grief of sin with the words "Buß und Reu knirscht das Sündenherz entzwei" [Penitence and remorse rend the guilty heart in two]. Another example is in the St. John Passion; when the Jews tell Pontius Pilate "wir dürfen niemand töten" [We are not allowed to execute anyone], Bach uses a five-note rising and falling chromatic line on the word "töten." Here the *passus duriusculus* is referring to the imminent sacrifice of Christ. For further discussion of Bach's use of chromaticism in a sacred context, see Eric Chafe, *Tonal Allegory in the Vocal Music of J. S. Bach* (Berkeley: University of California Press, 1991), 34f.

77. Schweitzer, *J. S. Bach*, trans. Newman, 1:115.

78. *WA* 7:25; *LW* 31:351.

79. Emil Platen, *Johann Sebastian Bach. Die Matthäus-Passion* (Kassel: Bärenreiter, 1997), 60. Here Platen draws attention to "Ich will bei meinem Jesu wachen" from the St. Matthew Passion, where this paradox is clearly expressed in musical terms.

80. Lothar Steiger and Renate Steiger, *Sehet! Wir gehn hinauf gen Jerusalem. Johann Sebastian Bachs Kantaten auf den Sonntag Estomihi* (Göttingen: Vandenhoeck & Ruprecht, 1992), 134.

81. See also BWV 22/3, where the bass has a joyful melisma on the word "Freuden," representing the joy in taking up the cross of Christ.

82. *NBR*, 20.

83. *NBR*, 20. See *NBR*, 230 for a facsimile of the title page of this canon. See also *Dok* I, No. 174.

84. This idea of opposites is seen in the aria "Kreuz und Kron sind verbunden" from the cantata *Weinen, Klagen, Sorgen, Zagen* (BWV 12/4). Here the text shows how cross and crown are connected; Christians have their pain but also consolation in the wounds of Christ. In this aria Bach makes consistent use of the *figura corta*, as well as employing cross figures (for example, m. 37 twice on the word "Wunden"). This is another example of Luther's "joyful exchange" as referred to previously.

85. Schweitzer, *J. S. Bach* (1966), 1:74; Keller, *Die Orgelwerke Bachs*, 191; Keller, *The Organ Works of Bach*, 259.

86. *BC* 1:256.

87. There is a striking resemblance between this aria and the fanfare motive of the *et expecto* of the B Minor Mass. The text of the *et expecto* refers to the resurrection of the dead at the final coming, a similar theme to that of the aria in BWV 145.

88. A similar example can be found in BWV 162/1, the bass aria "Ach, ich sehe, itzt, da ich zur Hochzeit gehe" with a *descensus* on the words "Hölle," "Tod," and "Höllenflammen."

89. *NBA KB* IV/2:84.

90. *NBA KB* IV/2:84.

91. Schützeichel, *Albert Schweitzer*, 259.

92. Luedtke, "Seb. Bachs Choralvorspiele," 42.

93. Luedtke, "Seb. Bachs Choralvorspiele," 42.

94. Terry, *Bach's Chorals Part III*, 236.

95. Grace, *The Organ Works of Bach*, 280.

96. Steglich, *Johann Sebastian Bach*, 125f.

97. Taylor, *The Chorale Preludes of J. S. Bach*, 109.

98. Taylor, *The Chorale Preludes of J. S. Bach*, 119.

99. Albert Clement, "'O Jesu, du edle Gabe': Studien zum Verhältnis von Text und Musik in den Choralpartiten und den Kanonischen Veränderungen von Johann Sebastian Bach," PhD diss., University of Utrecht, 1989, 182.

100. See Renate Steiger, ed., *Johann Sebastian Bachs Kantaten zum Thema Tod und Sterben und ihr literarisches Umfeld* (Wiesbaden: Harrassowitz, 2000).

101. Albert Clement, *Der dritte Teil der Clavierübung von Johann Sebastian Bach: Musik, Text, Theologie* (Middelburg: Almares, 1999), 276; see Günther Stiller, "Beicht und Abendmahlsgang Johann Sebastian Bachs im Lichte der Familiengedenktage des Thomaskantors," *MuK* 43 (1973): 182–186.

102. This is also clear in the setting of *Nun komm der Heiden Heiland* (BWV 660), where Bach uses the technique of canon to symbolize Christ fulfilling the will of the Father (see the discussion in chapter 8).

103. *WA* 401:560.

104. *CoG*, 240.

105. See the discussion in chapter 11.

106. See Anne Leahy, "Bach's Prelude, Fugue and Allegro (BWV 998): A Trinitarian Statement of Faith?" *JSMI* 1 (2005): 33–51.

107. Wolfram Syré, "Zur Polarität des Weihnachts- und des Passionsgedankens im Orgelwerk von Johann Sebastian Bach," *MuK* 56 (1981): 23.

108. Clement, "O Jesu, du edle Gabe," 182.

109. Clement, "O Jesu, du edle Gabe," 131, where Clement refers to Bach's use of this precise motive throughout BWV 768/7. Here the text of the hymn "O Jesu, du edle Gabe" refers to the fact that the crucifixion of Christ eliminates the fear of death. Significantly this variation is also in 12/8 time.

110. Neumeister, *Tisch des Herrn*, 187f.

111. See Clement, "O Jesu, du edle Gabe," 127–132.

112. This can be seen also in BWV 78/2 where Bach uses the hard interval to depict "die Kranken und Irrenden."

113. Renate Steiger, "'Die Welt ist euch ein Himmelreich.' Zu J. S. Bachs Deutung des Pastoralen," *MuK* 41 (1971): 1–9 and 69–79.

114. Steiger, "'Die Welt ist euch ein Himmelreich,'" 1f.

115. Clement, "O Jesu, du edle Gabe," 129–132.

116. *BSLK*, 721.

117. *BkC*, 454.

118. This same theme can be found in the tenor aria, the second movement of BWV 62.

119. Neumeister, *Tisch des Herrn*, 187f.

120. Platen, *Bach. Die Matthäus-Passion*, 207. Platen also links these two arias although he does not comment on the significance of the 12/8 meter in the latter aria.

121. That Bach did not include a setting of an Easter hymn in the "Leipzig" chorales might imply that, like the *Orgel-Büchlein*, the extant preludes were part of a more extensive plan. On the other hand, Bach may have felt that he had already dealt sufficiently with all aspects of Christ's life and death in these extended chorale preludes.

· 11 ·

Komm Gott Schöpfer heiliger Geist

THE HYMN

Komm Gott Schöpfer heiliger Geist is Luther's translation and revision of the Latin hymn *Veni Creator Spiritus*. It has traditionally been associated with Pentecost (Vespers) and ceremonial services such as ordinations and consecrations. Many authors have been credited with writing this ninth-century text, but it has been most frequently associated with the Benedictine theologian and archbishop of Mainz, Hrabanus Maurus. It is also thought that Hrabanus was the composer of the melody, its earliest record being a manuscript originating before 1026 from the Benedictine monastery of Kempten in Allgäu.[1] In 1524 it was published in the two Erfurt *Enchiridia* and in Johann Walter's *Geystliche Gesangk Buchleyn* at Wittenberg,[2] and in a slightly different version in Joseph Klug's hymnbook of 1529. The basic Latin melody was revised by Luther to make it more suitable for congregational singing. In the middle ages, *Veni Creator Spiritus* was one of the oldest, best loved, and most widely used invocations addressed to the Holy Spirit. Its singing was marked with special dignity, the ringing of bells, the use of incense, and the best vestments. Several German translations were made of *Veni Creator* before Luther's, including one by Thomas Münzer.[3]

Komm Gott Schöpfer was the only one of Luther's Pentecost hymns to appear in the appropriate place according to the church year in Walter's hymnbook of 1524. The other two are placed at the beginning of the hymnbook because in Wittenberg, and in early Lutheran liturgies that followed Wittenberg use, the hymn was frequently sung at the beginning of worship. Walter used the original melismatic plainchant melody for the German words, but the Erfurt *Enchiridia* used a simplified syllabic version of the melody for Luther's

251

text. For his translation of the Latin text, Luther modified the Latin meter of 8.8.8.8. to 8.8.8.7. A few of the hymnbooks in use during Bach's lifetime deliberately altered Luther's poetry in their published versions of *Komm Gott Schöpfer heiliger Geist* in order to restore the Latin meter of four lines of eight syllables.[4] In order to accommodate these modified texts, additional notes were added to the final line of the tune, such as in the Weißenfels hymnbook of 1714. Bach's harmonized chorale (BWV 370) is a setting of the earlier version of the melody, the seven-syllable final line, and this is the form that Bach employs for the *cantus firmus* in BWV 667 and BWV 631. The hymn in the Weimar hymnbook of 1713 appears in the section "Vom Heil. Pfingstfest":

1. KOmm GOtt Schöpffer heilger Geist/
   besuch das Hertz der Menschen dein/
   mit Gnaden sie füll/ wie du weist/
   daß dein Geschöpf vorhin sey.

2. Denn du bist der Tröster genant/
   des Allerhöchsten Gabe theur/
   ein geistlich Salb an uns gewand/
   ein lebend Brunn/ Lieb und Feur.

3. Zünd uns ein Licht an im Verstand/
   gib uns ins Hertz der Liebe Brunst/
   das schwach Fleisch in uns dir bekant/
   erhalt fest dein Kraft und Gunst.

4. Du bist mit Gaben siebenfalt/
   der Fing'r an GOttes rechter Hand/
   des Vaters Wort giebst du gar bald/
   mit Zungen in alle Land.

5. Des Feindes List treib von uns fern/
   den Fried schaf bey uns deine Gnad/
   daß wir deinm Leiten folgen gern/
   und meiden der Seelen Schad.

6. Lehr uns den Vater kennen wohl/
   darzu JEsum Christ/ seinen Sohn/
   daß wir des Glaubens werden voll/
   dich beyder Geist zu verstahn.

7. GOtt Vater sey Lob und dem Sohn/
   der von den Todten auferstund/
   dem Tröster sey dasselb gethan/
   in Ewigkeit alle Stund.[5]

1. Come, God Creator, Holy Ghost,
   visit the heart of your people,
   fill them with grace, for you know,
   that your creation should be yours.

2. For you have been called the comforter,
   precious gift of the Most High,
   a spiritual salve used on us,
   a living well, love and fire.

3. Ignite a light in our understanding,
   give love's ardor in our hearts,
   the weak flesh which is known to you,
   make strong by your power and favor.

4. With sevenfold gifts
   you are the finger on God's right hand,
   You soon give the Father's word,
   in tongues in all lands.

5. Drive the cunning of the foe far from us,
   let your mercy create peace among us,
   so that we gladly follow your lead,
   and avoid whatever endangers the soul.

6. Teach us to know the Father well,
   and his son, Jesus Christ,
   that we may be full of faith,
   the spirit of both to understand.

7. Glory to the Father and to the Son,
   who rose from the dead,
   the Comforter has done the same
   in all the hours of eternity.[6]

The Latin text of the hymn *Veni Creator Spiritus* as found in the *Liber Usualis* is as follows:

1. Veni Creator Spiritus,
   Mentes tuorum visita,
   Imple superna gratia
   Quae tu creasti pectora.

2. Qui diceris Paraclitus,
   Altissimi donum Dei,
   Fons vivus ignis caritas,
   Et spiritalis unctio.

3. Tu septi formis munere,
   Digitus paternae dexterae,
   Tu rite promissum Patris,
   Sermone ditans guttera.

4. Accende lumen sensibus,
   Infunde amorem cordibus,
   Infirma nostri corporis
   Virtute firmans perpeti.

5. Hostem repellas longius,
   Pacemque dones protinus:
   Ductore sic te praevio,
   Vitemus omne noxium.

6. Per te sciamus da Patrem,
   Noscamus atque Filium,
   Teque utriusque Spiritum
   Credamus omni tempore.

7. Deo Patri sit gloria,
   Et Filio qui a mortuis
   Surrexit, ac Paraclito,
   In saeculorum saecula. Amen.[7]

In his German version, Luther altered the original Latin order of stanzas 3 and 4 and omitted stanza 6, thus making the sequence more logical, creating three couplets of two stanzas plus a doxology.[8] As a result, the text relating to the Holy Spirit teaching the Father's word, a statement crucial to the Lutheran faith, was now in central position in the hymn.[9] The first two stanzas are an invocation to the Holy Spirit, that he may fill the hearts of the faithful; the third and fourth stanzas seek the gifts of the Holy Spirit; and the fifth and sixth speak of faith.

Central German hymnbooks continued to publish both the Latin hymn and its German version side by side. In Saxony and Thuringia, the chorale was variously used throughout the three festival days of Pentecost. For the first day of Pentecost, the Weißenfels hymnbook of 1714 lists it as the hymn to be sung after the cantata during the morning service; for the second day of Pentecost, as the hymn after the *Magnificat* in the afternoon Vesper service; and for the third day of Pentecost it was sung as the Gradual hymn in the morning Hauptgottesdienst.[10]

During his tenure at Weimar, Bach made a complete handwritten copy of Nicolas de Grigny's *Premier Livre d'Orgue* with its versets on *Veni Creator Spiritus*, the first of which uses a particularly florid version of the tune.[11]

Komm Gott Schöpfer is one of the four hymn tunes adapted by Luther himself that Bach chose to set in the "Leipzig" chorales (BWV 651–652, BWV 659–661, BWV 665–666, and BWV 667). This hymn has historically been linked with another of Luther's Pentecost hymns, *Komm heiliger Geist, Herre Gott*, with the two hymns often appearing together in central German hymnbooks. *Komm heiliger Geist, Herre Gott* was the title that Bach listed in the *Orgel-Büchlein* autograph immediately before his setting of *Komm Gott Schöpfer*. Of the two, however, Bach only left a setting of the latter (BWV 631) in the *Orgel-Büchlein*.

In the "Leipzig" chorales, both BWV 667 and the following setting, *Vor deinen Thron* (BWV 668), bear a direct relationship to *Orgel-Büchlein* settings. BWV 668 is, by way of BWV 668a, an expansion of the *Orgel-Büchlein* setting *Wenn wir in höchsten Nöten* (BWV 641), with an added interlude and a simplified *cantus firmus*. Excluding inner-voice ornaments, the first eight measures of BWV 668 are identical to Bach's single elaboration of the melody in the *Orgel-Büchlein*. BWV 667 is an expanded version of BWV 631, with two distinct sections and the *cantus firmus* stated twice in its entirety.

BWV 667, BWV 631, and BWV 370 each use a chromatic variant in the melody's third phrase. This version was transmitted in a number of seventeenth- and eighteenth-century collections including those of Schein (1627) and Vopelius (1682) at Leipzig, and Weißenfels (1714).[12]

KOMM GOTT SCHÖPFER HEILIGER GEIST (BWV 667)

This chorale prelude exists in three versions: an early Weimar fragment (BWV 667b), which is a sketch for an early Weimar complete setting (BWV 667a), and the final Leipzig version (BWV 667). BWV 667 is headed "*Komm Gott Schöpfer Heiliger Geist. in Organo pleno con Pedale obligato* [*sic*]." in P271, in the hand of Bach's son-in-law Johann Christoph Altnickol. As mentioned above, BWV 667 is an expansion of BWV 631. Measures 1–8.3 of both settings are identical. Peter Williams views mm. 8–12 of BWV 667 as an interlude, with the remainder of the piece forming the second half.[13] This so-called interlude could be seen as a conclusion to the first section of the piece, with its use of a final tonic pedal being similar to many other settings in this collection as well as being an introduction to the second part.

This piece is in G mixolydian with many diatonic cadences and is set in a 12/8 gigue rhythm. The first section presents the chorale melody in the soprano voice. The alto, tenor, and bass parts are characterized by motivic writing, as with so many of the chorale settings in the *Orgel-Büchlein*. Two main motives dominate the inner parts: one of three eighth notes and one of an eighth note, two sixteenths, and an eighth note. The pedal part consists of an eighth note on the third eighth note of each beat. With the exception of the cadential moments, this part moves by step for the first two phrases. The tonality is governed by the mixolydian qualities of the chorale melody. The first phrase concludes with a perfect cadence to C major (m. 2.2–3). The second phrase closes with a plagal cadence to G (m. 4.2–3). Bach introduces a *c-sharp²* in phrase 3 where the original melody was a *c-natural²* (m. 6.2). This creates a strong cadence toward D, which is immediately canceled by the introduction of an *f-natural¹* (m. 6.3). The final phrase of the chorale ends with a plagal cadence to G at m. 8.1–3. This phrase represents Bach's most adventurous harmonic writing thus far in the piece, with a move toward D minor in m. 7.

An interlude linking the first and second sections of BWV 667 follows (mm. 8–12), where Bach introduces new motivic material over a tonic pedal, which will be developed in the second section of the piece. This material contains increased sixteenth-note movement in the manual parts. The *cantus firmus* is presented in the pedal in this section of the piece. Above this, Bach develops the kind of writing that Peter Williams has described as being typical of the type found in the prelude of BWV 547.[14] The first phrase of the *cantus firmus* enters in the pedal at m. 13.1. A similar motive to that found in the opening measures of BWV 679 appears first in the alto at m. 15.4 and subsequently in mm. 16 and 19. The second phrase of the *cantus firmus* enters at m. 16.3, finishing with a diminished-seventh cadence to D in m. 18. Bach uses more chromatic harmony here than in the opening section. There is also much use of suspensions and other dissonances. Phrase 3 of the *cantus firmus* enters at m. 20. Here Bach uses a *c-sharp* as in the first section. The presence of a *b-flat* and *f-natural* in m. 21 confirms the D minor tonality at this point. From m. 22 to 24, there is much writing in parallel sixths and thirds. The final phrase of the *cantus firmus* enters at m. 23.3. This final cadence is similar to that found at the end of the fugue of BWV 541. It is highly chromatic, leaning toward the subdominant minor with a final diminished-seventh cadence.

Interpretations by Other Authors

As with the opening Pentecost piece in this collection, *Komm heiliger Geist, Herre Gott* (BWV 651), the image of the fires of Pentecost has inspired many writers on the subject of *Komm Gott Schöpfer heiliger Geist* (BWV 667).

Albert Schweitzer claims that in the undulating motives of the first section of BWV 667, Bach was symbolizing the Holy Spirit hovering over the water at the beginning of creation, referring to the biblical conception of the Holy Spirit as "Creator," as implied in Genesis 1:2.[15] He substantiates this claim by stating that in the first section of BWV 667, the fact that the middle voices move without a fundamental bass is deliberate on Bach's part. According to Schweitzer, the first section of BWV 667 was too short to portray the beautiful text of the hymn, so therefore Bach proceeded with a second, equally pictorial section. He proposes that it is now the burning flames of the Pentecostal Spirit that Bach is portraying, as exemplified in the text of stanza 2.[16] Schweitzer points out that the early dogmatists made much of the connection between the Old and New Testament Spirit, a fact of which Bach would have been well aware.[17]

Charles Sanford Terry suggests that Bach had Acts 2:2–3 in mind when he set BWV 667 ("And suddenly there came a sound from heaven as of a rushing mighty wind, and it filled all the house where they were sitting. And there appeared unto them cloven tongues like as of fire, and it sat upon each of them").[18]

Stainton de B. Taylor considers that Terry's opinion regarding the "cloven tongues of fire descending from heaven" is a little far-fetched.[19] He acknowledges that the sudden change of style in m. 9, with the broken-chord passages in m. 10, might portray the "sound from heaven," with the conclusion regarding the tongues of fire following on from there. In general, however, he seems doubtful, concluding that the music is highly effective in its own right (whatever that might mean) and that this setting is not among the most inspired of the collection.[20]

Rudolf Steglich makes many comments regarding the relationship between text and music in BWV 667. He initially relates the text of stanza 1 to the first half of the piece, continuing to comment on the lively middle voices, suggesting that they represent the Pentecostal tongues of fire sent from above as in stanza 3: "Zünd uns ein Licht an in Verstand/ gib uns ins Herz der Liebe Brunst."[21] Steglich observes that the next step is to see an obvious picture of the heart in the triplets of the middle voices. In addition, he considers that the middle voice at m. 1.1 (e^1-c^1-f^1) forms a cross symbol.[22] In referring to the repetition of the chorale that begins at m. 13, he states that now the divine might does not come from above but is on earth. Commenting on the lighter close of the piece, he suggests that it was as if Bach made the image of Passion and salvation grow dimmer. He sees the text of the penultimate stanza being portrayed here: "Lehr uns den Vater kennen wohl, dazu Jesu Christ seinen Sohn, das wir des Glaubens werden voll."[23]

Hermann Keller states that as with all of Bach's settings with the *cantus firmus* in the bass, the meaning conveyed is that of all-penetrating power. He adds that the use of the minor subdominant at the end is to be interpreted, as in the G major fugue (BWV 541), not as intense sorrow, but as the ultimate heightening of joy and trust.[24]

Arnold Schmitz considers that there is much to be learned from this piece by examining the figures in the composition. He refers to the *figura corta* of the middle voices and the *syncope consonans desolata* of the bass voice.[25] Johann Gottfried Walther defines the *syncope consonans desolata* as "wenn nur eine Stimme, und zwar ohne *dissonanz* sich rücket" [when only one voice is shifted without incurring a dissonance].[26] Schmitz comments on the animation of the *figura corta*, which helps to convey the *vivificantem* of the Nicene Creed.[27] He also quotes Luther in the third article of his Small Catechism as follows:

Und am jüngsten Tage mich und alle Toten aufferwecken wird und mir sampt allen Gläubigen in Christo ein ewiges Leben geben wird.[28] [On the last day (the Holy Spirit will) raise me and all the dead and will give to me and all believers in Christ eternal life.[29]]

Ulrich Meyer quotes the views of Schmitz and Steglich, regarding them as plausible and corresponding to the opening stanza.[30] He suggests that Bach was thinking of the final stanza in the second half of BWV 667.[31]

Peter Williams does not consider that the two sections of this piece constitute a representation of two separate stanzas.[32] He states that it is not difficult to interpret the second part, which suggests the same verses in Acts as in BWV 651. He refers to the cadential harmony of the final two measures but proposes that this seems to have been a formula associated with this key rather than having any textual or modal character.[33] According to Williams, the second section is in answer to the first, the Holy Ghost answering the invitation.[34]

Russell Stinson comments on the use of two stanzas in this setting, seeing no obvious rationale for this, since it does not correspond to the number of stanzas in the hymn as it did with *O Lamm Gottes unschuldig* (BWV 656).[35] Stinson considers that the two variations of this work may well represent two different Pentecost themes.[36] He suggests that in the first variation, pedal notes normally sounding on the third eighth note of the beat depict the third person of the Trinity, and in the second, fast sixteenth notes in scalar motion run through every measure like a giant gust of wind.[37]

Assessment

Many of the writers on *Komm Gott Schöpfer heiliger Geist* (BWV 667) refer to Acts 2:2–4 and see this work as a portrayal of the rushing wind and tongues of fire (Terry, Grace, Steglich, and Williams). Bach sets the *cantus firmus* twice: once in the soprano and once in the bass. The continuous nature of this setting may mean that Bach is setting two consecutive stanzas.

Further striking musical elements of BWV 667 are the lively 12/8 meter and the important descending motive that first appears at m. 15.4. The lively meter is present in both sections of BWV 667 and so could be considered a depiction of the life-giving character of the Holy Spirit. The Holy Spirit is implicated in all stanzas, since this is a Pentecost hymn, and therefore the animated writing may not necessarily lead to any stanza(s) in particular. Stanza 2 mentions "ein lebend Brunn," but if Bach was inspired in this regard by stanza 2, more proof is required than this aspect alone.

Bach sometimes appears to be making theological statements in the register of a *cantus firmus*. The title of the hymn and line 1 of stanza 1 invite "Gott Schöpffer heiliger Geist" to visit the hearts of the faithful. It is likely that Bach may have portrayed God Creator, Holy Spirit, in the uppermost position of the *cantus firmus*. How can this relate to the following section? Following the invitation to come on earth, one might expect that the Holy Spirit would indeed descend. Bach could portray the Holy Spirit in the bass in, for example, *Komm heiliger Geist, Herre Gott* (BWV 651) and *Kyrie Gott heiliger Geist* (BWV 671). The use of the bass register can be an expression of the Holy Spirit of the New Testament who has descended to earth. A similar meaning could be found for the second half of BWV 667. It is conceivable that in moving the *cantus firmus* from the soprano to the bass, from section 1 to section 2, Bach is symbolizing the journey of the Holy Spirit from heaven to earth.[38] If it is true that God the Creator in stanza 1 is symbolized in the position of the *cantus firmus* of section 1, then it may be reasonable to suggest that the New Testament "Tröster" of stanza 2 is depicted in the second section.

The opening line of the text of stanza 1, "Komm Gott Schöpfer Heilger Geist," specifically mentions God Creator who is in heaven. God the Creator who is in heaven is asked to visit the faithful in the person of the Holy Spirit. One of the books that Bach possessed during his education at the Lutheran Latin schools of Eisenach and Lüneburg would have been Leonhard Hutter's *Compendium Locorum Theologicorum* (Wittenberg, 1610), a basic theological textbook that was widely used in German schools, including the Thomas School in Leipzig. In the second article, "Von Gott, der da ist einig im Wesen, und dreyfaltig im Personen?" [Of God who is one in essence and threefold in persons?], Hutter asks and answers:

> 2. Was ist dann nun GOTT?
> GOTT ist ein Geistlich/ Verständig/ Ewig/ Warhafftig/ Gütig/ Keusches/ Gerechtes/ Barmhertziges Wesen/ freyes Willens/ unermeßlicher Gewalt und Weißheit: . . . Inmassen dann die Gottheit sich also im Wort/ unnd Göttlichen Zeugnissen geoffenbaret hat/ daß der ewige Vater/ sampt dem Sohn und heiligen Geist/ Himmel und Erden und alle Creaturen erschaffen/ unnd erhelt/ auch allen Creaturen/ zu Erhaltung derselben gegenwertig sey.[39]
> [2. What is God then?
> God is a spiritual, wise, eternal, truthful, benevolent, pure, righteous, merciful being of free will and of immeasurable power and wisdom: . . . As such, then the Godhead has revealed itself in word and in divine testimonies, that the eternal Father, together with the Son and Holy Spirit, created heaven and earth and all creatures, and saves, it will also be present in order to save these same creatures.]

It is clear from the above quotation from Hutter that Bach's understanding of the Trinity in relation to "Gott Schöpffer" would have been that the three persons of the Godhead created the world. Therefore, in the opening invocation of "Komm Gott Schöpffer heilger Geist," he is referring to the Trinity. This is confirmed by the second point of article 4 of Hutter's paper "Von der Schöpfung" as follows:

> 2. Was ist die Schöpffung?
> Die Schöpffung ist ein eusserliche Handlung der gantzen H. Dreyfaltig-keit/ durch welche GOtt alle erschaffene/ sichtbare unnd unsichtbare Ding/ innerhalb sechs Tagen/ nach seinem blossen Willen/ auß nichts erschaffen.[40]
> [2. What is creation?
> Creation is an external act of the whole Holy Trinity, through which God created all created things out of nothing, visible and invisible, within six days, according to his will.]

It seems very likely that Bach is depicting stanza 1 in the first section of BWV 667. God is in heaven above, and therefore the *cantus firmus* is in the soprano part. The light dancing setting illustrates the *spiritum vivificantem* as described by Williams. The portrayal of the life-giving Spirit is enhanced by the use of the parallel thirds and sixths of the middle parts and the fact that the bass appears on the third eighth note of each beat in section 1. This is not a reference to the third person of the Trinity as described by Stinson, but it does provide the lightness necessary to portray the life-giving Spirit. Luther's description of this feast as "ein lieblich Fest" is appropriate in this context.

The third important aspect of BWV 667 mentioned above is the motive that first appears at m. 15.4. Albert Clement has related this motive to *descendit in coelis* in the context of variation 1 of BWV 769a. In stanza 1 of *Vom Himmel hoch*, the angel descends from heaven with the message of the precious gift of the birth of Christ.[41] Bach could be using this motive in a similar context in BWV 667. He introduces this motive in m. 15.4, a half measure before the entry of line 2 of the *cantus firmus* in m. 16.2 (see example 11.1). Investigation into the second line of all stanzas may provide a reason for Bach's use of this motive. It appears that the only suitable line is that of stanza 2. If the words of stanza 2 are applied to the second appearance of the *cantus firmus* in BWV 667, then the text at this point is "allerhöchsten Gabe theuer." As observed in chapter 1, the concept of the gift of the Holy Spirit is discussed liberally in Luther's various Pentecost sermons. It cannot, therefore, be a mere coincidence that Bach chooses to employ this exact motive in the Pentecost cantata *Erschallet, ihr Lieder, erklinget, ihr Saiten!* (BWV 172), movement 1, m. 13. Here, as in BWV 667, the gift of the descending Holy Spirit, which in turn results in the gift of salvation for humanity, is represented in the descending melodic (see example 11.2). Alfred Dürr has suggested that because of its secular celebratory nature, the opening chorus may be taken from a missing congratulatory

Example 11.1.   BWV 667 (mm. 15.4ff.)

cantata.[42] This does not seem to be likely since this motive appears to be very clearly tied in with the gift of the Holy Spirit. The only possibility could be that when Bach composed this supposed other movement, he already knew that he would use it in the context of a Pentecost cantata.

The association of the previously mentioned motive with "allerhöchsten Gabe theuer" seems a strong argument in support of the fact that Bach is depicting stanza 2 of the hymn.[43] Additionally, the position of the *cantus firmus* in the bass implies that this great gift indeed descended to earth. Since the *Orgel-Büchlein* setting BWV 631 and the first half of the "Leipzig" chorales setting BWV 667 are identical, this makes the solution easier. As BWV 667 sets the *cantus firmus* twice within a continuous setting, it would seem logical to propose that stanza 2 should follow stanza 1.[44]

The opening two lines of stanza 1 of *Komm Gott Schöpfer heiliger Geist* reflect the opening stanza of the Gospel for Pentecost, John 14:23–31, which includes the following:[45]

> Jesus answered and said unto him, if a man love me, he will keep my Word: and my Father will love him, and we will come unto him, and make our abode with him.

Example 11.2.   BWV 172/1 (mm. 13–15)

The text of the hymn, "Komm Gott Schöpffer heilger Geist/ besuch das Herz der Menschen dein," shows how God will dwell in the hearts of those who love him. In the Gospel, Christ is seen as referring to the Trinitarian Godhead, and Bach seems to be making a similar statement in BWV 667. The word "Gnade" is a keyword for Pentecost, found in line 3 of stanza 1 of the hymn. Bach depicts it with parallel thirds and sixths. Steglich's vision of the inner parts forming a heart may seem a little far-fetched, but the notion is consistent with Bach's musical ideas: the warmth of the human heart that welcomes God, as well as the warmth of the love of God. The condemnation of law has been abolished with the New Testament Pentecost, and therefore Bach uses no canonic or strictly imitative writing. Instead he writes music mainly in parallel motion.

Schweitzer's suggestion that Bach was representing the Holy Spirit of the Old and New Testaments in the two sections of BWV 667 is difficult to accept. As discussed previously, the reference to Creator appears to be God the Creator in heaven, before the descent of the Holy Spirit, not as he was at the beginning of creation. The text of lines 2–4 refers to the Holy Spirit dwelling in the heart of the believer, as in the New Testament, but there is no dichotomy of Testaments implied in BWV 667.

Another important issue is that of the time signature. Bach chooses a time signature of 12/8 time. Since this is discussed at some length in chapter 10, it may be sufficient here just to state that Bach frequently used 12/8 time in the context of eternal salvation. Similarly, the role of the Holy Spirit in relation to salvation is investigated in chapter 1; the Spirit teaches the believer to know Christ, and it is in knowing Christ that there is eternal salvation. In all of his Pentecost sermons, Luther stresses the role of Christ as mediator within the context of the provision of salvation by the Holy Spirit. Therefore, the time signature of 12/8 seems to be very logical for BWV 667. The 12/8 time signature in combination with the musical figures employed by Bach give a dance-like character, in particular that of the gigue. The dancing *figura corta* helps to portray the *spiritum vivificantem*: the life-giving Spirit described in the text of the hymn. This idea belongs to the New Testament as described in John 6:63: "It is the spirit that quickeneth; the flesh profiteth nothing: the words that I speak unto you, they are spirit, and they are life."

BWV 667 is identical to the *Orgel-Büchlein* setting up to m. 8. Measures 8–12 have been described by Williams as an interlude that serves to introduce the figuration that becomes so important in the second section of BWV 667. It appears that the grace of the feast is being portrayed here in the dancing sixteenth notes, many of which are in parallel sixths. Particularly striking are the dancing sixteenth notes of mm. 10 and 13.

The text of stanza 2 of *Komm Gott Schöpfer heiliger Geist* describes the characteristics of the Holy Spirit, the Comforter, precious gift of the most high, a spiritual salve, a living well, love and fire.[46] As is clear from these references, the Father sends the Spirit, and then Jesus also sends him, thus stressing the equality between Father and Son. Each person of the Trinity is very much involved in the feast of Pentecost in equal ways. The Spirit is the final link to salvation; Jesus refers to him as the Spirit of truth, and with him there is certainty of salvation. He therefore is deserving of the title of "allerhöchsten Gabe theuer."

Johann Christoph Altnickol inserted the inscription *in organo pleno / con pedale obigato-* [*sic*] at the beginning of this piece. It seems possible to connect this registration designation to the courage and faith of the message of Pentecost. In the first section, a light pedal registration may be appropriate, reflecting the *spiritum vivificantem* of the New Testament. In the second section, the organist might draw a sixteen-foot reed before the entry of the *cantus firmus*. Other chorale preludes on hymns related to the Holy Spirit also call for an *organo pleno* setting, for example, *Komm heiliger Geist, Herre Gott* (BWV 651) and *Kyrie Gott heiliger Geist* (BWV 671). A similar interpretation may be applied to the bass aria "Heiligste Dreieinigkeit" from the cantata *Erschallet, ihr Lieder, erklinget, ihr Saiten!* (BWV 172), where the three trumpets and timpani of the accompaniment also bring to mind the courage and faith of Pentecost.

★ ★ ★

In his setting *Komm Gott Schöpfer heiliger Geist* (BWV 667), Bach has presented a clear image of the Holy Spirit. Key words such as "Gnade," "Lieb," and "Feur" are singled out for special prominence. Grace and love are portrayed in the use of the *figura corta* and the many parallel thirds and sixths. The journey of the Holy Spirit from heaven to earth is symbolized in the registers of the *cantus firmus*. The life-giving character of the Holy Spirit is demonstrated in the pedal part of section 1 and the dancing 12/8 rhythm. The raging fire of Pentecost is seen in the use of *organo pleno* and the rushing sixteenth notes of the second section. As Bach contemplated the role of the Holy Spirit in eternal salvation in BWV 667, so he prepared the way for the final chorale of the collection *Vor deinen Thron* (BWV 668) with all its attendant eschatological implications.

NOTES

1. Johannes Kulp, *Die Lieder unserer Kirche* [Handbuch zum Evangelischen Kirchengesangbuch, Sonderband], ed. Arno Büchner and Siegfried Fornaçon (Göttingen: Vandenhoeck & Ruprecht, 1958), 162.

2. For the text, see Philipp Wackernagel, *Das deutsche Kirchenlied von der ältesten Zeit bis zu Anfang des XVII. Jahrhunderts* (Leipzig: Teubner, 1864–1877; reprint, Hildesheim: Olms, 1964), 3:14f. (No. 20); for the melody, see Zahn 294–245. The

most common Lutheran form of this tune was a further revision of it printed in a series of Joseph Klug's Wittenberg hymnbooks.

3. *LW* 53:260; *WA* 35:161f. All following information is based on these two sources.

4. For example, in Schemelli's hymnbook of 1736, for which Bach acted as musical editor, the final line of the first stanza, "daß dein Geschöpf vorhin sey," becomes "daß dein Geschöpf soll für dir sein." See the facsimile, *Musicalisches Gesang-buch herausgegeben von George Christian Schemelli* (Hildesheim: Olms, 1975), 241 (No. 361).

5. *SLG*, 171f.

6. Translation based on Mark Bighley, *The Lutheran Chorales in the Organ Works of J. S. Bach* (St. Louis: Concordia, 1986), 161f.

7. *The Liber Usualis with Introduction and Rubrics in English* (Tournai: Desclee, 1961), 885f.

8. *WA* 35:162; *LW* 53:260. See also Wichmann von Meding, *Luthers Gesangbuch. Die gesungene Theologie eines christlichen Psalters* (Hamburg: Kovac, 1998), 136–139.

9. Von Meding, *Luthers Gesangbuch*, 138.

10. The instructions regarding the hymns varied from region to region; See Robin A. Leaver, "Bach and Hymnody: The Evidence of the Orgelbüchlein," *Early Music* 13 (1985): 229. In central German liturgies for the festival days of Pentecost, the only hymn that was specified more often than this one was Luther's *Komm heiliger Geist, Herre Gott*; see Detlef Gojowy, "Kirchenlieder im Umkreis von J. S. Bach," *JbLH* 22 (1978): 108.

11. Kirsten Beißwenger, *Johann Sebastian Bachs Notenbibliothek* [Catalogus Musicus 13] (Kassel: Bärenreiter, 1992), 56, 191ff; *Dok* 3:634f. (No. 147a).

12. In these chorales, the chromatic variant is confined to the third phrase. They do not employ a chromatic alteration of the melody's fourth note, which also appeared in each of these three hymnbooks. Similarly, neither in BWV 665 nor BWV 666 does Bach use the chromaticized fourth note of *Jesus Christus unser Heiland* which was given in the same three hymn collections.

13. Peter Williams, *The Organ Music of J. S. Bach*, 2nd ed. (Cambridge: Cambridge University Press, 2003), 380.

14. Williams, *The Organ Music of J. S. Bach*, 2nd ed., 380.

15. Harald Schützeichel, *Albert Schweitzer: Die Orgelwerke Johann Sebastian Bachs. Vorworte zu den "Sämtlichen Orgelwerken"* (Hildesheim: Olms, 1995), 259.

16. Schützeichel, *Albert Schweitzer*, 259.

17. Schützeichel, *Albert Schweitzer*, 259.

18. Charles Sanford Terry, *Bach's Chorals Part III: The Hymns and Hymn Melodies of the Organ Works* (Cambridge: Cambridge University Press, 1921), 241f.

19. Stainton de B. Taylor, *The Chorale Preludes of J. S. Bach* (London: Oxford University Press, 1942), 119.

20. Taylor, *The Chorale Preludes of J. S. Bach*, 119.

21. Rudolf Steglich, *Johann Sebastian Bach* (Potsdam: Akademische verlagsgesellschaft Athenaion, 1935), 122.

22. Steglich, *Johann Sebastian Bach*, 123.

23. Steglich, *Johann Sebastian Bach*, 123.

24. Hermann Keller, *Die Orgelwerke Bachs. Ein Beitrag zu ihrer Geschichte, Form, Deutung und Wiedergabe* (Leipzig: Peters, 1948), 192; Herman Keller, *The Organ Works of Bach: A Contribution to Their History, Form, Interpretation and Performance*, trans. Helen Hewitt (New York: Peters, 1967), 260.

25. Arnold Schmitz, *Die Bildlichkeit der wortgebundenen Musik Johann Sebastian Bachs* (Mainz: Schott, 1950; reprint, Laaber: Laaber Verlag, 1980), 77.

26. Walther B, 590, and Bartel, 404.

27. Schmitz, *Die Bildlichkeit der wortgebundenen Musik*, 77.

28. *BSLK*, 512.

29. *BkC*, 356.

30. Ulrich Meyer, "Zur Frage der inneren Einheit von Bachs Siebzehn Chorälen (BWV 651–667)," *BJ* 58 (1972): 71.

31. Meyer, "Zur Frage der inneren Einheit," 71.

32. Williams, *The Organ Music of J. S. Bach*, 2nd ed., 380.

33. Williams, *The Organ Music of J. S. Bach*, 2nd ed., 380.

34. Williams, *The Organ Music of J. S. Bach*, 2nd ed., 380.

35. Russell Stinson, *J. S. Bach's Great Eighteen Chorales* (New York: Oxford University Press, 2001), 7.

36. Stinson, *J. S. Bach's Great Eighteen Chorales*, 103.

37. Stinson, *J. S. Bach's Great Eighteen Chorales*, 103.

38. The successive registers of the *cantus firmus* in *O Lamm Gottes unschuldig* (BWV 656) may symbolize the journey of the Lamb from heaven to earth; see the discussion in chapter 5.

39. Leonhard Hutter, *Compendium Locorum Theologicorum, ex scripturis sacris et libro concordiae . . . Ist aber jetzo . . . Die Deutsche Version / Wie sie der Herr Autor Seel. Selbst übersetzt hat* (Hildesheim: Hageman, 1661), 11.

40. Hutter, *Compendium Locorum Theologicorum*, 53.

41. Albert Clement, "'O Jesu, du edle Gabe': Studien zum Verhältnis von Text und Musik in den Choralpartiten und den Kanonischen Veränderungen von Johann Sebastian Bach," PhD diss., University of Utrecht, 1989, 180ff. Clement also mentions the presence of this motive in BWV 619, 738a, 738, 666, and 667; "'O Jesu, du edle Gabe,'" 182.

42. Alfred Dürr, *Die Kantaten von Johann Sebastian Bach. Mit ihren Texten* (Kassel: Bärenreiter, 1985), 394.

43. This motive is also discussed in chapter 10; see pages 237f.

44. In *Clavierübung III* where Bach sets three versions of one chorale, such as *Allein Gott in der Höh sei Ehr*, he proceeds progressively through the stanzas with stanza 1 corresponding to BWV 675, stanza 2 to BWV 676, and stanzas 3 and 4 to BWV 677 with its two fugal subjects; see Albert Clement, *Der dritte Teil der Clavierübung von Johann Sebastian Bach: Musik, Text, Theologie* (Middelburg: Almares, 1999), 83–108, 334. In the "Leipzig" chorales, he also moves progressively through the stanzas; see the discussion in chapter 9.

45. Robin A. Leaver, "Bach's Understanding and Use of the Epistles and Gospels of the Church Year," *BACH* 6/4 (1975): 10; Albert Clement, "De orgelkoraalbewerkingen van Joh. Seb. Bach in het kerkelijk jaar," *Het Orgel* 86 (1990): 326.

46. Biblical references to the Holy Spirit as "Tröster" are discussed in chapter 9.

• *12* •

Vor deinen Thron tret ich

THE HYMN

*T*he hymn text *Für deinen Thron tret ich* was written by Bodo von Hodenberg (1604–1650) and is listed by Eduard Emil Koch as a "Mittagslied."[1] Georg Christian Schemelli placed it in the section under "Morgenlieder" in his hymnbook of 1736, with a provision for evening application in stanza 11. Albert Fischer and Wilhelm Tümpel refer to the Hannover hymnbook of 1646, where it was headed "Am Morgen, Mittag und Abend kan man singen" [in the morning, at noon and in the evening one can sing].[2] The hymn text in the Schemelli hymnbook is as follows:

1. Für deinen thron tret ich hiemit,
   o Gott, und dich demüthig bitt,
   wend dein genädig angesicht,
   von mir, dein armen sünder, nicht.

2. Du hast mich, o Gott Vater mild,
   gemacht nach deinem ebenbild,
   in dir web' schweb und lebe ich,
   vergehen müst ich ohne dich.

3. Errettet hast du mich gar oft,
   ganz wunderlich und unverhofft,
   da nur ein Schritt, ja nur ein haar
   mir zwischen tod und leben war.

4. Verstand und ehr hab ich von dir,
   des lebens nothdurft giebst du mir,
   darzu auch einen treuen freund,
   der mich im glück und unglück meint.

1. I come before your throne,
   O God, and humbly ask you
   turn not your gracious countenance
   from me, a poor sinner.

2. You have, O God Father mild,
   made me in your image,
   In you I move and live,
   I would have to perish without you.

3. You have often rescued me,
   miraculously and unhoped for,
   when only a step, indeed, only a hair,
   was between life and death for me.

4. Understanding and honor I have from you,
   You give me life's needs,
   and in addition, a true friend
   who loves me in good times and bad.

5. Gott Sohn, du hast mich durch dein Blut
erlöset von der höllengluth,
das schwer gesetz für mich erfüllt,
damit des Vaters zorn gestillt.

5. God the Son, you have through your blood
saved (me) from the flames of hell
and fulfilled the difficult law for me
to quiet the Father's wrath.

6. Wenn sünd und satan mich anklagt,
und mir das herz im Leib verzagt,
alsdenn brauchst du dein mittleramt,
daß mich der Vater nicht verdammt.

6. When sins and Satan accost me,
and my heart despairs in my body,
you need your office as mediator
so the Father does not condemn me.

7. Du bist mein vorsprach allezeit,
mein heil, mein trost, und meine freud,
ich kan durch dein verdienst allein
hier ruhig und dort selig seyn.

7. You are my advocate at all times,
my salvation, my comfort and my joy,
only through your merit can I
be at peace now and saved hereafter.

8. Gott heilger Geist! du höchste kraft,
des gnade in mir alles schafft,
ist etwas guts am Leben mein,
so ist es warlich alles dein.

8. God the Holy Spirit! You highest power
whose grace accomplishes everything in me,
if there is anything good in my life,
it is truly all yours.

9. Dein ists, daß ich Gott recht erkenn,
ihn meinen Herrn und Vater nenn,
sein wahres wort und sacrament
behalt, und lieb bis an mein end.

9. It is due to you that I recognize God aright,
call him my Lord and Father,
his true word and sacrament
uphold, and love him until my death.

10. Daß ich fest in anfechtung steh,
und nicht in trübsal untergeh,
daß ich im herzen trost empfind,
zuletzt mit freuden überwind.

10. That I stand firm in temptation
and do not succumb in adversity,
that I find comfort in my heart
and finally conquer with joy.

11. Drum dank ich dir mit herz und mund,
o Gott in dieser morgen-(abend-)stund,
für alle güte, treu und gnad,
die meine Seel empfangen hat.

11. Therefore I thank you with heart and mouth,
O God, in this morning (evening) hour,
for all the goodness, faithfulness and grace
which my soul has received.

12. Und bitt, daß deine gnadenhand
blieb über mir heut ausgespannt,
mein amt, gut, ehr, freund, leib und Seel
in deinen schutz ich dir befehl.

12. And ask that your gracious hand
remain spread over me today,
my position, property, honor, friends, body and soul
I commend into your care.

13. Hilf, daß ich sey von herzen fromm,
damit mein ganzes Christenthum
aufrichtig, und rechtschaffen sey,
nicht augenschein und heucheley.

13. Help me to be devout from my heart,
so that my whole Christendom
be upright and righteous,
not appearance and hypocrisy.

14. Erlaß mich meiner sünden schuld,
und hab mit deinem knecht geduld,
zünd in mir an glauben und lieb,
zu jenem leben hoffnung gieb.

14. Release me from the guilt of my sins
and have patience with your servant.
Ignite faith and love in me,
give me hope for the life to come.

15. Ein selig ende mir bescher,	15. Grant me a blessed death,
am jüngsten tag erweck mich, Herr,	and awaken me Lord on Judgment Day
daß ich dich schaue ewiglich,	so that I may behold you eternally,
amen, amen, erhöre mich.[3]	Amen, amen, hear me.[4]

In stanza 1 of *Vor deinen Thron*, the petition is that God will not turn his gracious countenance away from the poor sinner. This can be seen as a reference to the blessing from Numbers 6:26. Throughout the course of the next nine stanzas, the text devotes three stanzas to each member of the Trinity. Stanza 11 thanks the Trinitarian God for all the good done for the believer, while stanza 12 asks for a continuation of these blessings for the days to come. Stanzas 13 and 14 become more specific and ask that a true Christian life be led without hypocrisy, with release from the guilt of sin, igniting faith and love with hope in the life to come. The final stanza asks for a blessed death and links in with the first stanza by asking "daß ich schaue ewiglich"—the idea of looking on God's face. The melody of this hymn was originally Calvinist, first appearing in *La forme de prières* in 1542 (Calvin's Genevan Psalter) and was also associated with Paul Eber's *Wenn wir in höchsten Nöthen*.[5]

Vor deinen Thron tret ich (BWV 668) is closely related to *Wenn wir in höchsten Nöten* (BWV 641 and 668a). The latter hymn was written by Paul Eber (1511–1569) who was a professor at Wittenberg. *Wenn wir in höchsten Nöthen* first appeared in the *New Betbüchlein* (Dresden, 1566).[6] The following year it was to be found in the *Geistlich Zenghauß* of Esaiam Tribauer, which was published in Wittenberg.[7] *Wenn wir in höchsten Nöthen* was classified under the heading "Von Creutz, Verfolgung und Anfechtung" [Concerning Cross, Persecution and Trial] in the Weimar hymnbook of 1713.[8] The hymn's origins lie in 2 Chronicles 20 and in a hymn by Eber's former teacher Joachim Camerarius, *In tenebris nostrae*.[9] The sinner calls on God in his distress, asking to be rescued from fear and misery. In true repentance, he asks to be forgiven, which comes about through the sacrifice of Christ. In stanza 6, the plea for forgiveness of sin is reiterated, while the sinner also asks for support from God. The final stanza gives thanks to God, promising him obedience at all times. The text of this hymn as it appears in the Weimar hymnbook of 1713 is as follows:

1. WEnn wir in höchsten Nöthen seyn/	1. When we are in utmost distress
und wissen nicht/ wo aus noch ein/	and know not where to go,
und finden weder Hülf noch Rath/	and find neither help nor advice
ob wir gleich sorgen früh und spat.	whether we seek from early to late.

2. So ist diß unser Trost allein/	2. So this is our only comfort:
daß wir zusammen ingemein	that we together,
dich anruffen/ O treuer GOtt/	call on you, O faithful God
um Rettung aus der Angst und Noth.	for rescue from fear and distress.

3. Und heben unser Augn und Hertz
zu dir in wahrer Reu und Schmertz/
und suchen der Sündn Vergebung/
und aller Straffen Linderung.

4. Die du verheissest gnädiglich
allen/ die darum bitten dich/
im Namen deins Sohns JEsu Christ/
der unser Heyl und Fürsprechr ist.

5. Drum kommen wir, O HErre GOtt/
und klagen dir all unser Noth/
weil wir ietzt stehn verlassen gar/
in grosser Trübsal und Gefahr.

6. Sieh nicht an unsre Sünde groß/
sprich uns derselben aus Gnaden loß/
steh uns in unserm Elend bey/
mach uns von allen Plagen frey.

7. Auf daß von Hertzen können wir
nochmahls mit Freuden dancken dir/
gehorsam seyn nach deinem Wort/
dich allzeit preisen hier und dort.[10]

3. And lift up our eyes and hearts
to you in true repentance and pain,
and seek forgiveness of sins
and the alleviation of punishment.

4. Which you graciously give,
to all who ask you
in the name of your son Jesus Christ,
who is our salvation and advocate.

5. Therefore we come, O Lord God,
and complain to you all our distress,
because we are now abandoned
in great trouble and danger.

6. Do not regard our great sins:
by mercy free us from them,
support us in our distress
and make us free from all trouble.

7. So that from our hearts we
again with joy thank you,
be obedient to your word,
praise you always, now and hereafter.[11]

VOR DEINEN THRON TRET ICH (BWV 668)

Vor deinen Thron tret ich (BWV 668) was the final chorale copied into P271. In the hand of an as-yet-unidentified scribe, it is unfortunately incomplete, breaking off halfway through m. 26. It appears from the manuscript that the following page is missing, rather than that the original composition was incomplete, as the music continues to the end of the page. It is merely headed "Vor deinen Thron tret ich" in P271. There is a clear relationship between this piece and two other settings by Bach, the *Orgel-Büchlein* chorale prelude *Wenn wir in höchsten Nöten* (BWV 641) and that of the same name which was published with the Art of Fugue, BWV 668a. BWV 668a is an expansion of the *Orgel-Büchlein* setting (BWV 641), and BWV 668 is a revision of BWV 668a. Christoph Wolff has discussed all the issues relating to the sources of these three pieces, arriving at the following conclusions:

- The obvious original source for both BWV 668a and BWV 668 is the *Orgel-Büchlein* setting BWV 641.
- At some later point, probably during the Weimar period, but possibly the Leipzig period, a draft of BWV 668a was written down by Bach.

- BWV 668a was subsequently revised by Bach to produce the version attached to the Art of Fugue. This composition is not in Bach's hand and may have been copied by Bach's son-in-law, Johann Christoph Altnikol. BWV 668a could now serve the same purpose for Bach as did all the earlier versions of the "Leipzig" chorales—in the last decade of his life, Bach chose to revise all eighteen of these compositions, including BWV 668a.
- Someone close to Bach played BWV 668a for him during his illness and notated his revisions into a new draft copy. This new draft copy could now serve as a basis for the fair copy found in P271, which unfortunately is incomplete.

This hypothesis dispels the myth surrounding the so-called "deathbed" chorale, dictated by Bach on the spur of the moment. Hans Klotz has presumed that the dictated version was BWV 668a, whereas Wolff argues that it is a version of the final BWV 668 that is the "Diktatfassung."[12] Wolff also adds that the method of distribution of Bach's estate may have had something to do with the fact that it was the earlier BWV 668a that was published with the Art of Fugue. As an organist, Wilhelm Friedemann Bach probably inherited the collection of organ works bound together in what is now P271, while the harpsichordist, C. P. E. Bach, inherited the autograph and engraver's plates of the Art of Fugue. C. P. E. Bach was not in Leipzig at the time of his father's death and therefore did not know about the latest version, BWV 668. According to Wolff, this accounts for the publication of the older version with the Art of Fugue.[13] The important issue is the fact that Bach chose to change the title of BWV 668 by using a different hymn text.

The final version of this chorale, BWV 668, seems to be a revision of BWV 668a, with a similar approach to revision as seen in all the chorale preludes in this collection. The major alteration, which is not found with any other composition in P271, is that Bach changed the title of the hymn on which the composition is based from *Wenn wir in höchsten Nöthen* to *Vor deinen Thron tret ich*. As Wolff has stated, this is a fact that cannot be overlooked.[14] The common belief is that as Bach clearly approached the end of his life, his thoughts were on the life hereafter. The following questions arise out of Bach's choice of hymn. Did Bach originally compose BWV 641 with a particular stanza in mind? When he expanded BWV 641 to become BWV 668a—both compositions being based on the same hymn—is it still the same stanza that occupied him? When he changed to *Vor deinen Thron* for BWV 668, was he thinking of a particular stanza, and if so, what does it have in common with the stanza(s) of the two other settings? These are the questions explored below.

The opening motive of BWV 668 is a diminution of the first line of the chorale melody. This is answered strictly in inversion by the alto an octave higher in m. 2. The tenor part provides an interesting rising chromatic line beneath this. In m. 4, the process begins again, with the pedal starting on d^0 being answered in inversion an octave higher by the alto. In m. 6, the tenor and bass rise in chromatic thirds together. In m. 7, Bach has added sixteenth notes to the tenor on beats 1 and 3, thus creating the *figura corta* in the tenor as well as the alto. The first line of the *cantus firmus* enters in m. 8. In the sections of BWV 668a and 668 containing the *cantus firmus*, Bach clearly bases the musical material on BWV 641, although without the coloratura line. The alto and tenor rise in thirds, using the opening motive, while the pedal employs it in inversion. The tonality moves toward E minor, following the same harmonic pattern as BWV 641 and 668a at this point, until halfway through m. 10 where Bach substitutes the original perfect cadence with an interrupted cadence, only arriving at the tonic chord in root position at m. 11.3. Bach's addition of an *e-flat⁰* to the plagal cadence in m. 11 adds a particular poignancy.

Bach employs similar compositional means for the eight measures that precede the entry of line 2 of the *cantus firmus*. The notes of the second phrase of the chorale melody are heard in the tenor in diminution beginning at the second half of m. 11.3. This is answered in m. 12 by the alto in inversion. The pedal enters with the paraphrase of the second chorale phrase in its *rectus* form, while the alto provides some chromatic interest above. Bach repeats the process in a slightly varied manner before the entry of the second line of the chorale at m. 19.3. Meanwhile, the first four notes of the original opening motive are heard in its *rectus* and *inversus* forms. Measures 19–22 correspond to mm. 3–5 of BWV 641, following more or less the same harmonic and motivic pattern.

The third line of the chorale is heard in diminution, beginning at the second half of m. 22.3. The answer in inversion, heard in the alto, moves decisively toward A minor, with the pedal entry in m. 24 facilitating a modulation to E minor at mm. 25f. Unfortunately the music breaks off at m. 26.3 at the end of the page.

Since up to m. 26.3 of BWV 668 Bach has only made modest changes from BWV 668a, it seems reasonable to suggest that he might have continued in this way. Therefore, in order to aid an interpretation of the text-music relationships in BWV 668, I will continue with an analysis of BWV 668a from m. 25.3. The third line of the chorale is heard in the alto, in diminution and inversion from the second half of m. 25.3. This brings about a decisive perfect cadence to E minor at mm. 26.3–27.1. The bass answers at m. 27.3 with this motive in its *rectus* form, bringing the music to G major in m. 28, followed by a cadence to D at m. 29. At m. 29.3, the *cantus firmus* enters in the soprano. Meanwhile, the accompanying parts repeat the four-note opening motive in its *rectus* and *inversus* forms.

The final line of the chorale is heard in the tenor from m. 32.4, answered in the alto by an inverted diminution at m. 33.1. The *rectus* form of this diminution is heard in the bass at m. 34.1, answered in the alto at m. 35.3. During the course of this phrase, the music moves from G major to E minor, passing through B minor at m. 36 before arriving in A minor at m. 37.3. Four more entries of this line of the chorale follow: the *inversus* form in the bass at m. 38.2, in diminution in the tenor at m. 38.3, in the alto at m. 39.1, and in the tenor again at m. 40.1. At m. 40.3, line 4 of the *cantus firmus* enters in the soprano, concluding with a long-held tonic of three and a half measures. The cadence to the final note of the *cantus firmus* is to E minor. Under the final tonic, there are references to line 4 of the chorale in diminution in the alto (*rectus*) and the tenor (*inversus*). The composition closes with a plagal cadence, with a final reference to the chorale heard in mm. 44–45 in all three accompanying parts in parallel motion.

Interpretations by Other Authors

Very few authors have attempted to unravel the complex situation relating to text and music in *Vor deinen Thron tret ich* (BWV 668). Albert Schweitzer suggests that Bach changed the hymn title to *Vor deinen Thron* because he was already out of danger, stating,

> Er wollte damit ausdrücken, daß er schon über alle "höchsten Nöte" hinaus sei und sich bereite, vor Gottes Thron zu erscheinen.[15] [He wanted to express by it that he was already out of the greatest danger and prepared himself to appear before God's throne.]

Hans Luedtke sees a connection between stanzas 1–3, as well as with the final stanza and BWV 668.[16]

Harvey Grace speaks of the composition of this chorale setting in romantic terms, describing it as being full of placid charm, with a final cadence of great beauty (he is presumably referring to BWV 668a).[17]

Hermann Keller states that the peaceful calm of the melody is communicated to the whole composition and therefore seems to be discussing BWV 668a.[18] In his view, only in the last measures does he find the shades of death, apparently once more meaning BWV 668a.[19]

In his biography of Bach, Christoph Wolff makes some comments regarding the text:

> But the text that went through Bach's mind, in the face of near death, especially the first and last stanzas of the prayer hymn, may have redefined the setting and its function for a moment he had not anticipated earlier.[20]

Russell Stinson raises the question of the suitability of this hymn as a deathbed text. According to Stinson, since the hymn was designated for "Morning, midday or evening," it in essence summarizes the Christian faith. He comments on the change from a corporate perspective to singular expression: "Wenn *wir* in höchsten Nöthen sein" becomes the plea of an individual in "Vor deinen Thron tret *ich* hiemit."[21]

Assessment

No single writer on the subject of *Vor deinen Thron tret ich* (BWV 668) addresses the complex issues relating to text and music. Christoph Wolff argues convincingly on the question of the various versions and correctly points out that the change of hymn title is very significant. In order to try to unravel Bach's possible intentions regarding text and music, it is necessary to return to the two earlier compositions: BWV 641 and BWV 668a.

The nine-measure *Wenn wir in höchsten Nöten* (BWV 641) contains many musical features also present in the other two compositions. Its prominent musical features are as follows:

- a very ornate *cantus firmus*;
- persistent use of a four-note motive in its *rectus* and *inversus* forms, derived from the first line of the *cantus firmus*;
- much writing in thirds and sixths, with a particularly noteworthy rising scale in thirds in m. 1;
- the long alto d^1 in mm. 6–7;
- the *heterolepsis* of m. 7 where the accompanying voices rise above the *cantus firmus*; and
- the *anabasis* of the final measure with the very free presentation of the final notes of the *cantus firmus*.

Can these musical features be related to any stanza in particular of Eber's hymn? The parallel thirds and sixths may easily be seen to depict "Trost" (stanza 2), "gnädiglich" (stanza 4), "Gnaden" (stanza 6), or "Freuden" (stanza 7). It is possible that the constant repetition of the opening four-note motive indicates that the opening line of the text is important. If one only considers the opening four notes, then apart from "drum kommen wir" of stanza 5, no particular text seems applicable. It is conceivable, however, that Bach was using this motive as a reminder of the opening line, wishing to stress it without necessarily quoting it in full. In which case, lines 1 of stanza 1 ("Wenn wir in höchsten Nöthen seyn"), stanza 2 ("So ist diß unser Trost allein"), and stanza 6 ("Sieh nicht an unsre Sünde groß") seem most appropriate.[22] Is there any stanza that provides an explanation for the long alto d^1 of mm. 6–7, followed by the *heterolepsis* of m. 7 (see example 12.1)? This occurs in line 3 of the text. An explanation may be found in stanza 6: "steh uns in unserm Elend bey."[23] Another striking feature of this composition is the *anabasis* and free portrayal of the *cantus firmus* of the final measure (see example 12.2). With the exception of stanza 6, "mach uns von allen Plagen frey," there is no obvious connection with any other stanza. The freeing up of the *cantus firmus* may be a literal portrayal of being made free from all trouble.

The final musical characteristic that could help to solve the issue of text-music relationships is the ornate *cantus firmus*. It is not possible to say that Bach consistently used this kind of writing for a specific kind of text. In the *Orgel-Büchlein* it is utilized in *Das alte Jahr vergangen ist* (BWV 614); *O Mensch, bewein dein Sünde groß* (BWV 622); and *Wenn wir in höchsten Nöten* (BWV 641). It is immediately striking that the words "Sünde groß" occur in stanza 1 of *O Mensch bewein* and in stanza 6 of *Wenn wir in höchsten Nöthen*. Both chorale settings display a similar approach to the *cantus firmus*. This can help provide a solution to the question of text-music relationships in BWV 641. The combination of the beautifully shaped coloratura line with the constant use of double thirds and sixths brings to mind another composition, although on a much grander scale: *Allein Gott in der Höh sei Ehr* (BWV 662). Here the relevant stanza of the text is stanza 1, where the Trinitarian God is thanked for his goodness and mercy.

Following this discussion, it seems that the strongest arguments are in favor of stanza 6. There is no other stanza where an explanation for all the musical features previously mentioned may be found. The repetition of the opening motive could be a reminder of line 1 of the text, which asks God not to regard the great sins of humanity. The "Gnaden" of line 2 can be understood in the parallel motion, while "beystehen" can be related to the Halteton of mm. 6–7 and the *heterolepsis* of m. 7. In the case of BWV 641, the *heterolepsis* is caused by the overlapping of the accompanying parts of the left hand with the solo right hand in m. 7. The presence of the accompaniment in the pitch

Example 12.1. BWV 641 (mm. 6ff.)

Example 12.2.   BWV 641 (m. 9)

area of the *cantus firmus* reinforces the notion of "beystehen" initiated by the Halteton which begins in m. 6.

Finally, the liberation of the *cantus firmus* in the very ornate right hand of the final measure with its *anabasis* to g^2 may reflect the liberation from all trouble expressed in the final line of text of stanza 6. Moving on to *Wenn wir in höchsten Nöten* (BWV 668a), the following observations can be made:

- This is a much longer piece than BWV 641, now with interpolations between statements of the chorale.
- The musical material in the measures containing the chorale remains more or less the same as in BWV 641, but now the chorale is less ornate.
- The development of the opening motive is expanded to include longer imitations by inversion.
- Each line of the *cantus firmus* is preceded by a fore-imitation with inversion.
- The opening four-note motive prominent in BWV 641 remains prominent here.
- There are chromaticisms in mm. 2, 6, 11, 44, and 45.

It would seem that BWV 668a possesses all of the musical characteristics of BWV 641 and some additional significant ones. Is Bach portraying the same stanza as he did in BWV 641, or is it a new one? Do the new musical features enhance the text of stanza 6, or do they point to a depiction of a completely different stanza?

In m. 2 of BWV 668a, Bach adds a rising chromatic line that is not present in BWV 641. Since it is part of the fore-imitation for line 1 of the *cantus firmus*, it may be linked to line 1 of one of the stanzas. Conceivably, it might be possible to link this line to the opening line of stanza 1, "Wenn wir in höchsten Nöthen seyn," or of stanza 6, "Sieh nicht an unsre Sünde groß." None of the other opening lines seem appropriate.

In mm. 30–31, a long d^1 is held in the alto, as it was in BWV 641. If one counts the final d^1 of the *cantus firmus* at mm. 31.3–32.2, then this note is heard almost uninterrupted for eight and a half beats. It is possible that this Halteton has the same meaning as it does in BWV 641, where it appears to depict "beystehen."

A dominant feature of BWV 668a is the use of strict imitation, inversion, diminution, and stretto. Sometimes Bach appears to use the technique of inversion for a specific reason. It may be helpful to examine his use of this kind of writing in other works. In the *Missa* in F (BWV 233), the subject of the *Christe eleison* is almost exactly a mirror image of the *Kyrie eleison*. In the second *Kyrie*, the two themes are combined to make a double fugue. The text is a plea for mercy to the Father and the Son. It may be reasonable to suggest that Christ is portrayed as a mirror image of the Father in the inverted *Christe* theme. In the second *Kyrie*, the two themes are combined to perhaps symbolize the Holy Spirit who proceeds from the Father and the Son. Added to this, Bach superimposes the three stanzas of the chorale *Christe, du Lamm Gottes* successively over the three sections of the *Kyrie-Christe-Kyrie* on horns and oboes. Here Bach may be deliberately associating the plea for mercy with a hymn with strong Passion associations.[24]

Bach employs similar means in the *Missa* in G (BWV 236). In the opening fugal *Kyrie*, the tenor answers the bass with a strict inversion of the opening subject. The alto answers the soprano in like manner in the following entry. Here the prayer is to God for mercy. It seems possible that Bach is once more associating the technique of inversion with a plea for mercy. Christ's role is crucial to this. His involvement in the provision of mercy and salvation may be prompting the use of inversion. The same might be possible for BWV 668a.

BWV 233 has the added context of a reference to Passion in the superimposed hymn *Christe, du Lamm Gottes*. There may be a stanza in *Wenn wir in höchsten Nöthen* that contains similar ideas. Stanzas 3 and 6 seek forgiveness of sin. Stanza 6 is even stronger, asking additionally for deliverance from all trouble. Forgiveness of sin and salvation come about through the sacrifice of Christ. This makes Christ central to all pleas for mercy and forgiveness. It appears that the technique of inversion portrays Christ, in the image of the Father in the two *Missae* movements mentioned above, as well as in BWV 668a.

It seems logical to conclude from the above that as in BWV 641, Bach was setting stanza 6 of *Wenn wir in höchsten Nöthen* in BWV 668a. A convincing argument may be found first with regard to the chromaticism of the opening phrase. This may be related to the word "Sünd." Bach has used similar portrayals of this word elsewhere. In movement 2 of the cantata *Gottlob! Nun geht das Jahr zu Ende* (BWV 28), Bach depicts the text "Hat dir dein Sünd

Example 12.3.   BWV 28.2 (m. 51.2ff.)

vergeben" [has forgiven you your sins] in a rising chromatic line (see example 12:3). In the opening movement of the *Missa* in G (BWV 236), the musical portrayal of "Christe eleison" incorporates a descending chromatic motive (*passus duriusculus*). In this case, it is possible that the *passus duriusculus* is related to the plea for mercy. Bach may be giving a musical hint about how mercy and salvation will be provided—it comes through the sacrifice of Christ, symbolized in both movements in the chromatic harmony and jagged melodic lines.[25] These arguments help to support the position that in these chromaticisms in BWV 668a, Bach may have been portraying the word "Sünd." This leads to a second strong argument supporting the idea that Bach may have been thinking of stanza 6: the prominence of inversion. From the preceding discussion, it seems that this may be related to Christ who is the means of salvation and deliverance. This again leads to stanza 6. Third, as in BWV 641, the long d^1 in mm. 30–31 can be associated with "beystehen." The repetition of the opening motive could be related to the petition of this stanza: "Sieh nicht an unsre Sünde groß." From all this, it appears to be conclusive that Bach was indeed depicting stanza 6 of "Wenn wir in höchsten Nöthen" in BWV 668a.

Vor deinen Thron tret ich (BWV 668) is a revision of BWV 668a. With all of the other "Leipzig" revisions of the "Weimar" chorales, Bach presumably had the same stanza in mind. In the case of BWV 668, however, since there is now a different hymn text, it is necessary to examine again the musical features and relate them to the hymn *Vor deinen Thron tret ich*. The following musical alterations need to be noted:

- The delayed cadence at m. 10.3: Bach replaces the original chord of G with an E minor chord, thus creating an interrupted cadence, delaying the cadence to the tonic to m. 11.
- The added notes to the tenor in m. 7, resulting in the incorporation of the *figura corta* to balance the alto line.
- The first eighth note of the pedal part in m. 9 becomes dotted to complement the rising dotted line of the chorale on beat 2.
- A similar change to the dotted rhythm in m. 26.

In order to remain in keeping with ideas presented in BWV 641 and 668a, similar sentiments would need to be expressed in the new text. The provision of two texts for what is basically the same musical material was not a new process for Bach. It was a compositional technique that he employed time and again in his vocal works. A few examples may be mentioned to demonstrate this: The *Crucifixus* from the B Minor Mass was originally conceived in the first choral movement of the cantata *Weinen, Klagen, Sorgen, Zagen!* (BWV 12). The *Qui tollis* of the same work started life as the opening movement of the cantata *Schauet doch, und sehet ob irgendein Schmerz sei* (BWV 46). In both cases, Bach retains the overall *Affekt* of the movements in question.

Another significant example can be found in his organ music: the final Schübler Chorale, *Kommst du nun Jesu vom Himmel herunter* (BWV 650). Five out of the six Schübler Chorales, including BWV 650, are parodies of movements from extant cantatas. In the case of BWV 650, Bach uses the original music of the second movement of the cantata *Lobe den Herren, den mächtigen König der Ehren* (BWV 137) but changes to the text of Kasper Friedrich Nachtenhöfer's *Kommst du nun vom Himmel herunter*. Albert Clement has argued that Bach depicted stanza 2 of the latter hymn in BWV 650.[26] The connection with BWV 668 is clear. Here Bach is changing a hymn text while retaining the same music, and this was possible because the second text had the same theological content.

The change to the new text close to the end of his life has been acknowledged by many as being a very personal one. For example, Russell Stinson refers to the change from the corporate "wir" to the personal "ich."[27] With this in mind, can a solution be found relating to text and music in the case of BWV 668? Is there a stanza that contains some or all of the ideas of stanza 6 of *Wenn wir in höchsten Nöthen*? Stanza 6 of this hymn is a prayer for mercy from the sinner. This in itself is a fitting prayer at the end of life.

Stanzas 2–4 of *Vor deinen Thron* are more statements of fact than requests or prayers. God the Father is thanked for support and love. Similarly, stanzas 5–7 extol the good works of Christ, but he is not asked for anything specifically. Stanzas 8–10 address the Holy Spirit in the same manner. Stanza 11 is also more of a comment than a plea, thanking God for goodness, faithfulness, and grace. Stanzas 12–15 are prayers and petitions, asking for protection, righteousness, release from the guilt of sin, and a blessed death respectively. Stanza 1, however, is also a prayer asking for grace for the sinner as he stands before the throne of God. So it appears that the most likely stanzas may be 1, 12, 13, 14, or 15. Which one of these stanzas has the closest connection to stanza 6 of *Wenn wir in höchsten Nöthen*? This stanza is very specific about its prayer for liberation from sin. Neither stanza 12 nor 13 of *Vor deinen Thron* mentions sin at all. Similarly, stanza 15 only asks for a blessed death and does not mention sin particularly. This leaves stanzas 1 and 14. Stanza 14 asks for release from the guilt of sin and for an ignition of faith and love, with hope for the life to come. Stanza 1 places the sinner before the throne of God, asking that he will not turn away. Which of these two stanzas is it most likely that Bach is depicting in BWV 668? It does not seem likely that Bach would have been asking for faith and love at the end of his life. In addition, this was not an aspect of stanza 6 of *Wenn wir in höchsten Nöthen*. Consequently, it appears that Bach was depicting the text of stanza 1 of *Vor deinen Thron* in BWV 668. It also seems to be very likely that as Bach drew close to the end of his life, he would choose to depict the deeply personal and eschatologically strong stanza 1 in the final composition in this collection.

How do the musical features of BWV 668 relate to the new text, stanza 1 of *Vor deinen Thron*? The text of this stanza shows the humble sinner before the throne of God, asking that he not turn away. In effect, the sinner is asking for salvation and forgiveness of sin, as in stanza 6 of *Wenn wir in höchsten Nöthen*. Therefore, similar text-music interpretations may be applied to BWV 668 as those of BWV 668a. Christ remains central to the sinner as he stands before the throne of God. Consequently, the technique of inversion employed by Bach from the outset (see example 12.4) may have a similar meaning to that outlined above. The inversion itself serves as an image of the sinner turning into a liberated being. In chapter 8, the technique of inversion is discussed in relation to BWV 661. Here I suggest that Bach was portraying the idea of opposites in the employment of this technique. Equally in BWV 668, Bach could be depicting the two opposites of the sinner and the saved. The employment of the *passus duriusculus* could be interpreted as being related to a plea for mercy as seen in the *Kyrie* settings discussed previously.

The opening line of stanza 1, "Vor deinen thron tret ich hiemit," shows a certain act of faith on the part of the humble believer.[28] The entire hymn is taken up with statements of faith in salvation. Consequently, the unadorned *cantus firmus* is very suited to a prayer of the humble sinner.

★ ★ ★

The small alterations made by Bach to BWV 668 did not change or influence the text-music relationships. Although there is obviously a new text, the musi-

Example 12.4.   BWV 668 (mm. 1f.)

cal features are still associated with the same ideas. The change of cadence at m. 10 serves to delay the tonic chord by one measure and makes for a more satisfying musical conclusion to the phrase. The addition of dotted rhythms in mm. 9 and 26 and of the *figura corta* in m. 7 are typical of the kinds of revisions Bach made in the other Leipzig chorale preludes.

Many issues surround the progression from BWV 641 to 668a to 668. All three compositions contain similar musical ideas, implying that similar texts may be applied to all three works. The technique of inversion, as in other works by Bach, shows the idea of opposites, perhaps alluding to Luther's understanding of justification, that a Christian is *simul justus et peccator*, at the same time both righteous and a sinner. The employment of the *passus durius-culus* corresponds to its use in other works by Bach where the sinner asks for mercy. In BWV 668, the humble Christian begs for mercy, and its repetition underscores the prayer. It seems highly reasonable that Bach, conscious of his own mortality, decided to relate an eschatological text to already existing music from a deeply personal point of view (cf. BWV 650). As such, BWV 668 must be regarded as a most fitting final piece for this collection.

NOTES

1. Eduard Emil Koch, *Geschichte des Kirchenlieds und Kirchengesangs der christlichen, insbesondere der deutschen evangelischen Kirche* (Stuttgart: Belser, 1866–1876; Hildesheim: Olms, 1973), 3:239.

2. Albert Fischer and Wilhelm Tümpel, *Das Deutsche Evangelische Kirchenlied des 17. Jahrhunderts* (Gütersloh: Bertelsmann, 1904–1916; reprint, Hildesheim: Olms, 1964), 2:409f.

3. *Musicalisches Gesang-buch herausgegeben von George Christian Schemelli* [facsimile] (Hildesheim: Olms, 1975), 11f.

4. Translation based on Mark Bighley, *The Lutheran Chorales in the Organ Works of J. S. Bach* (St. Louis: Concordia, 1986), 233ff.

5. Koch, *Geschichte des Kirchenlieds und Kirchengesangs*, 8:164.

6. Koch, *Geschichte des Kirchenlieds und Kirchengesangs*, 8:161.

7. Koch, *Geschichte des Kirchenlieds und Kirchengesangs*, 8:161.

8. *SLG*, 360f.

9. Koch, *Geschichte des Kirchenlieds und Kirchengesangs* 8:161.

10. *SLG*, 360f.

11. Translation based on Bighley, *The Lutheran Chorales in the Organ Works of J. S. Bach*, 240f.

12. *NBA KB* IV/2:104; Christoph Wolff, *Bach: Essays on His Life and Music* (Cambridge, MA: Harvard University Press, 1991), 282–294.

13. Wolff, *Bach: Essays on His Life and Music*, 294.

14. Wolff, *Bach: Essays on His Life and Music*, 292.

15. Harald Schützeichel, *Albert Schweitzer: Die Orgelwerke Johann Sebastian Bachs. Vorworte zu den "Sämtlichen Orgelwerken"* (Hildesheim: Olms, 1995), 260.

16. Hans Luedtke, "Seb. Bachs Choralvorspiele," *BJ* 15 (1918): 88.

17. Harvey Grace, *The Organ Works of Bach* (London: Novello, 1922), 281.

18. Hermann Keller, *Die Orgelwerke Bachs. Ein Beitrag zu ihrer Geschichte, Form, Deutung und Wiedergabe* (Leipzig: Peters, 1948), 193; Herman Keller, *The Organ Works of Bach: A Contribution to Their History, Form, Interpretation and Performance*, trans. Helen Hewitt (New York: Peters, 1967), 261.

19. Keller, *Die Orgelwerke Bachs*, 193; Keller, *The Organ Works of Bach*, 216.

20. Christoph Wolff, *Johann Sebastian Bach: The Learned Musician* (New York: Norton, 2000), 450.

21. Russell Stinson, *J. S. Bach's Great Eighteen Chorales* (New York: Oxford University Press, 2001), 105.

22. In the *Estomihi* cantata *Herr Jesu Christ, wahr' Mensch und Gott* (BWV 127), the melody of the first line of Paul Eber's chorale is heard in diminution repeatedly throughout the movement, serving to emphasize the opening line: "Herr Jesu Christ, wahr' Mensch und Gott" [Lord Jesus Christ, true man and God]. Bach uses this motive to accompany the soprano in all the other lines of the chorale, thereby stressing the importance of line 1 of stanza 1. A similar technique is employed in movement 2 (soprano recitative and chorale) of the cantata *Gelobet seist du Jesu Christ* (BWV 91) and in variation 3 of the Canonic Variations (BWV 769).

23. Bach sometimes depicted the word "stehen" by a Halteton as seen in movement 2 of the cantata *Ich steh mit einem Fuß im Grabe* (BWV 156). The same approach can be seen in the tenor aria of BWV 78/5 where Bach employs a Halteton for the word "steh." There are of course many other examples throughout Bach's cantatas.

24. [With regard to the references in these paragraphs to the short Masses, there are notes in Dr. Leahy's computer files indicating that she intended to investigate the cantata movements parodied for these Masses to verify that the original versions of these movements exhibit the same characteristics as found in the later Mass settings—Editor.]

25. The two *Kyrie* movements from the B Minor Mass are also interesting in this regard. The text "Kyrie eleison" asks God for mercy. Chromatic harmony is a prominent feature of both of these movements.

26. Albert Clement, "'Sechs Choräle' BWV 645–650 von J. S. Bach und dessen Bedeutung," in *Das Blut Jesu und die Lehre von der Versöhnung im Werk Johann Sebastian Bachs*, ed. Albert Clement [Royal Netherlands Academy of Arts and Sciences: Proceedings of the International Colloquium The Blood of Jesus and the Doctrine of Reconciliation in the Works of Johann Sebastian Bach, Amsterdam, 14–17 September 1993] (Amsterdam: Royal Netherlands Academy of Arts and Sciences, 1995), 293.

27. Stinson, *J. S. Bach's Great Eighteen Chorales*, 105.

28. Stiller sees the change of text from BWV 668a to 668 as a convincing key to forming an estimate of the faith and piety of Johann Sebastian Bach, and he understands the final title as an expression of the last prayer of his life; Günther Stiller, *Johann Sebastian Bach und das Leipziger gottesdienstliche Leben seiner Zeit* (Kassel: Bärenreiter, 1970), 193; English: *Johann Sebastian Bach and Liturgical Life in Leipzig*, trans. Herbert J. A. Bouman, Daniel F. Poellot, and Hilton C. Oswald; ed. Robin A. Leaver (St. Louis: Concordia, 1984), 205.

Bibliography

Ameln, Konrad. *The Roots of German Hymnody of the Reformation Era.* St. Louis: Concordia, 1964.

Auhagen, Wolfgang. *Studien zur Tonartencharakteristik in theoretischen Schriften und Kompositionen vom späten 17. bis zum Beginn des 20. Jahrhunderts.* Frankfurt am Main: Lang, 1983.

Axmacher, Elke. "'Ich freue mich auf meinen Tod': Sterben und Tod in Bachs Kantaten aus theologischer Sicht." *Jahrbuch des staatlichen Instituts für Musikforschung Preussischer Kulturbesitz* (1996): 24–40.

Bartel, Dietrich. *Musica Poetica: Musical-Rhetorical Figures in German Baroque Music.* Lincoln: University of Nebraska Press, 1997.

Beißwenger, Kirsten. *Johann Sebastian Bachs Notenbibliothek.* [Catalogus Musicus 13]. Kassel: Bärenreiter, 1992.

Bighley, Mark. *The Lutheran Chorales in the Organ Works of J. S. Bach.* St. Louis: Concordia, 1986.

Blankenburg, Walter. "Die Bedeutung des Kanons in Bachs Werk." *Bachtagung,* 250–258.

———. *Das Weihnachts-Oratorium von Johann Sebastian Bach.* Kassel: Bärenreiter, 1982.

———. "Mystik in der Musik J. S. Bachs." In *Theologische Bach–Studien 1,* ed. Walter Blankenburg and Renate Steiger, 47–66. [Beiträge zur theologischen Bachforschung 4]. Neuhausen-Stuttgart: Hänssler, 1987.

Blume, Friedrich. "Umrisse eines neuen Bach-Bildes," *Musica* 16 (1962): 169–176; English: "Outlines of a New Picture of Bach," *Music & Letters* 44 (1963): 214–227.

Boyd, Malcolm, ed. *J. S. Bach.* Oxford Composer Companions. Oxford: Oxford University Press, 1999.

Breig, Werner. "The 'Great Eighteen' Chorales: Bach's Revisional Process and the Genesis of the Work." In *J. S. Bach as Organist: His Instruments, Music, and Performance Practices,* ed. George Stauffer and Ernest May, 102–120. Bloomington: Indiana University Press, 1986.

———. "Orgelwerke." In *Johann Sebastian Bach. Spätwerk und Umfeld,* 145–156. [Programmbuch 61. Bachfest der Neuen Bachgesellschaft, 24. Mai–5. Juni 1986, Duisburg]. Duisburg, 1986.

Brown, Raymond E. *An Introduction to the New Testament.* New York: Doubleday, 1997.

Bruggaier, Roswitha. "Das Urbild von Johann Sebastian Bachs Choralbearbeitung 'Nun komm der Heiden Heiland' (BWV 660)—eine Komposition mit Viola da gamba?" *BJ* 73 (1987): 165–168.

Chafe, Eric. *Tonal Allegory in the Vocal Music of J. S. Bach.* Berkeley: University of California Press, 1991.

———. *Analyzing Bach Cantatas.* New York: Oxford University Press, 2000.

Chailley, Jacques. *Les Chorals pour Orgue de J.-S. Bach.* Paris: Leduc, 1974.

Clement, Albert. "'O Jesu, du edle Gabe': Studien zum Verhältnis von Text und Musik in den Choralpartiten und den Kanonischen Veränderungen von Johann Sebastian Bach." PhD diss., University of Utrecht, 1989.

———. "De orgelkoraalbewerkingen van Joh. Seb. Bach in het kerkelijk jaar." *Het Orgel* 86 (1990): 322–331.

———. "'Zum inneren Zusammenhang der Sechs Choräle' BWV 645–650 von J. S. Bach und dessen Bedeutung." In *Das Blut Jesu und die Lehre von der Versöhnung im Werk Johann Sebastian Bachs*, ed. Albert Clement, 285–304. [Royal Netherlands Academy of Arts and Sciences: Proceedings of the International Colloquium The Blood of Jesus and the Doctrine of Reconciliation in the Works of Johann Sebastian Bach, Amsterdam, 14–17 September 1993]. Amsterdam: Royal Netherlands Academy of Arts and Sciences, 1995.

———. "'Alsdann ich gantz freudig sterbe, Zu' J. S. Bachs Deutung des 24/16 Taktes." In *Theologische Bachforschung heute: Dokumentation und Bibliographie der Internationalen Arbeitsgemeinschaft für theologische Bachforschung 1976–1996*, ed. Renate Steiger, 330–343. Berlin: Galda & Wilch, 1998.

———. *Der dritte Teil der Clavierübung von Johann Sebastian Bach: Musik, Text, Theologie.* Middelburg: Almares, 1999.

Dietrich, Fritz. "J. S. Bachs Orgelchoral und seine geschichtlichen Wurzeln." *BJ* 26 (1929): 1–89.

Dürr, Alfred. *Die Kantaten von Johann Sebastian Bach. Mit ihren Texten.* Kassel: Bärenreiter, 1985.

———. "Melodievarianten in Johann Sebastian Bachs Kirchenliedbearbeitungen." In *Das protestantische Kirchenlied im 16. und 17. Jarhrhundert: Text-, Musik und theologiegeschtliche Probleme* [Wolfenbütteler Forschungen 31], ed. Alfred Dürr and Walther Killy, 149–163. Wiesbaden: Harrassowitz, 1986.

———. "'Ich freue mich auf meinen Tod': Sterben und Tod in Bachs Kantaten aus musikwissenschaftlicher Sicht." *Jahrbuch des staatlichen Instituts für Musikforschung Preussischer Kulturbesitz* (1996): 41–51.

Eickhoff, Henry J. "Bach's Chorale-Ritornello Forms." *Music Review* 28 (1967): 257–276.

van Elferen, Isabella. *Mystical Love in the German Baroque: Theology, Poetry, Music.* Contextual Bach Studies 2. Lanham, MD: Scarecrow, 2009.

Fischer, Albert, and Wilhelm Tümpel. *Das deutsche evangelische Kirchenlied des 17. Jahrhunderts*, 6 vols. Gütersloh: Bertelsmann, 1904–1916; reprint, Hildesheim: Olms, 1964.

Gojowy, Detlef. "Kirchenlieder im Umkreis von J. S. Bach." *JbLH* 22 (1978): 79–123.

Grace, Harvey. *The Organ Works of Bach.* London: Novello, 1922.

Greer, Mary J. "The Sacred Duets and Terzets of Johann Sebastian Bach: A Study of Genre and Musical Text Interpretation." PhD diss., Harvard University, 1996.

Grüß, Hans. "Über die Tradition des Cantus-Firmus-Kanons." *BJ* 71 (1985): 135–146.

Honders, Casper. "'Allein Gott in der Höh sei Ehr' BWV 663: Vom Dank zum Trost." *MuG* 29 (1975): 106–110.

———. *Over Bachs Schouder. Een bundel opstellen.* Groningen: Niemeijer, 1985.

———. "Super flumina Babylonis. Bemerkungen zu BWV 653b." *Bulletin Internationale Arbeitsgemeinschaft für Hymnologie* 17 (1989): 53–60.

Hutter, Leonhard. *Compendium Locorum Theologicorum, ex scripturis sacris et libro concordiae . . . Ist aber jetzo . . . Die Deutsche Version / Wie sie der Herr Autor Seel. Selbst übersetzt hat.* Hildesheim: Hageman, 1661.

Jenny, Markus. *Luthers geistliche Lieder und Kirchengesänge.* Vollständige Neuedition in Ergänzung zu Band 35 der Weimarer Ausgabe. [Archiv zur Weimarer Ausgabe der Werke Martin Luthers 4]. Cologne: Böhlau, 1985.

Kappner, Gerhard. *Sakrament und Musik.* Gütersloh: Bertelsmann, 1952.

Keller, Hermann. *Die Orgelwerke Bachs. Ein Beitrag zu ihrer Geschichte, Form, Deutung und Wiedergabe.* Leipzig: Peters, 1948. English: *The Organ Works of Bach: A Contribution to Their History, Form, Interpretation and Performance,* trans. Helen Hewitt. New York: Peters, 1967.

Kelly, Clark. "Johann Sebastian Bach's 'Eighteen' Chorales, BWV 651–668: Perspectives on Editions and Hymnology." DMA diss., Eastman School of Music, 1988.

Kirkendale, Warren. "*Circulatio*-Tradition, *Maria Lactans*, and Josquin as Musical Orator." *AM* 56 (1984): 69–92.

Kloppers, Jacobus. "Die Interpretation und Wiedergabe der Orgelwerke Bachs: ein Beitrag zur Bestimmung von stilgerechten Prinzipien." PhD diss., Goethe-Universität, Frankfurt am Main, 1965.

Klotz, Hans. *Studien zu Bachs Registrierkunst.* Wiesbaden: Breitkopf & Härtel, 1985.

Koch, Eduard Emil. *Geschichte des Kirchenlieds und Kirchengesangs der christlichen, insbesondere der deutschen evangelischen Kirche.* 3rd ed. 8 vols. Stuttgart: Belser, 1866–1876; Hildesheim: Olms, 1973.

Kulp, Johannes. *Die Lieder unserer Kirche* [Handbuch zum Evangelischen Kirchengesangbuch, Sonderband], ed. Arno Büchner and Siegfried Fornaçon. Göttingen: Vandenhoeck & Ruprecht, 1958.

Leahy, Anne. "The Opening Chorus of Cantata BWV 78, *Jesu, der du meine Seele.* Another Example of Bach's Interest in Matters Soteriological." *BACH* 30/1 (1999): 26–41.

———. "Bach's Prelude, Fugue and Allegro for Lute (BWV 998): A Trinitarian Statement of Faith?" *Journal of the Society for Musicology in Ireland* 1 (December 2005): 33–51.

———. "Bach's Setting of the Hymn Tune 'Nun komm der Heiden Heiland' in his Cantatas and Organ Works." In *Music and Theology: Essays in Honor of Robin A. Leaver,* ed. Daniel Zager, 69–101. Lanham, MD: Scarecrow, 2007.

Leaver, Robin A. "Bach's 'Clavierübung III': Some Historical and Theological Considerations." *Organ Yearbook* 6 (1975): 17–32.

———. "Bach's Understanding and Use of the Epistles and Gospels of the Church Year." *BACH* 6/4 (1975): 4–13.

————. *Bachs theologische Bibliothek: eine kritische Bibliographie.* [Beiträge zur theologische Bachforschung 1]. Neuhausen-Stuttgart: Hänssler, 1983.

————. "Bach and Hymnody: The Evidence of the Orgelbüchlein." *Early Music* 13 (1985): 227–236.

————. "Bach's Mature Vocal Works." In *The Cambridge Companion to Bach*, ed. John Butt, 86–122. Cambridge: Cambridge University Press, 1997.

————. "Luther's Catechism Hymns 1: 'Lord Keep Us Steadfast in Your Word.'" *Lutheran Quarterly* 11 (1997): 397–410.

————. "Luther's Catechism Hymns 7: Lord's Supper." *Lutheran Quarterly* 12 (1998): 303–312.

————. "Eschatology, Theology and Music: Death and Beyond in Bach's Vocal Music." In *Irish Musical Studies 8: Bach Studies from Dublin*, ed. Anne Leahy and Yo Tomita, 129–147. Dublin: Four Courts Press, 2004.

————. "Ms. Bach *P271*, a Unified Collection of Chorale-based Pieces for Organ?" *Bach Notes: The Newsletter of the American Bach Society* 1 (Spring 2004): 1–4.

Leutert, Hansjürg. "Betrachtungen über Bachs Choraltriptychon 'O Lamm Gottes unschuldig' [BWV 656]." *MuG* 21 (1967): 21–25.

Little, Meredith, and Natalie Jenne. *Dance and the Music of J. S. Bach.* Bloomington: Indiana University Press, 1991; expanded edition, Indiana University Press, 2001.

Lohmann, Heinz, ed. *Johann Sebastion Bach. Orgelbüchlein.* Wiesbaden: Breitkopf & Härtel, 1983.

Luedtke, Hans. "Seb. Bachs Choralvorspiele." *BJ* 15 (1918): 1–96.

Marissen, Michael. "On the Musically Theological in J. S. Bach's Church Cantatas." *Lutheran Quarterly* 16 (2002): 48–64.

————. "The Character and Sources of the Anti-Judaism in Bach's Cantata 46." *Harvard Theological Review* 96/1 (2003): 63–99.

Marius, Richard. *Martin Luther: The Christian between God and Death.* Cambridge, MA: Harvard University Press, 2000.

von Meding, Wichmann. *Luthers Gesangbuch. Die gesungene Theologie eines christlichen Psalters.* Hamburg: Kovac, 1998.

Melamed, Daniel R. *J. S. Bach and the German Motet.* Cambridge: Cambridge University Press, 1995.

Meyer, Ulrich. "Zur Frage der inneren Einheit von Bachs Siebzehn Chorälen (BWV 651–667)." *BJ* 58 (1972): 61–75.

————. *J. S. Bachs Musik als theonome Kunst.* Wiesbaden: Breitkopf & Härtel, 1979.

————. "Über J. S. Bachs Orgelchoralkunst." In *Theologische Bach-Studien 1*, ed. Walter Blankenburg and Renate Steiger, 7–46. [Beiträge zur theologischen Bachforschung 4]. Neuhausen-Stuttgart: Hänssler, 1987.

————. "In profundis–in excelsis: Zu drei Orgelchorälen J. S. Bachs über 'Allein Gott in der Höh sei Ehr.'" *MuK* 58 (1988): 12–18.

————. *Biblical Quotation and Allusion in the Cantata Libretti of Johann Sebastian Bach.* Lanham, MD: Scarecrow, 1997.

Moser, Hans Joachim. *Die Melodien der Lutherlieder.* Berlin: Schloessmann, 1935.

Mudde, Willem. "Bachs behandeling van het lied 'O Lamm Gottes unschuldig' in zijn Matthäus-Passion en in zijn Achtzehn Choräle." *Musica sacra: orgaan van de Interdiocesane Kerkmuziekschool en van de Sint-Gregorius-Vereeniging* 62 (1961): 233–241.

Müller, Heinrich. *Himmlischer Liebes-Kuß / Oder Ubung deß wahren Christenthumbs / fliessend auß der Erfahrung Göttlicher Liebe.* Franckfurt am Mayn: Wilde, 1669.

———. *Evangelische Schluß-Kette / und Kraft-Kern / oder Gründliche Auslegung der gewöhnlichen Sonntags-Evangelien.* Frankfurt am Mayn: Wust, 1672.

———. *Geistliche Erquick-Stunden / Oder Dreyhundert Haus- und Tisch-Andachten.* Franckfurt am Mayn: Wust, 1672.

———. *Evangelisches Praeservativ wider den Schaden Josephs / in allen dreyen Ständen.* Franckfurt and Rostock: Wild, 1681.

Musch, Hans. "'. . . der von uns den Zorn Gottes wandt . . .' Zu Johann Sebastian Bachs Orgelchoral BWV 688." In *Musica-Scientia et Ars. Eine Festgabe für Peter Förtig zum 60. Geburtstag,* ed. Günther Metz, 91–108. Frankfurt am Main: n.p., 1995.

Neumeister, Erdmann. *Tisch des Herrn, In LII. Predigten über I. Cor. XI. 23–32. Da zugleich in dem Eingange der selben Unterschiedliche Lieder erkläret worden.* Hamburg: Kißner, 1722.

Paczkowski, Szymon. "Über die Funktionen der Polonaise und des polnischen Stils am Beispiel der Arie 'Glück und Segen sind bereit' aus der Kantate *Erwünschtes Freudenlicht* BWV 184 von Johann Sebastian Bach." In *Johann Adolf Hasse in seiner Epoche und in der Gegenwart: Studien zur Stil- und Quellenproblematik,* ed. Szymon Paczkowski and Alina Żórawska–Witlowska, 207–224. Warszawa: Instytut Muzykologii Uniwersytetu Warszawskiego, 2002.

Pelikan, Jaroslav. *Bach among the Theologians.* Philadelphia: Fortress, 1986.

Petzoldt, Martin. "Zur Frage der Textvorlagen von BWV 62." *MuK* 60 (1990): 302–310.

Pfeiffer, August. *Der wolbewärte / Evangelische / Aug-Apfel / oder / schrifftmässige Erklärung / Der / Augsburgischen / Confession.* Leipzig: Kloß, 1685.

Platen, Emil. *Johann Sebastian Bach. Die Matthäus-Passion.* Kassel: Bärenreiter, 1997.

Rössler, Martin. *Bibliographie der deutschen Liedpredigt.* Nieuwkoop: de Graaf, 1976.

Schmitz, Arnold. *Die Bildlichkeit der wortgebundenen Musik Johann Sebastian Bachs.* Mainz: Schott, 1950; reprinted, Laaber: Laaber Verlag, 1976 and 1980.

———. "Die Oratorische Kunst J. S. Bachs. Grundfragen und Grundlagen" [1950]. In *Johann Sebastian Bach* [Wege der Forschung 170], ed. Walter Blankenburg. Darmstadt: Wissenschaftliche Buchgesellschaft, 1970, 61–84.

Schützeichel, Harald. *Albert Schweitzer: Die Orgelwerke Johann Sebastian Bachs. Vorworte zu den "Sämtlichen Orgelwerken."* Hildesheim: Olms, 1995.

Schweitzer, Albert. *J. S. Bach.* Leipzig: Breitkopf & Hartel, 1908; reprint 1920. English: *J. S. Bach,* trans. Ernest Newman. London: Blach, 1923; reprint, New York: Dover, 1966.

Scooler, Evan. "J. S. Bach's Changing Conception of the 'Great Eighteen' Organ Preludes." PhD diss., Brandeis University, 2003.

Spitta, Philipp. *Johann Sebastian Bach.* Leipzig: Breitkopf & Härtel, 1873–1880; 4th ed., 1930; English: *Johann Sebastian Bach,* trans. Clara Bell and J. A. Fuller-Maitland, 3 vols. London: Novello, 1884–1885; reprint, New York: Dover, 1992.

Stapel, Wilhelm. *Luthers Lieder und Gedichte.* Stuttgart: Evangelisches Verlagswerk, 1950.

Steglich, Rudolf. *Johann Sebastian Bach.* Potsdam: Akademische Verlagsgesellschaft Athenaion, 1935.

Steiger, Renate. "'Die Welt ist euch ein Himmelreich.' Zu J. S. Bachs Deutung des Pastoralen." *MuK* 41 (1971): 1–8, 69–79.

———. "'Jesu, der du meine Seele' BWV 78." In *Johann Sebastian Bachs Choralkantaten als Choral-Bearbeitungen*, 57–87. [Internationale Arbeitsgemeinschaft für theologische Bachforschung Bulletin 3]. Heidelberg: Internationale Arbeitsgemeinschaft für theologische Bachforschung, 1991.

———. "'Gnadengegenwart.' Johann Sebastian Bachs Pfingstkantate BWV 172 'Erschallet, ihr Lieder, erklinget, ihr Saiten!'" In *Die Quellen Johann Sebastian Bachs. Bachs Musik im Gottesdienst*, ed. Renate Steiger [Internationale Arbeitsgemeinschaft für theologische Bachforschung. Bericht über das Symposium 4.–8. Oktober 1995 in der Internationalen Bachakademie Stuttgart]. Heidelberg: Internationale Arbeitsgemeinschaft für theologische Bachforschung, 1998, 15–57.

Steiger, Renate, ed. *Theologische Bachforschung heute: Dokumentation und Bibliographie der Internationalen Arbeitsgemeinschaft für theologische Bachforschung 1976–1996*. Berlin: Galda & Wilch, 1998.

———. *Johann Sebastian Bachs Kantaten zum Thema Tod und Sterben und ihr literarisches Umfeld*. Wiesbaden: Harrassowitz, 2000.

Steiger, Lothar, and Renate Steiger. *Sehet! Wir gehn hinauf gen Jerusalem. Johann Sebastian Bachs Kantaten auf den Sonntag Estomihi*. Göttingen: Vandenhoeck & Ruprecht, 1992.

Stiller, Günther. *Johann Sebastian Bach und das Leipziger gottesdienstliche Leben seiner Zeit*. Kassel: Bärenreiter, 1970. English: *Johann Sebastian Bach and Liturgical Life in Leipzig*, trans. Herbert J. A. Bouman, Daniel F. Poellot, and Hilton C. Oswald; ed. Robin A. Leaver. St. Louis: Concordia, 1984.

———. "Beicht- und Abendmahlsgang Johann Sebastian Bachs im Lichte der Familiengedenktage des Thomaskantors." *MuK* 43 (1973): 182–186.

Stinson, Russell. *J. S. Bach's Great Eighteen Chorales*. New York: Oxford University Press, 2001.

Syré, Wolfram. "Zur Polarität des Weihnachts- und des Passionsgedankens im Orgelwerk von Johann Sebastian Bach." *MuK* 56 (1981): 14–23.

Taylor, Stainton de B. *The Chorale Preludes of J. S. Bach*. London: Oxford University Press, 1942.

Terry, Charles Sanford. *Bach's Chorals Part III: The Hymns and Hymn Melodies of the Organ Works*. Cambridge: Cambridge University Press, 1921.

Unger, Melvin P. *Handbook to Bach's Sacred Cantata Texts. An Interlinear Translation with Reference Guide to Biblical Quotations and Allusions*. Lanham, MD: Scarecrow, 1996.

Wackernagel, Philipp. *Das deutsche Kirchenlied von der ältesten Zeit bis zu Anfang des XVII. Jahrhunderts*. 5 vols. Leipzig: Teubner, 1864–1877; reprint, Hildesheim: Olms, 1964.

Walter, Meinrad. *Erschallet, ihr Lieder, erklinget, ihr Saiten! J. S. Bachs Musik im Jahreskreis*. Zurich and Düsseldorf: Benzinger, 1999.

Walther, Johann Gottfried. *Praecepta der musicalischen Composition* [MS 1708], ed. Peter Benary. Leipzig: Breitkopf & Härtel, 1955.

———. *Musicalisches Lexicon Oder Musicalische Bibliothec* (Leipzig, 1732), ed. Friederike Ramm. Kassel: Bärenreiter, 2001.

Werthemann, Helene. "Johann Sebastian Bachs Orgelchoral *Nun komm, der Heiden Heiland, a due bassi e canto fermo*." *MuG* 13 (1959): 161–167.

———. "Bemerkungen zu Johann Sebastian Bachs Siebzehn Chorälen für Orgel." *MuG* 22 (1968): 154–160.

Williams, Peter. *The Organ Music of J. S. Bach.* 3 vols. Cambridge: Cambridge University Press, 1980–1986. A revision of vols. 1–2 was issued as *The Organ Music of J. S. Bach.* 2nd ed. Cambridge: Cambridge University Press, 2003.

Wolff, Christoph. *Bach: Essays on His Life and Music.* Cambridge: Harvard University Press, 1991.

———. *Johann Sebastian Bach: The Learned Musician.* New York: Norton, 2000.

Wollny, Peter, ed. *Die Achtzehn Grossen Orgelchoräle und Canonische Veränderungen über "Vom Himmel Hoch"* [facsimile]. Laaber: Laaber-Verlag, 1999.

Zeller, Winfried. "Vom Abbild zum Sinnbild: Bach und das Symbol." In *Theologie und Frömmigkeit. Gesammelte Aufsätze I,* ed. Bernd Jaspert, 165–177 [Marburger Theologische Studien 8]. Marburg: Elwert, 1971.

Index of Bach's Works

Index of Names

About the Author

The late **Anne Leahy**, musician, musicologist, and Bach scholar, lectured in academic studies at the Dublin Institute of Technology (DIT) Conservatory of Music and Drama and was the first Gerhard Herz Visiting Professor of Bach Studies at Louisville University in the fall of 2003. A Fulbright scholar with a doctorate from Utrecht University, Dr. Leahy was also a talented organist who had studied with the leading Dutch organist Ben Van Oosten. She was the organist and director of music at St. Michael's, Dun Laoghaire, where for many years she oversaw the prestigious summer organ recitals. As an editor and author, her work was centered in Bach studies.